The Restless Dominion

THE RESTLESS DOMINION

*The Irish Free State and the British
Commonwealth of Nations, 1921–31*

D. W. HARKNESS

*Lecturer in History
University of Kent at Canterbury*

New York NEW YORK UNIVERSITY PRESS
1970

First published 1969 by
MACMILLAN AND CO LTD
Little Essex Street London WC 2
and also at Bombay Calcutta and Madras
Macmillan South Africa (Publishers) Pty Ltd Johannesburg
The Macmillan Company of Australia Pty Ltd Melbourne
The Macmillan Company of Canada Ltd Toronto
Gill & Macmillan Ltd, 2 Belvedere Place, Dublin 1

Library of Congress Catalog Card Number 73-114761
SBN 8147-0463-8

Manufactured in the United States of America

To W. F. S. Harkness

Contents

Preface

In 1968 the Irish Republic plays an individual role in international affairs. An alert, small nation with a long civilisation and a distinctive anti-imperial history, it is peculiarly well placed in the world of emergent states. At the United Nations and in the trouble-spots of the world, Ireland's voice and participation belie its small size and recent freedom. Its authority, indeed, corresponds more to the wide-flung community of Irishmen around the globe: the Irishmen who in the past helped to build the United States of America and the several Dominions of the British Commonwealth. Today the Republic of Ireland is as consciously and undeniably independent as any nation, in a world of interdependent economies and major ideological blocs. Sovereign and free it plays its hand more or less according to its own decision.

But in 1922 the new-won Irish Free State was not so clearly master of its own destiny. Bound by the stipulations of the Articles of Agreement for a Treaty between Great Britain and Ireland it enjoyed mere Dominion status: a status analogous to that of Canada, but ill-defined and with specific additional restrictions. It is not the purpose of this work to explain why the Treaty was signed; why it was accepted by some and rejected by others. Nor is it its purpose to analyse the subsequent Civil War, or to try to explain that war in terms of personalities or social circumstances. Dominion status, on the other hand, is very much its concern. And, for the period up to the end of 1931, the role played by the youngest Dominion, situated as it was at the very heart of the British Empire, is its very special preoccupation. Too many commentators already have seized upon individual landmarks in the imperial development of this period, ascribing credit or censure to this or that Dominion. It is hoped that a consistent account of the role of the Irish Free State throughout these years will contribute, with greater continuity, a picture of greater clarity.

Lloyd George was perceptive when, on 14 December 1921, he said that 'the freedom of Ireland increases the strength of the Empire by ending the conflict which has been carried on for centuries with varying success, but with unvarying discredit'.[1]* The Canadian historian, Alexander Brady, was even shrewder when he added: 'it will accelerate the transformation of that Empire into an association of nations, knit together by various associative bonds rather than by the rigidity of an Austrian sovereign'.[2] But it is unlikely that even he foresaw the pace of that acceleration or fully understood the eventual form of the association.

The process of transformation had its own fascination. R. J. Manion, a Canadian 'of pure Irish descent' who had studied 'the terrible mistakes of England in Ireland', generously maintained in Ottawa, on 29 March 1927, that:

> there is no more fascinating study, probably, in the whole range of politics . . . than the study of the gradual constitutional development of the British Empire. . . . When one remembers that the British Empire comprises a quarter of the peoples and a quarter of the area of the globe, that it takes in all races, creeds and nationalities, that it touches all the continents of the world, and that it comprises practically all the various forms of government, from the most democratic constitutional monarchy to the government which is perhaps undemocratic because of the backwardness of the people concerned, it is easily understood why the question is so interesting.[3]

It is certain that between 1921 and 1931 lie ten of the most interesting years of that Imperial development. The First World War and the peace treaties at Versailles had thrust the adolescent Dominions towards maturity. They were joined in 1922 by an Irish Free State claiming to be not a Dominion but a nation,[4] and together they set about determining their international identities.

Superficially, the mighty Canada or the irascible South Africa may be credited with the achievement in 1931 of the Statute of Westminster, the charter of the new Commonwealth of Nations. Indeed Professor P. N. S. Mansergh, in his excellent survey of Commonwealth affairs,[5] argues that South Africa maintained at this time the strongest initiative, and that Canada, senior Dominion and a vital moderating force, has no cause to qualify Mr St Laurent's general claim, made in 1950, that 'Canadians have virtually shaped the Commonwealth as it stands today'.[6]

Mansergh also refers, however, to Mr J. G. Latham's claim that:

> In 1921 the immersion of a foreign body, the Irish Free State, disturbed the quiet waters of the Conventional Commonwealth. Out of the ferment which it created the Statute of Westminster, 1931, emerged.

adding on his own account that:

> If it be accepted that the immersion of the Irish Free State – and it was not a voluntary immersion – was the primary cause of the disturbance, then the wisdom of British insistence on dominion status for the Irish Free State in 1921 needs a more critical scrutiny in the field of intra-imperial relations than it has hitherto received.[7]

He further points out that the inclusion of the Free State in the Commonwealth gave heightened significance to 'Irish constitutional developments and legal precedents':[8] a significance that was Commonwealth-wide rather than merely domestic.

Professor Helen Mulvey also points to this decade as worthy of investigation. Writing on 'Ireland's Commonwealth years, 1922–40',[9] she repeats that it 'is deserving of more attention than it has received' and poses some vital questions:

> Was Lloyd George's hope of reconciling Irish national aspirations with membership of the British Commonwealth foredoomed to failure? . . . How significant was Ireland's responsibility for pushing the Commonwealth towards a sharper definition of status and function?[10]

It is to this period and to such questions that this book addresses itself. It sets out to illustrate the development of the British Empire at a time when it was becoming the British Commonwealth of Nations, and to claim that the most forceful inspiration in this direction derived from the Irish Free State: an Irish Free State which abroad was urging its fellow Dominions to a fuller national awareness, and which at home was explaining to its critics, that, in its widest freedom, it was a nation in which all Irishmen could take pride. Patrick McGilligan, Irish Minister for External Affairs and one of 'the two protagonists in the evolution of Dominion sovereignty',[11] put his country's effort in proper context in a speech in Dail Eireann, towards the end of the decade:

> Our Treaty with Great Britain and the Constitution of the Irish Free State gave a new direction to Constitutional thought and set going new forces and new processes in Constitutional speculation within the

Commonwealth of Nations itself. The Constitutional historians of this time will hereafter record the great achievement this has been. In a far larger field the historian of international politics will find the landmark of our progress.[12]

With the purpose, then, of demonstrating Ireland's contribution to Commonwealth development during the first ten years of its own statehood, the points of contact between Ireland and its fellow Dominions will be probed. The Imperial Conferences, above all, were the expression of inter-imperial thought and action, and if the official reports of their meeting give little more than a record of their eventual decisions, nevertheless Mr John Costello, for one, has endorsed their source value in the study of the period.[13] The Imperial Conference provides the main chronicle of imperial achievement, and the Conferences of 1926 and 1930, as well as the 1929 Committee on the Operation of Dominion Legislation, deserve close attention. These vital gatherings are given special emphasis below, but there is also an introduction to the conference system, a chapter on the 1923 Conference (in which the Irish delegation played no great part) and a chapter on the Statute of Westminster and the other constitutional events of 1931.

In between treatment of these landmarks, an effort has been made to recount the international innovations made by the Dominions in the decade. Here, too, a steady leadership emanated from Dublin. At the League of Nations the Irish delegates instructed their Dominion colleagues in the attributes of nationhood, and used the League itself to counter tendencies to dominate the Commonwealth association which Westminster still retained. No attempt is made, however, to give a complete account of international, or even purely Irish, events in this period.

One final point is perhaps worth making at this stage. In the Ireland of the twenties, anti-British sentiment was strong enough to prevent the Cosgrave Government from trying to make political capital of its contribution to what was popularly regarded in Ireland as the *British* Commonwealth. Dominion status was expanded to satisfy Irish nationalism, but no *esprit de Commonwealth corps*[14] was ever attained by the Irish Free State. The Irish contribution was, however, a very real one, not to be dismissed on the ground that it was made by an atypical Dominion, bent on pursuing its own selfish interests.

ABBREVIATIONS USED IN FOOTNOTE REFERENCES

United Kingdom and Commonwealth Parliamentary Debates

United Kingdom Debates are referred to as 'H.C. Deb.' (Commons), and 'H.L. Deb' (Lords). The volume number precedes this abbreviation, the series and column number follow it.

Abbreviations used for the Debates of the Commonwealth countries are as follows:

Australia, H. of R. (House of Representatives)
Canada, H. of C. (House of Commons)
New Zealand, H. of R. (House of Representatives)
South Africa, H. of A. (House of Assembly)

The Debates of the Irish Free State are referred to as Dail Eireann debates or Seanad Eireann debates. Dail Eireann, *Debates on the Treaty between Great Britain and Ireland, December 1921 and January 1922* (Dublin, Talbot Press), is referred to as Dail Eireann Treaty debates.

Colonial, Imperial and Prime Ministers Conferences

These are referred to by their Command number and year only, as follows, full reference being given in the Bibliography, section 4:

Cd. 3404, 1907: *Published proceedings and précis of the Colonial Conference, 15 to 26 April 1907.*

Cd. 5745, 1911: *Minutes of the proceedings of the Imperial Conference, 1911.*

Cd. 8566, 1917–18: *Extracts from proceedings and papers laid before the Imperial War Conference 1917–18.*

Cmd. 1474, 1921: Conference of the Prime Ministers and representatives of the United Kingdom, the Dominions, and India, held in June, July, and August 1921. *Summary of proceedings and documents.*

Cmd. 1987, 1923: Imperial Conference, 1923. *Summary of proceedings.*

Cmd. 2009, 1924: Imperial Economic Conference of representatives of Great Britain, the Dominions, India and the Colonies and Protectorates, held in October and November 1923. *Record of proceedings and documents.*

Cmd. 2768, 1926: Imperial Conference, 1926. *Summary of proceedings.*

Cmd. 2769, 1926: Imperial Conference, 1926. *Appendices to the summary of proceedings.*

Cmd. 3718, 1930–1: Imperial Conference, 1930. *Appendices to the summary of proceedings.*

Command Papers widely quoted

These are treated as above Conferences.

Cmd. 3479, 1929–30: *Report of the Conference on the Operation of Dominion Legislation and Merchant Shipping Legislation, 1929.*

Journals and books frequently quoted

C.H.B.E., *Cambridge History of the British Empire.*
J.C.P.S., *Journal of Commonwealth Political Studies.*

Other abbreviations

P.R.O., Public Record Office, London.

Acknowledgements

I would like to acknowledge with particular gratitude the assistance given to me by Mr Patrick McGilligan, who was extremely helpful both with recollections and with documents. The same also is true of Mr J. A. Costello, another leading figure in the events described in this book. I am also very much indebted to Mr Garret FitzGerald for his great kindness and hospitality and for allowing me to see and use so many of the records left by his father, Desmond FitzGerald. Without the assistance of these three it would have been extremely difficult to compile a documented account.

My sincere thanks go also to Professor F. S. L. Lyons for consistent advice and encouragement and to Miss Alice Martin, of the Fine Gael Headquarter Office in Dublin, for her patient attention and many kindnesses, in particular in helping me to establish contact with Irish political figures. I am also grateful to R. Mackworth-Young, M.V.O., Librarian, Windsor Castle, for confirming the text of the letter by Lord Stamfordham on page 233, and to Her Majesty the Queen for her gracious permission to reproduce it.

Finally in a near-contemporary subject unusual importance attaches to the personal interview, and I would like to thank all those listed in the Bibliography who so readily gave of their time and experience, often on a number of occasions, sometimes at very short notice. I must emphasise, however, that the final responsibility for the views and conclusions expressed below remains my own.

Canterbury, 1968   D. W. H.

We hereby proclaim the Irish Republic as a Sovereign Independent State, and we pledge our lives . . . to the cause of its freedom, of its welfare and of its exaltation among the nations. . . .

Poblacht Na h'Eireann

Proclamation of the Republic. Easter Monday 1916

The Restless Dominion

Introduction
A. The British Empire

That the British Empire was changing in 1921 was certain. What was not entirely clear was how quickly it was changing, or in what direction it was moving. In the past it had developed at its own pace, adjusted itself according to its own needs and avoided binding itself by any formal Constitution or rigid structure. But the First World War had placed new and unexpected demands upon it. And in the disturbed post-war world a ferment of national and international ideas moved questioningly around and through it. It seemed doubtful, to say the least, whether the British Empire could again enjoy the leisure of its former progress.

Throughout its fluctuating history, missionaries, economists and politicians had sought to realise in the British Empire their respective schemes; a Christian empire bringing the virtues of British civilisation to the ignorant; a federal empire developing its resources according to a comprehensive plan; a decentralised empire of friendly nations girdling the earth, spreading British influence but sparing the British taxpayer. Such strains had been part of an evolution which was steady enough to absorb one influence after another, and by 1921 the die was probably cast. There was no doubting the fact of Dominion self-government, nor the desire for full Dominion sovereignty. As far back as 1869, Sir Charles Adderley had affirmed that 'the normal current of colonial history is the perpetual assertion of the right to self-government',[1] and at the same period in Canada, John A. Macdonald had spoken of the Empire as 'an alliance of equal and autonomous states linked together by a common sovereign'.[2] New Zealand had seized the initiative during the early colonial conferences of the twentieth century to propose a central imperial council. In 1907 New Zealand was supported in this by Alfred Deakin of Australia, who launched a plan for a central secretariat.

But the New Zealand premier, Ward, added on this occasion that his country wanted to keep clear of British 'continental troubles' and affirmed that 'we want a distinct line of demarcation between the responsibilities which may be imposed on us without prior discussion'.[3] Already the international obligations of Empire were upsetting the Dominions which nevertheless were pleased to enjoy its benefits. Canada had previously rejected any imperial council, feeling that 'a permanent institution endowed with a continuous life might eventually come to be regarded as an encroachment upon the full measure of autonomous legislative and administrative power now enjoyed by the self-governing Colonies.[4] At the 1907 Imperial Conference itself Lord Elgin agreed with the Canadian, Laurier, thinking that 'the establishment of a body with independent *status* or authority . . . might be a danger to the autonomy of us all'.[5] It was at this conference that the term 'Dominion' was applied to the self-governing colonies.

At the 1911 Imperial Conference, meeting at the Foreign Office rather than the Colonial Office, presided over by Asquith, and including General Botha as Prime Minister of the new Union of South Africa, Ward had continued to urge his federal scheme. He wanted a New Zealand voice in such matters as peace and war, but Asquith curtly dismissed any notion that Britain could share her authority in regard to foreign policy. Though this conference had revealed a new appreciation of the importance of foreign affairs amongst the Dominions, Laurier had been true to form; wary of any foreign policy consultation lest it imply commitment to British ventures. He had advocated increased Dominion powers in the conduct of commercial affairs and had required that all British treaties hampering the independent wishes of the Dominions should go. In general terms this conference had marked a setback for the federal and a gain for the devolutionary conception of Empire. Its governing note, as Colonial Secretary Harcourt had said, was 'Imperial co-operation' not 'Imperial concentration'.[6]

Three years later, in the House of Commons, it was again Harcourt who rejected a demand for the exercise of central authority. Replying to Ramsay MacDonald on the issue of South African labour legislation, and carefully dissociating his remarks from Irish grievances at home, he had firmly stated that the Imperial Parliament could not grant self-government and then treat a Dominion as though it was a Crown colony. It was more important for a country to be self-governed than well governed, though fortunately the Dominions were both. Remember, he had said in conclusion:

It is your toleration and your restraint which can alone proclaim your confidence and your generosity and which alone can maintain the good fellowship of a united Empire.[7]

There had been divisions at home and abroad, and upon such divisions burst the Great War, temporarily submerging them. The whole Empire had to devote its energies to the task of winning the battle. But if the war tended to favour a central imperial executive and brought into being an Imperial War Cabinet, it also accelerated Dominion development, bringing a 'consciousness that the dominions had become adult nations',[8] and it encouraged at least one Dominion statesman to examine critically the whole nature of the imperial relationship.

General Smuts, as early as 1902, had foreseen a new imperial order, though he doubted 'if Empire was the right name for the free and fraternal association which he envisaged'.[9] Now, in 1917, in the midst of the struggle, when Lionel Curtis and the *Round Table* were urging a desperate, now-or-never, 'Federate or Disintegrate' policy, he made every effort to change that name of Empire. Co-operation in battle, the logic of central planning and an imperial trade preference, the shared values, loyalties and traditions of the British way of life argued at this time for a federal system. But Smuts saw beyond the demands of war to the aspirations of the separate self-governing Dominions, scattered and various as they were. And it was largely due to him that a resolution to the Imperial Conference, delivered by Borden but inspired by the South African general, urged that after the cessation of hostilities a readjustment should be made in the constitutional relations of the component parts of the Empire. It also put on record

that any such re-adjustment, while thoroughly preserving all existing powers of self-government and complete control of domestic affairs, should be based on a full recognition of the Dominions as autonomous nations of an *Imperial Commonwealth*, should recognise their right to an adequate voice in foreign policy and foreign relations, and should provide effective arrangements for continuous consultation in all important matters of common Imperial concern and for such necessary concerted action founded on consultation as the several Governments may determine.[10]

Clearly, this view negatived imperial federation. Smuts proceeded to develop the argument further. 'The British Commonwealth' must be transformed and the anomalous legal structure of former colonial subordination must be swept away: 'Too much of the old ideas still clings to the new organism which is growing. I think that although in practice there is great freedom, yet in actual theory the status of Dominions is of a subject character . . . theory still permeates practice to some extent.'[11] The 'basis of freedom and equality' of the Dominions must be assured and this would mean that machinery for continuous consultation would have to be devised. People were already talking of a League of Nations. Let the developing British Commonwealth become the pattern of such international co-operation.

Borden, who had remarked: 'The action of the Dominions in this war has made the spirit of nationhood splendidly manifest',[12] summed up the discussion by emphasising that: 'the Crown in its relation to any Dominion acts upon the advice of the duly constituted Government or Cabinet of that Dominion'. He pointed to the satisfactory Dominion representation in the Imperial War Cabinet, drew attention to the importance of such a convention, and then underlined the 'sharp distinction between legal power and constitutional right' in order to nullify British predominance. 'While there is the theory of predominance, there is not the constitutional right of predominance in practice, even at present.'[13] Smuts, speaking at a banquet given in his honour by members of both Houses of the British Parliament, on 15 May 1917, reinforced the anti-federalist cause:

> We have the so-called Dominions, independent in their government, which have been evolved on the principles of your free constitutional system into almost independent States, which all belong to this community of nations and which I prefer to call 'The British Commonwealth of Nations'. . . . This British Commonwealth of Nations does not stand for standardisation or denationalisation, but for the fuller, richer and more various life of all the nations comprised in it.[14]

As for keeping the association together, he held: 'there are two factors that you must rely on in the future. The first is your hereditary kingship, the other our Conference system.'[15]

After the First World War, which had thrust the Dominions on to the world stage, had ended, the Peace Conference carried them further, while their membership of the League of Nations consolidated their new position. By participating as national representatives in the Peace Conference and by signing the Versailles Treaty on behalf of their peoples, the Dominion leaders had baptised the sovereignty of their countries. A new nationalism had echoed round the parliaments of the Empire. To each Dominion had come the realisation that it was now 'of age'; that a new era had dawned which called for new adjustments.

But the Imperial Conference which met in 1921 did not recapture the spirit of 1917. Due mainly to the strong opposition of Premier Hughes of Australia (who had been unable to attend in 1917), the Conference passed over the suggested task of constitutional overhaul. Regretting that 'continuous consultation' could 'only be secured by a substantial improvement in the communications between the various component parts of the Empire', it concluded: 'Having regard to the constitutional developments since 1917, no advantage is to be gained by holding a Constitutional Conference.'[16]

It had been the declared intention of Hughes to prevent such a conference, and he returned home and reported to his Parliament that he was well satisfied.[17] At the Imperial Conference he had opposed Smuts and Meighen of Canada in forthright manner. 'Is it', he had asked,

> that the Dominions are seeking new powers, or are desirous of using powers they already have, or is the Conference to draw up a declaration of rights, to set down in black and white the relations between Britain and the Dominions? What is this Conference to do? ... Surely this Conference is not intended to limit the rights we now have. Yet what new right, what extension of power can it give us? ... What can they (the Dominions) not do, even to encompass their own destruction by sundering the bonds that bind them to the Empire? What yet do they lack? Canada has asserted her right to make treaties. She has made treaties. She is asserting her right to appoint an Ambassador at Washington. ... Either it [the Conference] must limit our rights of self-government, or it must weaken the bonds of Empire, or it must simply content itself with asserting rights and prvileges and responsibilities that are ours already and that none question. In effect we have all the rights of self-government enjoyed by independent nations.

And at General Smuts he had fired a final 'Let us leave well alone'.[18]

His strength and determination carried the day so that at the opening of our period the character of the new Empire remained undefined. But Premier Hughes was seeking the best of both worlds. It was he who had led the Dominion demand for separate representation at Versailles. It had suited him. He had not trusted the British to handle the Japanese problem in the best interests of

Australia, and he had wanted to supervise personally the destruction of German economic power, and to argue out the Australian Mandate. Borden and Smuts were interested in the status and prestige of representation, both having Opposition nationalists at home to silence, but they would have been satisfied with a Dominion Delegation. Hughes had had his way. But he was now unwilling, in 1921, to see the logical conclusions of separate representation implemented; separate national identities and separate attributes of sovereignty. He kicked against any inroads into the traditional diplomatic unity of the Empire which normally gave him the best of possible platforms. He insisted that things remain as they were.

Yet much work had been done for the 1921 Conference, and it was not to be wasted. In his book in 1920,[19] for example, Duncan Hall had recorded his views:

> The gradual transformation of the British Empire from a single state into a group of equal and autonomous states has been brought about by the restriction, point by point by means of successive declarations of constitutional right, of the legal power of the United Kingdom over the Dominions. . . . These declarations implemented where necessary by Imperial legislation have practically secured the constitutional equality of the Dominions with the United Kingdom; but they have left the legal authority of the Crown and the Imperial Parliament intact. It seems obvious, therefore, that by developing to its logical conclusion the distinction of the British Constitution between legal and constitutional right, it will be possible without destroying the legal unity of the Empire, to secure to the Dominions the absolute equality of nationhood which they desire.[20]

Mr Hall went on to suggest that the Imperial Conference should draw up now a 'general declaration of constitutional right covering the whole field of government'. But, thanks largely to Hughes, no such general declaration was made by the Conference. It also passed over even more specific proposals made by General Smuts.

Smuts had sent to L. S. Amery a set of draft proposals, of a most far-sighted nature, as a preparation to the 1921 Conference. These proposals, in a memorandum entitled 'The Constitution of the British Commonwealth', incorporating views which he had expressed as far back as 1910, and written in the mood of 1917, received the general approval of Amery, who must have been strongly influenced by them when he took over the Dominions Office in 1925 (a separate Office which Amery himself inaugurated). Smuts recommended that the Imperial Conference should draft detailed proposals for the future Constitutional Conference and so give a lead to public opinion. He thought that the only way to check separatist movements already under way in the Empire was to 'make them unnecessary by the most generous satisfaction of the Dominion sense of nationhood and statehood'.[21]

What Smuts anticipated as necessary was a new definition of the constitutional status of the Dominions, in the Commonwealth itself, and in the outside world. The practice of equal sovereignty was to be given the backing of theory. He pointed out that extraterritorial effect was desirable for Dominion legislation; and that each Dominion should have power to amend its own Constitution, thus enabling it to control appeals to the Privy Council and to ensure its own legislative supremacy (the Colonial Laws Validity Act of 1865, in fact, must no longer apply to Dominion Legislation). In the field of foreign affairs the Dominions should be given the same status and recognition as accorded at Paris, and there should be more clarity over treaty procedure and the appointment of Dominion ministers to foreign countries. He agreed that Hall's suggested declaration might be a good way of achieving the desired results, and he set out the changes required in the constitutional conventions, the law and the machinery of government of the Commonwealth. The Dominion Governments should become co-ordinate governments of the King with full equality of status.

This would involve:

(*a*) that the Dominions should cease to be placed under the Colonial Office or any other British Department.

(*b*) that the Dominion Governments should have direct access to the King who will act on their advice without the interposition of the British Government or a Secretary of State.

(*c*) that the Governor-General should become a vice-roy simply and solely and only represent the sovereign in his Dominion Executive, and not also the British Government.[22]

Smuts recommended closer consultation with Dominion representatives in London as a first step. There should also be established a quadrennial 'Commonwealth Congress' or 'Imperial Conference' more in the nature of a Commonwealth parliamentary conference; a 'Prime Ministers' Conference' instead of a misnamed 'Imperial Cabinet', meeting at least every two years; and a 'Dominions Committee' – Prime Ministers or their deputies as a continuous organisation.

Such measures would transform the British Empire into a society of free and equal states and 'a new name should mark this epoch-making departure ... such as the British Commonwealth of Nations'.[23]

Amery, inveterate believer in a unitary monarchy, agreed in general with Smuts but added that any set of declarations must include 'an affirmation not only of the complete independence and equality of the several partners but also the indissoluble unity of all of them under King and Crown'.[24]

The 1921 Conference failed to pronounce upon these topics and its failure was dubbed a victory for the forces of imperial centralisation, though, in fairness to the Dominion leaders present, it is probable that they were merely anxious to present a united front on broad matters of imperial concern. Their plan was co-operation, not federation. But the problems as stated by Smuts were very real. That independent national sovereignty was the status of the Dominions they did not deny, but they were evading the issue when they ignored altogether the fresh demands on the imperial relationship that this status entailed. Westminster still tended to confuse its thought with terms of colony status; and the law was founded on colonial precedents and characterised by a mother-country complex out of keeping with the new mood. British supremacy might be mitigated in practice, but it clouded constitutional issues as far as the Dominions themselves were concerned and completely mystified the rest of the world. It is therefore worth setting out clearly here, under the headings used by Smuts, the areas of maximum controversy which existed at the opening of our period. The ideas mentioned above are pointers to imperial development in the twenties. Here now are the facts of the imperial relationship in 1921.

1. Dominion Status

The Dominions were still placed under the British Colonial Office.

Though they had signed the Peace Treaty and were full members of the League of Nations, other international activity was lacking. However, the power to make treaties was tentatively being acquired by Canada, and it was a convention that the Dominions should have full say in commercial treaties affecting their interests.

Canada too had taken the unprecedented step, in 1920, of announcing its intention to appoint an ambassador to Washington.

While this had received British sanction, the appointment had not been made, and many Canadians felt that such action involved a scandalous breach in the diplomatic unity of the Empire, an unnecessary duplication of services, and a blow to the imperial connection in Canada.

The outward and visible signs of nationhood were, therefore, scantily arrayed. Any inner realities were also hard for a critical foreigner to penetrate, buried as they were under a colonial legal structure of imposing proportions.

The British Government retained the right to reserve and to disallow Dominion legislation, though this was more theoretical than practical, having fallen for the most part into abeyance. There remained real powers of reservation in connection with shipping, contained in British merchant shipping legislation (Merchant Shipping Act, 1894 and the Colonial Courts of the Admiralty Act, 1890) and in connection with the London finance market (Colonial Stock Act, 1900).

Also, the British Government did legislate binding the Empire, though now only with the consent of the Dominions. But the Colonial Laws Validity Act, 1865, could still be used to subvert Dominion legislation repugnant to British statute.

The Judicial Committee of the Privy Council provided further evidence of restricted Dominion sovereignty. By the Judicial Committee Act, 1844, the prerogative right of the Crown to hear appeals from any colonial court was given statutory validity. Though in different cases subsequent legislation modified this position, 'no limitation has ever been placed on Appeals from Canada, by Imperial Act'.[25] In the case of Australia, 'it was desired to retain the right to decide constitutional cases involving the rights of the States and the Commonwealth *inter se*, and this was finally accepted in the Commonwealth of Australia Constitution Act, 1900, after the Imperial Government had declined to concede any wider extension of exemption from the appeal'.[26] In the case of the Union of South Africa 'the appeal has been restricted to cases decided in the Appellate Division of the Supreme Court of South Africa, and permission to appeal is not freely granted'.[27] In both Australia and South Africa, legislation restricting the right of appeal to the Privy Council had to be reserved, while 'the New Zealand Parliament . . . cannot limit appeal by special leave'.[28]

2. The Governor-General

This official provided a wide range of anomalies in himself. There is little doubt that in 1921 the conception of a Colonial Governor had not been sufficiently challenged in the Dominions, nor adequately exorcised from British thinking. The Governor-General was still appointed and instructed by the British Government, and his instructions allowed him discretion to reserve Bills which he considered to have imperial significance.

He was still the agent of the British Government as well as the representative of the Monarch.

He was also the channel of communication between Westminster and the Dominion governments.

3. Constitutional Amendment

The Dominion Constitutions, even if drawn up in the Dominions, were enacted in Westminster. In each case there were reserved areas which required the intervention of the British Parliament to alter.

Canada had comparatively limited powers in this respect because the Federation was a compact between the provinces, and the Federal Parliament was not held to be allowed to alter the terms of that compact unless the general assent of the provinces had been obtained. Imperial Acts had been necessary 'in 1907, to alter the amounts of the provincial subsidies, in 1915 to readjust the representation of the provinces in the Senate, and in 1916 to extend the duration of Parliament by a year'.[29]

Australia had 'the widest of constitutional powers' but there was doubt 'whether any change abandoning the federal character of the constitution' was possible. To Professor Keith, in 1924, 'the answer would seem to be in the negative' while 'Bills effecting important alterations or dealing with the Governor's salary must be reserved unless approved in advance by the Imperial Government'.[30]

New Zealand, since the Act of 1865, seemed to have almost full powers of constitutional change,* 'though any important constitutional change would probably be effected by a bill reserved for the signification of the royal assent. The same position applies to *New-*

* See below, p. 153, on the other hand. It is clear that the British Government still felt in 1929 that New Zealand was unable to pass laws repugnant to the law of England.

foundland where the constitution rests on the prerogative.'[31] 'In the *Union of South Africa* . . . any bill affecting the constitution or powers of the Provincial Councils or the provisions regarding the Lower House must be reserved.'[32]

4. CONSULTATION

Because of their as yet uncompleted development, the Dominions in 1921 were glad to use abroad the services provided by the British Foreign Office. But they were increasingly reluctant to be implicated in British ventures over which they had no form of control. Laurier, Botha and Smuts demanded that the Dominions be conceded the right to neutrality in any future British war, and they desired to be kept informed of British intentions and consulted on any matters involving their own interests. The Canadian Liberals in particular rejected any form of central imperial committee, or advisory body, which might remove decisions affecting Canada from the Canadian Parliament; but no satisfactory substitute was found by which the Dominions could be kept up to date with fast-moving international events. New Zealand would have welcomed any central body which would have given that small country a share in the voice of the Empire, and Smuts did suggest a form of continuous central organisation, as we have seen above. But at this time only despatches to the Governor-General and the occasional imperial conference existed to meet this need and the comprehensiveness of the British Foreign Office ensured the mother country a clear predominance in the international field. Though the Dominions resented the implications of this predominance it was nonetheless real in 1921. It was to take only another year before the incident at Chanak exposed the glaring inadequacies of the system.

To Smuts these problems were urgent. Imperial relations must be rationalised or the Commonwealth would not survive. Nowhere more strongly than in South Africa was the voice of separation heard. South Africa with its Boer and British frictions and its Native difficulties resented every evidence of British interference in its affairs. And General Hertzog, leading the opposition to Smuts, did not hesitate to emphasise the areas of controversy.

The tradition in Australasia was different. Here there was no big minority problem. The population was largely of British stock, with an affectionate loyalty to the Old Country. Conscious too of their exposed position far off on the rim of Asia, Australia and New Zealand felt a real dependence on the British Navy. Australia with her federal constitution had more need of outside legal arbitration than unitary South Africa. Massey of New Zealand denounced attempts to define Dominion status and even denied that for international purposes the Dominions were sovereign states at all. They were, rather, in partnership with Great Britain for the management of 'the British Empire as a single undivided unity'.[33]

In Canada, the oldest Dominion and the pioneer of Dominion development, a different situation again existed. A federal country with a strong French minority group which looked to Britain to protect its rights, Canada also contained men with mature ideas of Canadian sovereignty and equality. Borden, and earlier Laurier and Macdonald, had represented a tradition of loyalty with independence. In opposition to Borden in the post-war parliament sat Mackenzie King, who now expanded traditional views to fit the post-war context. He sought then, as he expressed it in 1924, 'a more clearly recognised nationhood within the community of nations comprising the British Empire or the British Commonwealth by whichever term you may wish to call it'.[34]

Newfoundland, in theory a Dominion, regarded itself as the oldest colony, and was proud to be so.

It is important to stress these different needs and views. The Dominions varied in location, composition and aspiration. In 1921 they could not be represented as one entity with one outlook. Thus, when the Articles of Agreement for a Treaty between Great Britain and Ireland (signed on 6 December 1921) enshrined for the first time in an official document Smuts's new title 'The British Commonwealth of Nations', the relationships of that Commonwealth remained obscure and the status of Dominion, conferred by it upon Ireland, was not clearly defined. The 'Second British Empire' had passed away, and the Third, distinguished by a new name, and by a 'concept of equality' that marked it off 'from the older Empire and gave to it a distinctive character',[35] was in the process of evolution.

While the Irish Treaty negotiations were actually being conducted, Professor R. Coupland was assuring an Oxford audience: 'Nationalism is no new thing in the Dominions. It has yet to run its course. We cannot certainly foretell, however strong our belief may be, what spirit will inform it when it reaches its full power – the spirit of

Mazzini or another's.'[36] To its credit, however, it was still accurate to call the Empire, as Smuts had done in 1917, 'a system of States, and not a stationary system, but a dynamic evolving system, always going forward to new destinies'.[37] After a brief look at Ireland's position we will study its destiny in terms of the 1920s: one of the most crucial of all its evolutionary decades.

B. Ireland and the British Empire

'Freedom, not the ultimate freedom that all nations desire and develop to, but the freedom to achieve it.'[38] This was Michael Collins's memorable analysis of the Treaty with Great Britain, and this was the view more than any other which persuaded Dail Eireann to ratify that Treaty. It remained the guiding light of W. T. Cosgrave and his supporters throughout their tenure of office, from 1922 until 1932. Their objective was full and unrestricted sovereignty: their method became the peaceful transformation of the British Empire so that the definition of Dominion status might be synonymous with fullest freedom. In 1921, as indicated above, the state of the British Empire was far from clear, while Dominion status fell far short of complete independence. It is important to decide what the Irish leaders understood by that status in December 1921: and it will be useful first to glance at the position which the Empire occupied in Irish thought in the years leading up to the Treaty.

In 1882 F. H. O'Donnell, whose maiden speech eight years before had been in support of Indian nationalism, announced that the Irish Party in Westminster would make itself 'the natural representatives and spokesmen of the unrepresented nationalities of the Empire',[39] and this policy was pursued actively under Parnell. In 1903 the Canadian House of Commons, noting its Addresses to His Majesty for 'a just measure of home rule'[40] for Ireland, passed in 1882, 1886 and 1887, reiterated its plea in this direction. In 1906, the Australian House of Representatives and the Australian Senate, both underlining the benefits accorded to their country by Home Rule, urged that a similar blessing be bestowed upon Ireland, 'for never was a request more clear, consistent or continuous as theirs'.[41]

Isolated and at random, these incidents show that, at the turn of the century at least, Ireland was aware of the Empire, as the Empire was of Ireland. Indeed it would have been hard for it to have been otherwise, so many sons of Ireland being scattered by then through all the King's Dominions, and beyond.

Even in 1912, Redmond was careful to point out the benefits which would accrue to the Empire when his Home Rule Bill had settled Irish grievances. But by then there were many in Ireland who doubted whether even the limited freedom which this measure promised would be realised. When Ulster intransigence and the Great War intervened to keep the Bill from becoming law, the appeal of physical force as the method of achieving separation intensified. The Irish Parliamentary Party had played the game according to British rules. Now that its victory was in sight Britain was altering the rules. So Pearse and his men raised the flag of the Republic in 1916 and hallowed it with their blood: and the country moved steadily behind their banner in response to continued British miscalculation. In a desperate effort to reach an agreed solution which would not detract from the enormous war effort, Lloyd George called an Irish Convention on 25 July 1917. It was at this unlikely meeting, with Horace Plunkett in the chair, but with the newly strong Sinn Fein Republican movement deliberately boycotting, that the first authoritative appeal for home rule on a Dominion basis was made for Ireland. Already, in 1911, Erskine Childers had written a detailed, if isolated, plea for Home Rule: a Dominion Home Rule much less comprehensive than the one he was to scorn so soon and to die opposing. He had based his scheme on the precepts of Lord Durham, and he had concluded:

> It is being said that the freedom given to Canada cannot be given to Ireland, because the separation from the Empire theoretically rendered possible by such a step would be immaterial in the case of Canada, which is distant, but perilous in the case of Ireland which is near. If this be Imperialism it should stink in the nostrils of every decent citizen at home and abroad.[42]

Now in 1917, in the midst of quarrellings and bitter debate, in the darkness of disagreement and failure to compromise, two fresh schemes for Dominion Home Rule were proposed. Plunkett even harnessed George Bernard Shaw to the cause.[43]

The ground had been prepared by 'circulating a mass of information on previous Home-Rule schemes, Irish statistics and the constitutional position of the Dominions and other territories'.[44] As a result, the Convention, from which so much had been expected by those conscious of its South African precedent, but from which so little emerged, at least encouraged its chairman to pursue the Dominion ideal and to found, in 1919, an Irish Dominion Party.

On 28 June 1919 Plunkett's new weekly paper, the *Irish Statesman* (modelled closely on the British *New Statesman*), contained the manifesto of the Irish Dominion League, and for the year of its first production it gave expression to the League's principles. Reasoned, logical, honest and explicit, the Dominion League advocated much that was to be accepted in the end only after bitter fighting. It was a policy of compromise which hoped to satisfy all Irish aspirations in the status of a self-governing Dominion: a status which would include the recognition of Irish nationality, giving Ireland equal place in a great Commonwealth of free nations; which would provide an Irish share in the guidance of combined foreign policy and in the preservation of world peace. No advantage was to be had in Republican status, it held, but many disadvantages. The policy was hopeful and eminently sensible. But it stood no chance. It was crushed between the uncompromising and irreconcilable grindstones of Protestant Ulster and Catholic Ireland.* Already, in 1918, Sinn Fein had swept the election board in the South, and in that area the prevailing sentiment had become one of anti-British hatred. That the significance of this election had escaped the notice of Parliament in Westminster, overburdened as it was with post-war settlements, was further evidence, if further evidence was needed, that England was unable to cope with affairs in Ireland. While the Irish Dominion League was mustering a small and intellectual support in Dublin, and holding Peace Conferences and public meetings, Sinn Fein had established Dail Eireann and was labouring to make it the effective power in the land. In Belfast the Unionists were beginning to consolidate the six-county position, soon to be guaranteed to them by the Government of Ireland Act, 1920.

From 1919 to 1921, the history of Ireland is the history of Dail Eireann and its struggle for predominance. The extent to which this predominance was eventually compromised is written in the 'Articles of Agreement for a Treaty between Great Britain and

---

* It was, to use Plunkett's phrase 'like a cat in a tennis court', turned upon with equal venom by both opponents (Professor George O'Brien, in interview).

Ireland'.* The Treaty was not signed by men of Plunkett's following, but by men sworn to a Republic. But the work of the Irish Dominion League must surely have helped these 'Republicans' in their understanding of the position which Ireland was now offered. Collins at any rate signed the Treaty firmly believing that with it Ireland could progress to the fullest freedom. Tragically, Michael Collins was lost to Ireland and the Commonwealth in the following year. But his thoughts did not die and they are so fundamental to an understanding of the role which Ireland played that they must be recorded here. It is fortunate that the circumstances of the Treaty negotiations compelled him to commit himself to paper. On 25 November 1921 Austen Chamberlain sent to Lord Birkenhead a memorandum headed 'Personal and Unofficial', and written by Collins. It stated:

... While Anglo-Irish relations have taken on this aspect with an apparent suddenness which is almost bewildering to the ordinary British mind, it happens that at the same moment the relations between Great Britain and the Dominions have, by a different process, reached a stage in which the finding of a solution is almost as urgent in the interests of British security and world peace.

The history of Ireland as an ancient independent nation which is now at last receiving recognition, is utterly different from that of the Colonies who have outgrown the tutelage of their mother country. . . .

The Colonies, as full-grown children, are restive under any appearance of parental restraint, though willing to co-operate with the parent on an equal footing in regard to all family affairs.

Ireland as a separate nation, would be also restive under any control from the neighbouring nation, but equally willing to co-operate in free association on all matters which would be naturally the *common concern* of two nations living so closely together. The problem on both sides can only be solved by recognising without limitation the complete independence of the several countries, and only on that basis can they all be associated together by ties of co-operation and friendship. The only association which it will be satisfactory to Ireland to enter will be based not on the present technical, legal status of the Dominions, but on the real position they claim, and have in fact secured. . . . It is essential that the present *de facto* position should be recognised *de jure*, and that all its implications as regards sovereignty, allegiance, constitutional independence of the governments should be acknowledged.

An association on the foregoing conditions would be a novelty in the world. But the world is looking for such a development, and it is necessary if the old world of internecine conflicts is to emerge into a new world of co-operative harmony. For such an association would be the

* Referred to in Ireland, then and since, as 'The Treaty', and so described hereafter in the text.

pattern for national co-operation on a wider scale, and might form the nucleus of a real League of Nations of the world. . . .[45]

In this testimony, closely paralleling the vision of Smuts, Collins asserted the separateness of Ireland but recognised the advantages of co-operation.

The members of Dail Eireann were not drawn from the advocates of such ideas.* They had to think out the implications of the Treaty at the time, and to accept, for the most part, the judgement of their leaders. To some, freedom and a 'Republic' had become synonymous: to others less doctrinaire, and anxious only to be rid of England so that the Irish people could pronounce its voice, freedom meant freedom to choose.

The frustrated Republic, however, was still on their minds and in the imaginations of many of their constituents. The new Irish Free State was not even to be the whole of Ireland, at first, and it would be joining the 'free' imperial association only as a last resort and after tough bargaining. Ireland, after all, was a mother country, not a colonial settlement; it had emigrant, not immigrant problems; it hoped to be a Roman Catholic democracy, and anticipated difficulties about a Protestant monarchy; it had experienced no gradual devolution from British control, but rather a long history of enforced submission followed by a violent reaction; and it was European in orientation, unlike the other oversea Dominions. It may have had something in common with these Dominions, but it had much more affinity with the United States. The Irish in America were still mindful of Ireland, and in America Ireland still meant many votes at election time. But it was with the Dominions that Ireland was now to be associated.

As the attrition in Ireland between the I.R.A. and the British forces had progressed, so determination to be quit of Britain altogether had increased. But now a treaty of equality and co-operation with Britain was to be ratified. It seemed to many that Britain must somehow contrive to continue its domination. Thus the debate upon the ratification of the Treaty, which raged on and off from

---

* 'It was anything but a microcosm of the country, since Nationalists, Farmers, Labour and S. Unionists were completely unrepresented in it. Its members, who were all of one party, had been elected unopposed as a gesture of defiance to England and of hostility to partition at the height of the Black and Tan régime. Most of them were fighting men, or youths and lists had been scrutinised at Sinn Fein headquarters for the purpose of ensuring that none but politically "safe" candidates should be adopted' (Donal O'Sullivan, *The Irish Free State and its Senate*, p. 50).

14 December 1921–7 January 1922 was a bitter and passionate one. It provides a further insight into Irish opinion at the opening of our period and it puts the new Dominion accurately into its context.

Perhaps no one, not even Collins, understood the constitutional intricacies of the British Empire so well as Erskine Childers: and Childers, 'the most brilliant constitutional authority Ireland ever had',[46] was adamantly against accepting the agreement. This treaty, he declared, did not give Dominion status. Ireland was not responsible for her own defence and therefore could not claim a voice in foreign policy, treaties or decisions of war and peace. Ireland was too near to England: the British powers recognised as obsolete in Canada (to which the Free State was to be most closely likened) would not be treated as obsolete here.* Childers, with all the weight of his constitutional knowledge, declared that the Treaty 'places Ireland definitely and irrevocably under British authority and under the British Crown'.[47]

With passionate patriotism, with philosophy and theology, with emotion and with intellect both sides argued their case. Because Griffith and Collins prevailed and because their successors governed throughout our period, their arguments are the more instructive. Griffith, old dual-monarchist that he was, proudly proclaimed the equality with Britain which the Treaty gave, and he assured his audience that any royal representative in Ireland would have to be approved by the new Irish Government. Ireland would now take her place in the League of Nations. Collins pointed to the guarantee of freedom which the Commonwealth association gave. Shrewdly he underlined the value of partner nations in the troubled post-war world, and of these nations in particular which would jealously guard Ireland from any British interference deemed to reflect on their own position. Dominion status, too, was undefined: it gave Ireland the power 'to hold and to make secure and to increase what we have gained. . . . The fact of Canadian and South African independence', he urged, 'is something real and solid and will grow in reality and force as time goes on'. Ireland's status would not be

> the legal, technical status . . . but the status which enables Canada to sign the Treaty of Versailles equally with Great Britain, the status which prevents Great Britain from entering into any foreign alliance without the consent of Canada, the status that gives Canada the right to

* Childers has become disillusioned since his earlier work. See Introduction, note 42, above

be consulted before she goes into any war. It is not the definition of that status that will give it to us; it is our power to take it and to keep it. . . . I believe in our power to take it and to keep it.[48]

By the Treaty the word 'Empire' had been got rid of for the first time in an official document. Ireland had now a common citizenship instead of subjection. To Collins's view, the realist O'Higgins added that while the Treaty did not give everything hoped for, he believed that 'the evolution of this group must be towards a condition, not merely of individual freedom, but also of equality of status'.[49] O'Higgins's close friend, Patrick Hogan, thanked Childers for outlining the 'virtual independence' of Canada, and he assured the assembly that the Treaty gave Ireland just that: 'virtual independence'.[50]

W. T. Cosgrave also used Childers's analysis and rejected Childers's conclusion. 'Canada', he quoted, ' "is by the full admission of British statesmen equal in status to Great Britain and as free as Great Britain". "Canada alone can legislate for Canada." '[51] Cosgrave continued that while technically the British parliament alone could alter the Canadian constitution, in practice only Canada could alter it. ' "In fact" ', he said, ' "the Canadian owes obedience to his own Constitution only" ', and he added that ' "the Governor-General of Canada in law is the nominee of the British Cabinet only. In fact he is the joint nominee of the Canadian and British Cabinets" '.[52] Here Cosgrave was quoting Childers against himself. Professor Michael Hayes supplemented the evidence of Dominion nationhood by referring to the Dominion representation at Versailles and at the 1921 Washington Conference.

Meanwhile the lawyer Gavan Duffy exhorted the constitution-makers to

relegate the King of England to the exterior darkness as far as they can. . . . All our internal affairs so far as the Constitution is concerned are left to our fashioning and any government worthy of the name will be able to place that foreign King at a very considerable distance from the Irish people.[53]

Professor MacNeill in turn urged that in interpreting the Treaty the facts must be seized and not 'some antiquated theory'.[54] He stood for 'Ireland's equality of status with all the other members of that community and for the right of complete national sovereignty in our domain', and he believed that Ireland would have the support, in its interpretation, 'of South Africa, Canada, Australia and New Zealand, for it is to their selfish interest that that construction . . . be put upon these terms'.[55]

Ireland would not be free, Ireland would be free. The arguments alternated. With considerable insight and determination the case was put for Dominion status, and, trusting their leaders the Deputies of Dail Eireann voted. The views of Griffith and Collins were sustained. The Treaty was accepted and put to the test, and history has vindicated those who approved it. It was not so clear then, nor was it to be clear for some years. But the record of the Irish Free State in the British Commonwealth of Nations during the first ten years of its life, a decade which forms an era in itself, is an active and a positive one. From the very moment of its entrance into the Commonwealth, as well as by the very fact of that entrance, the Irish Free State began to change the imperial association.

I

The Irish Free State and the British Empire 1922

Dail Eireann accepted Dominion status on Saturday 7 January 1922, but the Treaty with Great Britain which brought this status carried a 'significance not limited to Ireland'.[1] It brought to that association, now officially described not only as the 'British Empire' but also as the 'British Commonwealth of Nations', a Catholic, European mother country which had arrived at its new status not by evolution but by revolution and which, by its arrival, 'raised again more fundamental questions about the ordering of imperial relations and definition of dominion status'.[2] A treaty was an unprecedented Dominion midwife, and this one not only marked a point in Dominion development, it contained within itself new advances towards full Dominion sovereignty.

The most fundamental advance embodied in the Treaty concerned the oath to be taken by members of Parliament in the new Dominion. The contentious Article Four had almost halted the Treaty negotiations, which were rescued only by the insight into Irish susceptibilities attained by Lord Birkenhead. The agreed formula involved no direct allegiance to the King.* As Henri Bourassa, the veteran Canadian nationalist, wryly demonstrated in the Canadian House of Commons, this oath was far removed from the obedient Canadian declaration: 'I do swear that I will be faithful and bear true allegiance to Her Majesty Queen Victoria.' It marked a further development of Dominion diversity by ending their 'common allegiance to the Crown'.[3] The Irish Deputy's allegiance was to the Constitution of the Irish Free State, and to the King only in his capacity as part of that Constitution. Though this should not be

---

* Article Four contained the following oath: 'I . . . do solemnly swear true faith and allegiance to the Constitution of the Irish Free State as by law established and that I will be faithful to H.M. King George V, his heirs and successors by law, in virtue of the common citizenship of the group of nations forming the British Commonwealth of Nations.'

over-stressed, the oath and the passions aroused by its discussion made clear the attitude of the new Dominion. Upholders of the unitary monarchy were issued with a warning.

Furthermore, although the Treaty laid down that the Governor-General should be appointed 'in the like manner as the Governor-General of Canada and in accordance with the practice observed in the making of such appointments',[4] there was a specific undertaking given by the British negotiators that the Irish Government should have a greater than usual share in the nomination and appointment of this officer.[5] The Irish delegation were able to insist that the King's representative would be an Irishman and a commoner, and they followed this up by naming their choice. Doubtless there was not much competition for the job amongst the English aristocracy, but it was nevertheless an important precedent when Timothy Healy* was appointed.

Though the Appeal to the Judicial Committee of the Privy Council was not specifically mentioned in the Treaty, the Irish delegates were assured that this provision, regarded as an essential safeguard for minority rights, would not be exercised except in accordance with the wishes of the Irish Government.[6] That this assurance was not adhered to caused much indignation later on.

But if the Treaty 'stretched the framework of dominion status in the attempt to make room within it for the national and self-derived statehood which Ireland claimed',[7] the Irish Constitution expressed the autochthonous basis of the state even more firmly. Henri Bourassa, trying to jolt Canada back into the vanguard of Dominion development, again pointed out the difference between Article Nine of 'our Constitution' and Article Two of 'the Constitution of Ireland, the latest in that magnificent development of self-government in the British dominions. . . .'[8] Certainly Article Nine: 'the executive government and authority of and over Canada is hereby declared to continue and be vested in the queen',[8] compared ill with: 'All powers of government and all authority legislative, executive, and judicial in Ireland, are derived from the people of Ireland and the same shall be

---

* Tim Healy had been a member of the Irish Party at Westminster, and had been of great assistance to the Irish delegation at the Treaty negotiations in London. He had a wide experience of men and affairs, and a shrewd grasp of character. His name was first suggested by Kevin O'Higgins, his nephew, with the disarming plea to his colleagues that they should not suspect him of nepotism! Though the bitter legacy of the Parnell split prevented unanimous approval in Ireland, his experience proved very valuable to the young government.

exercised in the Irish Free State (Saorstat Eireann) through the organisations established by or under, and in accord with, this Constitution'.[9]

Drafted by theorists,* who were without practical experience but who were able to draw widely from British and continental sources, the Constitution bore the impress of Hugh Kennedy, who was determined to exclude British impositions.† Embodying the actual rather than the legal status of the Dominions, the Irish Free State Constitution 'presented an unprecedented impact between the theoretic dogmatism of continental systems and the evolutionary empiricism of the British Constitution'.[10] The 'archaic symbols [of the British Constitution] had to be introduced, but their meaninglessness for Ireland was writ large on every page. The monarchical forms paled into insignificance in the light of the formal enunciation and the consistent application of the principle of the sovereignty of the people as the fundamental and exclusive source of all political authority'.[11] In it 'the sovereignty as well as the continuity of the native parliament could not have been expressed more emphatically',[12] though it is true that obligations contracted with the Southern Unionist minority and in the Treaty were included.‡

'A most comprehensive and, in spirit, essentially republican constitution on most advanced Continental lines',[13] the Irish Constitution was contained in parallel legislation in Dublin and Westminster. The Irish Act[14] 'decreed' and 'enacted' on an authority which came 'from God to the people'.[15] Its first article broke new Dominion ground by defining the Irish Free State as 'a co-equal member of the British Commonwealth of Nations'. Article Two was

* The Constituent Committee consisted of: Chairman, Michael Collins; Vice-Chairman and Secretary, James Douglas; Hugh Kennedy (Law Adviser to the Provisional Government); James Murnaghan; James MacNeill; The O'Rahilly; C. J. France; Kevin O'Shiel; John Byrne.

† When faced with a British requirement which he felt was not in accord with Irish aspirations, Kennedy would emasculate it as far as possible, so that it might work *his* way '*if at all*', as his phrase had it (W. T. Cosgrave, interview).

‡ Apart from the special restrictions imposed on her dominion status by the Treaty – the defence arrangements, the limitation of Irish forces, and the financial agreements – Hugh Kennedy maintained that Britain had no wish to interfere in the Irish Constitution. In order to avoid subsequent controversy the Provisional Government undertook to show the British the Constitution draft. This was done early in 1922 but the political chaos in Ireland led some in England to insist on the letter of the Canadian Constitution, ignoring the 'practice and constitutional usage'. Michael Collins travelled to London to counter this suggestion, and he 'successfully and cordially' accomplished this. (See H. Kennedy, 'The association of Canada with the Constitution of the Irish Free State', in *Canadian Bar Review* (1928) VI – also note on pp. 24–25.)

equally novel and we have already noted Henri Bourassa's comments upon it.

The Irish negotiators had won the right to nominate their Governor-General. The Constitution now went further than any other amongst the Dominions to reduce the status of this nominated official: the opening and closing of Parliament was fixed by the Dail; the choice of President was fixed by nomination from the Dail, and the other ministers by nomination of the President; the Governor-General had no powers of dissolution. A formal apex to the parliamentary framework, he was placed in fact on a lower level than the President of the Executive Council.

Article Fifty of the Irish Constitution emphatically established the indigenous national power of amendment ('within the terms' of the Treaty, which was scheduled to the Constitution). Article 66, dealing with the Appeal to the Privy Council, contained a self-contradiction without parallel in any other Dominion constitution. As Lord Buckmaster later explained, it was 'quite plain upon the face of it that, as far as possible, finality and supremacy are to be given to the Irish Courts'.[16] The primacy of the Gaelic language was a further departure from Dominion precedent. More important was the distinctive Irish citizenship instituted in Article Three, though this, it is admitted, was consistent with the 1910 Canadian immigration legislation. An effort was made also to repose in the Oireachtas the power to declare war.[17] The defence facilities afforded to Britain by the Treaty would no doubt have prejudiced this power in practice, but behind it lay the desire, common to all the Dominions, to escape involvement in British or imperial wars of no obvious local concern.*

The British Government accepted this individual and democratic Constitution, no doubt informed by the Irish leaders that if it was rejected the anti-Treaty group would surely triumph.[18] The Dail, further unbalanced by the withdrawal of the anti-Treaty faction, was bludgeoned into accepting some of the Constitution as it stood by the threat of the Provisional Government that it would otherwise resign.† Nevertheless, a vigorous and extremely detailed

* The desire applied equally to obligations to the League of Nations. Canada in particular was anxious to avoid being subject to advice from the League Council with respect to military obligations. See C. A. W. Manning, *The Policies of the British Dominions in the League of Nations*, pp. 32–3.

† In a letter to Mr Thomas Johnson, published in the *Irish Times* on Saturday 23 September 1922, Kevin O'Higgins described in full the details of the Constitution which they had agreed with Britain not to alter. This was because the British claimed

debate occupied the Dail from 18 September until 25 October 1922.

Perhaps it is simply stating the obvious to point out the concern of Irishmen at this time to remove British influence from Irish affairs, and to remove Irishmen altogether from British alliances. Later, admittedly, there was some modification. The Civil War in Ireland did give to the Treaty a measure of sanctity and the Cosgrave Administration, having fought to protect it, 'not without an austere pride . . . took its stand' upon it.[19] Later, some of what had become the inspiration of General Botha infected a few of the Irish leaders.* A feeling of greater security inside the Commonwealth association developed. On 15 December 1926, with commendable realism, Desmond FitzGerald admitted that:

> The League of Nations as its machinery and institutions develop may obtain such tangible recognition of the community and inter-dependence of all countries as will give sufficient guarantees for the elimination of war, the political and commercial integration of its members, and may make any other group arrangement unnecessary. But it would be foolish to imagine that the system of group association, whether engendered by geographical propinquity or by other ties, can cease to operate within any period susceptible of being estimated, even approximately, in our generation. No political regime in this country could ignore those agencies and remain isolated without substantial injury to this country. Our state is a member of the British Commonwealth, but if it were not so declared in the Treaty of 1921, I think it is pretty certain

---

that it was 'constitutional usage and practice to express certain matters in the name of the Crown', and these were listed as Parliament, which had to be summoned and dissolved in the name of the Crown; the King, who had to be a member of the legislature; Ministers, who had to be appointed in the name of the Crown; and Judges likewise. Legislation had to be assented to in the name of the Crown and every money vote at the request of the government of the day had to be presented in a message from the Crown or its representative. He explained also that 'several other clauses are agreed texts after discussion, and I think it will be found that these agreed texts are in no case to the disadvantage of Ireland'. O'Higgins then listed the preliminary clause and twenty of the Articles affected by this interpretation and agreement. He added a final paragraph on Article 66, emphasising that Ireland had been accorded the South African position in regard to the Appeal to the Privy Council, and that this Appeal would be allowed only in cases which affected other members of the Commonwealth.

* On 28 August 1919 General Botha died. Already he had come to see the British Empire in a new light. He had been able to say: 'I fought against the British, but I am a firm upholder of the Commonwealth. In South Africa we enjoy all the liberty we could have as an independent nation, and far greater security against external aggression; we have complete powers of self-government; we control the development of our country; and in the affairs of the world we take a place far higher and render a service more notable and useful than we could attain or give as a separate nation.' Cited in W. K. Hancock, *Survey of British Commonwealth Affairs*, p. 70.

that we should adhere to some group. And I am satisfied that geographical and other conditions, the natural flow of commerce and many other agencies existing at present, would lead us to associate with our nearest neighbour, Great Britain, and with the Commonwealth of which she is a member.[20]

In 1928, Mr Blythe, Minister of Finance and also at that time Vice-President of the Executive Council, was even more candid:

Are we seeking a Republic? We are not. We believe that this country as a member of the British Commonwealth of Nations can enjoy greater freedom and greater security than she could outside the British Commonwealth of Nations, and our policy within it is really to remove anomalies that exist in the relationship between the members of it.[21]

But these sentiments were rarely expressed, and they were not in accord even with the left wing of the government party. In 1922 the Treaty was fresh and so was the memory of the war with Britain: a war 'fought to stop Ireland being pink on the map'.[22] No one in Ireland believed that Ireland would be treated on a par with the other Dominions; everyone believed that Britain would still try to dominate the imperial association.*

In 1922, as Kevin O'Higgins was to recall to the Irish Society at Oxford University two years later: 'the Provisional Government was simply eight young men in the City Hall standing amidst the ruins of one administration, with the foundations of another not yet laid, and with wild men screaming through the keyhole.[23] This was not a time for political theories, incorporating visions of a far-sighted, supra-nationalist association. The Irish simply asked for a chance to make their own country. They were preoccupied with the practical business of state-building, and if a few appreciated the evolution which was transforming an Empire of domination into a Commonwealth of consent, they had little love for a settlement imposed on the aspiring Republic. There was little realisation in 1922 of the Commonwealth's promise of greater security and liberty. The wider co-operation and brotherhood of international association, surmounting the narrow isolation of nation-state, could be envisaged only after the nation itself had been confirmed.

Thus, in the interminable debate over the Constitution, there was,

---

* W. T. Cosgrave has said that the Irish Free State Cabinet lost its suspicion of Great Britain after about a year. It was some time longer before it realised it could go its own way, but even then there was little realisation of the true position in the rest of the country, which continued to agitate and criticise the government unjustly (interview).

understandably, no sense of coming-of-age, of reaching a new maturity within the Commonwealth, a maturity which would enable Irishmen to play a constructive part in moulding the destinies of all while securing the fullest freedom for themselves. The disappointed Republic was too close. The need to make the Treaty compromise acceptable to the whole country was too delicate a matter for the government to enthuse over anything British. Even though Gavan Duffy, Professor Magennis and Darrell Figgis had a knowledge of what Dominion freedom meant, and even though O'Higgins and Cosgrave had sufficient confidence in Ireland and sufficient optimism about the Commonwealth to recommend first the Treaty and then the Constitution, Ireland's role in the new Commonwealth was never outlined. Given time, Ireland could *get* everything for her freedom from this arrangement. What Ireland could *give* was so irrelevant to the mood of 1922 that it was only touched upon in isolated moments of anti-imperial fellow-feeling for Indians and Egyptians.

However, the few well-read, constitutionally-trained men in the Dail did describe the contemporary pattern of Commonwealth development, revealing considerable knowledge and foresight. Gavan Duffy, hair-splitter though he may have been, took pains to list the proposals made by Smuts in 1917, and, emphasising always the importance of 'practice and constitutional usage' as opposed to 'law', he begged the assembly not to rush into a definition of Commonwealth relationships. He looked to the promised Commonwealth Constitutional Conference (of the 1917 Resolution) to overhaul the old, archaic imperial relations and construct new forms: 'The British Dominions are asking that these things [new forms] shall be put down in black and white in the light of day. Surely an Irish Government is not going to ask us to indite them in red, white and blue in the dark of the present moment?'[24] Cosgrave retorted that Irishmen were good enough to resolve their own affairs without Smuts or any other Commonwealth leader: Kevin O'Higgins added that this promised conference had already met, in 1921, only to decide not to meet. Professor Magennis outlined the evolving international personality of Canada and South Africa and made a moving appeal to the Republican faction. If those outside, he pleaded,

> would only take the trouble to understand what we have got, and how our feet have been put on the path that leads to the realisation of all that the highest patriotism has ever desired from our country, if they

would stop to consider what partnership, fellowship in the great Commonwealth of Free Nations really involves, they would not be on the hillsides today, but here sharing with us the task of trying to frame the best of Constitutions for our country.*

This may have been a portent of a constructive Irish effort yet to come, but if so the urge unfortunately soon perished in the wordy heart of that over-splenetic academic.

As the Constitution wound through its five readings the amendments became more sophisticated, the quotation of outside authorities more numerous, and the marshalling of Dominion precedents more feverish. Gavan Duffy was again in the forefront. He returned to Smuts to show that Britain could no longer claim supremacy, and he insisted that the words 'sole and exclusive' be added to reinforce the legislative power of the Oireachtas over the Free State (Article 12). This was based on the advice of Professor A. B. Keith. To emphasise that the Governor-General must be advised, in Ireland, by his Irish Ministers only, he introduced the views of Henry Harrison, Professor Keith and Duncan Hall. With a final flourish he underlined the autochthonous nature of the Irish Parliament, which alone could truly 'enact this Constitution'. 'We are not made Dominions by this Treaty', he exclaimed, like the Dominions 'who had to go to England for a British Act of Parliament which was the very foundation of their new authority ... but we are accorded, if you like, the same status.'[25] Ireland was already a nation. Magennis added Lord Haldane to the list of authorities, while Deputy W. Cole quoted Borden's description of the Dominions as 'Ministerial republics',[26] and made tentative reflections pertinent to the 'several' nature of the monarchy. Darrell Figgis wanted a Commonwealth tribunal in the Australian tradition, instead of the Privy Council, and was astute in demanding a recognition of Ireland's right to extra-territorial jurisdiction. He, too, quoted Keith, but Kevin O'Higgins preferred this matter to be left as it was, so that the extraterritorial

---

* Dail Eireann debates, i, col. 569. There is an apt quotation in the South African House of Assembly, 22 April 1931, when Dr N. J. van der Merwe praised General Hertzog's contribution to the proposed Statute of Westminster. His words could so easily have been uttered by any of those 'on the hillside' had they had sufficient vision. 'I honour the Republican idea', he said, 'and for it I stand four-square behind the Prime Minister. He has written freedom on his banner and this will lead to a republic.' The passions of the Dail often found a parallel in South Africa. In 1934 Count John McCormack could write home in surprise that a speech by Smuts in the South African House of Parliament 'could have been uttered in the Dail, it was so apropos' (McGilligan Papers).

power could be assumed to exist. As Minister for Home Affairs and Vice-President, O'Higgins carried the burden of seeing the Constitution through the Dail and he was careful to assert that nothing they were doing was irrevocable: that they were fixing nothing 'in cast iron'.[27] He rejoiced that power was now in the hands of the Irish people and he took pleasure in the special relationship to Canada which the Treaty gave to the Free State. Here was the guarantee of future progress and the safeguard of present gains.

On his re-election to the office of President, on 6 December 1922, W. T. Cosgrave looked ahead, and, closing one era, he opened another with a note of appeal:

> The present position of the free nations which constitute the British Commonwealth is something which every Irishman should examine, know and dwell upon ... it was because of their vision and understanding of what it all meant and all it stood for that the two great leaders whom we have so lately lost, boldly asked the Irish people to accept that position and the almost unlimited measure of freedom and independence which the treaty offered. ... We appeal again ... to the people who stand in arms against this free Constitution ... to open their eyes and to realise ... the fact that freedom is in their hands though they know it not.[28]

By the time those eyes were in fact opened, however, many further steps forward had been taken. In 1932, while Leo Kohn was writing that 'it was the new conception of co-equality and national sovereignty embodied in the Constitution of the Irish Free State which inspired the re-definition of Imperial Relations by the Imperial Conferences of 1926 and 1931',[29] Mr de Valera was admitting in Seanad Eireann that since the Treaty 'there have been advances made that I did not believe would be made at the time'.[30] As the ensuing chapters hope to demonstrate, it was not simply the Irish Constitution which led to the 're-definition' and 'advances', but also the unmitigated pressure of successive Irish ministers and civil servants whose contribution, in the words of Patrick McGilligan, was 'positive, persistent and decisive'.[31]

2

External Relations 1922–3

In 1922 the Chanak incident profoundly changed Empire foreign relationships, and it was Canada, led by Mackenzie King, which set the Dominion pace. This incident, a feature in the Graeco-Turkish post-First World War struggle, threatened to involve Britain in an uncomfortably isolated military role in the Balkans. In September 1922 Lloyd George appealed to the Dominions to send troops to support Britain in her latest hour of need. But the appeal – in the form of an enquiry – was hopelessly bungled from the start. It antagonised loyal Australia and even the unquestioning New Zealand was unhappy, though not the same series of unfortunate circumstances occurred in New Zealand as in Canada. There, Mackenzie King, angered by a premature newspaper manifesto, by a complete lack of prior information from Britain and the unprecedented suggestion of sending troops, refused the British request. He threw the responsibility for action upon the Canadian Parliament, confident that it would not comply. Fortunately the crisis was resolved in the Balkans: but in the Commonwealth it simmered on and it left its permanent imprint.

It demonstrated, to begin with, the complete inadequacy of existing Dominion communications. Far more important, it revealed a fundamental divergence of ideas in the Commonwealth. Decentralisation and aggressive nationalism were on the move again. A Dominion, angered by the lack of courtesy and the playing of the 'Empire Game' by Britain, had for the first time refused to stand by the rest of the Empire in a serious emergency. Chanak was remote from Canada and from Canadian interests, and Canada had preferred not to become embroiled.* Its reaction was a timely warning to the

---

* For an outline of these events see R. M. Dawson, *The development of Dominion status*, 1900–36, pp. 234–50. Also R. M. Dawson, *W. L. M. King*, 1; Lord Beaverbrook, *The decline and fall of Lloyd George*; and *Round Table*, no. 230 (April 1968), pp. 169–77.

over-complacent Empire statesmen in London, too inclined to take the military support of the Dominions for granted.

Also in 1922 the new Irish Free State set about mounting the League of Nations stage at Geneva. The Irishmen who had fought against England in the early twentieth century for the independence of their country had, of course, followed the example of their fore-fathers: 'a nation once again' was their hope; rebellion was their traditional pursuit. But they had also another tradition. If we remember that Robert Emmet required that his epitaph should remain unwritten until Ireland had 'taken her place amongst the nations of the earth', we will remember too that Ireland had long looked to the continent of Europe and to America both for the inspiration of its freedom and the outlet of its energies, until that freedom should be grasped. In its final struggle it did not hesitate to court the German Empire in the moment of England's weakness, while after the Great War it made its plea in the name of self-determination for small nations, echoing the lofty sentiments of President Wilson of America. And when it finally came to terms with Britain it did so influenced strongly by two attributes of dominionhood which appealed to this tradition: firstly it could expect to join the League; secondly it would acquire the established right, albeit hitherto unexercised, of diplomatic representation in foreign capitals.

The use made of these attributes must not be ignored, and in particular the effects of that use on the British Commonwealth. For the Irish Free State was not content with a merely theoretical place amongst the nations of the world. In the capitals of a few relevant states, but above all at Geneva, it sought to proclaim its independence and secure its equality in real terms, and every step it took reverberated round the Commonwealth. At first the Irish Free State was subdued. Once it had settled its domestic strife, however, it threw itself with vigour into the maelstrom of post-war Europe. Even in the earliest days it studied its task with careful precision.

The first Free State Minister for Foreign Affairs was George Gavan Duffy. He was replaced by Desmond FitzGerald in the Cosgrave Government, which took office in the autumn of 1922, but he had by then blueprinted future Irish action. On 20 June 1922 he drew up for his successor a memorandum weighing the prospects for the young Free State. Its first objective must be to join the League of Nations. He paints the picture and he underlines the motive:

. . . our Envoys will be much sought after. The reasons are: first, that Ireland is a world-race with great possibilities; secondly that we are supposed to have great influence upon American politics and policy; thirdly, that we know England better than the continental peoples and that the friendship of an Ireland lying on England's flank may at any moment be very useful; moreover we have a reputation for frankness and fearlessness which stands us in good stead, and it has often been said that Ireland in the League of Nations will be invaluable, because she may be expected to say plainly the things that everyone is thinking and that other powers are too cowardly to be the first to say.

. . . All the principal countries, and most of the smaller ones want closer connections with us, and many of them are influenced by the fact that Ireland is believed to stand for democratic principles, against Imperialism and upon the side of liberty throughout the World.

. . . There is no doubt whatever that these various factors give us an international importance quite disproportionate to the size and population of this island and that we can enhance our international position, if we seize our obvious opportunities.

. . . The bigger our world-position becomes, the more increasingly difficult it will be for England to attempt any undue interference with us; for this reason, if for no other, money and trouble spent by the Irish Government upon foreign development will be amply repaid. There is no other sphere in which we have equal opportunities for making ourselves seriously felt by England; and it is urgently necessary that we should train some of the best of our young men for the international field.[1]

To Gavan Duffy the priorities were clear. He distrusted England – but there were few Irish leaders who did not in 1922 – and he feared the Commonwealth, which was surely dominated by Westminster. But there was at Geneva a platform in the spotlight of the world's press. Ireland must mount to this platform immediately and thereupon make fast her sovereign freedom. Gavan Duffy was himself soon replaced, but his policy survived, and if we view the succeeding ten years of busy international life in the light of his observations we will understand the role of the Free State. Gavan Duffy's policy was implemented: and what advanced the status of his Dominion advanced the status of all.

As we have seen from the Introduction the international position of the Dominions was far from clear in 1922. They had joined the League as founder members – indeed, General Smuts was one of the chief architects of the League Covenant – but they belonged nevertheless in a somewhat ambiguous category: they were 'Dominions', and they were listed together after the mother country, Great Britain, and not in alphabetical order as were other members. The

British Empire, furthermore, was represented permanently on the League Council, not just Great Britain. To many foreigners it appeared that Dominion membership was simply a device to give the Empire seven votes.

In practice, of course, the Dominions quickly disproved this charge. They were young nations detached from the atmosphere and influences of Europe and they tended to speak their minds and to support only what they believed to be worth while. Foreign affairs were new to them but they were at pains to demonstrate to the world that they could stand on their own feet. As C. A. W. Manning pointed out: 'That the plurality of British Commonwealth votes were not always, if ever, to be placed at the unfettered disposal of England, became manifest from the start.'[2] If it was not quite a question of *quot* Dominions *tot sententiae*, the world soon became aware that the Dominions could vote as they liked. But the Dominions did have their difficulties.

All of them were far removed from Geneva. South Africa and Australia and New Zealand in particular could not hope to spare ministers for the length of time that representation at the Assemblies required. Once at Geneva a Dominion delegation could not easily maintain contact with its home government. Expense too was a problem, for there was seldom enough interest in foreign affairs in the Dominions themselves to justify adequate expenditure. These factors inhibited participation in the Committees and the specialised work of the League, further reducing interest at home. Canada was in a slightly better position and usually managed to include a Minister in its delegations. It carried a little more weight, too, as the sole representative of North America, but it must be realised that while the Dominions might often impart a high moral tone to the Geneva debates, through speaking their minds, they nevertheless possessed little political force. Collectively they did lend Great Britain a greater authority, and the Commonwealth did make an effort to consult and reach a common policy on major issues. But there was no machinery of discussion, apart from the Imperial Conference, and suggestions for group conferences before the Council or Assembly meetings were not acted upon: discussions during the Assembly were 'informal and occasional', their frequency and intimacy varying 'from year to year'.[3]

It must be admitted, too, that the Dominions maintained a certain amount of suspicion and doubt about the League. None of them,

Canada least of all, was enthusiastic about acquiring new obligations in Europe. World peace was a cause to which they were prepared to sacrifice and stint themselves but they did not approve of League requirements of a military nature, which placed authority in the hands of the Council and took from the individual members their power of decision. Canada had been the pioneer of early Dominion status, and from their first days at Geneva the Canadians had sought to alter Article 10 of the Covenant: that Article which guaranteed 'against external aggression the territorial integrity and existing political independence of all Members'. Canada, in the spirit of American continentalism, but also sharing a common Dominion reluctance towards overseas commitments, had opposed this clause lest it be involved in some remote war. In 1923 it did manage to achieve an interpretation of the clause which allayed its fear. Australia and New Zealand were afraid that the League might break up the Commonwealth, which was already doing for part of the world what the League might one day achieve for the whole world: with South Africa, however, they willingly shouldered the responsibility of Mandate Territories.

Membership of the Commonwealth did give the Dominions a certain stature. They were used to Imperial Conference negotiation and to the principle of agreement with unanimity. Canada also brought long experience of a successfully demilitarised border, and a proven system of joint international investigation of border disputes. With South Africa it had experience of harmonising disparate national groups.

This was the sort of Dominion involvement and reaction which was to emerge in Geneva. In 1922 the situation had not become clear but at least the Dominions were there upon the stage. They may not have appreciated the *inertie courtoise* that inhibited their more sophisticated European colleagues from expressing their minds lest they offend their allies; they may not have appreciated some of the finer subtleties of international intrigue; but they were learning to make themselves known abroad and in fairly harmless circumstances. Even though L. S. Amery might later regret 'the distraction created by the League of Nations' where the Dominions were enabled 'to assert their individual international status without, in fact, incurring any serious individual responsibilities',[4] and even though they were, to adopt Hughes's phrase, 'like little boys who swim on bladders'[5] – for they could get out of their depth with relative impunity – the

Dominions found the League an invaluable training ground in diplomacy, which came at a most opportune moment in the development of their national awareness. The League provided a training ground, a platform, a collective security and a means of self-assertion. It is not surprising therefore that the Irish Free State was anxious to join and use it.

From the outset, of course, the Irish Free State was unique amongst the Dominions. Even more so than in its 'internal' imperial situation, its position in the outside world differentiated it sharply from its Commonwealth colleagues. To begin with it was not a 'new' country in the sense that the other Dominions were. It was a mother country in its own right with a long and proud history. More important, it was European. It was favourably and securely placed in the shadow of Britain and had easy access to the Geneva deliberations. Furthermore, it had nationals well versed in European politics and it had the 'feel' of a continent often baffling to other Dominions. Manning takes trouble to establish that the Free State was a Dominion, for the sixth Committee's Report, upon which it was elected to membership, notes that the Free State was 'a Dominion forming part of the British Empire upon the same conditions as the other Dominions which are already members';[6] but his subsequent analysis is forced to exclude the Free State so frequently from the convenient generalisations which fitted the other Dominions that it soon becomes apparent that it was of a quite exceptional nature. It was exceptional from the start and it took pains to point this out.

In 1922 the Free State had established Michael McWhite in Geneva. This ex-officer of the Foreign Legion had a flair for diplomatic activity and his hard work and astute management played a notable part in establishing the Free State at the League. As early as 17 January 1922 he was interviewing Sir Eric Drummond, the Secretary-General of the League, about the requirements of membership and the form of application. Ireland was also helped, while the negotiations for membership proceeded throughout that year, by E. J. Phelan, of the International Labour Office, a man whose 'remarkable knowledge of European politics and of technical matters connected with the League'[7] was put at the disposal of his native country. On 17 April 1923 a formal application was submitted by Desmond FitzGerald to Sir Eric Drummond,[8] and in the following September President Cosgrave journeyed to Geneva to see his country admitted on the tenth of that month.

The Free State did not apply to join the League as a Dominion but as 'Saorstat Eireann . . . a fully self-governing state'.[9] President Cosgrave underlined this status in his speech to the Assembly which he closed with a dignified statement of the value of the League; a statement which Manning thought worthy of inclusion as the best description of the Dominion attitude towards international co-operation: '. . . as the life of a man is bettered and fructified beyond measure in a harmonious society of men', President Cosgrave averred, 'so must the life of nations reach a much fuller liberty and a much fuller dignity in the harmonious society of States.'[10] The Irish Free State took its place. How would it use it?

A clue to this question is quickly supplied. Cosgrave could not delay long in Switzerland, for he had to return to the new Dail about to meet in Dublin. But he left behind John MacNeill, the multi-lingual Marquis MacSwiney and Kevin O'Sheil, as well as McWhite. MacNeill was in charge and on 4 October reported how the Irish baptism had proceeded:

> The Irish delegation maintained throughout the position of representa-tives of a foreign, independent state linked by the terms of the Treaty to Great Britain and the Dominions States and cultivating a spirit of friendship and friendly consultation with these. This is also the attitude of Canada, South Africa and Australia. New Zealand claims this status less pronouncedly though I do not know if anything inconsistent with it could be specified.[11]

MacNeill went on to assure his government that 'the full status of Ireland was universally admitted', and he recounted how Marquis MacSwiney had corrected a Japanese delegate who suggested that the Dominions were of a subordinate status to Great Britain. A British delegate, Sir Hubert Llewellyn Smith, had corroborated MacSwiney's statement and the Canadian, Graham, was 'warmly appreciative' of the Irishman's intervention. MacNeill praised the discretion and effectiveness of the Marquis, who was perhaps the best linguist in the Assembly, and the efficiency with which O'Sheil had set about winning goodwill for Ireland. His highest tribute, however, is for McWhite, who had 'good tact and judgement and a remarkable knowledge of political personages and the press', and who, besides being an active member of the delegation, had under-taken all the secretarial work as well. To him, and to E. J. Phelan,*

---

* E. J. Phelan was Chief of the Diplomatic Division of the International Labour Office.

who 'always watched for the advantage of Ireland and whose advice never failed us', the Irish delegation owed 'the fact of being able to keep up in spite of the inexperience of the rest of us'.[12]

MacNeill was able to recognise the disadvantages of power groupings in the League along the lines of the old balance of power system, but he was convinced of the overriding utility of the organisation, and he echoed Gavan Duffy's plea that a greater interest should be taken, and adequate staff in the Department of External Affairs be provided. When he left Geneva, MacNeill travelled straight to the 1923 Imperial Conference. There he urged support for the League's principles as the basis for Commonwealth co-operation in foreign policy.

Before turning to Imperial Conference considerations, however, we must take note of a further Canadian initiative of great Commonwealth significance. On 22 March 1923 Canada signed with America a treaty 'to secure the Preservation at the Halibut Fishery of the North Pacific Ocean'.[13] In so doing Canada took a major step forward in the conduct of foreign affairs by the Dominions. Its attitude was entirely logical and reasonable and was born out and endorsed by the Imperial Conference later in the year,* but it was the first Dominion assertion of the treaty-making power. Mackenzie King, indeed, emphasised three precedents: first, the appointment of a Canadian plenipotentiary on the advice of the Canadian Government; second, the signing of the Treaty by that minister alone; and third, the ratification by the King on the advice of the Canadian Government.[14] But for Canada it did even more. When the Treaty had been ratified in Washington,[15] 'the Canadian Government had succeeded in securing from the United States that recognition of its international status of which it had been disappointed when the Senate rejected the Covenant of the League of Nations'.[16] Needless to say this action like the earlier stand over Chanak, was observed with considerable approval in Dublin.[17]

* See Chapter 4.

3
The Imperial Conference

Before observing the Imperial Conference of 1923, it is important first to examine the Imperial Conference itself as an institution, for the conference system was perhaps the greatest expression of the Commonwealth as a reality.* It must be seen as it was, and how the diverse statesmen and commentators of the Commonwealth regarded it.

By 1914 the Imperial Conference had a regular composition, regular sessions, and customary methods of procedure, and in the Imperial War Conference it reached a peak of concerted effort and a comradeship in arms facilitated by continuous contact. After the First World War it altered somewhat in emphasis so that at the beginning of our period the purpose and powers of the Conference were as uncertain as those of the Empire itself. There were many suggestions, there were supporters and detractors; and throughout our period voices for change were freely raised. Confident centralists advised consolidation and continuous machinery; anxious devolutionists suspected and resented the very existence of the Conference. To many in the Dominions these London sessions were the basis of the federalists' dream. Dominion premiers met there to discuss. Did they not also decide and commit? Such conferences might usurp Cabinet decisions, might effectively create a central authority, might develop an imperial parliament. Dominion representatives were warned to beware of taking decisions proper only to Dominion parliaments, and even such determined statebuilders as Mackenzie King and W. T. Cosgrave were suspected. Would not the crafty English in their citadel ensnare and bamboozle their guests, committing them to British policies by a combination of Court dinners

---

* Or, in the phrase of Nicholas Mansergh, the Imperial Conference was regarded as 'the chief buttress of imperial unity and the tangible expression of imperial co-operation'. P. N. S. Mansergh, *Survey of Commonwealth Affairs, 1931–9*, p. 34.

and high-flown phrases? Critically, jealously, the stay-at-home opposition nationalists of the Empire watched each conference for evidence of imperial encroachment.

The Dominion representatives at each conference did all in their power to allay such doubts. In a series of references in 1926, for example, Desmond FitzGerald explained the Conference to Dail Eireann.

> The Imperial Conference is a body which meets, but which has no absolute power. It is not able to control anybody. It is a meeting of representatives of those States which form the British Commonwealth of Nations coming together pre-eminently for the purpose of deciding what the relations of those States will be. . . .[1] [It] has no powers whatsoever, but nations working together find it useful to come together at times and consider any difficulties that may arise in their so working.. . .[2] It has no powers delegated to it . . . none of the attributes of a supreme federal council and it does not claim to have them. It is simply a meeting of the representatives of the independent governments of the Commonwealth for the purpose of conferring together to discover the most effective means of furthering the interests of each member of the group and of the group as a whole. With this end in view it formulates certain conclusions, the acceptance or rejection of which depends on the will of the governments.[3]

More succinctly, Mackenzie King had defended the system in 1923. 'The governments of the Empire must confer; the Parliaments of the Empire, if needs be, must decide'.[4] His Minister for Justice reinforced this claim:

> The Imperial Conference is not an executive, nor a government, nor a cabinet: it is a consultative body and nothing else. . . . It is a consultative body composed of representatives of the various units of the Empire who meet, get each other's opinions, discuss conditions and problems which affect all or some of them, and, in the light of knowledge and impressions received and communicated to them, may afterwards, if necessary, recommend to their respective parliaments any legislation or executive act which may best suit the need. . . .
>
> We want to preserve as much as possible the association of the nations of the Commonwealth, and the Imperial Conference is one of the means of preserving if possible this association by promoting friendly meetings, friendly discussions of problems and friendly intercourse.[5]

The Conference, then, was a conferring together of Dominion leaders, without sinister intent. But it was an intermittent arrangement and it was not immune from further criticisms. The opinions

of some of its detractors are illuminating. Henri Bourassa was particularly scornful, and he was pointing to the central difficulty of the
Conference and to the heart of the imperial problem, when in 1927,
he debated the 1926 Conference:

> If you take into account the circumstances – the peculiar and very
> different circumstances – under which the representatives of the various
> dominions have to carry on their internal government and their external
> policies, you will readily understand that in this conference, as in every
> other conference, a formula had to be found without any regard to
> logic, without any regard to harmony of thought and purpose but in
> which something had to be inserted to please everybody. . . . There
> will never be an Imperial Conference, or any political body in which
> the representatives of Great Britain and the various self-governing
> dominions meet to discuss various propositions of internal economy or
> external policy upon which they can agree. If they are bound to agree in
> formulas they must lie to each other in their expression of their thought;
> and also lie to their respective peoples; or if they want to tell the whole
> truth, if they want to express the thoughts and aspirations of their
> respective peoples, they must express differences of opinion because the
> conflicting interests cannot agree, because the aspirations are not the
> same, because differences are caused by geographical, historical and
> economic conditions.[6]

The difficulty of reaching a Conference Report congenial to all
parties was ever present. Another Canadian had said of the 1923
Report that it was more significant for what it left out than for what
it contained: that in their desire for unanimity the Dominion representatives had been forced to emasculate many of their resolutions
and to ignore others completely.[7] Lester Pearson's general description of the typical conference report is only too true. If such a report
had been written after Runnymede, he explained, it would have said
no more than that 'there had been a full and friendly discussion of
feudal rights and the Conference decided to make some recommendations to King John'.[8]

In Australia the requirement of unanimous decisions at the Conference was deplored as having the effect only of levelling everything
down to 'the lowest degree of loyal sentiment'.[9] Conference reports
contained 'a great deal in the way of high-sounding phrases but very
little of a substantial character',[10] according to at least one critic in
New Zealand. Even the very atmosphere of the Conference was
criticised by Patrick McGilligan, who attended all the Conferences
in our period in one capacity or another. The Commonwealth was a
gentleman's group, he explained, and it was very important to 'play

the game'. While Ireland was no longer threatened with 'immediate and terrible war' it was often isolated in embarrassing silences. To speed progress the British would make concessions and then appeal to 'our Irish friends' to make concessions too. To stand fast was to feel a heel and a cad, even though one knew that wheedling and deliberate staging had played their part in such incidents.[11] Mackenzie King noted similar feelings in 1923.[12] And all Dominion statesmen were aware that the home advantages of initiation and the first draft, which lay with Britain, were very important factors operating against them.*

The Imperial Conference, then, had its shortcomings and its critics. Yet those who went to these meetings and met and conferred there were conscious of its great value and potential. The warm, world-wide contacts, the comradeship and the genuine spirit of co-operation left them in no doubt that such meetings were more than just a showpiece expression of the Commonwealth tie. They were inspiring and useful in themselves. The problem was how to make the most use of them; constructive suggestion was needed, not mere condemnation.

We have seen in the Introduction some of the suggestions put forward by General Smuts in 1921. In that year the Imperial Conference itself recorded the value which it felt it contained. Here was the best method of reconciling Dominion differences and of understanding one another's point of view. At the time the need for full consultation upon which to base co-operative action was keenly felt. As ever, the difficulty was how to consult soon enough and often enough to meet the demands of international politics. L. S. Amery was then formulating his own views, and in letters written to Sir Edward Grigg in June 1921, he outlined his thoughts. As a commentary on the past system and as an insight into the wishes of one of the chief actors upon this particular stage, these thoughts are instructive. On 1 June 1921, a time when the idea of a Constitutional Conference to redraw the relations of the Commonwealth was still fresh in the air, he wrote:

> My feeling about the old regular Imperial Conference is that it was not differential enough. Once the novelty of the mere fact of the Dominion

---

* See L. S. Amery, *Thoughts on the Constitution*, p. 145. Writing in 1946/7 L. S. Amery recognises the existence of this and claims that it also embarrassed and inhibited the British Delegation. The situation has changed little even today. For the comments of Premier Eric Williams of Trinidad and Tobago in 1965 see Chapter 10, p. 254 below.

Ministers being over here ceased, it lacked the element of publicity and debate. On the other hand the fact that its proceedings were enshrined in a blue book and that it was a conference and not an intimate personal meeting, made it unsuitable for the discussion of executive policy and more particularly of foreign affairs and defence. The latter need was met by the creation of the Imperial War Cabinet which was a real Cabinet in the sense that it discussed in intimate confidence and with a view to immediate decisions, the great problems of foreign policy and defence. . . . A directly elected Assembly or Convention might conceivably come at a more distant date, but the most obvious and simple way of providing this need is a conference of small Parliamentary delegations in which not only the Governments but the Opposition Parties are represented. All that is wanted is some reasonable excuse for bringing such a Conference into being without dropping what has been gained by having instituted the Imperial Cabinet system. . . . Another Committee will also be required to go into the question of more effective co-operation and consultation on foreign affairs. This is an issue separate from the question of the constitutional conference, though of course, any satisfactory arrangement arrived at in this respect might be amplified or at any rate officially endorsed by the constitutional conference when it does meet. I quite know all the reluctance there is to face the giving of any real responsibility to a Minister over here, but the objection is not really one of substance, but only a part of the unfamiliarity of the Dominion statesmen with external affairs generally. . . .

On 24 June 1921 he added a further thought:

The more I think of it the clearer it is to my mind that a committee ought to be appointed without delay to go into the constitutional question, viz the machinery for co-operation and the agenda for the Constitutional Conference. These two matters really hang together, for if the Conference is not to take place till 1923 that is all the more reason for setting up some sort of effective machinery for consultation and co-operation for the immediate future.*

The Federation-fearing Dominion nationalists had definite grounds for their suspicions, had they but known. For it was just this central machinery, which must necessarily assume some of their own sovereignty, that they feared most. Mackenzie King was later to

---

* L. S. Amery to Sir Edward Grigg, 1 June and 24 June 1921, in Sir Edward Grigg's papers, in the possession of John Grigg (hereafter cited as Grigg papers). Amery added further interesting details at the close of his letter of 24 June 1921 on the content of the Committee he desired: 'I wonder whether it would be possible to suggest to the Prime Minister appointing Milner Chairman of the Committee? He would be able to give the time and would be trusted equally by Smuts and by the Massey–Hughes wing. The Prime Minister might also possibly like to add Fisher as a representative of liberalism. . . . I should be only too delighted if I got the chance of going on to it myself. And of course, you ought to be Secretary' (Grigg Papers).

become suspicious simply because Amery, as Dominions Secretary, began regular tea-parties for the Dominion High Commissioners in London. Any suspicion of extra-parliamentary commitment was to him anathema. And so the problem of consultation remained a problem.

In 1924 the Labour Government in Britain, responsible for many gaffes in its brief term of office, made its own effort to solve the problem. The atmosphere was not propitious and the mention of 'some sort of workable machinery'[13] did not meet with approval. Neither did the mention of Opposition Party representation, to which Amery also alluded above. This was a recurring suggestion and an easy one to refute. In 1927, while leader of the Opposition in New Zealand, W. E. Holland hoped that 'the time will come when the Imperial Conference will cease to be a Conference merely of the dominant parties in the different dominions – when it will in reality represent the people of the countries within the Empire'.[14] But, as Premier Forbes pointed out, 'the Conference can only be a Prime Ministers Conference, for only the Prime Ministers can "deliver the goods" '. Only discord could result if the Opposition was there too.[15] On the occasion of the Labour Party's suggestion in 1924, Canada was even more vehemently opposed:

> We regard the Imperial Conference as a Conference of Governments of which each is responsible to its own Parliament and ultimately to its own electorate, and in no sense as an Imperial Council determining the policy of the Empire as a whole. We would deem it most inadvisable to depart in any particular from this conception, which is based on well-established principles of Ministerial responsibility and the supremacy of Parliament. We consider that with respect to all Imperial Conference resolutions or proposals, each government must accept responsibility for its attitude and the Oppositions or Opposition be free to criticise: with Parliaments and, if occasion arises, peoples deciding the issues.[16]

The dilemma remained. Towards the close of our period the *Saturday Review* could still complain:

> there can be no co-operation without co-operative organs of some kind: and the Imperial Conference has never yet provided itself with any organs except the Imperial War Graves Commission. ... Had the Imperial Conference been a living institution, equipped with a permanent secretariat representing all the member states, these officials would have been studying for months in advance the various matters which the governments intended to bring forward, and preparing memoranda for them.... In default of such elementary organisation

and preparation we have again had [the 1930 Conference] the spectacle of feverish rush, with its overstraining of minds, fraying of nerves, and, in the end, next to nothing done.[17]

Criticised but also appreciated, the Imperial Conference went on being used, subject to the tensions of the particular international situation at the time of its meetings, and handicapped by the *ad hoc* nature of its secretariats. In its very nature it contained contradictions and inhibitions, but it continued to be useful, and, in spite of its centralising nuances, it remained the chief stage upon which the dominions advanced towards full and independent sovereignty. To see how it was so used in this decade we shall look at each Conference in turn. And we shall regard particularly the contribution of the delegates from the Irish Free State. Irish statesmen did much to transform the Empire from a standpoint outside the Imperial Conference orbit, in the diplomatic, legal and economic controversies that swept in succession across the international landscape. But here at the Imperial Conferences they were working inside: inside at the heart of the British Empire, at the representative meetings of all the Dominion leaders, in London, centre of the British world. Perhaps this work was primarily dedicated to the advancement of Ireland, not the Commonwealth *per se*. But, most particularly inside the Conference system, both the deliberate and the secondary Irish achievements had far-reaching effects on the Commonwealth. It is of little use to examine the Empire as though the Irish Free State never existed.[18] It did exist, and in the 1920s its capable leaders supported, equalled and finally commanded the forces of Dominion evolution. Their main battleground was the Imperial Conference.

4
The Imperial Conferences 1923

It is impossible to approach any imperial conference without reference to the international conditions under which it met. In 1923 the European scene was one of squabbling uncertainty: Germany was disintegrating, France and Britain were out of tune, communists and fascists were flourishing amidst post-war depression and disillusion. Nearer home, in the Dominion sense, the incident at Chanak and the Canadian Halibut Treaty with the United States dominated the Conference preparations and influenced its decisions. Foreign policy and a united Empire front appeared more important to Britain than inter-Dominion details, so that international affairs and defence accordingly occupied a large part of the Conference agenda. Canada, loyal but anxious to justify its recent national self-assertiveness, kept up the momentum of Dominion development. No constitutional conference ensued, but the meeting nevertheless occupies an important place in Commonwealth evolution: through it co-operation emerged as the chosen way and centralisation was discontinued.

No great Irish contribution was forthcoming, but the Irish leaders were introduced to 'new experiences and responsibilities'.[1] If they were content to follow their Dominion colleagues on this occasion, then that was a natural response of beginners. They were never to be so quiescent again.

The Conference assembled in London on 1 October without Premier Bruce, who did not arrive from Australia until the fifth. It was heralded enthusiastically by the press, and for a week or two the Dominion statesmen held their own on the centre pages amidst German revolutions, Japanese earthquakes, royal weddings and election speculations. At the funeral of Mr Bonar Law and at the Armistice Services they received honourable mention. But their deliberations, some necessarily in secret, could not hold the public imagination for long.

As they foregathered, *The Times* recommended to them the virtues of a calm and united Empire in a troubled and divided world.[2] Mr Baldwin in his opening speech revealed how near Europe had been brought to renewed hostilities by the Italian bombardment of Corfu. The Dominion leaders responded, in reply, to the warm brotherhood of their association. Mr Cosgrave, graciously and sincerely welcomed, made a short speech of good faith and co-operative intention,[3] and then returned to his work in Dublin. Desmond FitzGerald was appointed chief Irish representative, and he attended for the team photograph. When Professor MacNeill arrived from Geneva, however, he was given charge of Irish opinion, with Mr McGrath appearing at the concurrent Economic Conference. The Irish leaders were too busy to give the Conference the attention it merited. They had a state to build at home.

The Conference followed upon considerable advance preparation, and informed commentators had already predicted its likely moods. The *Round Table* had been realistic enough to depart from its federal dream and had appreciated the growing preoccupation of the Dominions with their own domestic affairs. 'The *Round Table*', it proclaimed,

> does not consider that, under the present circumstances, with the German menace gone, with the problems of their own internal development, with the disparity in the population of Great Britain and the overseas nations, and above all, perhaps, with the uncertainty that attaches to the part that the United States is going to play in the world, that any organic reconstruction of the Constitution of the Commonwealth is practical.[4]

Mackenzie King of Canada emphasised this same conclusion before leaving for London. Canada did not 'propose to raise any questions of constitutional changes,' he said. As he had advised on a previous occasion, he repeated, 'no steps should be taken in any way involving any change in the relation of Canada to other parts of the Empire'.[5] Yet Canada was expected by many in Britain to prove this time to be an awkward partner. More than the other Dominions it had demonstrated its rejection of a British diplomatic monopoly. In the emergency of Chanak it had underlined the sovereignty of its own Parliament and exposed the inadequacy of imperial communications: Canada would not be stampeded into an unquestioning acceptance of British decisions. By negotiating a treaty with the United States itself, without requiring the signature of a British representative,

Canada had given notice of maturing status and of its own special relationship to its great southern neighbour. The 1923 Conference, called to consolidate the Dominion harmony of 1921, found the atmosphere less congenial to the centralist plan. Dominion interest in world politics had waned. Canada was wary of European entanglements, and South Africa too was reluctant to accept commitments far from home. The new Irish Free State was quick to endorse these views.

From 1 October until 8 November the Conference deliberated the problems of the Empire and of the world. It held sixteen plenary sessions. The Economic Conference, in which the Dominion premiers took a great interest, lasted from 2 October until 9 November, with twenty-three plenary meetings. *The Times*, which had at the beginning recommended the importance of foreign affairs to the Conference, summarised its discussions on a similar note: 'The Prime Ministers of the Dominions found that the chief issues awaiting settlement were not so much concerned with the future conduct of their own affairs as with the present state of Europe.'[6] Mr Baldwin, speaking at the Lord Mayor's banquet on 9 November, made a similar summary of the Conference, placing foreign policy and imperial defence above all else in importance.[7]

The Conference, indeed, had given much of its time to the state of the world. Keen discussions had followed the comprehensive review of the League of Nations, given by Lord Robert Cecil, and the outline of colonial affairs given by the Duke of Devonshire,[8] as well as the masterly survey of foreign affairs which Lord Curzon had conducted on 5 October.[9] Curzon was not unique among British Foreign Secretaries in wishing to have the whole strength of the Empire behind his pronouncements and he fought hard at this Conference to have the Dominions accept a united foreign policy for the Empire. Bruce was an enthusiastic supporter, and with him his satellite Massey; Smuts was deeply concerned to restore European peace, and it was left to Mackenzie King to hold out for the right of the Dominions to pass judgement in foreign affairs. Here was the crucial parting of the ways. Would the Conference draw the Empire closer together in order to give strong leadership to a chaotic Europe, or would it recognise the growth of Dominion autonomy as an inevitable development? Mackenzie King made it clear from the start that he was out to justify his stand at Chanak and his assertion of the treaty-making power. He would not allow the Conference to usurp Cabinet powers, and he would not approve British foreign policy without full information and without parliamentary authority. He had no ambitions to share in the reshaping of Europe and he threatened a separate Canadian resolution and support for a potential Irish paragraph of dissociation from British policy in Egypt, unless he got his way. The Canadian premier was consistently wary of any centralising suggestions and he went so far as to hint that future Conference invitations would have to be closely considered by his country if there was going to be pressure to conform in this respect.[10] He confessed later that he did not enjoy being so outspoken, but he succeeded in making his point. The Empire did not pursue its wartime centralisation further. It began to adjust to a condition based on the nationalism and independence of the Dominions.

A combined defence policy did not fare much better. Here again the Canadian leader was reluctant to accept centralising commitments, and *The Times* gloomily asserted that 'it is in the very important question of defence that the results of the Conference are least conclusive and least satisfactory', regretting that there was no 'constructive suggestion embodied in the Report as to how the burden should be shared'.[11] J. W. Dafoe, the shrewd Canadian journalist who was covering the Conference, added a list of defence and foreign policy topics upon which the Conference was unable to reach unanimous decisions.[12] There was no declaration on the Singapore naval scheme (merely 'interest' noted), and no naval plans were agreed; nor was an expeditionary force founded to deal with sudden emergencies; there was no Near East policy agreement, and there was no strong condemnation of French obduracy, which the British had sought; the 1921 assurance that the British Foreign Secretary spoke with the weight of the Empire behind him was not repeated.

In the discussion of inter-Dominion affairs, also, Mackenzie King was outspoken, and the most important resolution respecting 'Negotiation, Signature and Ratification of Treaties' was an official blessing of the Canada–United States Halibut Treaty precedent. As the Report explained:

> The word 'Treaty', is used in the sense of an agreement which in accordance with the normal practice of diplomacy, would take the form of a Treaty between Heads of States, signed by plenipotentiaries provided with Full Powers issued by the Heads of the States, and authorising the holders to conclude a Treaty.[13]

The procedure for negotiation' signature and ratification was then set out, with an explanatory note outlining the existing practice for ratification, which was to be maintained. This was the one clear achievement of the Conference. It was a definite recognition that the Dominions had the right and power to look after their own treaties: and this implied looking after their own foreign affairs.

Mackenzie King did not insist on his own view that the Dominion High Commissioners should have their status increased, as there was no general demand from the other Dominions, and this issue was side-stepped. The Conference discussed at length the position of Indians throughout the Empire, but it was able to give the Indian delegation no more than an assurance that disabilities placed on Indians in other parts of the Empire were not the result of colour prejudice. The problems of instituting the 1921 Conference resolution on this matter was passed on to a Committee of enquiry.

The Economic Conference made tentative steps in the direction of an imperial preference, upon which Amery, Lloyd-Graeme and, not least, Bruce, hoped to build an impregnable Empire. Here the full proceedings were published and the difficulties of the Conference were exposed to the public. Everyone had different points of view, or at least a difference of emphasis. With reference to the British gesture on Preference, Mr Burton of South Africa said:

> While we welcome what you propose to do . . . we claim the right in our Dominion to settle our own fiscal policy, and therefore we do not claim any right, whether by actual motion or even by 'methods of education' to interfere in the right of the British people here to settle their own fiscal policy for themselves.[14]

Mackenzie King adopted a similar line, feeling that such a Preference should be based on goodwill only. Bruce, on the other hand, had put forward detailed proposals, hoping to strengthen the Empire by economic bonds. Britain refused some of Bruce's proposals but did make concessions respecting dried and fresh fruit. Bruce also proposed, on 6 November, the appointment of an imperial economic committee. In spite of characteristic opposition to this from King, it was generally approved, though it did not come fully into operation until 1925. Overseas settlement, co-operation in imperial development, and steps to improve mutual trade were debated in detail, but further conflicting views inhibited dynamic action. This Economic Conference was not a success. Most of the issues debated were either too big for its scope, or too small. It was not repeated in this form again.

The Conference Reports roused few passions in any quarter. Sir Keith Hancock has said of this Imperial Conference that 'for joint control and responsibility it substituted separate control and responsibility', with the obligation to consult.[15] But there was little realisation in the Dominions at the time that anything remarkable had happened. According to one Canadian historian, for example, 'Canadians were more concerned with domestic problems than with external affairs. Few realised the new orientation in imperial relations; it would be many years before they would boast of their distinctive autonomy.'[16]

In Australia, the *Round Table* reported that there had been little public following of proceedings, and that no one really understood Canada's assertion of the treaty-making power. The imperial preference debates aroused most interest, but in spite of Premier Bruce's proposals there was little to cheer about. Bruce, a Cambridge rowing blue and a strong imperialist, a handsome man with a permanent limp sustained in the Empire's defence, had come to London to strengthen that Empire by economic and military agreements. The Conference must have been a disappointment to him. And what disappointed Australia had a similar effect on New Zealand, especially when in the following year, the British Labour Party undid what little advance there had been in regard to preferential tariffs.

South Africa did not react at all to the new treaty resolution, but was particularly interested in the preference which was accorded to dried fruit, sugar, tobacco, wine and some fresh fruits. General Smuts, with his comprehensive interests and duties and his particular concern for the peace of the world had tended to support Britain and a strong Empire foreign policy, to the detriment of inter-Dominion constitutional matters.

Canada was well content. Mackenzie King had proved immune to the blandishments of the imperial capital and had defended successfully the interests of his country. Even if domestic issues overshadowed external affairs, the Canadian Government was congratulated on its stand in London, and loyal pleasure was recorded that Canada was recognisable as an autonomous entity in the galaxy of nations surrounding the British throne.

There is little doubt that this was indeed Mackenzie King's conference, and he was himself pleased with his first appearance. 'The Imperial Conferences', he wrote in his diary, 'have broadened my vision and added fresh and larger interests . . . the experience has left me with added confidence.'[17] At its close Smuts is reported to have turned to him and said: 'You ought to be satisfied. Canada has had her way in everything.'[18] J. W. Dafoe, who had been attached to the Canadian party in London, was agreeably surprised by King's firmness of purpose.[19] R. M. Dawson, outlining the developments in Dominion status between 1900 and 1936, attributes to King credit for the fact that in 1923 the 'centralising characteristics of the Imperial Cabinet dropped quietly, and the non-committal conversations of the old Imperial Conference as quietly resumed'.[20] But though Mackenzie King is indeed to be congratulated, some responsibility must also be given to his able lieutenant Dr O. D. Skelton.

Oscar Skelton was to play a continuous and important part in imperial affairs, and in particular in the field of Irish-Canadian co-operation.* University lecturer and biographer of Laurier, he was chosen by Mackenzie King, in 1923, to serve as Secretary to the Canadian Delegation. In 1924 he became a Counsellor in the Department of External Affairs, then a tiny department with only three administrative officers; and in 1925 he became Deputy Minister, in effect Under-Secretary of State, for that department. He was one of the ablest men in Canada,[21] came from Queen's University, Ontario, and was married to an Irish-Canadian who had written a biography of D'Arcy McGee.[22] For two months before the 1923 Conference he prepared memoranda on every topic. He was particularly opposed to a common Empire foreign policy. This, he felt, offered Canada a maximum of responsibility with a minimum of control. To ensure real influence and responsible control the Dominion must reserve ultimate decisions to its own Parliament. Skelton had great influence in Canadian foreign policy decisions. He proved to be a powerful friend to Ireland, and there was considerable correspondence between his department and Dublin, and occasional exchanges of views in Geneva.[23] At future imperial conferences he was to co-operate closely with his Irish counterparts. If he was sometimes over-cautious it was in deference to Mackenzie King's considerable British veneer, and because on some issues the reality of French Canada at home allowed him less room to move than the Irishmen. It is fitting, and significant, that Vincent Massey,

* 'He was influenced throughout his life by strong Irish . . . sympathies.' See W. A. Mackintosh, 'O. D. Skelton', in R. L. McDougall (ed.), *Canada's Past and Present* (series five), p. 60.

reviewing his long association with the Department of External Affairs, should have concluded as follows:

> Skelton is often referred to as the creator of our diplomatic service. This is not entirely true, although he made a great contribution to the service as its able permanent head for sixteen years, approached his work in a spirit of very real loyalty to the post and brought to his task a brilliant academic mind. . . . One might have expected that a person with so scholarly a mind as Skelton would be objective in outlook, but in certain matters this was not so. He had a strong and lasting suspicion of British policy and an unchanging coldness towards Great Britain. In other words, to put it bluntly, but I do not feel unfairly he was anti-British. No one who had worked with him, or who knew him well, could, I think, fail to recognise this.[24]

We shall see more of Dr Skelton later.

The British Delegation at the Conference was not entirely of one mind, and party politics and traditional tariff prejudices were accorded undue weight by the prospect of a general election. Baldwin was a gracious host but was never decisive (except on motions to adjourn). According to the brilliant if wayward Curzon 'nothing can exceed the cheerfulness, good temper and courtesy of Baldwin, except his impotence. At the Conference he never opens his mouth and leaves the entire lead to me.'[25] Baldwin did, however, opt for Protection in his Plymouth speech, on 25 October, and he called an election for 6 December to confirm his radical gesture. But when the British Government was defeated at this election more problems were created than if the Dominions had been given no encouragement in the first place. The British Labour Party repudiated the Conference agreements, causing increased disappointment and harshly exposing the problems involved in conducting an Empire of co-operation. Curzon, Amery and Lloyd-Graeme were the chief 'Empire' protagonists at the Conference, but Amery, as First Lord of the Admiralty, was not then so well placed as he was to be in the future.

The part played by the Irish Free State at the Conference has been deliberately left to the end. It was not a large part, and its context was to some extent explained by Lord Balfour when he spoke on the subject of the Conference at Nottingham University in 1924:

> The part of the Irish Free State in the Conference was a difficult one. They had no experience of Imperial Conferences, and they had made up their mind that they had come to listen on this occasion and not to offer very much advice; and they listened, and finally they became impressed

– in spite of everything deeply impressed – with the significance of the British Empire, and towards the end, without knowing it, they joined in.[26]

Perhaps this was not completely the mood of the Irish leaders. They had approached the Conference with a certain amount of misgiving, and with suspicion. Furthermore they were preoccupied at home: the strike at Dublin docks, the launching of a National Loan, and the introduction of the 'Courts of Justice Bill' to the Dail were sufficient problems for a country still in its birth pangs, without looking for more. Home issues dominated the public interest and there was no enthusiasm for a London Conference which might involve participation in policies of little concern to the Free State. Britain was presumed to control these imperial meetings and Cosgrave expressed his anxiety before he set out. He had seen his country welcomed into the League of Nations in the previous month, however, and he was characteristically prepared to accept the new experiences and responsibilities attached both to the League and to the Commonwealth associations.

Denis Gwynn, who was amongst the crowd assembled at Whitehall to watch the delegates arriving, describes vividly the enthusiasm and heightened interest displayed when the modest Irish contingent appeared, and he recounts how, from the moment of their warm reception, the Irish responded to the friendship and understanding shown them by their Dominion colleagues.[27] Smuts in particular was consistently kind, and day by day the confidence of the Irish representatives increased. They discovered that the opinions of every Conference member counted, theirs no less; that everything was to be gained and nothing lost by a full and candid participation. It was these discoveries which enabled them, before the end, to join in wholeheartedly. The experience was a valuable one. The Irish leaders realised that they need stand in no awe of their fellow Dominion statesmen. They were impressed by the comprehensive nature of the subjects and the complete trust shown in their integrity. Patrick McGilligan, who was Secretary to the Irish Delegation, has stressed the good effect of this complete acceptance of the Irish Free State; this complete assumption of its good faith.* The Irish

* Mr McGilligan was amazed at the freedom of speech and the trust placed in the Irish ex-rebels, even though some confidential matters were kept from the Irish Free State and India by the device of calling a meeting of 'Prime Ministers'. Many defence details – naval, military and air – were outlined without inhibition. McGilligan, who had been Secretary to the Irish High Commissioner James MacNeil, was persuaded

inferiority complex, or, more simply, the natural reaction of a country
which had so recently achieved its freedom by war, had assumed
that Ireland would not receive equal treatment. This Conference
dispelled that illusion. They were ready to play a full part next time.
· The Irish had not had time to prepare for this Conference. The
Civil War and the establishment of the State were scarcely behind
them when the Conference assembled. Cosgrave's opening speech
was no more than a gesture. He did not appear again. Mr FitzGerald
was more concerned with Dublin than London at this time, and
though he represented the Irish Free State on the Treaty Resolution
sub-committee, recorded a handsome but painless expression of
sympathy with the Indian delegation, and added half a dozen lines
in the tariff debate, his contribution was not weighty. Professor
MacNeill, scholarly, eminent, but by then more interested in other
things, hardly ever appeared. In reply to Lord Robert Cecil's survey
of the League of Nations' activities he stated bluntly that 'the Irish
Free State has arrived at nothing nearer to a definition of Foreign
Policy than is expressed in its adhesion to the League of Nations'. [28]
He added that if all pursued policies in conformity with the underlying principles of the League, there would be no difficulty in steer-
ing a common course. At the end of the Conference he did dig his
heels in and insist that references to 'The British Empire', in the
final address to the King, be changed to the 'British Commonwealth
of Nations', and references to 'the throne' be replaced by 'the
Crown'. He had little enthusiasm for the trappings of a colonial
age.* Kevin O'Higgins crossed to the Conference to attend and to
speak at the foreign affairs discussion: General Mulcahy joined only
the defence deliberations.

   At the Economic Conference, the Irish Minister for Industry and
Commerce, Mr J. M. McGrath, made a suitably non-committal

---

to act as secretary to his brother Professor John MacNeill for the conference. He had
complete freedom and a front line seat on most occasions, as the Professor was an
infrequent attender.
   * John MacNeill to Executive Council, 26 October 1923 (FitzGerald Papers). In the
same letter MacNeill notes that time is ripe for the Registration of the Treaty at Geneva.
A story is told of his only other contribution to this august assembly. Bored by the
rambling dissertation of Massey of New Zealand on frozen mutton, sheep farming and
his constituents (referred to as sheep, whether by intention or mistake) MacNeill passed
back the following note: 'The only difference that I can detect between this delegate and
his constituents (sheep) is that they have their wool outside their heads.' The note was
unintentionally circulated and was only just retrieved before it reached the New Zealand
benches.

opening.* On 2 October he told the other delegates that 'The Free State Government and people have as yet had no time to evolve an economic policy',[29] and so he could not lay any plans before the Conference. To the *Irish Times*, this was the more relevant of the two conferences, and it desired the Minister to co-operate closely with the Commonwealth, to gain preferential rates in the British market.[30] *The Times*, while pointing out that the Irish people took note of little outside their own country, commented that Irish interests were closely involved. Imperial preference, it argued, would do more than anything to kill republicanism, while there was a real need for an imaginative Empire settlement programme, now that the new American immigration laws were restricting the entry of Irishmen there.[31]

Though he may not have had a plan to lay before the Conference, there is no doubt that Mr McGrath was alive to the advantages a preferential entry into the British market would bring. He was bound, however, to agree with South Africa on this matter. Ireland had fought hard to win her own fiscal autonomy and it could not now dictate terms to England. Had a comprehensive list of Empire goods been favoured, an effort to add butter and beef would have been made. Ireland also shared Mackenzie King's distrust of central agencies based on London, be they economic or political.

Ireland at the Conference, then, did not play an important role. There is little doubt, however, that the tenor of the Report was in accord with Irish aspirations, and that the one positive achievement, the treaty resolution, suited Ireland's book perfectly. 'Time spent on reconnaissance' according to the military maxim, 'is seldom wasted.' The 1923 Conference was an Imperial recce by the Irish Free State. It was in due course put to good use, as the Irish achievements in 1926 and 1929 affirm.

* Mr E. J. Riordan, Secretary to the Trade and Shipping Department of the Department of Industry and Commerce, attended in the absence of Mr McGrath.

5

External Relations 1924-6

(i) 1924

At the Imperial Conference the Irish Free State had made a cautious beginning. MacNeill, the chief Irish delegate, had come straight from the League of Nations, and his sole contribution had been to urge respect for the ideals of that body. The League meant so much to the young Free State: membership was itself the guarantee and the expression of its nationhood. Geneva was a place to make friends and to counter potentially undesirable Commonwealth tendencies; Geneva was a centre of world affairs infinitely more acceptable than London, and the Free State could play there an international role clearly more independent. O'Higgins in particular recognised the value of the conference table and at Geneva the table was bigger and more representative than in London.* Costello, too, saw greater security in the League for an Ireland so lately freed from British domination.† Membership was itself a prize. But there was also an immediate object in joining the League. The Free State wished to register the Ango-Irish Treaty as an international agreement under the terms of Article 18 of the Covenant.

This contentious move soon opened up the *inter se* controversy which was to trouble the Commonwealth for the rest of the decade.‡

* O'Higgins, Kevin Christopher (1892–1927), elected Sinn Fein M.P. for Queen's County, December 1918. Appointed Assistant Minister for Local Government 1919 and Minister of Economic Affairs in the Provisional Government 1922. After the deaths of Griffith and Collins he became Vice-President of the Executive Council and Minister for Justice.

† Costello, John Aloysius (20 June 1891–), Assistant Law Officer, Provisional Government 1922; Assistant to Attorney-General 1922–6; Attorney-General 1926–32; T.D. 1933– ; Taoiseach 1948–51, 1954–7.

‡ This whole topic has been treated by J. E. S. Fawcett in his *The 'inter se' Doctrine of Commonwealth Relations*, University of London Institute of Commonwealth Studies, Commonwealth Papers no. v (1958). This particular Irish incident is mentioned on p. 16 though J. E. S. Fawcett wrongly attributes registration to January 1924.

It represented a major assertion of independent Dominion thought and gave unequivocal notice that the Free State had a mind of its own, and that it was prepared to follow it to the extent of taking independent international action. To the Free State itself, the implications were more vital and more personal. Successfully to register the Treaty was to establish the Free State as an international entity. If the Treaty was ever to be repudiated by Britain, the *status quo ante* could not then be restored, for the Irish Free State would have received recognition as a treaty-making state, rather than a mere adjunct of Great Britain. The attempt to register provoked firm opposition from Britain, but it had not been lightly undertaken by the Irish leaders. The same thorough preparation which was later to characterise their conduct of imperial affairs fortified their registration bid here.

THE REGISTRATION OF THE ANGLO-IRISH TREATY (1921) AT GENEVA, 1924

The Irish Free State began by establishing a permanent delegation at Geneva, giving Michael McWhite full official status in 1923.* He established his headquarters at 35, Quai du Mont Blanc, and on 17 September 1923 he wrote home for the requirements necessary to proceed. On behalf of his delegation he sought from the Minister for External Affairs:

(1) Instructions empowering them to take the necessary steps to have the Anglo-Irish Treaty registered;
(2) That the date of registration be left to our discretion as to whether it should be done immediately or left over until the Assembly adjourns;
(3) That a certified copy of the Treaty be sent to us. We can supply the French translation.
   This matter should be seen to immediately so that we may be prepared for any eventuality.[1]

Already the British had wind of what was intended and a letter two days later from MacNeill in Geneva refers to British 'Die Hard' suspicions and to the fact that the Irish were already circulating copies of the Treaty in French. The reply to McWhite's letter was sent on 22 September and it contained three requests for further information:

* The Irish Free State was the first Dominion to establish a permanent delegation at Geneva. Canada followed suit in 1924 and South Africa in 1929.

(1) If the Treaty were presented in the ordinary way for registration, would it be accepted by the usual registering authorities, or would it be referred to the General Secretary for his decision?
(2) What were the implications attached to the date of registering with special reference to (1) above?
(3) What form meets the League view of a 'certified copy' of the Treaty?[2]

McWhite's reply on 25 September indicated the need for caution and enclosed detailed information on procedure. He answered the Minister's questions in order, stating:

(1) That any Treaty presented to the League for registration should, in the first instance, pass through the hands of the Secretary General.
   We are not in a position to make any authoritative statement as to the possible lines of action on the part of the League authorities following an attempt to register.
(2) It would be advisable to make no attempt at registration whilst the Assembly is sitting, and
(3) The meaning of the term 'certified copy' is explained in Article 6 of the accompanying Memo.[3]

The 'accompanying Memo' was a copy of a memorandum dealing with the Registration of Treaties, which was approved by the League Council in 1920. It clearly stated the obligation imposed on members to register every form of international treaty or agreement, and it suggested that 'Parties presenting a Treaty or Engagement for registration should do so by depositing a textual and complete copy thereof with all appurtenant declarations, protocols, ratifications, etc., at the Treaty Registration Bureau of the International Secretariat'.[4] It merely remained for the Irish Government to prepare the relevant documents and to await the propitious moment.

On 3 November 1923, Diarmuid O'Hegarty, Secretary to the Executive Council, enquired of MacNeill, then attending the Imperial Conference in London, if the moment really was right to proceed.* MacNeill may now have advocated delay, for the next mention available is a request, made in Dail Eireann on 9 April 1924 by the leader of the Opposition, that action be taken on the matter. Deputy Johnson,† who was supported in his plea by Deputy Milroy, was anxious to see the Treaty officially safeguarded. Desmond FitzGerald admitted that steps were being taken.[5]

These steps resulted in the Treaty being registered on 11 July

* See note, p. 54 above.
† Thomas Johnson: Leader of the Labour Party and Leader of the Opposition 1922–7; Senator 1928–36.

1924. The Free State formally informed the British of their intentions six days in advance, on 5 July. The formal British reply to this letter was not written until 4 November and it puts the Irish action firmly in its Commonwealth context. Meanwhile there had been conversations and correspondence backstage. President Cosgrave and Whiskard, of the Colonial Office, conferred early in August. On the thirteenth of that month Whiskard wrote his Government's views to the President, and these were summarised as follows in an Irish Cabinet memorandum:

> In the opinion of the Colonial Secretary, the action of the Irish Free State Government raised questions of very great Constitutional importance as to the relations between the component parts of the Empire. In order to make their own position clear the British Government would feel bound to inform the Secretariat that the Treaty was not, in their opinion, an instrument proper to be registered under Article 18 of the Covenant.[6]

In his reply the President made it quite clear that he regarded the Treaty as 'a matter between two nations'[6] and as such there was a clear obligation to register under the said Article.

On 4 November J. H. Thomas amplified the British statement. His words were repeated in the letter to the Secretary-General of the League on 27 November, signed by Alexander Cadogan.

> ... Since the Covenant of the League of Nations came into force His Majesty's Government have consistently taken the view that neither it nor any Convention concluded under the auspices of the League are intended to govern the relations *inter se* of the various parts of the British Commonwealth. His Majesty's Government consider, therefore, that the terms of Article 18* of the Covenant are not applicable to the 'Articles of Agreement of 6 December 1921'.[7]

Thomas informed the Irish that he was conveying this information to the Secretary-General and he repeated the conclusions of the Barcelona Arms Traffic Conference of 1921 to support his contention.†

In Irish eyes this view was quite indefensible. Mr J. P. Walshe, later to become Secretary of the Department of External Affairs, drafted an exhaustive commentary on the situation, expressing the frustration felt by the Dominions in the League and underlining

---

* 'Every Treaty or international engagement entered into hereafter by any member of the League shall be forthwith registered with the Secretariat and shall, as soon as possible, be published by it. No such Treaty or international engagement shall be binding until so registered.' Article 18 of Covenant of League of Nations.

† See below, Ch. 6, p. 118, and Ch. 8, pp. 209–16.

the illogicality of the British theory. In it are contained the roots of
Irish foreign policy and the portents of its Imperial Conference
arguments. Walshe argued:

> The British obviously do not want to sacrifice their pet principle of the
> oneness of the sovereignty of the Commonwealth. They cannot allow
> two portions of the Commonwealth to bring a dispute before the
> League, the International Court or any other external body. If a single
> member of the Commonwealth brings a dispute with an outside State
> before the League, the fiction of the whole acting for the part will save
> the situation. The effort to maintain this fiction at all costs is at the
> bottom of the present ridiculous position of the Dominions in the
> League. They are actually members twice over and they have less power
> than the smallest State in the League. The Member of the League
> represented by the British Delegate is not the late United Kingdom, not
> the United Kingdom plus Crown Colonies and Protectorates, but the
> British Empire in the most comprehensive sense of the term with the
> result that the signature of the British Delegate necessarily binds every-
> one of the Dominions unless there is an express reservation in each case
> excluding them.
>
> The possibility of the Dominions being regarded as High Contracting
> Parties and independent Sovereign States was also faced at the Barce-
> lona Conference and a remedy was sought in the division of the
> Conventions into two parts: (*a*) A covering convention between High
> Contracting Parties and (*b*) An agreement between Contracting States.
> Sir Hubert Llewellyn Smith* explained to the Conference that this was
> necessary because 'the League of Nations included a certain number of
> Members which are Dominions and not Sovereign States. In diplomatic
> language they cannot properly be described, therefore, as High Con-
> tracting Parties.'
>
> There was no Dominion represented at the Barcelona Conference to
> defend the individual sovereignty of the Commonwealth States, hence
> it seems to be taken for granted by League Members that the British
> Empire Delegation, as the British now call the combined delegations, is
> one for all effective international purposes. The League Members have
> not so far objected to the anomaly of plural representation by the
> British Empire. No really big issue involving jealousy between the big
> powers has been pushed to such a point at the League that a few votes
> one way or the other have made any matter. But at the Dawes Report
> Conference in London in July this year France objected to the separate
> representation of the Dominions. The sop given to the Dominions was
> representation on the panel system which simply meant that the
> Dominion Representatives in turn acted as substitutes for one of the
> British Delegates.
>
> ... The British refusal to recognise the registration of the Treaty simply
> because Great Britain has always held the view that the Covenant does

---

* This gentleman seems to have had very flexible opinions. See above, Ch. 2, p. 36.

not apply to intra-Commonwealth relations is the most barefaced explicit denial of equality of which we have an instance. Up to this they had confined themselves to little manoeuvres more or less subtle and difficult to combat.

At the moment I can only suggest that we should emphatically declare that we joined the League of Nations believing the Covenant to be of universal application to all members without exception. We accepted the obligations of the Covenant fully believing that we were getting all the rights of Member States.*

If at the mere wish of Great Britain, the League decides that the Covenant does not apply to our relations with that Member State, we can give notice that we intend withdrawing at an early date.[8]

No such drastic action proved necessary, but the Irish drafted two firm replies to the British despatch, on 5 December 1924. The second of these, milder and more strictly relevant, was favoured by Desmond FitzGerald. Both are set out in Appendix B, together with the letter sent by the Irish Free State Government on 18 December to the League,[9] to counter the British protest there. The Irish letter of 18 December was referred to at question time in Dail Eireann on 19 December, but as it would not by then have reached Geneva no information was divulged. The Irish point of view had already been explicitly stated by FitzGerald on the fifteenth:

The Covenant of the League of Nations set out the duties undertaken by every member of the League. There are no distinctions between Members – none has special privileges and none is exempt from the obligations set forth in the Covenant. Article 18 means that every treaty and international engagement entered into after January 1920 shall be registered. The Irish Free State as a Member of the League, as well as every other Member, is bound by this Article. As the Treaty is the basis of the Free State relations with the other members of the British Commonwealth of Nations, it was pre-eminently our duty to register. To have failed in this would have been to repudiate the Covenant, which can be done neither by the Free State nor by any other member of the League.[10]

On 15 December, when this statement was being made, E. J. Phelan wrote in anger from Geneva condemning the British attitude and their action in circulating their views through the Secretary-General of the League. He urged the Irish to reply strongly in like manner as their case was 'irrefutable'.[11] On the twenty-ninth he

---

* See A. B. Keith, *Speeches and Documents*, p. 358, A. Chamberlain's speech in the House of Commons, 18 November 1925: 'No member can enter the League except with the same rights and obligations as every other member . . . the very foundations of it is that all nations in it are equal.'

wrote again to congratulate FitzGerald on his League letter and he mentioned the illuminating fact that in talking with the Canadian delegation he learned that Canada fully approved the Irish action.[12]

The Treaty was registered. On 16 December the Irish sent a further despatch (no. 462) to Britain. This was acknowledged by the new Conservative minister, L. S. Amery, on 9 March 1925. He was anxious to re-state the British view, as expressed by Thomas both on 4 November and in his letter to the League, and he made the additional point that had the British regarded the Treaty as international they would have registered it themselves at that time. But their view was then, and was still, based 'on the fundamental principle that the relations of the British Members of the League of Nations *inter se* are essentially different in character from those substisting between other states Members of the League of Nations'.[13]

A year later, on 4 February 1926, Amery repeated his Government's views, this time in connection with the Supplementary Agreement to the Treaty, signed on 3 December 1925.* The Irish reply on 15 February felt equally unable to concur in the British views. On 16 April Amery acknowledged this letter and expressed the hope that an opportunity to re-examine the whole question would arise at the forthcoming Imperial Conference. In the meantime he was reminding the Secretary-General of the British views on the matter, and sending copies of the correspondence to all the Dominions.

Thus the family quarrel dragged on. It is summarised neatly in a letter written by the Irish Minister for External Affairs, on 9 April 1925, to Professor Kennedy of the University of Toronto, who had on the previous December proffered some gratuitous advice. 'It seemed to me', wrote FitzGerald:

> that the British letter [to the League] was a statement of intention and of opinion. They stated that in agreeing to the Covenant they had intended that the Article dealing with the Registration of Treaties should not cover any arrangements *inter se* between the various parts of the British Commonwealth, and they stated their opinion that because of this intention of theirs the Article 18 was not applicable to the Anglo-Irish Treaty.
>
> On the face of it this obviously might be regarded as a protest against registration: I considered that we had to deal with it with regard to its existing wording. The Treaty was already registered: that was our

* This Supplementary Agreement closed the Boundary Dispute arising from Article 12 of the Treaty.

business. The question whether or not the British had in mind the reservation they implied and whether they were justified in making it lay between the British Government and the League of Nations. We, in joining the League had made no such reservation, nor had we any such reservation in mind.

You will notice that my letter to the League is written on these lines. Meanwhile the treaty remains registered, and I may add for your strictly private information, that the British Government, while still maintaining their own opinion on the matter don't intend to pursue the matter any further. . . .[14]

The matter had reflected little credit on the British, but they were no doubt extremely reluctant to give up that position of strength so precisely observed above by J. P. Walshe at the beginning of his memorandum. In an interesting postscript at the 1930 Conference, Sir William Jowitt confessed to Patrick McGilligan his amazement at the line taken by the earlier British Government. He could see no valid reason for that line. He himself would have welcomed the registration, which would have made it necessary to register every successive advance in Dominion freedom. This view is not far removed from the view held at the time by de Valera, for, as a violent opponent of the Treaty, he had had no wish to see it enshrined as an international document. However, the policy of the Free State Government, thanks not a little to the British reaction, served its purpose well enough. The Treaty was registered and the Free State rested on a more solid foundation.

But the year 1924 was not only remarkable for this Dominion display. In the international field the Free State managed to complete another notable chapter: and this chapter too had its preface in 1922.

In that year Professor T. A. Smiddy was at work on behalf of the Saorstat in Washington. Described as the Irish Free State Commissioner at Washington, Professor Smiddy had been 'one of the advisers on economics to Michael Collins during the Treaty negotiations in London'.[15] On 22 March 1923, Smiddy was officially informed by the Minister of External Affairs that he could regard himself as a Permanent Official of the Free State Government.[16] They had a high purpose in mind for him. Meanwhile he gave lectures and conducted top-level liaison in the United States and Canada.

The objective of the Free State Government was to appoint the first Dominion ambassador to a foreign capital. They relied on the precedent established on 10 May 1920 when permission was granted to Canada to attach a Canadian Minister to the British Embassy at Washington. This permission had not yet been taken up in fact, and it had also contained certain qualifications unacceptable to the Irish. But it was a good basis for their case, and this case was now pursued with vigour in 1924.

Early in the spring of that year, FitzGerald admitted in Dail Eireann that his government was arranging to accredit a minister at Washington, and he assured the Chamber that no difficulty was being put in the way.[17] On 24 June the British ambassador in Washington, Sir Esmé Howard, informed the American Government of the request of the Irish Free State: 'His Majesty's Government have come to the conclusion that it is desirable that the handling of matters relating to the Irish Free State should be confided to a Minister Plenipotentiary accredited to the United States Government.'[18] On 28 June a reply in the affirmative was received from the American Secretary of State, Charles E. Hughes.[19]

Meanwhile on 25 June, in the House of Lords, the alarm signals were raised. Lord Selborne wanted to know what clause of the Treaty allowed this, and how would Britain harmonise views in Washington on Irish and Empire matters? Lords Arnold and Parmoor quoted the Canadian precedent and assured the alarmists that here was no departure from the diplomatic unity of the Empire. Curzon, for one, was not convinced. The Canadian precedent bore no relation to this. Canada had 3000 miles of border with the U.S.A. and had anyway not yet implemented the scheme. This matter should be reserved for an Imperial Conference. Lord Chancellor Haldane reassured him that the unity of the Empire was maintained, that it was not possible to define Dominion status and that there existed a special relationship between the Free State and the United States.

In the Commons the following day there were more protests, but J. H. Thomas made the best of a bad job and said that he was glad to see the Free State assuming the privileges to which it was entitled. A slightly different story emerges from an interesting letter from the Irish Minister for External Affairs to Senator Belcourt, of Canada.*

* Senator Napoleon Antoine Belcourt (1860–1932) was M.P. for Ottawa in the Canadian House of Commons 1896–1907, being Speaker from 1904–6. In 1907 he became a Senator, which he remained until his death in 1932. He concerned himself with foreign affairs and in 1924 was Minister Plenipotentiary at the Inter-Allied Conference and at the International Conference of London.

On 9 July FitzGerald had announced in the Dail that the appointment in Washington was near at hand. On the twenty-fifth, Senator
Belcourt wrote to him seeking full details of the appointment: the
procedure adopted, 'were his powers sanctioned or not by His
Majesty, or was it merely by an Order-in-Council of your own
Government? – also the terms and conditions of the appointment
and the financial arrangements.'[20] The Canadian was under the
impression that the appointment was already completed, but it was
not, in fact, until October that Smiddy was officially gazetted.[21]
In his long reply on 13 August, FitzGerald painted the picture to
date. His letter is indicative of the warm and frank relationship
which already existed between Canada and the Free State, and it
illumines the background negotiations. 'In the first place', wrote
FitzGerald, filling in the details,

> we wrote to the British Government that we found it necessary to have
> a fully accredited representative in Washington, and we asked them to
> approach the American Government through their diplomatic channels
> to ascertain if the American Government would be willing to receive
> such a representative from us. In that despatch we also asked that if the
> American Government replied in the affirmative they should then be
> asked for their agreement with regard to Professor Smiddy as the
> person to be appointed, and if the American Government found
> Professor Smiddy *persona grata* we asked that His Majesty would
> forward to us a letter of Credence for us to transmit to Professor
> Smiddy.
> The British Government notified this proposal to the other Domin-
> ions: Canada and South Africa approved: New Zealand disapproved
> and Australia thought the matter should be left for the next Imperial
> Conference. The British Government had made long delays, and as I
> impressed upon them that this matter was urgent a conference was
> arranged in the Colonial Office. At the conference it was agreed that the
> British Government would approach the American Government, and if
> America accepted the proposal the Free State Minister should be the
> official channel of communication with the United States Government
> for dealing with matters exclusively affecting the Free State.[22]

FitzGerald now added further details of agreed administration
and co-operation between the British and Irish ministers and then
turned to the specific Canadian questions:

> As regards credentials: the British Government had previously for-
> warded me a copy of the credentials which had been proposed for the
> Canadian Minister in 1920. There were three things in that document
> which were objectionable to us. In the first place the use of the term
> 'United Kingdom of Great Britain and Ireland' in His Majesty's title.

In the second place the phrase 'to attach him to our Embassy', and in the third place the counter-signature of the British Secretary of State.

With regard to the first point: as I was assured that steps were already being taken with a view to changing His Majesty's Title, I agreed that if the change could not be affected before the credentials were to be issued that I would agree to the title in its present form.

With regard to the second point: the British agreed to eliminate the words 'to attach him to our Embassy'.

The third point I considered very important as it seemed to me that the counter-signature of the British Foreign Minister carried with it an implication that His Majesty could only act on the advice of the London Ministers. Sir Cecil Hurst of the British Foreign Office agreed with me in this, and it was agreed that the counter-signature of the British Foreign Minister should not be included in this or in any similar documents in the future.

The British then showed me the telegram they proposed sending to their Ambassador. In due time we were informed that the American Government agreed to receive a Minister from us. We immediately asked the British to inquire if Professor Smiddy would be *persona grata*. They delayed doing this for a considerable time so that only two days ago did I get word that the American Government would accept Professor Smiddy. We have now asked the British Government to forward us a Letter of Credence signed by His Majesty.

You will observe from the above that the terms of the Letter of Credence were agreed to in conference between the British Government and me. I interpret the omission of the Foreign Secretary's counter-signature as meaning that His Majesty empowers Professor Smiddy directly on the advice of the Free State Government. We also shall forward to Professor Smiddy a letter of Authority, and the appointment of Professor Smiddy will be covered either by an Order by our Executive Council (which is our equivalent to an Order in Council) or by a Resolution of the Dail.[23]

Further financial details follow and the letter ends with promises of additional information when the situation became clearer, and assurances of the utmost warmth and desire to co-operate. An interesting if somewhat cynical footnote is provided by an assertion later in the year in a memorandum by J. P. Walshe. 'The fact that he [Smiddy] was deliberately made a Minister Plenipotentiary', wrote Walshe, 'was only in order that he should never take precedence of the British Chargé d'Affaires (who, henceforth is to be a Minister Plenipotentiary and Envoy Extraordinary).'[24] Happily, when the United States had reciprocated the appointment, Smiddy's credentials were revised, early in 1927, to add 'Envoy Extraordinary'.

The Irish Free State had penetrated the diplomatic unity of the

Empire, successfully establishing in the American capital the first Dominion ambassador. Though it was not until December 1926, after the notable Imperial Conference of that year, that the American Government intimated its desire in turn to appoint its own envoy at Dublin, there was no denying that the 1924 achievement was one of major significance for the Commonwealth. No matter how much British statesmen reassured one another that nothing had changed things could never in fact be the same again.*

1924 had thus been a worrying year for British diplomacy. It was also the year of the first Labour Government, and thus of other considerable controversies and self-examination in the Commonwealth. We must first note that following the Chanak incident, peace negotiations had been entered into with the Turks. A conference began in 1922, in Lausanne, and, considering that they had just been asked to prepare to fight the Turks, it is an extraordinary fact that the right of Dominion representation was completely abandoned for this conference. It is clear from remarks made by Mackenzie King in the Canadian Parliament[25] that Britian was not entirely free to control the issue of invitations, but at any rate the Dominions were not to be represented at the Conference, nor were they informed of the arrangements until these had been completed. Canada, for one, raised no objection, provided that it was quite clear that Canada alone would determine the extent to which it would be bound by the resulting treaty. Considerable confusion and misrepresentation resulted from the Canadian attitude. When the Treaty was signed, on 24 July 1923, it was signed by the British plenipotentiary on behalf of the British Empire. But when, in 1924, the Dominions were asked to ratify, Canada very properly refused to bring the treaty before its Parliament. In March Ramsay MacDonald wrote to Mackenzie King expressing the hope that Canada would ratify. King wrote back saying that Canada would not, and for four months misunderstanding reigned. Mackenzie King was adamant. He was supporting 'the conception of the British Empire as a community of nations possessing equality of status'.[26] In his own words he was 'helping to make History in the lines along which I am defining relations between different parts of the Empire and asserting equality of status in fact not in name'.[27] Canada might in fact be legally bound

---

* P. Gordon Walker, in his book *The Commonwealth* (p. 99), is somewhat misled on the position of the Irish Minister, believing him to be a member of the British Embassy.

by Britain's signature, but Canada would decide the extent of the fulfilment of this binding, in her own Parliament, as the occasion arose. As King's second official biographer puts it, while 'Chanak had drawn a distinction between active and passive belligerency ... Lausanne implied a distinction between active and passive responsibility'.[29]

The Irish Free State had not got under way when the Lausanne negotiations were opened. It too was unrepresented and in 1924 it too refused to accept any definite responsibility for that treaty, adopting in the end a more recalcitrant position even than Canada. On 9 April, Deputy Johnson, in the Dail, had been highly critical of the uninformed, unrepresented position of the Free State with respect to this treaty. On 1 July 1924, Desmond FitzGerald assured the House of the anger and dissatisfaction of the Irish Government at the way the whole business had been handled. Nevertheless, to the extent that the Treaty brought peace to certain peoples of Eastern Europe, the Free State would comply with it. But this must not be taken as a precedent, nor would the Free State be bound by the whole treaty.*

Unfortunately, the ratification of the Lausanne Treaty, which caused such a stir and which stemmed originally from coalition policy, came to the forefront of Dominion affairs in a year studded with Labour Party errors. One of the first steps taken by the British Labour Administration on reaching office – and it did so just after an Imperial Conference which had established the principle of Dominion consultation as the guide to foreign affairs affecting the Empire – was to recognise the Government of Soviet Russia, without the slightest effort at consulting any of the Dominions. This was no doubt the result of ignorance and inexperience. But their next gaffe was inexcusable. The Dominions were not given the representation to which they felt themselves entitled at the London Conference on the Dawes Plan for Reparations. This was a matter in which all the Dominions were very interested. Professor Sir Keith Hancock has written with some justification that: 'It was negligence rather than

* A note on this treaty incident is made in an Irish Free State Memorandum headed 'Lausanne Conference – Irish Nationality'. Undated, the note reads as follows: 'This Treaty gives a chance to Ireland to take the first tentative steps in differentiating between her Nationals and British Nationals – by refusing to ratify the Commercial Convention and the 'Convention respecting Conditions of Residence and Business Jurisdictions'. Rejection would be an interesting step in the process of establishing *de facto* the gradual differentiation and recognition of Irish Nationality abroad' (FitzGerald Papers).

necessity which accounted for the British Labour Government's action in recognising the U.S.S.R. without first consulting the Dominions. There was, on the other hand, some element of necessity in its acceptance of a Conference on the Dawes Reparations Plan without ensuring separate representation for each Dominion.'[29] But it is nevertheless impossible to condone the way the Labour Government undertook the preparations for the Conference. Evasion and suppression of information and a final embarrassed presentation of a long-established *fait accompli* seemed to reproduce some of the worst features of the Lausanne preparations, 'to which', the Canadians protested, 'exception has been taken . . . and which we had hoped would not be repeated'.[30] Canada had demanded separate representation, as in the Versailles settlement. The Free State had made the same demand, but was quietened by the assertion that as it had not been a signatory it had not been deemed eligible for this conference. However, the British Government had once more been careless of Dominion rights and indifferent to Dominion sentiment. The conditions may have been exceptional and Ramsay MacDonald did repeat his Russian-recognition assertion that the matter was not to be regarded as a precedent; but the manner in which the affair was handled was undeniably outrageous. The Dominions were tolerant and reasonable in accepting, finally, a reduced membership on the Empire delegation system.*

The year 1924, then, was a bad year: a bad year, that is, for anyone who still cherished hopes of a centralised and unified Empire. At the League, which in a sense provided the basis for a common foreign policy, the Dominions were able to develop individual attitudes. And that experience gave them new confidence. Professor Zimmern was later to argue that the British Commonwealth and the League of Nations were 'inseparably interdependent'[31] – vital to one another in the quest for lasting peace. But the League was clearly a problem to London as it was an opportunity to the more nationalistic Dominions. The registration of the Anglo-Irish Treaty there was both problem and opportunity. Some matters admittedly were less controversial. The Geneva Protocol of 1924, for instance, the Dominions unanimously condemned as unhelpful to the cause of peace. In the

---

* Desmond FitzGerald had made it clear in Dail Eireann, however, that if the Irish Free State was not at the Conference it would not be bound and he did not think there could be 'such a thing as a British Empire or Commonwealth representation'. Dail Eireann debates, VIII, col. 838.

following spring, in Dail Eireann, Desmond FitzGerald explained
that he agreed with the aims of the Protocol but rejected its terms –
though not, he assured the Dail, through desire for Commonwealth
solidarity, but on purely ethical grounds.[32] He did, however, look to
the League to provide the ultimate safeguard against war. To the
Irish Government Geneva was a forum not only for the furtherance
of their ideas of independent sovereignty but for the general lessening of international tension through discussion. They believed of
themselves that they would prove 'not the less good Europeans for
being also good Irishmen'.[33]

The Free State leaders, as we have seen, had broken fresh ground
in this year at Washington. There they had made the first breach in
the hitherto unassailed field of diplomatic representation. There is
little doubt that this 'innovation of a Dominion diplomat at a
foreign capital could only be construed as a blow against a common
imperial foreign policy'.[34] But they did not stop there. They also
launched their own passports, opened a passport office in Washington and established a passport control officer in New York, where
visas too were issued.

The matter of Free State passports had involved, and indeed
continued to involve, a bitter struggle with the British Foreign
Office. In July 1923, FitzGerald had satisfied himself that the
necessary documents could be manufactured inside the Saorstat. But
he encountered considerable trouble with Britain about the wording
to be used within them. He assured the Dail, on 9 April 1924, that
the difficulties were being cleared up and that Irish passports were
now in general issue.[35] In fact the confusion of nationality, citizenship and allegiance, supplemented by the Irish desire to avail themselves of British diplomatic services abroad, remained unsettled, to
be wrangled over at successive Imperial Conferences throughout the
decade. But a start had been made. Other Dominions had so far been
content to describe their citizens as British subjects. The Irish Free
State now challenged this description. As well as its own diplomats
it wanted its own nationality, its own passports and its own flag.
Irishmen claimed, in 1924, to be recognised at least as 'Citizens of
the Irish Free State and of the British Commonwealth of Nations'.*

---

* Irish Free State passports, as issued from 3 April 1924. They did not contain the
words 'British Subject', upon which Great Britain had insisted, and so the British
Foreign Office refused to honour them, leaving the holders without protection where
there was no Free State representative.

In 1924 a pessimist looking at the Empire might have been excused for wondering if it could long survive the stresses to which it had lately been subject. Even the least perspicacious of observers must have noticed the new temper of Dominion assertiveness. Canada, the senior Dominion, had taken the lead in the development of Dominion equality, but now the Irish Free State was beginning to challenge that lead with a determined and explicit demand for full national dignity and international recognition. South Africa too indicated a change of mood. In June 1924, General Hertzog defeated Smuts to become Prime Minister of the Union. In the same month at home in London, Ramsay MacDonald, with little Dominion success so far, made an extra effort to gain sympathy by proposing a small conference to discuss Commonwealth consultation. Clearly communications were insufficient to the demands of the time, and so he called for suggestions from the Dominion leaders to remedy the obvious deficiencies.[36] The response was not encouraging. The Dominions were not in the mood to send representatives, angered as they were by the Dawes Conference affair, and, apart from Bruce of Australia, they sent little constructive advice. The straws were in the wind for 1926.

(ii) 1925-6

In the international sphere in 1925 the major event – and it had considerable Commonwealth importance – was the signing by Great Britain of the Locarno Treaties of Mutual Guarantee between Germany, Belgium, France, Great Britain and Italy on 16 October. Here, for the first time, it was the mother country which put its own particular interests before those of the individual Dominions or the Commonwealth as a whole. Not that the British policy was a selfish one. On the contrary, the Dominions welcomed it, and passed a motion of approval at the 1926 Imperial Conference. Britain was at pains to secure world peace. Her European commitments and her recognition of Dominion sovereignty determined her signature to this Treaty of Mutual Guarantee, which specifically exempted any Dominion from its obligations 'unless the Government of such Dominion, or of India, signifies its acceptance thereof'.[37] Britain would have liked to have had full consultation with the Dominions, but this was not found to be possible. This, at least, was how Austen Chamberlain as Foreign Secretary justified his action to the House of Commons. Other members were not so sure. The German offer to treat had come in February. Did that not give sufficient time to consult the Dominions? To Lloyd George, for one, the failure to consult the Dominions was a blot on an otherwise good agreement, 'a serious error which may have grave consequences'.[38] To prove his point he quoted the disappointment of General Smuts, who, recognising the centrifugal tendencies at work in the Empire, 'feared that Locarno had given some impetus to them'.[39]

Naturally, the *Round Table*, which believed that the Commonwealth rather than the League was the true expression of political reality, was dismayed by the Treaty. 'The new system inaugurated at Locarno', it cried out, 'strikes at the very root of the efficacy of the British Empire, whether it works through the Council of the League of Nations or through ordinary diplomacy in promoting world peace.'[40] Certainly this treaty crowned the efforts of the forces of decentralisation. It was indeed a major landmark 'in the evolution of dominion external policies',[41] for in the event, none of the Dominions did undertake any of its obligations. They approved, but they kept their hands free.

Quoting Article Nine, which exempted the Dominions, Desmond FitzGerald explained to the Dail that the Treaty of Locarno in his opinion overruled Article Seven of the Anglo-Irish Treaty, and reinforced the Irish Parliament's claim to be the sole arbiter of peace and war, so far as the Saorstat was concerned. The Locarno Pact was therefore welcomed in Ireland.

Perhaps the main virtue of this treaty was its realism. By rejecting the Geneva Protocol the Dominions had underlined their determination to avoid military obligations. They distrusted such arrangements and their distrust was to last until the Second World War. Locarno was the first treaty concluded by Great Britain which took this distrust fully into account.

1925 was dominated, so far as the Irish Free State was concerned, by the Boundary Commission; its work, its unhappy dissolution and the settlement which eventually resulted from it. This settlement was debated with considerable heat in Dail Eireann from 7–15 December 1925, but although it was a matter of vital importance to the relations between Ireland and Great Britain, it was principally a domestic issue and in no sense a Commonwealth concern. Its story does not properly belong here.

In other fields, 1925 was calm enough. FitzGerald, in a letter to

Oscar Skelton at Ottawa, outlined the current state of affairs regarding Irish passports. He emphasised that it was harmful to the Irish image in America that Irishmen without passports should have to go to a British Consul, and added: 'I believe I told you that there is a sort of deadlock between us and the British on the passport question, as they insisted that we should describe our nationals as British Subjects, which would be interpreted by our people as meaning "Subject to the Parliament of Great Britain".'[42] The deadlock continued, to be attacked once more at the Imperial Conference.

At Geneva, the Irish grew a little more cynical. They regarded disarmament as the fundamental purpose of the League, and it was because the Protocol involved sanctions and the waging of war to stop war, that they rejected it. In the September session Kevin O'Higgins capably refuted a statement by Sir Cecil Hurst which gave a misleading sense of unity to the Commonwealth representation and implied that Hurst himself spoke for all.[43] O'Higgins himself was somewhat disillusioned. He regretted that even at Geneva 'a crafty imperialism' could flourish and that there, 'as elsewhere "God is on the side of the big battalions" ', no matter what 'lip service is paid to idealism', or how many references were made to 'Justice, Truth, Right, etc.'.[44] He had some unflattering remarks to make about Sir Robert Cecil and he also concluded grimly that 'Security, Disarmament, Arbitration is a wonderful trilogy, if it didn't mean – security in my ill-gotten gains, disarmament for the other fellow and arbitration with the court well packed'.[45]

In Britain, by the end of 1925, preparations had begun for the 1926 Imperial Conference. L. S. Amery, who had created the Dominions Office* and who held the Secretaryships of State for colonial as well as Dominion affairs, recognised that a great deal had to be done if the Commonwealth was to be brought up to date and moulded into a form capable of survival. Throughout the Commonwealth in 1926, therefore, the scene was dominated by the detailed work required to make this conference a success.

Work proceeded, that is, in all the Dominions, except Canada. There, the political struggle was at white heat. The Canadian elections at the close of 1925 had left the Conservatives the biggest party, but they did not have an overall majority, and the Liberals remained in office. It was not a satisfactory position. Parliament met in January 1926 and Mackenzie King determined to carry on. By the

*The Dominions Office was established on 11 June 1925.

end of June, however, he realised that it was in his best interests to dissolve Parliament and seek a firmer mandate. He went to Governor-General Byng, and to his astonishment was refused a dissolution. Thus the historic King–Byng dispute, so graphically described in H. Blair Neatby's volume of the King biography, began. The issue, to the Liberal leader, was one of fundamental imperial significance, involving the constitutional position of the Governor-General as the Representative of the Crown. Canada was plunged into controversy and eventually into an election which absorbed its attentions until the Imperial Conference had almost begun.

In Ireland, as Chapter Six relates, tremendous energy was put into preparing a logical and detailed case to present to the Conference. But just before this conference an incident of considerable Commonwealth importance occurred at Geneva, for which the Dublin leaders were responsible.

The year 1926 had been a year of self-examination for the League. Following the Treaty of Locarno, Germany had applied for membership of the League, and, as Austen Chamberlain told the House of Commons in February, this had opened up 'the whole question of the composition of the [League] Council'.[46] This was to be discussed at Geneva in March, and it was rumoured that Spain, Poland and possibly Brazil were to apply for permanent council seats at the same time as the German bid for entry. The Dominions Office kept up a steady stream of information to the Dominions. At the end of February, it was disclosed that the Western Pact wished Germany to have a permanent Council Seat, which would mean enlarging the size of the Council.[47] The Dominions hastily replied that while Germany was an acceptable addition, there should be no others. In March it became apparent that the Dominions would object less to additional non-permanent members.[48] The subject was debated in the House of Commons on 4 and 5 March and discussion continued throughout April and May. On 10 May a Committee met at Geneva to decide on the matter. The Committee adjourned on 17 May, but on the request of the Spanish Government it reassembled on 30 August. It was decided to increase the number of non-permanent seats to nine.

The Plenary Session of the League began on 6 September, the Irish Delegation consisting of Desmond FitzGerald, Ernest Blythe and John MacNeill, with Michael McWhite and Dan Binchy as their substitutes, and Joe Walshe as Secretary. The main issue was the principle upon which the extra seats would be filled, and there was a sharp division of opinion. The Free State, a small nation, had no liking for big-power politics and the steam-rollering alliances of the major states, which seldom considered the wishes of the smaller countries. Its faith was in the League as a forum for equal nations, where democratic principles might thrive. For practical purposes a small council, including the major nations, was essential, but to the Free State the League could only live up to the sacred hopes of its Covenant if this Council remained firmly under the control of the Assembly. In the Assembly, each nation had one vote: here the principle of democratic equality was enshrined. But another theory had been insidiously advanced, which, the Irish leaders felt, denied the very principles of the League. Freedom, like road traffic, ran the argument, must be organised, or else it becomes meaningless. The increase in seats on the Council would permit a greater geographical representation and allow to the various League groupings a spokesman.

On 14 September Ernest Blythe argued that whichever countries were elected to the Council vacancies, the League must retain the power to withdraw their mandate if they fulfilled their roles in an unsatisfactory way.* This point was repeated by FitzGerald on the following day when he argued the Irish case with great conviction. And he added, with reference to the Council:

> We deny the right of any particular groups to be at any time represented thereon in any specified proportion and we deny more emphatically still the right of any group to choose from among themselves a State which the Assembly would be under an obligation to elect. . . .
> . . . we control the Council by our power to elect the majority of its Members. That I consider to be the greatest and the most important power possessed by the Assembly.

His speech was full of practical awareness of the human and political problems at stake and he ended:

> To our minds, the very essence of voting is choosing, and it seems to us that behind all these arrangements is an attempt to let us vote but not let us choose those who are to represent us on the Council.[49]

There is nothing remarkable in this point of view, but a dramatic element was introduced when the Spanish Government withdrew its

---

* Though not included in the published Records, Desmond FitzGerald comments on his own speech of 15 September that he himself repeated this point made by Blythe on the fourteenth. See FitzGerald Papers, 'Ireland and the League Council 1926'.

Council application. The Free State felt very strongly that its own view was right and it therefore decided to become a candidate on the anti-group principle. The matter was argued in a Commonwealth Delegates Meeting on 14 September, and in spite of strong opposition from Great Britain, the Free State decided to stand. Terence de Vere White has suggested that FitzGerald himself was persuaded by Chamberlain 'to forgo the claim', but that he was overruled by the rest of his Delegation.[50] Whatever his personal wishes might have been, the following letter was sent to all Dominion delegations on the evening of the fourteenth:

> Sir,
> I am instructed by the Irish Delegation to request you to be good enough to inform your Delegation that after careful consideration of the position reviewed at the meeting of heads of the Commonwealth Delegations this afternoon it has been definitely decided to proceed with our candidature for a seat on the Council. The Irish Delegates believe that this step will serve the best interests of the Dominions and they hope that their candidature will meet with the support of your Delegation.[51]

A separate letter was sent by FitzGerald to Austen Chamberlain in the friendliest terms, regretting the difference of opinion. The following day a reply from Chamberlain, appreciating the kindness of the Irish letter but regretting its decision, stated the official British objection:

> We hold as strongly as anyone that every State Member of the Assembly has an equal right to seek election in the Council and if we thought that that right was challenged in the case of the Dominions or India we should be among the first to uphold it. But the question does not so present itself to our mind at this moment. To us it seems to be not a question of the right, which is not challenged, but solely of the expediency of a Dominion candidature at this particular election. On this point, as you know, we share the view expressed yesterday by the representative of every other Dominion that the moment is inopportune for such a candidature, which we cannot but fear may set back rather than advance the position of the Dominions.[52]

Britain, therefore, could not give its support.

The election took place the following day, and, almost inevitably, in view of the lack of canvassing time, the Free State was not successful.* But the precedent it had set was extremely important. When in 1919 the Dominions had become members of the League,

---

* On the first ballot Colombia (46), Poland (45), Chile (43), Salvador (42), Belgium

Lord Robert Cecil had convinced Wilson to allow the Dominions to be eligible for Council seats but had argued that none wanted, nor were likely to seek, election. The position in 1926, with its larger Council, was different, but it was perhaps a compliment to the Free State that its right to stand was not challenged. Altogether the Irish Free State made an extremely good impression on the League, much bigger than the ten votes cast in its favour might indicate, and it showed the other Dominions what could be done. It took the first step. Extracts from two letters which Desmond FitzGerald wrote home from Geneva help to fill in some of the background.

On the seventeenth, the day after the election, FitzGerald was not downhearted in defeat. He was:

> Very satisfied with all we have done. If you read my speech (it will not be fully reported) you will see that we did not go up representing the Dominions but the Assembly. Did well with 10 votes. In spite of opposition of big ones – Britain etc. . . .[53]

Two days later he gives more detail and expresses his disgust at the lack of accuracy in the Irish press:

> The Irish newspapers that I have seen have been worthy of themselves – they seem to get the wrong end of everything with perfect genius. If we had a proper press we should have had good publicity. . . . We probably got a better show in practically every other press. We have been one of the most prominent countries here . . . and these damn fools haven't sense enough to make anything of it. But of course it doesn't really matter whether they do or not. The foreign papers have done well by us – and from the point of view of prestige that matters much more. . . . The Irish papers quite misunderstood our going up for the Council. We not only defended Dominion rights but also countries like Austria, Hungary-Bulgaria, Abyssinia etc, etc. We got the ten votes with the British against us. And only appearing on the scene the day before the election – I am quite satisfied that we could have been elected with a proper canvass in good time. Quite a lot practically blamed me for not telling them before they had promised their votes. But of course it was only when Spain definitely went out that we could do anything. And if another had gone up on our principle we should have left the field clear for them.[54]

On the seventeenth the Irish Department for External Affairs

---

(41), Roumania (41), Netherlands (37) and China (29) were elected, leaving one seat still to be filled. (Irish Free State with 10 votes was thirteenth.)

On the second ballot only four nations received votes, Czechoslovakia was elected with 27; Finland (11), Portugal (7), and Irish Free State (4) were runners up. See League of Nations, 7th Assembly, p. 82.

received the following telegram in Dublin. It adds a little more detail.

ESTERO DUBLIN
BRITAIN EVERY EFFORT MAKE US WITHDRAW
CANDIDATE STOP AFRICA GAVE STRONG SUPPORT
AND ONLY COMMONWEALTH VOTE STOP SATISFIED
OBJECT ACHIEVED.
SECRETARY DELEGATION.[55]

So the Commonwealth opposition had not been entirely unanimous.

In a report on the Session later, the Delegation repeated the old request that greater interest should be taken in the League and far more preparation made possible. Delegates, it argued, should be selected as far as possible twelve months ahead to give time for study. This year, though the Minister for Foreign Affairs* did useful work as Chairman of the Second Commission, the other members of the Delegation were a waste of money, for they had no proper preparation. Months of preparation and policy discussion were needed for an adequate performance. Had it not been for the accident of FitzGerald's chairmanship,

> and the fact that Spain's withdrawal provided an opportunity for raising the question of Dominion seats on the Council, we should have attended a third Assembly in succession in the work of which we should certainly have found ourselves unprepared to take a sufficient part.[56]

The candidature, it seems, was not solely to fight against group representation. Certainly the precedent once established was quickly followed and a year later a successful candidature was pursued by Canada. In 1930 the Free State was itself elected to the Council.

The reference which FitzGerald made to the Irish press could not have applied to the Irish correspondent of the *Round Table*, who had taken the trouble to read the Irish minister's speech. This speech, he commented, should be applauded by 'every honest European'[57] and the Irish candidature had been a natural corollary of it. The *Round Table* Geneva correspondent was less sanguine. He wondered quite who had voted for the Free State[58] and reflected that the League was becoming too much a place of intrigue.[59] There was a wide gulf growing between the Assembly and the Council and between the big and small nations. Great Britain's weight there amongst the Dominions was decreasing.

* FitzGerald found the session exceptionally busy. He as usual found the social life very hectic while the demands of working in French were an additional strain.

The *Round Table* may have been right in its surmise. In 1926, though a more settled peace was being established in Europe, there was much that was unharmonious about the Commonwealth relationship. But then that was why the Imperial Conference had been convened.

6

The Imperial Conference 1926

(i) INTRODUCTION

> Tonight I am able to describe foreign affairs as essentially more satis-
> factory than at any time since the end of the war . . . [Recovery of
> Europe is started] and this is what chiefly distinguishes November 1926
> from November 1923, the time of the last Imperial Conference. There
> has been definite, tangible advance towards more settled and more
> stable economic conditions. You have now France, Italy, Germany and
> ourselves working together for reconstruction and reconciliation.[1]

Thus Stanley Baldwin surveyed the world around him at the time of
the Imperial Conference of 1926: a world which had been severely
troubled but which now appeared more confident and more hopeful.
By the autumn of 1926 the danger of renewed war in Europe had
receded, while in Britain the Conservative Party had once more
gained control. Also, throughout the Dominions, the political situation was extraordinarily stable, with only the Irish Free State Government expecting an election in the coming year. This latter fact in
particular augured well for a fruitful Imperial Conference: the
Dominion leaders could all speak with authority; none would need
to indulge in vote-catching. Furthermore, the time now seemed ripe
for constitutional decision and for a concentrated programme of
economic development.

The world in 1926 was more settled. But as we have seen the
Empire had suffered a number of upheavals which affected the
outlook of its several Dominions and the atmosphere of their meeting. The handling of the Treaty of Lausanne had occasioned
Canadian resentment, in particular, while the British Labour Party
had managed to antagonise all the Dominions by its sudden recognition of the U.S.S.R. and by its failure to ensure separate Dominion
representation at the Dawes Reparation Conference. Then by the
Locarno Treaty, Great Britain had found it necessary to give a

military guarantee to her European commitments, and to exempt the Dominions from participation unless they chose to adhere individually. This treaty contributed to the new feeling of international security, but, as Mackenzie King said, it had a far more potent Empire significance: 'for the first time the assertion of national self-interest at the expense of the diplomatic unity of the Empire had come from the British Government'.[2]

In the imperial world itself we have noted the Irish innovations. The Irish Free State had sent the first Dominion ambassador to a foreign capital; it had registered at Geneva the Anglo-Irish Treaty, flouting the British theory that inter-imperial agreements were not international. We must also note that in Canada the controversial Nadan case[3] had brought the Judicial Committee of the Privy Council into disrepute in that country and had provided the Irish with additional ammunition in their campaign against appeals to it. Finally, the dispute between Mackenzie King and his Governor-General, Lord Byng, had spotlighted the anomalies inherent in the Governor-General's office, and had ensured that this subject too would be reviewed at the Conference. Each of these developments had initiated correspondence and discussion at the time, but was in need of fuller examination. No adequate solution had yet been found to the recurring imperial problems of consultation and co-operation, and two attempted conferences to improve these matters had failed to materialise.* Much, therefore, was expected of this agreed meeting scheduled for the autumn of 1926.

Exactly what was expected, however, differed from Dominion to Dominion. Britain was not immediately worried about imperial diplomatic unity but looked to the Conference to solve the problems of economic development. Australia and New Zealand, too, were hopeful of agreements to develop imperial resources and trade.

---

* In a telegram dated 23 June 1924 Ramsay MacDonald had set out the difficulties of Imperial consultation and called, not for a full Imperial Conference, but for suggestions for improving the situation and for a gathering in London of perhaps two representatives from each Dominion to work out a solution. This came to nothing, though Bruce of Australia did send a constructive reply on 16 July 1924. (See A. J. Toynbee, *The Conduct of British Empire foreign relations since the Peace Settlement*, pp. 75–7.)

L. S. Amery, taking over Dominion Affairs from the fallen Labour Government, withdrew MacDonald's invitation on 2 December 1924. However, he himself wished to call a full Imperial Conference in March 1925 to discuss the General Protocol for the Pacific Settlement of International disputes. This proved to be difficult and correspondence had to suffice. (See Toynbee, *The Conduct of British Empire*, p. 80: also L. S. Amery, *My Political Life*, II 375.)

Canada had shown no outstanding preferences, being absorbed in its own constitutional struggle, but South Africa had deliberately broadcast its sole intention of achieving a public acknowledgement of Dominion equality with the mother country. The Irish Free State had said little but had disclosed its desire for equal status and its determination to remove certain legal anachronisms which stood between it and that status. The Dominions were expecting action. The more self-conscious of them wanted their status to be defined before the world so that there could be no further mystery about their international identity. They wanted action on this immediately. As Professor Mansergh has pointed out,

> by 1926 the risks of inaction were acknowledged to be greater than the risks of definition even by those temperamentally allergic to such an exercise. The demand for the definition of intra-Commonwealth relations was in essence a demand for full equality of status as between the United Kingdom and the self-governing Dominions.[4]

Preparation for the Conference had begun in the new Dominions Office in the December of 1925, under Dominions Secretary Amery. A survey had been prepared of all matters likely to be raised and in February 1926 an inter-departmental committee had been established at Westminster to consider the agenda. Detailed reports had been drawn up and many points listed which were designed to formulate the equality of status of the Dominions, but also to preserve the unity of the Crown. Amery wished to concentrate on defence, foreign policy and Empire marketing, but he recognised that anxiety to remove archaic forms was felt in Canada and South Africa and particularly in the Irish Free State.[5] He circulated the Dominions, first with the proposed agenda, and then with 'a multiplicity of memoranda'.[6] He resisted attempts in Britain to over-centralise the Empire, knowing full well that such moves were out of harmony with Dominion sentiment. He saw that the coming conference would have a mass of technical questions to tackle and he did his best to prepare the ground and to anticipate the special committees which would be required. Sir Maurice Hankey has assessed for us Amery's planning during that summer. As he wrote to Sir Edward Grigg:

> Amery is very keen on getting the principle of an Imperial Conference every year. Of course he realises that he cannot get a first-class Conference, including the Prime Ministers for the Dominions. His idea is, I think, so far as it has taken shape at all, to try and get intermediate

Conferences on particular questions, e.g. co-ordination of research; particular trade and shipping questions etc. . . .[7]

Amery in his own way, perhaps hoping to divide and rule, was getting down to details.

The *Round Table*, as we might expect, was also reviewing the situation. One of the main difficulties it observed was that of how to reconcile unity and responsibility in the conduct of foreign affairs. 'The dislike of definite committal' was only natural to Canada and South Africa which could have no enthusiasm towards 'the vortex of European militarism'.[8] Australasian attitudes it correctly ascribed to geography and dependence on the Royal Navy. Irish policy, it confessed, was uncertain. The *Round Table* hoped that some arrangement could be made for dividing external problems into categories of local and imperial concern, but it pointed out that war anywhere was of concern to all, for war could spread. Sea trade, communication lines and Anglo-American relations were also of common interest. The vital question, however, went deeper still for 'the real alternatives before the Dominions are not between a dependent status and independent nationhood, but between a nationalism which sees its fulfilment in isolation and a nationalism which sees it in an active participation in the world's affairs'.[9]

The Dominions themselves had been preparing, and they had scrutinised the whole field of inter-imperial relations. The position had clarified a little from the mists of 1921, but too much still remained obscure. If the direction of Dominion advance was now unquestionably towards national independence, no constitutional conference had yet tidied the anomalous legal restraints surviving from the colonial era. A Dominions Office might be better than the Colonial Office but it did not confer equality of treatment with the other nations of the world; only the first breach in the unity of diplomatic representation had been made, though Canada was about to follow up the Irish precedent; at Geneva no strong Dominion individuality had manifested itself to the world, though the Irish were taking a stubborn line regarding intra-imperial agreements. Further, a brief term of Labour office in Britain had emphasised the deficiencies of imperial consultation and had thrown doubt even upon the value of negotiated economic agreements. But what was to be done? As the danger of war had grown less, the Dominions had turned inwards, desiring to develop their own nationhood yet reluctant to face up to the distraction of distant problems. By now whatever the solution envisaged for the Empire, it clearly could not rest on theories which ignored Dominion diversity. Each Dominion had different needs, different views and different political traditions. Their common starting-point had been a shared belief in the value of the Empire, to themselves and to the world. In the autumn of 1926, however, it was not entirely certain that even this fundamental criterion was held by all. Political Jonahs had enough evidence to forecast the disruption of the Empire. If more sanguine commentators assured their readers that there could be no danger to the Empire whenever its leaders were together in council, that only when these men were apart need fear be entertained, it was nevertheless clear that some decisive action was overdue.

South Africa had no doubt about what was needed. General Hertzog had familiarised himself with the achievements of past Imperial Conferences and with the views of his predecessor in office, General Smuts: views which he had found neatly summarised in memoranda and letters in the Prime Minister's office on his assumption of power in 1924. Hertzog had determined that nothing less than a full statement of Dominion equality, supported by the whole Conference and clearly setting out the international character of the Dominions before all the world, would suffice. At Stellenbosch University, in March 1926, his jealousy for South Africa's freedom, his suspicion that an Empire superstate was growing, and his desire for quick action combined themselves in a single demand: 'a formal declaration of Dominion status was necessary in order to put the matter beyond the reach of further controversy'.[10] 'The status of the Union', he said in his speech at the University,

> is, as you see, by no means clear to the outside world and notwithstanding the events of 1919 we have not progressed in improving this state of affairs. . . . There are two ways out of our difficulty. Either a frank acknowledgement to the outside world by an Imperial Conference of our real status, or each Dominion will have to take such independent action as may be necessary to clarify the position.[11]

General Hertzog issued his demand and his warning and the imperial pigeons fluttered in alarm. In letters to Amery, Hertzog repeated his view. It was not enough for the Dominions to be free: they must be seen to be free.

Canada was in a different position. Mackenzie King had been the champion of Dominion independence in 1923, and there is no doubt that he expected to be so again in 1926.[12] But he had no time to prepare himself for this conference. All his energies were absorbed by the constitutional struggle in Canada, which stemmed from the action of Lord Byng and which resulted in a hectic but triumphant election campaign for himself. To him, if perhaps not to the rest of Canada, this campaign had centred on the unconstitutional attitude of the King's representative, who had not acted in Canada as the King himself would have been bound to have acted in Britain. He had refused a dissolution to King, the legal Prime Minister, but had granted one to his successor in office, Meighen. This was intolerable interference in the Dominion's affairs by a Governor-General whose powers were obviously in need of clarification and restriction.

However, if Mackenzie King left little doubt about his view of the role of the Governor-General, he had time to examine nothing else. Earlier in the year telegrams from Ottawa had made it clear that Canada did not welcome a Conference in 1926 at all. The Canadians preferred 'early in October 1927',[13] but stated that because 'the general view of the governments of the other Dominions and of India is in favour of a Conference in October 1926, and that this view is shared by the British Cabinet, the Canadian Government is prepared to concur in the proposal to set October 1926, as the date of the Conference'.[14]

The Canadian election subsequently forced the Conference to meet a fortnight late and Mackenzie King recorded in his diary the effect it had on his own position. 'I am leaving for the Conference', he wrote, 'without any preparation whatever.'[15] But he was not distressed. The British had circulated agenda and memoranda and had indicated the broad divisions into which they expected the Conference to fall. These would be: 'foreign policy and defence, inter-imperial relations and problems of economic co-operation, with the latter being given the most attention'.[16] Oscar Skelton had been preparing the Canadian brief 'on all topics to be discussed at the Conference',[17] and there would also be Ernest Lapointe to help in London.* Mackenzie King was cock of the walk after his election victory. He was a little tired; he had become stouter than in 1923, but he could afford to be benign.

* To Vincent Massey, 'Ernest Lapointe . . . represented Canadian statesmanship in the best sense – with a quiet and distinguished assertion of the principle of nationality, tempered by a deep sense of tradition and belief in the blessings of the British connection'. V. Massey, *What's past is prologue*, p. 152. He was a popular member of successive imperial conferences and an excellent Committee chairman.

Australia and New Zealand were worried. The frankness of General Hertzog's demand, which included the right of South Africa to secede from the Empire, and which mentioned neutrality in future British wars, alarmed them. Bruce of Australia was an imperialist prepared to agree with Britain on constitutional issues, but who wanted a greater concentration on economic development. He shared with Coates of New Zealand a determination to preserve the Empire and to restrain the hot-heads. Coates himself had no other ambition. Like Monroe of Newfoundland he was perfectly content with the position of the Empire as it then stood. The Australasians approached the Conference on the defensive, constitutionally, but anxious to attack on what was to them the far more urgent ground of economic co-operation.

To the outside world, the Irish Free State was as yet an unknown quantity, though some British observers feared that it would make trouble. It had not made public its views but it was nevertheless taking this conference very seriously. The leaders of 'that little Dominion so surprisingly established almost in sight of our English coasts',[18] had carefully examined the whole legal and constitutional structure of the Empire and had noted where its theory was at variance with accepted practice. Sensitive of their new-won independence, taunted with subservience to Britain by opponents within and without their Parliament, they had listed the anomalies and the anachronisms of the colonial era which still remained to hamper their sovereignty and support their detractors. The British Government was still deeply rooted in the system of their state; the monarch remained too obviously 'British' and was not recognisable in his 'several' capacity, which was alone acceptable to them; the appeal to the Judicial Committee of the Privy Council remained as a standing insult to the competence of their judiciary. This latter resentment, like the others, was carefully analysed and annotated. The Irish Free State knew what had to be done and it was making sure that when the time came it would have a clear plan of how to do it.

There had been little evidence of Irish intentions, but in June, Desmond FitzGerald, the Minister for External Affairs, had given an indication of the mood of his colleagues. Co-equality with Britain was their aim, he said and, despite the assertions of General Hertzog, at Stellenbosch, that 'nowhere was an attempt made by a Dominion to obtain formal recognition of its international status by a foreign state',[19] FitzGerald was proud of the Irish record. 'During the existence of this Department', he was able to assure the Dail:

> we have brought home more clearly to the nations of the world than
> has ever been done before what exactly was the status of a country
> known as a Dominion. The advent of Ireland, from the fact that the
> Irish nation was known historically and culturally, made known to
> people abroad, even to a greater extent than did the event of the
> signature to the Treaty of Versailles that these nations known as
> Dominions, were full sovereign States, exercising the full rights of
> sovereign States in the world.[20]

He was forced to admit, however, that the status of the Free State
was at that time 'adolescent, but not entirely adult'.[21]

Kevin O'Higgins too had spoken, and it was to him rather than the
official minister, FitzGerald, that the brunt of the Conference
negotiation was to fall. For all his courage and culture, FitzGerald
lacked the dynamism required for such a job. O'Higgins, the Vice-
President of the Executive Council and Minister for Justice, who
had conducted the Free State Constitution through the Dail and
who had proved himself at Geneva, was developing a keen enthusiasm for foreign affairs and a ready appreciation of the value of
Commonwealth membership. If he now required the removal of
'anomalies and anachronisms', he also felt that the direction
of advance was more important than the pace, and the nervous
anticipators of imperial demise could have taken comfort from
his assurance, recorded by the *Round Table* Irish correspondent,
that the Irish Free State Government, 'challenged from the right,
challenged from the left ... will keep to the middle of the
road'.[22]

(ii) THE CONFERENCE

The Conference sat down to the first of its sixteen plenary sessions
on 19 October 1926. Vincent Massey, attending to prepare himself
for his new appointment as Canadian ambassador to Washington,
succinctly recorded his impressions that night, in his diary. 'Canada',
he wrote, was:

> conciliatory and contented: Australia impatient for material results;
> New Zealand placid and unobtrusive; South Africa polite, but restless
> and ominously determined on a new definition of status; Newfoundland
> purely Colonial and proud of it; the Irish Free State polite and

non-committal; India unctuously loyal in a speech that bore the sign manual of the India office.[23]

Later, in his biography he expanded this theme:

> There could hardly have been greater disparity between the view of those assembled at this gathering: on one flank Australia and New Zealand, who were content with things as they were; on the other South Africa and the Irish Free State, who formed a fellowship of disaffection. Harmony was not reached without patience and effort. The greatest contribution towards conciliation was made by Mackenzie King, who was always at his best in the role of mediator.[24]

The stage was set, and outside the Conference the newspapers waited and wondered. They also advised. It was clear to the Press that 'Dominion status' would have to be examined, that attention must be paid to imperial communications and that diplomacy and the representative of the Crown required consideration. But the essential business of the Conference, to *The Times* at least, was 'the organisation of the Empire resources in men and material'.[25] In Dublin, the *Irish Times* piously urged its leaders to forget their 'rights' and remember the 'privileges' of membership.[26] Let them work closely with the British and keep clear of foreign affairs which were of no concern to them.[27]

As usual, the Conference began in a blaze of publicity, and the various delegates were photographed and quoted in every newspaper. Their opening statements were carefully weighed, and it was observed that only General Hertzog struck a discordant note. Baldwin extolled the Empire as a stabilising force in a troubled world; King underlined, in his characteristic vein, the diversity of Dominions that were united in Empire; Bruce wanted construction for the future. But Hertzog, starting as he meant to proceed, called out for a clarification of Dominion status.

In its first five working days the Conference held no less than nine plenary meetings. On 20 October the Foreign Secretary gave a comprehensive statement, supplemented by the High Commissioner for Egypt. The next day disposed of the official statement on the colonies, protectorates and mandated territories, while that on inter-Empire trade was carried over to the twenty-second, when economic problems in general were also discussed. On Monday, the twenty-fifth, the statement on foreign affairs was debated, and the first of the specialist committees appointed. On the twenty-sixth the subject was defence. This, however, was not open to examination by the newspapers and, in London at least, their interest waned. The Conference was now becoming absorbed in committee work, the programme was growing more diffuse and the discussions appearing more technical and less exciting. The British coal strike, the twentieth Motor Show and the Cambridgeshire claimed public attention, and the Dominion leaders were left to draw up a new charter for the British Empire almost ignored by the British people.

In the Dominions, however, interest did not decline. To their press the London scene provided novelty, and the movement of their own leaders upon this strange stage retained its fascination. The special correspondent of the *Irish Times*, R. M. Smyllie, noted that the British were taking their Empire for granted as usual, but did his best to inform his readers of the day-to-day progress of the Conference and the business and social engagements of its members.* Far more clearly than in the home Press, he unfolded a continuous story, and, as the Conference approached its climax, he made it abundantly clear that exciting achievements could be expected.

On the second day of the Conference, Smyllie forecast that a great deal of time would have to be devoted to the constitutional issues. He added that President Cosgrave would not be able to stay long in London and that the Irish advocacy would fall on the shoulders of O'Higgins and FitzGerald. On 25 October the first soundings were taken on the question of status during the discussion on foreign affairs. Hertzog denied that South Africa had any wish to secede, and Smyllie noted that the Irish Free State also accepted that its future lay within the Empire. But both countries desired changes, Hertzog in particular wanting to uphold South Africa's treaty-making rights. At the end of his despatch Smyllie mentioned that a special Committee of Premiers had been set up to deal with the whole problem of Dominion relations: the Report of this committee would be keenly awaited. South Africa, he said, wanted a Declaration of Status, and while this did not appeal to the Irish who wished to remove legal anomalies, the two countries would work together and the Irish would not make trouble. Even the most conservative delegates were already impressed with the helpful attitude of the Free State party. It was clear that they would not try to set the pace for General Hertzog or for anyone else.

* These articles were unsigned but they were of very high quality and it comes as no surprise to learn from the *Irish Times* Office that Smyllie, destined to become one of the most famous editors of this leading Irish newspaper, was responsible for them.

Day by day Smyllie described the scene. When there was no full meeting he listed the committees which sat and he attempted progress reports and supplied 'inside' information. He admitted that the Conference was keeping its secrets well, but he emphasised with growing assurance that it was in the Committee on Inter-Imperial Relations, that body established on 25 October, that the real work was being done.

Yet, as the Conference completed its third week, there seemed little progress to report. The social events went on feverishly and with the pace of work so very high, little rest was allowed to anyone. Smyllie made guesses as to the views of individual delegations, as communications, and air, military and naval defence were discussed in committee. The eleventh Plenary Conference Meeting did not take place until 5 November, and by Sunday, the seventh, Smyllie paused to take stock. It was clear now that Hertzog, having shot his bolt at the beginning, was a man of courtesy and culture and not at all as difficult a colleague as had been expected. Hertzog might have dominated the Conference, Smyllie thought, but 'he has failed in some unaccountable way'.[28] Perhaps he had an insufficient grasp of the English language: maybe he did not know precisely what he wanted. He had been saved only by the fact that everyone liked him. Of the Canadians, Mackenzie King lacked the force of his previous visit, while the cheery Lapointe was one of the most popular members. For Australia, Bruce was verbose but very capable on technical issues, and he had a publicity man with him to look after his press image. Coates, the New Zealander, was quieter, a whole-hearted imperialist, 'a big, honest bluff Colonial' who wanted 'no more than he has', and who was not worried about 'constitutional subtleties' or 'metaphysical word nuances'.[29]

With the Irishmen Smyllie was well pleased. 'If anybody', he wrote,

> had made a name for himself at this year's Conference it is Mr Kevin O'Higgins. . . . The Free State Minister for Justice has impressed his colleagues in two ways – first by his economy of words and his knack of putting his point of view into the condensed compass of an incisive phrase, and second, by his insistence on essentials. In both these attributes Mr O'Higgins excels.[30]

Another Irish commentator gave even more lavish praise to O'Higgins, who was

> perhaps the most vital and the ablest figure among all the assembled

political leaders of the Dominions; and his personal activity and decided ideas concerning the lines upon which Dominion rights ought to be developed, set the pace, to a great extent, for the spokesmen of the other Dominions.[31]

General Hertzog, looking back from the vantage point of the next conference in 1930, added his own tribute to the Irish leader when he remembered 'the determined manner in which he fought for Dominion independence and freedom'.[32]

O'Higgins's impact, however, was as yet little known. This forthright and energetic figure was busy arguing the Irish case in several branches of the Conference. But happily he found time at this juncture to write home his impressions to his wife thus leaving us with a record of his thoughts:

> We have made substantial headway and are likely to make more next week. We have shoved round some excellent memoranda. . . . We are by far the best team at the Conference – bar one – and one would need to have been here in 1923 to realise the vast change in our position. If that change continues progressively, by 1929 things should be ripe for changing the name 'British Empire' to 'Irish Empire'.[33]

He commented on his fellow Dominion leaders, and his assessment parallels that of Smyllie. Hertzog, 'while a very decent, likeable kind of man, has not been a success – he talks a lot and none too clearly'. Mackenzie King had ' "disimproved" since 1923 – gone fat and American and self-complacent. The onus of the "status" push – anomalies and anachronisms – has fallen very largely on ourselves', he felt, 'and while it has made some headway it would be greater if Hertzog was more effective and King a stone or two lighter'. 'Bruce', he commented, 'is too much concerned getting himself into print to have much time to spare in attempting to keep in touch with the work of the Conference.' As for New Zealand, it 'must be like Northern Ireland – it produces the same type of Jingo reactionary'. Meanwhile, he laughed, over the all-important Inter-Imperial Relations Committee, Arthur Balfour presided 'with a smile "like moonlight on a tombstone" '.[34]

O'Higgins fretted at the lack of help which Canada and South Africa were providing, but he did find that Oscar Skelton made up somewhat for his leader's unexpected complacency.* Skelton understood the breadth of O'Higgins's Commonwealth vision and he arranged for Canada to put forward suggestions upon which the two

---

* FitzGerald had already liaised with Skelton on a number of points. See Appendix C.

delegations had previously agreed. Thus it transpired, as Terence de
Vere White has remarked, that 'many of the balls fired at the Conference by the Canadians were, unknown to the other delegations,
manufactured by the Irish'.*

The Conference however, had still almost three weeks to run. If
there was a lull in the plenary meetings for another ten days, the
committees, of which there were now many, remained at work as
hard as their constantly interrupted sessions would allow. Defence,
nationality, communications, oversea settlement, workmans' compensation, research, forestry and a host of economic subjects had
their own separate committees, but the Inter-Imperial Relations
Committee continued to hold the centre of the stage and to pre-
occupy the Dominion leaders.

L. S. Amery, in his autobiography,[35] has shown how even this
committee split up into an inner and an outer group, the one headed
by Balfour, dealing with constitutional forms and the adjustments
required, the other under Austen Chamberlain, concerned with
imperial relations in general. It is with the inner meeting, sitting in
Balfour's room in the Privy Council Office in Downing Street, that
we are principally concerned. Amery relates how it dealt in turn with
the King's Title, which the Irish rightly felt ignored their new
standing; with the office of Governor-General and in particular with
his function as the channel of communications between the British
and Dominion governments; with the reservation and disallowance
of Dominion legislation, and with the conduct of international
treaties by the Dominions. Amery, too, describes the Dominion
leaders, and he sees heresy in the attitude of Hertzog and O'Higgins

---

* T. de V. White, *Kevin O'Higgins*, p. 222. Note the similar reactions of Desmond
FitzGerald, writing to his wife on 20 November. Describing the Report he says: 'We of
course were the people who did the fighting in it. K. O'Higgins was at dinner with the
Simons last night and he is quite indignant about Mack K. who spoke of the way he and
we worked together when as a matter of fact we did the fighting and got damned little
support. However Mackenzie K. also spoke of the way we fought, how ineffective the
usual methods were to get us off the track etc. etc. Of course it doesn't matter who does
the thing as long as it gets done – but if these people had gone about things as we did
our line would have been much easier and we should have got more done.' Desmond
FitzGerald to his wife, 20 November 1926 (FitzGerald Papers).

Note also the observation of the Canadian D. B. McCrae. Representing the great
J. W. Dafoe – editor of the Manitoba Free Press, and adviser to Mackenzie King in 1923
– McCrae was in an inside position. He records that '. . . the Canadians and Irish worked
closely together and pushed hard'. See Ramsay Cook, 'A Canadian account of the 1926
Imperial Conference' in *Journal of Commonwealth Political Studies*, III (no. 1) 60 (1965).
See also Ramsay Cook, *The Politics of J. W. Dafoe and the Free Press*, ch. 10.

towards the Crown. They would have a several monarch to replace that unitary Crown which is the keystone of the imperial edifice. But otherwise they were reasonable men and they were at one with their colleagues in contributing to a Conference of unusual friendliness and warmth of fellowship. Amery relates the events, afterwards, at leisure. But by returning to the despatches of R. M. Smyllie we can better catch the drama of the unfolding Conference and the eager anticipation with which the report of this most vital committee was awaited.

On 8 November Smyllie surveyed the mass of material which the Committee had yet to handle. The Judicial Committee of the Privy Council, which during this very Conference was sitting on important Canadian and Irish cases, was under fire from both countries. The Irish wanted to remove the Appeal, but Mackenzie King was torn between the French Canadian desire to maintain this minority safeguard and the Canadian Liberal demand that ultimate decision should rest with Canada's Supreme Court. Premier Taschereau of Quebec was in London to observe. Ernest Lapointe appeared to be unconcerned.* Only a compromise appeared possible here.

The Colonial Laws Validity Act, reported Smyllie, was another thorn in Canadian flesh, affecting as it did British merchant shipping in Canadian waters. No one could say definitely whether this Act applied to the Irish Free State, but it could only cause trouble, had no value and should go. The Irish delegates were continuing to show moderation and willingness to co-operate, the governing notes of the Conference. They had learned the value of compromise in international affairs.

On the ninth, the Governor-General's position was discussed, all the Dominions having grievances to air except New Zealand. The Irish did not want the Governor-General to be an official of the Colonial Office, nor to be a channel of communication. Smyllie hoped a British High Commissioner would be appointed soon to Dublin. Progress was achieved in the debate on treaty powers, in

* J. A. Costello recalls the Irish expectation that Canada would support them after the flagrantly provocative Nadan Case judgment. This had outraged many Canadians, but with the understatement of the year Lapointe had merely agreed cautiously that 'there was much dissatisfaction in Canada'. He was unable to act. The inference in K. C. Wheare, *The Constitutional Structure of the Commonwealth*, pp. 47–8, that this Canadian case was a major factor in leading to the declaration of equality of status is misleading if it implies that Canada took any initiative on the matter. The initiative was Irish, though it is probable that O. D. Skelton was sympathetically helpful. For details of the case see note, p. 113, below.

which FitzGerald argued with great tenacity. South Africa and the Free State were fighting, with Canadian support, for recognition of the Dominions as equal to Britain in every respect, and of the Commonwealth as a completely free association. In a leading article on 11 November, the *Irish Times* forecast that 'when the history of the Conference comes to be written, the part that is being played by the Free State delegates will receive generous recognition'.[36]

On Friday the twelfth, the position of the High Commissioners was discussed. Smyllie referred to the Committee's difficulty of working in bursts of one and a half hours, with some delegations holding back their hands and others showing a distinct lack of preparation. 'All', he exclaimed, 'realise that there are certain matters to be reformed, but very few of them have any precise solution to offer.' But, he added:

> In this respect the Free State delegation is a marked exception. On the economic side as well as the political side the Irish case has been very well prepared, and it is hardly an exaggeration to say that the Free State Government takes the Imperial Conference more seriously than the Government of any other Dominion.[37]

The Free State looked for more co-operation in international affairs, contending that this could best be achieved on a basis of complete equality. FitzGerald and Austen Chamberlain held a discussion on passports, while agreement was sought generally on how the King might be separately advised, regarding treaties, by the separate Dominions. Smyllie noted that while Canada and the Free State talked in terms of the 'Commonwealth', Hertzog was still unconcernedly using the word 'Empire'.*

By now it was clear that while the other committees were doing valuable work, the only one that really mattered was the one which Balfour chaired. On the fifteenth the Report seemed in sight. No one now believed that any single Dominion would have all its grievances answered, for all recognised the paramount importance of the welfare of the Empire as a whole. Eagerly Smyllie awaited the outcome while the reports of minor committees began to trickle in.

In the background George Bernard Shaw refused a Nobel Prize for Literature, and the Conference delegates glimpsed the R101,

---

* P. McGilligan recalls that during one session Prime Minister Baldwin turned in exasperation towards himself and S. M. Bruce: 'If you, Mr Bruce, would use the word "Empire" a bit less', he expostulated, 'and you Mr McGilligan would use it a bit more, then we would make better progress.'

Britain's new and secret airship. The suspense mounted. By the ninteenth Smyllie felt able to risk a forecast. The Report was completed but not published. Smyllie had good information: with enthusiasm he assured his readers that when the Report appeared it would be seen that nine-tenths of the points urged by the Free State had been adopted. The Report would add a new dignity to the status of the Free State and it would toughen the whole imperial fibre. Smyllie forecast a wider status and changes in the office of Governor-General. He said with confidence that the Report was based on memoranda submitted by the Irish delegates, and he emphasised that 'the Free State delegation was the only one that really knew its own mind from the start and had a fully documented case'.[38] He paid tribute not only to the Irish leaders, but to the Secretariat – J. P. Walshe and Diarmuid O'Hegarty in particular. All the Canadian, South African and Irish complaints had been resolved better than had been deemed possible at the beginning. It was a distinct triumph for Free State advocacy: the 'co-equality' of FitzGerald had been implemented; the 'anachronisms and anomalies' of O'Higgins had been removed. The South Africans had come to the Conference, he maintained, with a vague notion of what they wanted and 'a still vaguer notion of how they proposed to get it':[39] not so the Irish Free State. 'General Hertzog shot his bolt the first day of the Conference.'* He got no further than his first rather tactless statement and was at sea in the Inter-Imperial Committee. The Irish on the other hand, 'by virtue of a well prepared case'[40] were able to direct progress very largely. 'They had memoranda for everything . . . and the Committee was often glad to seize on their cut and dried solutions of knotty points as a basis of final settlement.'[41] O'Higgins and Fitz-Gerald, Smyllie concluded, had no comment to make that night. They had been very discreet throughout the Conference, but he was confident that they were now well pleased.

The ebullient *Irish Times* correspondent continued his loud praises on the Sunday night after the Report had been printed in full. This was one of the most important imperial documents: it accepted the Free State's case; the King was now King of Ireland. Then the plenary Conference itself met for the last time, on the

* *Irish Times*, 20 November 1926. The Canadian, Oscar Skelton, supplements this observation: 'Hertzog stuck to his one point and the Irish Free State pressed from many angles.' O. D. Skelton to J. W. Dafoe, 8 January 1927, cited in R. Cook, 'A Canadian Account of the 1926 Imperial Conference' in *Journal of Commonwealth Political Studies*, III (no. I) 52.

twenty-third, and that evening the full *Summary of proceedings* was issued. With modest understatement Kevin O'Higgins informed the *Irish Times* direct that he was 'pleased with the general result. Matters raised by our delegation received fair and friendly consideration.'[42] To the Conference itself he had used the same words along with his appreciation that 'proposals which we felt necessary to bring forward were considered at short notice and with the greatest care and the fullest desire to meet us in a reasonable way on every issue that was raised'.[43] Smyllie took to himself the opportunity of adding a final word. It was in the sphere of personal relations that the Conference had been the greatest success. 'In this respect the Irishmen have scored heavily.'[44] Now the Dominions understood each other's point of view and no longer would the others regard all Irishmen as rebels and trouble-makers. Ireland was not a daughter nation but a mother country whose sons held trusted positions all over the Empire. Her special position was now understood: 'it has been dignified enormously by the work of the last few weeks and Mr O'Higgins has good cause for satisfaction.'[45] As we step down from the heights of journalistic exuberance to examine the facts we will find that to a surprising degree they underline the soundness of Smyllie's political instinct.

(iii) THE CONFERENCE REPORT

The first real section of the Report of the Inter-Imperial Relations Committee deals with the 'Status of Great Britain and the Dominions', and it includes the Declaration so persistently advocated by Hertzog. Known, in tribute to the Committee chairman, as the 'Balfour Declaration', it has become the most familiar of all modern Commonwealth statements. It refined the crude initial draft of the Boer leader into a single flowing sentence. Of the Dominions it proclaimed:

> *They are autonomous Communities within the British Empire, equal in status, in no way subordinate one to another in any aspect of their domestic or external affairs, though united by a common allegiance to the Crown, and freely associated as members of the British Commonwealth of Nations.*[46]

This constitutional equality, it explained, has now 'in all vital matters, reached its full development'.[47] In four additional paragraphs, this time actually the work of Lord Balfour, it proceeded to outline the 'true character of the British Empire', its 'historic situation' and its 'positive ideals'.[48] In a more controversial final explanation, the Committee chairman drew a distinction between equality of 'status' and equality of 'function'.[49] Britain was still to remain paramount in the fields of diplomacy and defence.

The Balfour Declaration itself was undoubtedly the direct result of Hertzog's determination that Dominion status should be defined and declared to the 'world at large'.[50] The story of the composition of this declaration is dramatically set out by C. M. van den Heever[51] and by Oswald Pirow,[52] both of whom emphasise the role played by Lord Birkenhead in persuading the British trio – Amery, Balfour and Chamberlain – that Hertzog meant business, and that such a statement was essential to the preservation of the Commonwealth. They detail the first draft and the subsequent amendments which preoccupied the Committee from 27 October until 9 November, though they do not perhaps give sufficient attention to the role of Mackenzie King or O'Higgins. Mackenzie King was not anxious to get involved in this controversy of definition, preferring a pragmatic approach, but he was conscious of his position as Canadian Prime Minister. 'Canada', as Blair Neatby has written, 'was the senior Dominion. She was recognised as being resolutely hostile to the vestiges of subordination. At the same time King believed that full autonomy was possible without separation. If a definition there must be, King would be the logical mediator in the discussion.'[53] The story remains an exciting one, however, worthy of a document which was to reverberate round the world from the moment of its publication: a document which, both because of what it said and what it omitted to say 'could be all things to all men'.[54]

But van den Heever and Pirow are both concerned to vindicate their own champion and to reveal how much wiser he was than his political opponent, Smuts. They do not trouble to examine the whole report and it has been left to Duncan Hall in recent years to point out their unfairness to Smuts and to underline the continuity of South African thought despite its changes of government.[55] But even Hall is concerned too exclusively with this one item of the Report. Perhaps the cynical comment of the Canadian, Dafoe, is the most apposite: 'We shall owe the Declaration', he wrote, '. . . chiefly to Hertzog and probably Ireland. It is also possible that the representatives of the British Government played a considerable part. There is this to be said for them, that they are always ready to abandon a position when they think the time has come when they can no longer safely hold it.'[56]

The British naturally played the Declaration down. They were not anxious to give the impression that the mother country would hence forward speak with a voice of lesser authority. The Declaration was simply a synopsis of established practice. How the other Dominions reacted to the Report will be treated later in this chapter, but in the meantime it is worth noting that hitherto most accounts of this conference and its achievements have been written by biographers anxious to explain the paramount influence of their own subject-statesman, with little interest in painting the full picture. There have been no Irish biographies to contribute to an overall balance, but if the Irish role is here emphasised it is because it was the Irish delegation which knew best where it wanted to go. This was a gentleman's club. Britain was reluctant to give a retarding impression. Canada, Australia and New Zealand were content and passive. Inevitably the more aggressive Dominions made an impact. South Africa had only one idea. Ireland alone had a consistent and practical programme.

Yet it is quite possible to read Duncan Hall's detailed account of the 'Genesis of the Balfour Declaration',[57] without knowing that the Irish Free State existed at all. He is preoccupied with South Africa and with Leopold Amery. He has found unexpected documents amongst the Hughes Papers, in Australia, and in his anxiety for these to right an old wrong against Smuts, he creates a new slight of omission against the Irish leaders. Professor Mansergh, surveying Commonwealth development up to the point in 1931 where he begins his own scholarly analysis, is sure that South Africa would have achieved the Declaration whether the Irish were there or not. South Africa was more senior and carried more weight. Hertzog was determined to obtain 'an explicit definition of Dominion Status', and he was prepared to threaten secession if he was not given his way. Furthermore,

> while South African secession from the Commonwealth would have been a serious, perhaps fatal blow to its prestige and pretensions, Irish Free State secession would have had no such disastrous consequences. The Irish Free State was a Dominion in name, not in spirit, and the failure of the Dominion experiment there would not necessarily have had disruptive consequences overseas.[58]

* This in spite of the central position of the Irish Free State at the heart of the Empire a position of real importance surely at this formative Commonwealth stage when

But Mansergh, like Hall, concentrates his attention on the Declaration. To the Irish, the Declaration was of no importance: worse still, it was a distraction from the real issues. Hall is right to leave the Irish out of his list of Declaration advocates, but he is wrong to overlook the real work which they did at the Conference. Mansergh, I think, underrates both the initiating significance of the Irish and the importance of their geographic position. But there was confusion at the time over the Declaration and it is worth asking how this arose.

Desmond FitzGerald supplies a clue. He had made co-equality one of the issues at stake for the Irish delegation and it was natural that afterwards, in the Dail, he should welcome its formal enunciation and enlarge upon the Irish contributions to it. But to the more forceful Kevin O'Higgins there was little to be gained from pious declarations. The British would glibly agree to say anything so long as they were asked to do nothing. O'Higgins had a strong belief in the efficacy of the conference system. He liked to get his feet under the same table as the other Dominions, for concrete decisions were likely to be adhered to by the British Government and not be subject to party fluctuation. He was confident that the Dominions were progressing towards full sovereignty, and that conference 'give and take' would ultimately achieve freedom, without the cost of further Irish lives. But he was anxious to get to work to make the Commonwealth a better institution, not simply to make it sound better. Where Dominion sovereignty was still circumscribed by legal anachronisms he would sweep those anachronisms away. He looked to Mackenzie King to back him here, and was disappointed at the Canadian's complacency. He argued the issue with Hertzog but was forced to bow to the Boer's inflexibility. J. A. Costello, the Irish Attorney-General at this time and a key member of the Irish delegation, has painted the picture with vividness and economy: 'At the outset', he explained, 'some of the members were almost openly hostile. Others from whom much was expected, were only occasionally helpful. General Hertzog's policy was concentrated on one line,

---

the world at large had no clear idea of Dominion status. What was true in 1949 – or even 1936 – was not true in 1926. In 1932, commenting on the Anglo-Irish economic dispute, General Smuts could still opine that 'If by chance Ireland leaves or is left out of the Commonwealth, irreparable damage may be done to the cause – infinitely greater than what is involved in the present dispute'. See Public Archives of Canada, 'Murphy Papers, Correspondence', pp. 977–88, letter to R. B. Bennet, 18 April 1932. Senator Murphy quotes other Dominion leaders to reveal Commonwealth-wide anxieties.

to secure a declaration of freedom and equality of status. The Irish policy, suspicious of phrase making, proceeded on the assumption of co-equality, and demanded its detailed and practical application.'[59] O'Higgins, accepting that the direction of Dominion advance mattered more than the pace, threw himself into the formulation of the Declaration once it had become inevitable. After all, it would openly declare that equality which was the basis of the Irish case. O'Higgins contributed his own draft and he was a joint critic with Hertzog of other drafts; he ruled out 'common bonds of allegiance';[60] he ensured that the final result was acceptable to Ireland. Then he and his delegation got down to the real work. If it is misleading of A. E. Malone to remark, as he does in his article on 'Party Government in the Irish Free State', that 'the famous so-called "Balfour Memorandum" owes more to the late Kevin O'Higgins than it does to Lord Balfour', he was doing no more than justice when he claimed that 'the Irish Ministry for External Affairs has done much to clarify the meaning of "Dominion status".[61]

The major Irish work of 'clarification' is contained in a remarkable memorandum drawn up by the Irish delegation on 2 November 1926. It is a document of great breadth and it recognises that matters which affected one dominion had repercussions upon all. Far from being a list of domestic grievances its aim was to create throughout the whole Commonwealth an atmosphere of co-operation based on the fellowship of equality. This comprehensive paper itself underpins the basic assertion of this book. Here lie the roots of the Statute of Westminster. Here the seeds of the 1929 Committee on the Operation of Dominion Legislation, which drew up that Statute, are sown. This document was the considered view of the Irish leaders. It raised questions of a penetrating nature that went to the heart of the imperial structure: questions that required the closest scrutiny at the highest level. So much time was taken up at the 1926 Conference by the insistent, compulsive Declaration, that there was not sufficient left to examine fully the Irish points. The British were ready to give Hertzog his formula, his painless paragraph of polished rhetoric. They were not ready to concede a radical uprooting of the whole British system of legal and constitutional supremacy from the fabric of the Empire, just to please the Irish. They proposed a special committee to examine in detail the items raised. Perhaps they hoped thus to turn the Irish lance, to side-track and so prevent any such examination. If they did, then events conspired against them. When

the 'Committee of Experts' met in 1929, the Conservative government had fallen from power, and Labour was in control in Australia
as well as in England. The Irish were left in a commanding position.
Patrick McGilligan, then head of the Irish team as Minister for
External Affairs and Minister for Industry and Commerce, took
O'Higgins's place to give his country once again the ablest and most
forceful delegate present.

If we break the chronology of events to look ahead here to 1929,
it is with a purpose. Only so can we throw proper perspective upon
this important memorandum. Dated 2 November 1926, and written
at the Hotel Cecil, the headquarters of the Irish Delegation, the
memorandum is listed E(IR/26)3 of the conference documents. It is
worth quoting in full:

Existing Anomalies in the British Commonwealth of Nations

The principle of the absolute equality of status and the legislative
judicial and constitutional independence of the members of the British
Commonwealth of Nations is now admitted beyond controversy. It is
accordingly thought that it would be opportune to direct attention to
some of the more outstanding anomalies and anachronisms which
appear most to detract from that principle with the object of abrogating
anything which in form or substance interferes with its complete application in practice.

2. The fundamental right of the Government of each separate unit of
the Commonwealth to advise the King in all matters whatsoever
relating to its own affairs should be formally affirmed and recognised in
practice.

3. The following are instances in which that fundamental right is
contravened:—

(*a*) The claim of the British Government to control legislation of the
other legislatures of the Commonwealth by means of the disallowance or reservation of the statutes of such legislature.

When the Secretary of state for Dominion Affairs receives each year or
more frequently certified copies of Acts of the Dominion Parliaments,
he requests the Governor-General to inform his Ministers that His
Majesty will not be advised to exercise his powers of disallowance in
respect of these Acts. Similarly, the reservation of statutes for His
Majesty's pleasure implies action solely on the advice of His Majesty's
British Ministers. Those powers of veto are obsolete and should be
formally abandoned.

(*b*) The issue of exequaturs to Consuls operating within the Dominions on the advice of His Majesty's British Ministers with the
counter-signature of the British Foreign Secretary.

In the case of Consuls *de carrière*, the Dominions are merely informed
that the exequatur is being appointed, but the exequatur issues on the

advice of the British Ministers. The consular commission should be sent direct by the foreign Government to the Dominion Government, and the exequatur should be issued on the advice of His Majesty's Dominion Ministers counter-signed by the Dominion Minister for External Affairs.

(*c*) The assumption in international treaties and conventions that the signature of the British plenipotentiary appointed on the sole advice of His Majesty's British Government binds the Dominions.

The principle should be formally accepted that no Dominion can be bound in any way except by the signature of a plenipotentiary appointed on its own advice. When there is a common plenipotentiary for two or more members of the Commonwealth, separate full powers should be issued in accordance with this principle.

4. The Governor General at present fills a dual role. He is at the same time the representative of the King and the representative of the British Government, thus giving credence to a common misapprehension that there is no distinction in practice between the British Government and the King as far as the Dominions are concerned.

Furthermore, it is not in conformity with the principle stated in paragraph 1 of this memorandum that a Government chosen by the people should be affected in any of its actions by the representative of another government. Accordingly, it is suggested that his functions should be confined exclusively to representing the King. He should act solely on the advice of the Dominion Ministry, and should not be the recipient of any instructions from the British Government. He should no longer discharge any functions as the representative of the British Government or of any Department thereof, nor act as the channel of communication between the British Government and the Dominion Government. The choice of the representative of the King should lie with the Dominion Government, on whose advice alone the appointment should be made. Similar principles should prevail when a change falls to be made in the holder of the office.

5. It has been sought to impose limitations on the legislative competence of the Members of the Commonwealth of Nations other than Great Britain by insistence on the contention that the laws of such members – except where extra-territorial operation is given to them by the British Parliament – operate only within the territorial area of such member. Such a contention is inconsistent with the legislative autonomy necessarily following from equality of status. Moreover, it is nowhere expressed in any of the Constitutions of the States of the Commonwealth that there is any territorial limitation to the operation of laws duly enacted. It is obviously necessary in modern conditions that the legislatures of those States should exercise authority with extra-territorial effect when necessary for the peace, order and good government of their countries. It would be absurd, for example, to suggest that legislation making it a crime to conspire outside the Dominion against the peace, order and good government of that Dominion, or to defraud the customs of that Dominion or otherwise

violate its laws, would be invalid. It should be made clear that a law passed by the legislature of any part of the Commonwealth cannot be invalid or fail to have effect by reason merely of extra-territorial operation, or of the fact that its provisions are repugnant to the provisions of any statute passed by the British Parliament.

6. The exercise of legislative authority by the Parliament of Great Britain as regards the other members of the Commonwealth of Nations would clearly be inconsistent with the principles upon which the Commonwealth of Nations is founded. The very title of such an Act as the Colonial Laws Validity Act (which would appear from a recent judgement of the Judicial Committee of the Privy Council to be still of technical legal effect in some parts at least of the Commonwealth of Nations) implies subjection, and the doctrines embodied in that Act are subversive of the principles of autonomy and constitutional co-equality.

No law can bind a member of the Commonwealth of Nations except its own law, and the function of enacting every such law belongs exclusively as of right to the Parliament of such member.

Uniformity of laws and of administration of laws where desirable or necessary can best be secured by the enactment of reciprocal statutes based upon consultation and agreement.

7. The Royal Titles are still as they were before the separation of the Irish Free State and the United Kingdom. For that reason, and in order to emphasise the dignity of the individual nations of the Commonwealth, it is suggested that these nations should be set out by name in the King's title, which would then read as follows:—

King of the United Kingdom of Great Britain and of Canada, Australia, New Zealand, South Africa, and the Irish Free State, Emperor of India.

In international treaties this title set out in full before, or in reference to, each of the national plenipotentiaries on the advice of whose Government the King acts will remove all doubt about the equality of status of the Commonwealth nations, both *inter se* and *vis-à-vis* non-Commonwealth states, and will at the same time indicate the bond upon which the real unity of the Commonwealth depends.

8. The position in regard to the Judicial Committee of the Privy Council and to matters relating to Merchant Shipping is dealt with in separate memoranda (see E.115 and E. (E.) 24 respectively).

9. The channel of Communication between Foreign Governments and the Dominions is still the British Foreign Office. It is clear from the text of Foreign Communications that Foreign Governments regard the Dominions Governments as subordinate to the British Government. This can best be illustrated by a recent and typical example. The Belgian Ambassador in London, in a letter to the British Foreign Secretary on the 30 September last, concerning the issue of fresh exequaturs in respect of altered jurisdiction in the Irish Free State, writes as follows:—

'Je me permets de recourir à l'obligeant intermédiaire de Votre Excellence aux fins que les titulaires de ces postes soient officiellement reconnus par les *Autorités britanniques* dans la nouvelle juridiction qui leur a été confiée.'

In all matters concerning the Dominions as individual states, correspondence should take place direct between the Departments of External Affairs of the Dominions and Foreign Countries. The members of the Commonwealth would, of course, keep each other informed of such correspondence in all matters of common interest in conformity with the spirit of the 1923 treaty resolutions.

Approval of this procedure should be intimated by the British Government to foreign Governments.

CONCLUSION

If the British Commonwealth of Nations is to endure as the greatest factor for the establishment of peace and prosperity throughout the world, its cohesive force must be real and permanent, whether viewed from within or without. It cannot be held together by a mere collective expression, which only serves to create doubt in the minds of Foreign Statesmen and discontent amongst the diverse nationalities of which it is made up.

The King is the real bond, and forms used in international treaties will be devoid of all meaning so long as they do not give complete expression to that reality.

The co-operation resulting from the bond of a common King will be effective only because it is free co-operation and to the extent to which it is free. Antiquated forms dating from a period when common action resulted from the over-riding control of one central Government are liable to make co-operation less efficacious, because they make it seem less free.[62]

The document is forceful but reasonable. In both its detailed and its general recommendations it forms the basis of the Report of the Inter-Imperial Relations Committee. It was not the only Irish memorandum submitted to that Committee, but it is a summary of an Irish point of view which was to be argued consistently until 1931, and most of the other Irish documents were expansions of points mentioned in it. The full Report of the Committee is too long to reprint here, but its conclusions must be examined in order to elucidate the Irish contribution to them.

After a note on the special position of India, the first major section following the Balfour Declaration is entitled 'Relations Between the Various Parts of the British Empire'. It contains a number of sub-sections, the first of which deals with the 'Title of His Majesty the King'. This subject occurs in item seven of the Irish Memorandum. According to Amery[63] it was the first question of principle decided by the Committee, and although the finally agreed change was not in accord with the original Irish suggestion it does represent a victory for O'Higgins. The title recommended by the Conference, and put into effect by the Royal and Parliamentary Titles Act, 1927, was: 'George V, by the Grace of God, of Great Britain, Ireland and of the British Dominions beyond the Seas, King, Defender of the Faith, Emperor of India'.[64] As far back as April 1924, the Royal Title had become an issue in Dail Eireann.[65] O'Higgins was anxious now that a new title should not only reflect the new status of the Free State, but should if possible clarify the royal signature on treaties concluded on behalf of the Dominions. The British were willing enough to drop the phrase: 'of the United Kingdom', from the original but they wished to retain 'of Great Britain *and* Ireland'. O'Higgins preferred the comma of the final result and this was accepted and became known as the 'O'Higgins Comma'. Its virtue was that it would need no alteration if Ireland became united, and the British were glad enough to retain the old triple division of the British Isles, the Overseas Dominions and the Indian Empire.

The subject was not merely of grammatical importance. The old Title did not recognise the existence of the Free State and a change was necessary. But as soon as so fundamental a part of the British Constitution as the Royal Title was challenged, a host of other issues arose. The concepts of nationality, of allegiance, of the Crown as the central imperial bond became involved, along with the very mystique with which the British loved to surround their deepest constitutional theories. Amery proudly affirms in his biography that he had coached the British Cabinet for two years into the acceptance of 'the right point of view',[66] no doubt based on the unitary, indivisible Crown as the ultimate safeguard of Empire. But O'Higgins and his men, drawing on the legacy of Griffith and Sinn Fein, held a quite contrary view. The monarchy was several. The only king acceptable in Ireland was the King of Ireland, and O'Higgins looked for the clarification of the King's several identity as head of the seven dominion-kingdoms. This point was to recur in the discussions on international agreements. At this stage, O'Higgins, who passionately hoped to restore the unity of Ireland and who saw in his 'Kingdom of Ireland' theory the best chance of unification, fought for a title which could include that whole kingdom without further change. Later, a leading article in the *Irish Times*, commenting on the Report, fervently hoped that 'one day the problem of Irish Unity will be solved by the aid of this formula',[67] and O'Higgins himself was to forecast that 'some day Anglo-Irish relations will be represented by a Dual Monarch – two quite independent kingdoms with a common King and, perhaps, a Defence Treaty'.[68]

So keenly did O'Higgins feel about this point that he used the opportunity of his presence in London to put the idea to the old Unionist leader, Carson. He did not ask for Carson's active support, but was anxious that no objection should be raised. In his own sitting-room, the former Ulster champion gave O'Higgins his passive approval,[69] and at two dinners – one legal,[70] the other a Canadian reception[71] – O'Higgins and Carson met on friendly terms. Perhaps the old bitternesses were already beginning to fade.

In Ulster itself, needless to say, the change was viewed with alarm. Immediately after publication of the Report a deputation from Belfast descended on London. The Ulstermen complained that they had become 'outcasts',[72] and argued that there was no need for the Title to be so incorrect. It could easily include the phrase 'of the United Kingdom of Great Britain and Northern Ireland, of the Irish Free State, and of the British Dominions. ...'[73] Only an assurance from Baldwin that the title had no Dominion significance, that it was purely descriptive of the King's territorial sovereignty and therefore was accurate, and that it was simply the shortest way of changing the Title, pacified them.[74] They did have the cold comfort that 'Defender of the Faith' remained in to mock their Roman Catholic neighbours.*

The next sub-section of the Inter-Imperial Relations Report is devoted to 'The position of Governors-General'. The emphatic conclusion reached was that

> the Governor-General of a Dominion is the representative of the Crown, holding in all essential respects the same position in relation to the administration of public affairs in the Dominion as is held by his Majesty the King in Great Britain, and he is not the representative or agent of His Majesty's Government in Great Britain or of any Department of that Government.[75]

The Governor-General need no longer be the channel of communication between the British and Dominion Governments: communication should be between government and government direct.

---

* This inclusion was resented in the Dail. See Deputy Baxter, Dail Eireann debates, XVII, col. 894 (1 December 1926). Note also that in 1928 it was proposed to omit the words 'By the Grace of God' and 'Defender of the Faith' from Free State passports, but no agreement could be reached.

It was left to the Dominions to implement this as they wished, but it was agreed that in all events Governors-General would be kept fully informed.

As far back as 23 June 1920, General Smuts had pointed out to the South African parliament the anomaly of the dual role which the Governor-General then played as the representative of the Crown and of the British Government, and he had called for clarification.[76] In Canada, in June 1924, an Opposition member had challenged the existing means of inter-governmental communication.[77] But the King–Byng dispute of the summer of 1926 had magnified the problem fourfold and, at the Conference, rectification of this muddle had become Mackenzie King's one insistent demand. As his biographer affirms:

> If the prejudices of a British Governor could nullify the Constitution, then Canada was not a self-governing Dominion. Autonomy was the foundation upon which Canada and the entire British Commonwealth stood.[78]

King had long regarded the Governor-General as 'the representative of the Crown in the Dominions and in no sense as an agent of the British Government'.[79] After the Byng controversy he was anxious for this to be recognised officially. He wanted the Governor-General's role to be defined, and also a new 'channel of communication between the Canadian and British Governments which would by-pass the Governor-General' to be created.[80] This would involve the British Government in establishing diplomatic representatives in Dominion capitals, a procedure which would in turn enhance the status of the Dominion High Commissioners in London. It would also lead to a greater degree of mutual understanding, the written word being augmented by personal explanation. Not all the Dominions were anxious for this new channel, but Amery conceded its value and helped to overcome British Cabinet opposition. Amery regretted the breaking of the useful private correspondence link between the Governors-General and the Dominions Secretary, but he recognised that greater issues were at stake. If this move put into the hands of the Dominion governments the 'exclusive initiative'[81] in the appointment of future office-holders, in place of the old joint Dominion–British discussions, then this was an inevitable development and constitutionally correct. Blair Neatby, in this section of the King biography, declares that once the Governor-General was no longer an agent of the British government, then 'the eventual appointment of a Canadian Governor-General for Canada was predictable'.[82] He seems to have overlooked the pioneering work done by Ireland in this respect. In fact there is little doubt that by 1926 both South Africa and Canada were anxious to attain what was then the accepted Irish position.

The approved recommendation is in triumphant accord with section four of the Irish Memorandum, which could not be more explicit. There is no doubt that the Irish and Canadians worked closely on this matter,* and if the final Irish sentences were omitted from the Committee Report then it is perhaps because this particular point could not find over-all approval. Certainly by including this latter demand the Irish were arguing from their own established position for the benefit of the Dominions in general. The Irish leaders did not doubt that their own nominee would be accepted and though they would have liked Dominion nomination to have become standard practice they would hardly have wished to force its adoption on the others.

From the beginning the Irish had been instrumental in transforming this office. In their view the Governor-General was an entirely colonial figure who should never have survived into the dominion era. Having accepted him, however, they desired to make him compatible with the status of equality. In Ireland he was no longer the representative of a foreign power but an integral part of the Oireachtas. Now he could be advised solely by his Irish ministers. Whatever functions His Majesty exercised in Great Britain in relation to the administration of public affairs, the Governor-General would exercise in the Irish Free State. The Royal Prerogative was now at the discretion of the Irish Government with respect to its own territory. In the words of a contemporary Irish lawyer, the Governor-General 'does not govern and has not the power to govern. He simply acts for the King.'[83]

Just as it had pioneered this particular ground, so the Irish Government was the first to implement the new procedure. In Canada and South Africa the recommendations came into force in July 1927, but in Ireland they were introduced in May.† As Mr

---

* See Appendix C.

† The story of Dominion implementation is revealed in telegrams from the Dominions Office in 1927. In reply to a Canadian request to implement the new procedure L. S. Amery notified the Dominions on 24 January 1927 that 1 July would be a suitable date. On 19 February the Irish Free State informed Amery that the change was desired as

Ernest Blythe explained, on the appointment of Ireland's second Governor-General: 'The Governor-General has ceased to be the channel of communication between the Irish Free State Government and the British Government since 1 May last.'[84] And lest there be any doubt about the method of the new appointment, he added categorically:

> the appointment of the Governor-General is entirely a matter for the Dominion Government concerned, and he is appointed by the King on the advice of the Government: the new Governor-General of the Irish Free State is being appointed by the King on the advice of the Saorstat Government.

From the office of Governor-General the Report moves on to the 'Operation of Dominion Legislation'. Under this single heading a number of very important subjects were examined, sub-sections being devoted to Disallowance of Dominion Legislation; Reservation; the territorial limitation of Dominion legislative competence; and the supremacy of the Westminster parliament, with particular reference to the operation of the Colonial Laws Validity Act. In regard to the latter it was actually suggested that 'in future uniformity of legislation as between Great Britain and the Dominions would best be secured by the enactment of reciprocal Statutes based upon consultation and agreement'.[85] But the Committee recognised that these subjects, all of which were emphatically raised in the Irish Memorandum (Sections 3a, 5, 6), required fuller treatment than the Committee itself could give. Accordingly it recommended that a further expert committee should be set up to 'enquire into, report upon, and make recommendations concerning'[86] these selfsame topics, the position of the Dominions at that time and how this position could best be reconciled with the new principle of equality of status. Thus the Committee of Experts (which met in 1929) was conceived.

Until this expert committee could meet, however, the Report

---

soon as possible, and suggested 1 May. This would be an easy matter as, Ireland was so close to Great Britain.

On 20 April this date was accepted and on 1 May the new procedure was initiated for the Irish Free State.

On 1 July Canada and S. Africa adopted the new procedure. New Zealand had already signified on 5 March that it desired no change. Australia welcomed the new procedure but owing to the Government's move to Canberra it did not adopt it until 1 January 1928.

placed on record two main assertions. The first of these, echoing
Section Two of the Irish Memorandum, stated that:

> apart from provisions embodied in constitutions or in specific statutes
> expressly providing for reservation, it is recognised that it is the right
> of the Government of each Dominion to advise the Crown in all matters
> relating to its own affairs.[87]

Reservation of Dominion legislation fell into two categories – obligatory and discretionary. Article 41 of the Irish Free State Constitution included discretionary reservation. As in Canada, the
Governor-General (now to be advised by his Dominion ministers) had
to signify, withhold assent or reserve the bill for the signification of the
King's pleasure. This now contained a contradiction in terms which
was ridiculous. There was no obligatory reservation, nor was there
provision for Disallowance of Irish statute, in the Irish Constitution,
but once again the Irish delegates had seized upon general conditions
which they felt derogated from Dominion status as a whole. Though
these conditions had little direct application to the Irish case they
served no useful purpose and should be cleared away, the better to
reveal the true position to the Dominions themselves and to the
outside world.

The second assertion which the Committee felt bound to place on
record referred to the

legislative competence of members of the British Commonwealth other
than Great Britain, and in particular to the desirability of those members
being enabled to legislate with extra-territorial effect.[88]

The Committee stated that

> the constitutional practice is that legislation by the Parliament at
> Westminster applying to a Dominion would only be passed with the
> consent of the Dominion concerned.[89]

More in line with Section Five of the Irish Memorandum, the terms
of reference for the Committee of experts looked for

> the most convenient method of giving effect to the principle that each
> Dominion Parliament should have power to give extra-territorial
> operation to its legislation in all cases where such operation is ancillary
> to provision for the peace, order and good government of the
> Dominion.[90]

From a brief prepared by the Irish Government for the 1929 Expert
Committee, some interesting light emerges on the position of this
subject in 1926.

Even at this time the extra-territorial rights of the Dominions had never been admitted. However, in June 1920, Canada had sought from the Crown an amendment to the British North America Act to the effect that competent Canadian legislation should have the same extra-territorial effect as United Kingdom legislation. This request had been refused in this form, and agreement was not reached until, on 18 July 1924, it was decided that:

> an enactment *intra vires* of the Parliament of Canada, if expressed to operate extra-territorially, shall have, and is deemed to have had, that operation if and in so far as it is a law for and ancillary to the peace, order and good government of Canada.[91]

To the Irish, the history of these addresses to the Crown was quaint comment on the asserted equality of status, and at the fifth Meeting of the Inter-Imperial Relations Committee (3 November 1926) Patrick McGilligan, Irish Free State Minister for Industry and Commerce, sought assurance that:

> Legislative functions which previously belonged to the British Parliament now belong to the Parliaments of the other members of the Commonwealth as well. Whatever the Parliament of the United Kingdom can do, the Parliament of any other of the Associated States can do: whatever the Parliament of any other of the Associated States can do, the Parliament of the United Kingdom can do, but no more.[92]

He wanted to make the position clear, and he wanted no qualifying statements in any way limiting the Dominion position. At the Imperial Conference of 1911, Sir Joseph Ward had placed on the agenda a resolution, namely:

> that the self-governing overseas Dominions have now reached the stage of development when they should be entrusted with wider legislative powers in respect to British and foreign shipping.[93]

This, McGilligan pointed out, was an approach entirely unacceptable from a constitutional point of view, and being 'conscious that a Resolution placed on the agenda of an Imperial Conference in the year 1926 would inevitably be framed in terms widely different from those of the Resolution of the Government of New Zealand in 1911', he hoped that it would 'reflect faithfully the existing position of the States of the Commonwealth of Nations'.[94]

The Irish did not regard any limitation as existing in respect to their own legislation, though there had been a difference of opinion on the matter early in the history of the Free State when, in 1923,

His Majesty's Law Officers in Britain had opined to the Governor-General in Dublin that 'the powers conferred on your Ministers and the Oireachtas respectively are not such as to enable them to make new byelaws or pass further legislation having extra-territorial effect'.[95] Whatever the British opinion, in 1925 FitzGibbon J., in the case of Alexander v. the County Court Judge of Cork (2 I.R. 1925, p. 165), stated a view more acceptable to Irish aspirations:

> As at present advised I am not prepared to hold that legislation in this country making it a crime for persons to conspire elsewhere, meaning outside the country, against the peace, order and good government of this country, or to defraud our Customs, or to violate our laws is necessarily invalid because of the secondary opinion of the Judicial Committee in McLeod's Case,[96] nor that our Courts would not have full jurisdiction to deal with such offenders if they should happen to come within the limits of the Saorstat. The Free State would not in the cases I have supposed, be enacting laws for itself with regard to persons or acts beyond its limits and if these laws were essential to the peace, order and good government of the Free State I see no ground for doubting that they would be valid.[97]

It was an integral part of the Irish argument that if a parliament was sovereign, then there could be no outside authority capable of pronouncing upon the laws passed by that parliament. McGilligan was primarily concerned, therefore, to establish that in respect of extra-territorial jurisdiction, as in all respects, the Dominion Parliaments, not least that of the Irish Free State, were sovereign.

'Merchant Shipping Legislation' is the next sub-division of the Inter-Imperial Relations Report. Here again the vast range of legislation concerned was too great for the Committee. Again they proposed a special sub-committee, to advise on the following general lines:

> To consider and report on the principle which should govern, in the general interest, the practice and legislation relating to merchant shipping in the various parts of the Empire, having regard to the change in constitutional status and general relations which has occurred since existing laws were enacted.[98]

In a separate memorandum (E.(E)24) the Irish had pointed out this large field of British legislation, which, though it did serve a purpose in preserving a uniform set of maritime laws, nevertheless contravened the equal legislative competence of the Dominions. The problem was dealt with by a sub-committee of the Committee on

Dominion Legislation (the 1929 Committee), under the chairmanship of the Canadian, Charles Burchell. To the Irish the main concern was that they should be able to fly their own flag on their own ships.

After merchant shipping, the Committee turned to the inflamatory subject of 'Appeals to the Judicial Committee of the Privy Council'. This was a subject upon which the Irish had particularly strong feelings. An emphatic memorandum (E.115) contained their view:

> It is an essential incident of the equality of status and the legislative judicial and constitutional independence of each member of the British Commonwealth of Nations that the question of appeals to the Judicial Committee of the Privy Council should be dealt with upon 'principles of autonomy'. In accordance with such principles, it is the right (which ought to be unquestionable and indisputable) of each individual State of that Commonwealth to decide, through its legislature, whether or to what degree and in what circumstances (if any) an appeal should lie from a decision of its own Courts to any tribunal outside the State. While it is in strict accordance with such principles that an appeal should lie to the Judicial Committee from the Courts of any State in the Commonwealth which desires the continuance of such an appeal, it would be a violation of such principles to deny the right of a State which desires that finality on judicial questions should be reached within its own area, to determine that such shall be the case.[99]

That the Appeal still existed in 1926 was one of the more regular taunts which the Irish Opposition could fling at their Government, and that Government itself felt that it was the chief slur on its claim to sovereignty. The Nadan Case in Canada – a criminal case accepted by the Judicial Committee against all tradition – had come at a most opportune moment and the Irish looked to their Canadian colleagues for support on this issue above all others.* But to their great disappointment support was not forthcoming. In spite of the fact that the

* The Case of Nadan *v.* the King was a Criminal Case and it had been Canadian law for twenty years that Appeals from judgments in criminal cases could not go before the Judicial Committee of the Privy Council. In accepting this Appeal, however, the Judicial Committee ruled that this Canadian law was *ultra vires* Dominion legislation, being repugnant to British law which allowed all His Majesty's subjects the right of appeal to the foot of the Throne.

The case was dismissed but it was significant because it kept alive the principle of the right of appeal. It was felt at the time that the whole affair was a deliberate attempt to preserve the principle, not for Canada so much as for the Irish Free State. (For an example of this view see Thorsen, Canada, H. of C., 1926-7, II 1756.) Details of the Privy Council judgment are most conveniently found in F. Madden, *Imperial Constitutional Documents 1765–1965, a Supplement*, pp. 47–54.

principle on which the Nadan Case was decided – 'that Dominion legislation was *ultra vires* if it conflicted with British legislation'[100] – was a contradiction of equal status, the Canadians could not contemplate outright abolition of the appeal. Premier Tascherau of Quebec was in London at the time perhaps keeping an eye on this very issue; Lapointe himself was a French Canadian; there was even currently a most important Canadian boundary case before the Privy Council – a dispute between Canada and Newfoundland over the Labrador border, the evidence for which had taken twenty years to prepare.* Mackenzie King, with one eye on the French Canadians who regarded this as the guarantee of their minority rights, and another eye on the Provincial Parliaments which saw in the appeal to the Privy Council the safeguard of the Provincial–Federal allocation of powers, could do no more than hedge. The Irish had to fight alone and their righteous indignation lent them considerable force. They had been accorded the South African position, they said, and Lord Chancellor Haldane had established a principle, in connection with the first Irish appeals in 1923, that in as far as possible matters would be settled in the Irish Courts: only issues affecting other members of the Commonwealth would be accepted by the Judicial Committee.† Then in 1925 an appeal from the Supreme Court on a private Land Bill had been allowed. If this was a precedent, where would the practice stop? The only answer was abolition. The Appeal was unconstitutional and it served no practical purpose. It provided no guarantee of minority rights (which were not needed anyway), for the Government had already evolved an 'effective and ingenious'‡ way of circumventing Judicial Committee decisions by passing retrospective legislation to make their own Supreme Court decisions law.

But Lord Birkenhead, accepted as a real friend of Ireland, and a close personal associate of Kevin O'Higgins, advised caution. At a

* For a full account of this dispute see St John Chadwick, *Newfoundland, Island into Province*, ch. 11.

† Lord Haldane: 'It becomes with the Dominions more and more or less and less as they please. We go upon the principles of autonomy on this question of exercising the discretion as to granting leave to appeal.' Quoted by D. J. O'Sullivan in *Neuphilologische Monatsschrift* (December 1930) p. 585. See also Lord Buckmaster: 'As far as possible finality and supremacy are to be given to the Irish Courts' (Hull *v.* M'Kenna 1926 I R 409).

‡ These are the words of Lord Cave, though he was no ally of the Free State, being 'the worst reactionary in the lot' at this Conference. He also 'finally stamped out of the Conference, saying he was not going to be a party to the breaking up of the British Empire'. D. B. McCrae, cited in R. Cook, *J.C.P.S.* (no. 1) III 60–1.

breakfast meeting with O'Higgins, Patrick McGilligan, John A. Costello and the British Attorney-General, Hogg, Birkenhead asked the Irish to allow a little more time to pass. The Irish were pre-occupied enough with the problems of establishing their State: the British too had troubles in unquiet Europe. If they would wait until the next Imperial Conference, he, Birkenhead would throw his entire weight behind their demand for abolition.* A compromise was required, and the Irish yielded. But by the next Imperial Conference, both Birkenhead and O'Higgins were dead.

O'Higgins, however, was not unduly dissatisfied in 1926, for he firmly believed that the resolution incorporated in the Report meant that appeals would only be allowed to the Judicial Committee with the permission of the Irish Supreme Court. The resolution that:

> it was no part of the policy of His Majesty's Government in Great Britain that questions affecting judicial appeals should be determined otherwise than in accordance with the wishes of the part of the Empire primarily affected.[101]

seemed clearly to establish this principle, and of course the Irish Supreme Court would never give such permission. That events turned out differently was not the fault of O'Higgins, and anyway the Irish had not left everything to chance. They had made it clear in the Report itself 'that the right was reserved to bring up the matter again at the next Imperial Conference for discussion in relation to the facts of this particular problem.'[102]

The fifth major division of the Report is concerned with 'Relations with Foreign Countries', as distinct from the former sections concerned with 'the relations of the various parts of the British Empire with one another'. The Committee took as its starting point the resolution of the 1923 Conference on the negotiation, signature and ratification of treaties, and in its first sub-section here, entitled 'Procedure in Relation to Treaties', examined the working of that resolution and considered 'whether the principles laid down with

---

* McGilligan and Costello both recounted this story with vigour at separate interviews. D. B. McCrae added a paragraph on this subject (cited by R. Cook, *J.C.P.S.* (no. 1) III 60): 'The Privy Council is left in abeyance but will likely come up at the next conference. The Irish had the British pleading to let the matter rest for the time being as they were having a hard time with their "die hards" and wished to have something to show that they had not given up. They promised that they would see that the Privy Council would hear no cases from Ireland unless by consent of the Irish Parliament: which might indicate that there is political pressure behind the P.C. when necessary.'

regard to Treaties could not be applied with advantage in a wider sphere'.[103]

Treaty procedure was in fact entrusted to a sub-committee under the chairmanship of Ernest Lapointe, who had pioneered this field by conducting the Canadian–American Halibut Treaty in 1923. Canada, South Africa and Ireland were all deeply interested in this subject, for the exercise of the treaty power was taken to be one of the hallmarks of independent statehood. The substance of the Irish case, prepared by Mr J. P. Walshe, is contained in sections three (*c*) and seven (second paragraph) of the Irish Memorandum, and it is here that Irish opinion identified itself with Hertzog's demand for a declaration of status. The Irish did not want to be bound by British-conducted treaties. They wanted to make it clear that only when they themselves signed were they involved. Because of the current form of the Title of the King, whose common kingship was the source of confusion to foreign governments, they had asked for that title to be changed. The problem was how to have the King advised separately by the individual Dominions and to have this recognised abroad. As the Memorandum explained, they wanted to 'remove all doubt about the equality of status of the Commonwealth nations, both *inter se* and *vis-à-vis* non-Commonwealth States'.[104] As stated before, the Dominions must be seen to be free.

The subject was a delicate one. Hertzog had already hinted at neutrality for South Africa in future British wars – a hint that had brought an immediate denunciation from the leader of the Opposition in Canada.* But such a theory had great attraction for the pacifist Johnson, leader of the Opposition in Ireland. And in the discussions on treaties, which might concern the sanction of military operations, such a matter was seldom far away. South Africa and Ireland argued the point, with Mackenzie King mediating as best he could. Skelton had already warned King against the British preference for an imperial diplomatic unity, conducted by the Foreign Office. 'Imperialist theories', he said, 'have for years been trying to foist upon us a doctrine of diplomatic unity, which had no relation to present realities and in practice would mean acknowledging the

* Guthrie, 21 October 1926: 'General Hertzog, the Prime Minister of the Union of South Africa, wants to have his cake and eat it. His attitude is that his country should remain in the Empire when all is well but be able to declare its neutrality in case of trouble.' Guthrie went on to warn Mackenzie King that in the East of Canada there was no sympathy towards this, while any that might exist in the West was due solely to ignorance. See *The Times*, 22 October 1926.

right of the Foreign Office, with more or less formal consultation, to bind the Dominions.'[105]

Mackenzie King's biographer describes the conflicting viewpoints:

The Conference also modified other surviving forms of colonialism. The initiative came from South Africa and Ireland, but again Canadian support helped to persuade the British to yield gracefully. The now accepted principle of equality of status proved to be a powerful solvent. Treaties could no longer be signed on behalf of the Dominions by British plenipotentiaries. Separate signatures by each Dominion, on the other hand, would contradict the principle of imperial unity. The Irish rather favoured such a contradiction. One Irish delegate suggested to King the 'extreme view' that each Dominion should sign as a distinct nation 'each with a separate King'.[106]

Britain of course was reluctant to accept this idea of distinct nationhood and Skelton suggested that treaties should be signed in the name of the King 'as the symbol of the special relationship between the various parts of the Empire'.[107] It has been suggested* that this wording was originally a Dominions Office solution, but, wherever it originated, it was adopted as a compromise and included in the Report.

The method of ratifying treaties was also discussed and a sample treaty *pro forma* was annexed to the Report. In most points the conclusions reached by the Committee were in harmony with those of the Irish Memorandum: no Dominion was to be committed to obligations by another Dominion; full powers to sign for their respective Dominions would be issued to Dominion plenipotentiaries; consultation would be the key to co-operation.

In a long speech in Dail Eireann, on 15 December 1926, Desmond FitzGerald took considerable pains to underline the success of the Irish Free State in this section, and there are good grounds for his assurances.

He underlined the necessity for each Dominion to control its own foreign affairs and pointed out that if there had been more infringement of this basic right up to that date, than there had been in internal affairs, then this was because the Dominions had only lately turned their attention to this subject, and because the machinery which they had used was so frequently that of the British Foreign Office. But the situation would be quite different henceforward. The

---

* Sir Charles W. Dixon, of Commonwealth Relations Office, suggested in interview that this was perhaps a co-operative contribution from Britain and Canada.

Irish Free State did not want to be involved even in passive obligations, and FitzGerald made it clear that the last sentence of the
section on treaty negotiation was for Irish benefit:

> In the case of a government that prefers not to concur in the ratification
> of a treaty unless it has been signed by a plenipotentiary authorised to
> act on its behalf, it will advise the appointment of a plenipotentiary so
> to act.[108]

Similarly, the ending of the practice of signing treaties either with
reference to the British Empire, or with the Dominions listed under
Great Britain, would clarify the position and enhance the status of
the Free State, particularly at the League of Nations. FitzGerald,
while paying tribute to the British that they 'accepted'[109] these new
formulas, discloses that most originated in his own department.
Each State of the Commonwealth would now be represented by its
own plenipotentiaries, appointed on its own advice. The King
remained as the symbol of the Commonwealth tie – but now 'acting
in a several capacity',[110] 'instead of one high contracting party . . .
acting in a distinct capacity on behalf of each State of which he is
King'.[111]

There is no doubt, however, that the conclusion was a compromise
one and FitzGerald was skating round one particularly distasteful
paragraph. This referred to the King as 'the symbol of the special
relationship between the different parts of the Empire', and denied
that treaties made in the King's name would regulate the relations of
the Empire members *inter se*.[112]   The point had already caused friction in 1924, when the Irish Free State had insisted on registering at
Geneva the Anglo-Irish Treaty as a full international agreement.*
It was to cause further bitterness at the 1930 Imperial Conference
when the whole matter was scientifically dissected by the Irish
delegation.†

A further sub-section in this part of the Report deals with representation at international conferences. Predictably, the Irish preferred
representation of a direct nature, and disapproved of method (ii) in
the second part of this sub-section, which outlined the possibility
of a single Empire delegation under certain circumstances. The
guiding light in all such conferences, however, would be the consultation recommended in the section on 'Treaty procedure'.

* See above, Ch. 5, pp. 57–63.
   † See Ch. 8, 209–16: there the circumstances of the 1926 compromise are explained
by Desmond FitzGerald in a letter to E. J. Phelan, p. 212.

The next sub-section deals with the 'General Conduct of Foreign Policy' and brings us back to the controversial Balfour paragraphs which followed the Declaration. His claim for a separation between 'status' and 'function' was not recognised by the Irish, who agreed here to its inclusion only in the spirit of give and take.* They intended to prove in practice that they could look after their own foreign affairs and they determined that, whatever facilities it might care to provide to Irish citizens abroad, the British Foreign Office would in no respect usurp the 'function' of the Irish Government. The Irish Free State was prepared to admit that divergent advice might be tendered to the King by his different Dominions, but they saw no stumbling-block in this, provided the Crown was seen to be 'several'. They were in advance of the other Dominions here, and their view was anathema to Amery, but it was to prevail.

The two small sub-sections which complete this division of the Report are almost exclusively of Irish inspiration. The examination of 'The Issue of Exequaturs to Foreign Consuls in the Dominions' is clearly initiated in section three (*b*) of the Irish Memorandum, and the full Irish suggestion is adopted. Though the point raised in section nine of the Irish Memorandum was not included, the paragraph 'Channel of Communication between Dominion Governments and Foreign Governments' accepted the ending of diplomatic unity with good grace and welcomed the appointment of the Irish ambassador to Washington and the announcement, made during the Conference, that Canada was at last to follow suit.

There remain only three other topics in this vital Inter-Imperial Relations Report. The first of these, given a full short section to itself, was the perennial problem of 'Communication and Consultation'. This was now further complicated by the new position of the Governor-General, and the Committee, while leaving solutions to the individual Dominions, urged that a system of personal contact be established 'both in London and in the Dominion capitals to supplement the present system'.[113] Mackenzie King was particularly anxious to establish British High Commissioners in the Dominions, and Canada was the first to follow up this resolution. Sir William Clarke was soon appointed to Ottawa, and other British High Commissioners followed elsewhere.

---

* J. A. Costello interview. Desmond FitzGerald has made the same observation about the *inter se* clause in this Report. See below Ch. 8, p. 212 (D. FitzGerald letter to E. J. Phelan, 24 March 1927 (FitzGerald Papers).

The second issue was a more contentious one, involving the whole theory of international status once more. It was an unvarying British policy that disagreements within the Empire should be settled within the Empire, preferably by resort to the Judicial Committee of the Privy Council. But the Permanent Court of International Justice was now established as a possible alternative, and Article 36 of the constitution of this court, the so-called 'Optional Clause', provided for compulsory submission of certain classes of cases to it. The Dominions subscribed to the Court but their attitudes to this clause had yet to be resolved.

The Irish Free State disliked the Judicial Committee of the Privy Council in principle. It also felt that if it was ever to be in dispute with another member of the British Commonwealth, that member was most likely to be Britain, and Britain had a predominant weight in the Judicial Committee. Furthermore, it was desirous of being a model member of the League of Nations.* Even during this Conference it had registered at Geneva certain postal conventions with Canada, and India (as well as U.S.A. and Germany) in spite of the disapproval Britain was bound to feel at such moves. It was anxious to adopt Article 36 without reservation, and it hoped that all the Dominions would adhere likewise, thus demonstrating their equality with the other nations of the world.

Unfortunately, however, only twenty-two other nations had so far signed the Clause and most of these only for a limited period of five years. The Dominions would not accept obligations without the assurance that most other countries were equally committed, and the Irish could not win their point. The Committee did not make a resolution to the Conference but felt that it was 'premature to accept the obligations under the Article in question'.[114] It also agreed that no Dominion would sign the Clause 'without bringing up the matter for further discussion'.[115] Perhaps this was to baulk the Irish. In the event the Irish were to lose patience. In 1929, pursuing their policy of independent action, alone of the Dominions, they accepted the Clause without any reservation.

The final section is innocuous in the extreme and consists of an expression of satisfaction at the efforts made by Britain to ensure the peace of Europe, culminating in the Locarno Treaty. The phrase was drafted by King,[116] the conciliator, and was a fitting note of unanimity upon which to close so hard-fought a Report.

* It must be admitted this was in some respects to offset its association with the Empire.

A great deal of this important report, then, is an expression of the Irish viewpoint. In its detail and in its spirit it reflects the Irish Memorandum. The wealth of that detail leaves little room for doubt that the Irish Free State above all, for better or for worse, for selfish or for altruistic reasons, had seized the helm of the British Empire ship: the spirit, and it must be accepted as genuine, reveals a realistic insight into a changing world, and a statesmanship fully attuned to that world. The Irish Free State had joined the British Empire at a crucial stage in the Empire's development. As a newcomer and an outsider it was perhaps better placed to judge the position of that development and to decide the direction in which it could most profitably proceed.

The rest of the *Summary of Proceedings* (the full Conference Report), of which the Inter-Imperial Relations Committee Report forms only a section, is a considerable anticlimax. The *Summary* has four main divisions apart from Inter-Imperial Relations: Defence; Nationality Questions; Communications; and Economic Questions.

The first of these divisions, 'Defence', failed to realise anything more startling than approval of several Dominion trends. Liaison of officers throughout the Empire was encouraged and the advantages of the new Imperial Defence College underlined; it was determined that naval strength would be maintained at the Washington Conference level and that air bases and refuelling stations should form an adequate chain. Kevin O'Higgins stressed the interdependence of Ireland and Britain in this sphere and offered full discussion on mutual interests.[117]

'Nationality' must have raised again many of the old imperial icons. The Irish were anxious to establish their own nationality: the British were determined to allow only Irish citizenship within British nationality. To Britain, allegiance to the Crown was involved, and the national flag was also threatened. The Irish were determined to refute what they regarded as the British 'umbrella theory': that all the Empire should shelter under the umbrella of British nationality. This theory was in accord with diplomatic unity, with unequal Dominion status, and with the resented view that the Dominions were something apart from the rest of the world, whose disputes should not be adjudicated by an international court. The Irish Attorney-General assured the Conference members that they belonged to the British Commonwealth of Nations, not the Commonwealth of British Nations,[118] but he could not mobilise sufficient support. The Report contented itself with minor legal amendments to the British 'Nationality and Status of Aliens Act, 1914'. It was not possible for the committee which was devoted to nationality questions, under the chairmanship of Joynson-Hicks, to reach a unanimous opinion on the nationality of married women,* and the subject was referred forward until after the Committee of Experts had met to discuss the Operation of Dominion Legislation. The British were always able to plead for the preservation of uniformity, the blessing of the *status quo*. They considered it their job to hang on to what they had, and only to yield graciously when forced. They were not forced on this occasion.

'Communications' were discussed, and recommendations in this technical field were unsullied by political rivalries. Ocean Communications, the Pacific Cable and Imperial Air Communications were all reviewed.

The important sphere of economic development, so passionately championed by Bruce in his 'Men, Money and Markets' speech of 22 October, produced disappointing results. All the committees, listed earlier by Smyllie, reported in due course and made useful technical and organisational recommendations. But there was no tariff or development breakthrough comparable to the results of the Inter-Imperial Relations Report. Here the Irish were prepared to play a waiting game: to leave the running to others and then to 'tack on' appropriate Irish products. But again the only areas of agreement proved to be in technical and organisational fields: standardisation, oil pollution of navigable waters, wool statistics and empire films received appropriate resolutions. There was then one final resolution – of loyalty to the Sovereign – and the Conference was over, on 23 November.

(iv) REACTIONS

Immediate world-wide reaction to the Conference was to assume that this was an imperial meeting of unusual importance and to confirm that it was in the Report of the Committee on Inter-Imperial Relations that its major achievements were to be found. The reaction of individual Dominions sheds further light on the attitudes adopted at the Conference itself, and the motives of the chief delegations.

* This topic aired at length in 1930. See p. 204 (and footnote) below.

The Times found to be most important the fact that the leaders of the Dominions had agreed. What they had agreed was less important than the principle of agreement. The Balfour Declaration, however, was 'essentially a register of conditions as they exist already, rather than a programme for the future'.[119] There was nothing new here, but some anomalies and anachronisms had received a timely treatment. Of the Judicial Committee of the Privy Council it made a surprisingly advanced observation. Noting that appeals would now be heard 'in accordance with the wishes of the part of the Empire primarily affected',[120] *The Times* remarked that 'all talk of equal status and autonomy would be meaningless except on that understanding';[121] a complete acceptance of the Irish point of view. It welcomed the Report as 'an agreed and authoritative picture of the Empire as it is',[122] and two days later urged the Dominions to go forward now in a spirit of co-operation.[123]

Some of the British leaders were anxious to emphasise other points. Balfour himself, in his lectures and in his letters, agreed that there was nothing new, but was glad that the facts of Empire would now be made clear to all. The Conference Report would 'bring their true character home to many on both sides of the Atlantic who did not so thoroughly realise the situation'.[124] He was more anxious, however, to underline the basic truth: 'one of the most fundamental considerations in the Report' . . . 'the distinction drawn between "status" and "function".' 'Status is immutable', he wrote:

> It is fixed, so far as my hopes go, for ever. Function is mutable. It depends upon circumstances. At present it is not an exaggeration to say that the whole defensive power of the Empire depends upon the British Fleet, for which the British taxpayer pays. That is the particular function which falls upon Great Britain for historic, economic, geographical and other reasons.[125]

L. S. Amery, in an address on 30 November, only a week after the Conference ended, also stressed that nothing new had taken place, and took pains to declare that equality of status did not mean equality of stature. Great Britain must still play the major part in foreign policy and defence for some time to come. Amery, the great imperialist, preferred to compare the British Empire to the coming together of the Italian and German nations, rather than to talk of the centripetal forces at work. He welcomed the Irish and Canadian embassies in Washington but did not think diplomatic unity endangered: while they represented 'a case where a general principle is conceded', it was nevertheless 'quite clear from the expression of views of all those concerned that it is only in those cases where a very special interest arises that any Dominion is likely to wish to take the actual step of trying to find a suitable representative and of burdening itself with the expense of separate representation'.[126] Then he moved on to his favourite ground with a long eulogy on the undivided and indivisible Crown, the rock upon which the Empire stood. It was, however, a rock which, unnoticed by him, had been submerged by a gentle but inevitable tide of Dominion nationalism. Perhaps he was on steadier theoretical ground when he urged that the Empire should now concentrate on economic achievement.

In the Dominions opinions on the Conference varied wildly, both from Dominion to Dominion and from party to party. But even Premier Bruce of Australia, who had set his heart on economic achievement, was forced to admit the success of the constitutional work of this Conference. 'Some day in the future I believe that Conference will be recognised as one of the great landmarks in our imperial history,'[127] he wrote to Lord Balfour. To the Australian Parliament he reported that much had been done which would 'cement the unity of the Empire and promote amongst its constituent parts a broader spirit of co-operation than has existed in the past';[128] and he gave generous pride of place to the constitutionalists who had attacked the dead wood and cleared the air, for all other progress depended on 'cordial relations and willing co-operation'.[129] While still in London he had remarked: 'I feel that our status as individual nations has been increased, while the prestige of the whole Empire has been considerably enhanced.'[130]

This was not the view of ex-Premier Hughes however. To him it was criminal even to try to write down the sacred bonds of Empire and to define Dominion status. Better by far to leave well alone, for the Dominions had already every power they could require. Let the disruptive Dominions pay more attention to their obligations and to strengthening this association which alone gives them meaning, instead of cutting themselves adrift.[131] Five years later, in the parliamentary debate on the Statute of Westminster, he resumed his attack with characteristic vigour, and he suggested his own definition: a sufficiently general one carrying none of the dangers inherent in that of Balfour: 'Whatever power is necessary for the well being of this Commonwealth or of any Dominion, that is compatible with the unity upon which every Dominion depends for its safety and existence, is vested in the Dominions by virtue of their equality of status with Britain and can be exercised.'[132]

But Hughes was an Australian, out on a limb and conscious of his country's dependence on the Royal Navy. J. G. Latham, who had been at the 1926 Conference in the capacity of Attorney-General, expressed a calmer and more convincing view in the same debate. Australia might have had no cause for change, he said, for Britain would never overrule her. But this was not so clear in the case of some of the others, 'particularly the Irish Free State, South Africa and to some extent Canada',[133] who opposed existing legal formalities. Harmony had required that misunderstandings be removed. Later, W. K. Hancock was to conclude that 'the Balfour Report recognised that Liberty and Unity were now reconciled through the free association of equals': it 'exorcised . . . the inequality-complex'.[134]

In New Zealand, insecure and remote and too utterly dependent on British protection and British markets, the Conference Report was not welcomed. Premier Coates in London had expressed pleasure that the Dominions had been able to agree, but hoped that Canada and South Africa would not insist on all their privileges.[135] Back in his own parliament he outlined the policy he had pursued at the Conference. On the subject of imperial relations he admitted that 'no suggestions or demands whatever were put forward on behalf of New Zealand'.[136] New Zealand was satisfied with its position in the Empire and its imperial relationships before this Conference, and so 'modesty and helpfulness . . . rather than initiative or assertion'[137] characterised its contribution. New Zealand, he announced, would not alter the Governor-General's position, and would continue to communicate through him.

Like a good Leader of the Opposition anywhere, Holland protested at this attitude and expressed his entire dissatisfaction even with the progress the Conference was alleged to have made. Perhaps his attack was born of mere political expediency, but it looks more like a genuine Dominion nationalism and a reflection of some of the motives which inspired the Irish Free State leaders. In contrast to the unimaginative unconcern of his premier, Holland demanded a greater say for New Zealand in the decisions most affecting it – in defence and foreign affairs. He resented the distinction between 'status' and 'function', which was a denial of equality: the high-sounding platitudes were not in accord with the facts.

Australasia reacted much as expected. South Africa was positively exuberant. Party politics were never far from the surface of South African events, and partisan enthusiasms and denunciations greeted this as any other party achievement. Soon it was seen, however, that both sides could approve the principles of the Report and that it promised a new opportunity for ending national strife and beginning to build up a prosperous and unified country. General Hertzog did not disguise his pleasure. He expressed his satisfaction in England and assured everyone that as his country had got all it required there would be no further talk of secession. He was received with adulation on his return to South Africa and his followers humbly criticised themselves for not anticipating that he would achieve the impossible. In Parliament Hertzog announced the end of the old British Empire. 'The British Empire has been broken up by the declaration of the Imperial Conference',[138] he claimed. An association of independent states remained.

Smuts's first reaction to the Conference Report was that of regret at the unstatesmanlike attitude of Hertzog. He did approve of the achievements of the Conference, however, and was concerned that Hertzog should not take all the credit. Calm reflection in South Africa did reveal that the two policies of Hertzog and Smuts had both been vindicated in this report, and many began to urge a new era of domestic co-operation. *The Times* supported Smuts and reported the South African opinion that 'the Conference Report is a triumphant vindication of General Smuts's creed of Dominion status which is now recognised by the Nationalist leaders as a most important reality and not the "slim trick"* which they always represented it to be before they got into power'.[139] In reply to Hertzog in the parliamentary debate Smuts re-emphasised that the Report said nothing new, and that he had been putting it into practice since 1917. Let us not be so bitterly partisan, he pleaded, and then he congratulated his opponent in so far as he had participated in the Conference.

In Canada the Report was received with enthusiasm and with misgiving, with disdain and even contempt. Mackenzie King was pleased enough and called the Conference Report a Magna Carta for the Commonwealth,† which recorded once and for all the unques-

---

* 'Slim' in the same sense as in England 'smart' is used in 'smart Alec'. The Nationalists referred to Smuts as 'slim Jan Smuts'.

† And J. W. Dafoe called the Balfour Declaration a 'Charter of Dominion Independence', R. Cook, *The Politics of John W. Dafoe and the Free Press*, p. 181.

tionable rights of the Dominions. He had set out for the Conference full of 'goodwill' and 'with no grievances and no requests',[140] and he admitted that once there 'Canada did not put forward concretely any particular matters to be taken up'.[141] His biographer, who remarks that the Irish and South African delegates were still impatient at the restrictions which remained after the Conference, and that the Australian and New Zealand delegates were regretting the extension of Dominion autonomy, suggests that 'Mackenzie King was probably the only Prime Minister who believed that the Commonwealth had been made stronger by the Conference'.[142] In the debate in the Canadian House of Commons King took trouble to set out this opinion at length.

This debate was acrimonious and protracted. It expressed fears for the Canadian Constitution, and it denied any extension of equality by this wasted Conference. Studded with the contributions of constitutional lawyers it pointed fingers at the Irish Free State as the source of gains and losses alike, in a division of opinion that was to re-echo round the Canadian Parliament for the next three years.[143]

Mackenzie King began by outlining the changes, pointing out that their object was to remove misunderstandings and to disarm 'agitators'. Disallowance might be dead in Canada, he said,

> but take the position of Ireland, and then you begin to see why this question was brought up at the Imperial Conference, and why the interpretation which the British ministry has placed upon it is a wise one. The Irish Free State came into existence in 1921, and one of the clauses of the act bringing it into existence provided with respect to constitutional questions, that matters affecting the Irish Free State would be carried out in accordance with the practice and custom of Canada. That is what made it important to have an interpretation, so far as Canada is concerned, of the significance of disallowance. . . . If you grant that the power of disallowance lies in the hands of the British government, then, so far as the Irish Free State is concerned, the situation is this: that the men who within the last three or four years have been given the right of self-government are obliged to have all their legislation subject to disallowance by a government that politically may be hostile to them. Does not my honourable friend agree with me that I am entitled to say that that is the kind of situation which agitators delight in ? All that is needed to create trouble in Southern Ireland with respect to the power of disallowance is to point out that gentlemen sitting at Westminster, who politically are the sworn enemies of the right of self-government in the Irish Free State, have the right to disallow any act of the Parliament of that State. The British government took the broad view that such a situation should not be allowed to

develop in that way, and they have given in clear terms their own interpretation of what their course of action with respect to disallowance will be ... they have said with relation to legislation passed by the parliament of the Irish Free State that they would not disallow such legislation, except upon the advice of the ministers of the Free State parliament, not the ministers of the British parliament. Is not that the sort of thing that makes for unity and harmony within the Empire? And the same thing is true in its application to South Africa. ...[144]

So Mackenzie King proceeded, and he made similar reference to the Privy Council: 'it was for the Dominion itself, possessing self-government to the fullest extent, to say whether or not it wished that the right of appeal limited, cancelled or continued'.[145] This was Mackenzie King's view: whether it was the truth or not is less important than the fact that he believed it to be so.

Leader of the Opposition Guthrie wanted the Privy Council left alone:

The only real difficulty which arose at the Conference in connection with appeals to the Judicial Committee was in the case of the Irish Free State. ... In regard to appeals from the Irish Free State the whole question was postponed until the next Imperial Conference, because there were special difficulties in regard to the Irish Free State which did not exist in connection with other Dominions.[146]

Next the cynical Henri Bourassa exposed the weaknesses of the conference system calling the Declaration a mere formula in which something had been included to please everyone, without any regard to logic. He suggested a sentence which met the Irish and South African view but which was unacceptable to Australia and New Zealand:

Great Britain, Ireland, Canada, Australia, New Zealand and South Africa are autonomous communities equal in status, in no way subordinate one to the other in any aspect of their domestic or external affairs, though united by their allegiance to the same crown and freely associated on such terms as they determine from time to time between themselves.[147]

And how was unanimity achieved in the rest of the Report? First the title of the King had been changed to please the Irish 'who are a good deal like our French Canadians – they are very often too apt to be content with words'. Of course the Irish asserted that their country was not a Dominion but a nation. When would Canada claim to be such a nation? When would Canada be in the same position as Ireland in respect to the King – and not in the same boat as the 'black tribes of Africa'[148] and the colonial Empire?

The Governor-General change was a bouquet for the Canadian Prime Minister, asserted Bourassa, and the recognition of the Washington embassies was evidence of a British desire to please both Canada and Ireland. The clause on exequaturs to foreign consuls was a specifically Irish one.

Lapointe poured oil on the waters. The Conference was a friendly consultative body making suggestions agreeable to all. J. T. Thorsen denied the validity of the Balfour Declaration. It might give 'equality of status within the Empire' but this was 'in law a contradiction in terms'.[149] H. C. Hocken was irate. The Conference, he said, had been faced with three major problems: inter-imperial trade, imperial defence and immigration. Their impractical Prime Minister had brought back an answer on none of these things, having wasted his time on academic constitutional questions. To Canada this declaration meant nothing at all. Canada's representatives had left over the major issues and co-operated with the representatives of South Africa and the Irish Free State, putting them in a position to disrupt the Empire.[150]

Other Canadian opinions were expressed outside Parliament. The Canadian historian, R. M. Dawson, thought that while the Conference had emphasised the moral unity of the Commonwealth, it also represented a victory for the advocates of decentralisation. 'Empire diplomatic unity, which had already disappeared from practice, was formally and quietly abandoned; Empire diplomatic individualism and co-operation took its place.'[151] From the Senate, in the following April, the old imperialist Sir George Foster wrote sadly to Balfour that now 'special efforts must be made to link together in sentiment and co-operation the various parts of the Empire, clustering around and converging towards the greatest possible imperial unity'.[152] But it is Sir Robert Borden, speaking in England on 14 June 1927, who brings us most sharply back to reality and, intentionally or unintentionally, returns us to the philosophy of the Irish leaders. At the close of an address to the Royal Institute of International Affairs, he reminded his audience that 'In broad consideration of the whole subject it is essential ... to remember that nationhood cannot be created or maintained by phrases in resolutions or reports. It must be founded on achievement and the acceptance of responsibility.'[153]

Practical achievement and the acceptance of responsibility

amongst the nations of the world, as well as in their own domestic sphere, were the very aims of the Irish leaders who had attended the 1926 Conference. They had taken the initiative and urged the other Dominions to a realistic approach to world affairs; to a view of themselves as international persons with the obligations and the attributes suitable to that estate. 1926 was a beginning. As Kevin O'Higgins wrote reluctantly to his wife from Geneva in 1927:

> Canada and South Africa will only fight in *support* of us. They have not yet learned to take a stand on their own and in any case they only see things when they are pointed out to them. Their own vision is entirely second-hand and derivative.[154]

The story of the next five years is a repetition of this summary by the Irish Vice-President. But 1926 *was* a beginning.

The Report of the Conference echoed around the world. How was it received in Ireland, and what remains for us to add to our earlier comments on the Irish effort so instrumental in bringing it about? The Irish correspondent of the *Round Table* was pleased enough with the results and he gave full credit to O'Higgins and FitzGerald. They may not have got their way over the Privy Council, but this was Canada's fault, not Britain's, he thought. He took seriously the subject which O'Higgins had mentioned in jest, and, noting the impressions of the Irish delegation to the concurrent Empire Parliamentary Union, he emphasised that the Empire was in fact as much an Irish Empire as a British one. Finally, he was glad to see the Government promoting in Dail Eireann a policy of friendly co-operation with England and their fellow Dominions. Only in this direction lay unity with Northern Ireland.[155]

In the Dail itself, however, we are told that the Report was received 'in chilly silence':[156] there was no enthusiasm in the Dail for the work of the Inter-Imperial Relations Committee nor was there any in the country. Admittedly, this was an Opposition observation. Ireland was not like the other Dominions. The others, perhaps, had gained something from this Conference but there were many in Ireland who were dismayed that their country,[157] which had gained entry to the League of Nations as a 'fully self-governing state'[158] should now be forced to appeal to Westminster for recognition of a status which was less than that which they had assumed hitherto. This Report was a derogation of status and not an amplification; it was full of the word Empire and spoke little of Commonwealth; it drew an unacceptable distinction between status and function and would have only a retarding effect on the development of the country; 'equality' might be an effective sop for the gullible but it was completely controverted by this 'function' clause. Even the matter of exequaturs was criticised: there would be no improvement until foreign nations applied direct to an Irish Minister. As usual there were persistent queries regarding British wars: would foreign nations draw the subtle distinctions of the Minister for External Affairs, or would they attack?

FitzGerald and O'Higgins replied with tact and patience. From the beginning the Irish Government had protested its full independence in order to protect the Treaty settlement and disarm its critics. It was difficult now to be excited about a report which only brought that full independence nearer. But they could and did point to the benefits of membership of the Commonwealth: a Commonwealth which they were guiding towards an association of free nations. FitzGerald in his opening speech had asserted that the status of equality was now fully accepted and the way had been made clear for 'the gradual elimination of legal machinery and administrative practices which are not in conformity with that principle'.[159] He now picked his way carefully through the Committee Report, first stating the policy which he had followed:

> Mutual interests necessitate certain mutual arrangements. The attitude of the Government is that those mutual arrangements should be dictated by that mutual interest and by that only. Forms and practices still existing merely as remnants of a time when the Government in Great Britain retained authority and power over the Dominions were not calculated to assist harmony and co-operation but might . . . be actually dangerous to the necessary co-operation. . . . They should be eliminated. . . .[160]

The Report had borne out this policy and was, he now concluded, 'eminently satisfactory'.[161] O'Higgins merely amplified this point:

> Anything, everything that to us appeared to conflict with the conception of the fullest co-equality of status was raised by us in that Conference. . . . The matters raised by us at the Imperial Conference were exhaustive of the points of practice, the points of constitutional machinery, which struck us as being in conflict with the conception of co-equal status, and they are set out in this Report.[162]

Outside the Dail there was little public enthusiasm. The Commonwealth was regarded as a British institution and there was as yet no love for the British. More political capital might have been made by staying away from the Conference. If the Irish leaders chose to transform the Commonwealth from the inside it was not for political reasons but for the achievement of practical advances. It is well to keep this truth in view. For O'Higgins, though the Conference had been a great personal success, there was little acclaim in Ireland. When Hertzog, surrounded by his adulators in South Africa, was reported as saying that he had 'brought home the bacon', O'Higgins is said to have added, wryly, 'Irish Bacon'.[163] He was satisfied with this.

Hertzog, too, of course, had his difficulties in his homeland, and he must have been glad to declare that the British Commonwealth was acceptable to him. At that time the pro-British element in South Africa controlled industrial resources, though the electoral system favoured the Afrikaner outback. Not until the 1930s did the population shift and the industrial boom bring wealth to the Dutch descendants. In 1926 Hertzog was too dependent on financial backing from the British South Africans to go so far as he sometimes threatened. Yet his stand had been of some value, and John A. Costello[164] has since described how South Africa and the Free State were able to work at this Conference:

> Working from completely different angles the South African and Irish delegations eventually co-ordinated their efforts, and, be it said, with no small measure of assistance from the broadminded attitude of some members of the Conservative British Delegation,* achieved a triumph. The mutual assistance which accrued to South Africa and Ireland by the adoption of their different methods at the Conference of 1926 was commented upon to me by General Hertzog at the conclusion of that Conference.[165]

In 1919, Hertzog had appealed, like the Irish Nationalists, to the speeches of President Wilson in seeking recognition of the rights of his nation.[166] Yet Botha and Smuts were gaining those very selfsame rights in practice by utilising the process of constitutional evolution which was taking place in the British Empire. It is tempting to observe that Hertzog was bent on a similar tactical mistake at the 1926 Conference by appealing to mere words, and that the more expedient policy of the Irish leaders on this occasion had mitigated his error and realised the more substantial practical gains.

As Costello wrote, however, benefits had accrued to both the Irish and South Africans from each other's efforts. There is no doubt that the Balfour Declaration, which enunciated the principle

* He must here be thinking primarily of Birkenhead.

behind the Irish policy, helped considerably to bring that policy to fruition. Professor Keith called the Declaration 'exaggerated language', 'careless phraseology' and 'rhetoric'.[167] President Cosgrave has expressed his doubts that Balfour actually meant what he had written.[168] But once this Declaration was accepted the Irish went ahead to take every word literally and to implement in every sphere that principle of equality. Mackenzie King noted that even for the rest of that same Conference 'Dominion representatives were quick to refer to equality of status in subsequent discussions of Imperial relations. The effectiveness of these references should dispel any doubts about the importance of the definition.'[169] We shall see that the 'root principle' of 1926 was made instinct in every corner of the Report drawn up in 1929.

As we have noted earlier, other commentators have not seen Irish achievements in so kindly a light. Professor Mansergh, as well as crediting South Africa with more influence at this conference, endows General Hertzog with a clearer foresight than Kevin O'Higgins, even if he was less articulate. He plays down the Irish part in the 1926 Conference but he also pays little attention to the 1930 Conference and ignores the 1929 Committee of Experts, which drew up, in effect, the 1931 Statute of Westminster. He does admit that the Statute of Westminster, 'this one great landmark in the history of the Commonwealth, has remained of preponderent importance not merely in defining Commonwealth relations but in determining their later development.'[170] But he has not pointed out that this statute was conceived in the Committee on Inter-Imperial Relations and brought to the light of day in the 1929 Committee. This sequence was a continuous process and the Irish drive was present at the beginning and throughout. Removing out-of-date legal anomalies from the structure of the Commonwealth and the body politic of the several Dominions, they were creating from a still colonial Empire a new association of free Commonwealth nations. Mackenzie King clearly accepts the positive nature of this achievement. As Blair Neatby observes: 'The gradual extension of autonomy was for him a constructive policy which would preserve the Commonwealth.'[171] By their practical, constitutional work the Irish made the Commonwealth an acceptable association in an age of nationalism. Without their achievements would India and Pakistan and the succession of liberated colonial territories have agreed to become members?

The Irish Free State was simply in advance of the other Dominions, as O'Higgins had claimed. Sir Keith Hancock has written of the Dominions at this time, that they were more concerned with their domestic affairs than their international role. 'In practice', he says, 'Dominion nationalism generally concentrated on "inward" aspects and was disinclined to think out clearly the full meaning of equal status in a world of sovereign states.'[172] This is perfectly true, but it is less so of that dominion which was not a dominion but a nation. The Irish Free State was conscious of its past, concerned about its present and determined for its future. National self-interest was inherent in every Commonwealth move it made, but it was genuinely anxious to make Commonwealth and its national interests agree. It sincerely believed that concluding statement of its principal memorandum to the Imperial Conference:

> If the British Commonwealth of Nations is to endure as the greatest factor for the establishment of peace and prosperity throughout the world, its cohesive force must be real and permanent, whether viewed from within or without. It cannot be held together by a mere collective expression, which only serves to create doubt in the minds of Foreign Statesmen and discontent amongst the diverse nationalities of which it is made up.
>
> ... The co-operation resulting from the bond of a common King will be effective only because it is free co-operation and to the extent to which it is free. Antiquated forms dating from a period when common action resulted from the over-riding control of one central Government are liable to make co-operation less efficacious, because they make it seem less free.*

The strongly nationalistic Walshe recognised the value of what had been done. To him: 'The 1926 Imperial Conference began a new era in the history of the Saorstat and its sister states and the favourable results are due in no small measure to the work of the Irish Delegation. An Irish Republic could not achieve a position of freedom better calculated to promote in peace our prosperity and our national institutions.'[173] Sir Keith Hancock himself concluded that, whereas Canada hitherto had borne the brunt of Dominion advance, the Irish Free State 'from now on ... was ready to lead the march towards equality'.[174]

* Imperial Conference 1926 E(IR/26)3 (Memorandum by Irish Free State Delegation). See above, p. 104.

7

Committee on the Operation of Dominion Legislation 1929

(i) External Affairs 1926–9

In the year following the 1926 Imperial Conference the Dominions set about adjusting themselves to their newly recognised status. An interesting memorandum by Joe Walshe, written on 4 January 1927, gives a hint of what this meant in one small particular.[1] Before this conference, Walshe pointed out, it had been the practice for plenipotentiaries, appointed on the advice of the British Government, to negotiate a treaty while holding unlimited powers. They were regarded as acting for the Commonwealth as a whole although the Dominions were often asked later to concur in their work by ratifying the Treaty. The Saorstat had objected to this procedure, but the other Dominions had accepted it as a matter of course, taking little notice of obligations arising therefrom. The Saorstat, simply in order to make its point, had usually failed to ratify, even though this made little difference in international law. But now no active obligations could be undertaken except on the advice of a plenipotentiary appointed by a Dominion, so the Saorstat need no longer make its gesture.

In March, however, the new harmony appeared to be threatened by an action of Austen Chamberlain, at Geneva. Explaining the Imperial Conference treaty-procedure changes to the League of Nations Council, he was reported in the Press as having spoken as the representative of all the Dominion governments. The alert E. J. Phelan, in Geneva, was horrified, and he wrote to FitzGerald immediately.[2] (In fact he had already warned the Irish Minister of Chamberlain's intention to speak, so keen was he to protect Irish interests.)[3] In a further letter Phelan urged that the Saorstat should continue its bid for the League Council as the best way of clearing up any misapprehensions which might remain about Dominion subservience.[4] Ultimately a Downing Street despatch denied the accuracy of the report of Chamberlain's speech, pointing out that he had in fact made it clear that he was the 'Representative of Great Britain only, not the Dominions',[5] but the affair had soured the Commonwealth atmosphere.

During June, however, the Dominions got a chance to underline their new position, and characteristically it was the Free State which took the opportunity. In an External Affairs paper of 1 June the situation was described:

> for the first time in history the States of the Commonwealth will be represented on this basis of complete independence at a Naval Disarmament Conference to be held in the middle of June at Geneva. No international obligations whatever can in future be imposed on the Saorstat, except on the advice of the Saorstat Ministers.[6]

This Naval Conference did not turn out to be a success and it might be wondered what an unarmed, small country, scarcely able to protect its own fishermen, had hoped to gain there. A Japanese delegate supplies the answer: 'the Conference has been a failure for all except the Irish. They have used it to assert their international status, in which they have fully succeeded.'[7] Kevin O'Higgins had made sure that his country had taken the earliest opportunity afforded to be represented by her own plenipotentiary with full powers, and he had made it quite clear that on no account did anyone else speak for the Free State.*

With the prickly self-consciousness of a new nation, still precarious in a changing world, the Free State had asserted itself. But a much more important recognition had already been afforded the young Irish State in the early days of 1927. The United States of America had decided to reciprocate in the field of diplomatic representation. As the same 1 June paper put it: 'The Government of the most powerful State in the world had formally recognised our status of absolute equality by appointing a Minister Plenipotentiary to

---

* Soon after this Conference at which he had represented his country, Kevin O'Higgins, on Sunday 10 July 1927, was brutally murdered while on his way to Mass. Perhaps one of the cruellest self-inflicted injuries perpetrated by any nation, his death was of incalculable loss to Ireland and the Commonwealth. To quote the appreciation of but one Dominion statesman, Vincent Massey noted later of the 1926 Conference: 'The most striking figure from Ireland was Kevin O'Higgins. . . . Thinking of his assassination which came so soon, one can only murmur sadly, "what a waste of goodwill" ' (Vincent Massey, *What's past is prologue*, pp. 112–13).

Dublin.'[8] On 28 December 1926 a letter from L. S. Amery had disclosed that the United States was intending to appoint ambassadors to Dublin and Ottawa. On 31 December T. M. Healy had expressed his satisfaction on behalf of the Irish Free State and proposed a form of procedure. On 31 January 1927, F. A. Sterling, Counsellor of the United States Embassy in London, had been suggested for the post of Envoy Extraordinary and Minister Plenipotentiary, and this choice had been quickly approved. Mr Sterling had presented his credentials on Wednesday 27 July. In Washington Professor Smiddy had had his credentials suitably revised* and in Geneva the ever watchful Phelan had recorded his pleasure.† The Irish Free State had arrived.

Early in 1927 Canada followed the Free State by establishing an embassy in Washington. Vincent Massey had attended the 1926 Imperial Conference in preparation for this post, and correspondence between Downing Street and Washington had been circulated amongst the Dominions during November and December 1926. On 11 January 1927, Massey had been gazetted, and he took up his appointment on 16 February. In his memoirs he described the volume of work that awaited him:

> It did not take me long to discover how much business awaited the establishment of a Canadian legation.
>
> The British Embassy had very loyally looked after Canadian affairs but, needless to say, no one in that mission was personally familiar with the Canadian scene. Our problems presented the heavily-laden Embassy with an added burden which it was unfair to impose on them. According to Esmé Howard, who as British Ambassador when our legation was established could speak with real knowledge, 'the affairs of Canada supplied the Embassy with fully one-third of its work'.[9]

Thus a Canadian summed up the value of his post: it is safe to assume that the other Dominion embassy in Washington was no mere ornament either.

In September 1927, at Geneva, Canada was again in the limelight. This was the Diamond Jubilee year of Canadian Confederation and it was fitting that when three seats on the League Council became

* The words 'Envoy Extraordinary' were added to his title.

† 'I hope', wrote Phelan, 'it is not too late to congratulate you on the results of the Imperial Conference and in particular on the appointment of a U.S. Minister to Dublin which I take it is really one of them. It is I think extremely important. It completes the Smiddy appointment, which was an anomaly so long as the U.S. did not reciprocate, and it establishes our right of Legation beyond challenge.' E. J. Phelan to D. FitzGerald, 18 February 1927 (FitzGerald Papers).

vacant, Canada was put up for election. There is little doubt that the Free State had been considering its own candidature, but Canada was a very close partner, and although the Irish were firmly opposed to group representation, they recognised that two Dominions could not be successful. Canada was the senior partner, Canada stood, and Canada was elected. Canada 'got in' by a narrow margin,* and thereafter took a decided and independent line, Senator Dandurand being its Council representative. In Ireland, the League of Nations Society, in the first issue of its newspaper, *Concord*, welcomed the success of Canada and noted: 'The Irish Free State went forward last year rather to assert a principle than expecting to be elected. Our turn will come later.'[10] The following month saw a more specific comment: 'It was not difficult for a close observer to perceive that the great part of the work involved in securing Canada's election was done by the Irish Free State delegation.' Canada's cause, it asserted, had been pleaded to delegation after delegation by the Irish during the pre-election week. Furthermore, *Concord* concluded:

> the Eighth Assembly, by electing Canada to the Council, has made it definitely clear that the nations of the world accept the members of the Commonwealth group as being on a footing of complete equality with all other states. It has given international sanction to the declaration of the Imperial Conference.[11]

The year ended, then, with Canada once more in the van of the Dominion advance. But she was a champion following in the footsteps of the Free State, in Washington and now also at Geneva, where the considerable groundwork done by the Irish was undoubtedly helpful to her once the Irish themselves decided not to compete.

In the purely intra-Commonwealth field, one incident in 1927 is worth mentioning before passing on to 1928. On 26 May 1927, a letter to Dublin from L. S. Amery, on the subject of Dominion membership of the Judicial Committee of the Privy Council, proposed that this court be modernised by a Bill enabling two additional Indian judges to be appointed. It was also suggested that the Irish Free State, which had not been in existence at the time of the Judicial Committee Bills, might like to put itself in the same position as the other Dominions. The Irish reaction was characteristic.

* C. A. W. Manning, *The policies of the British Dominions in the League of Nations*, pp. 145–8. See also: League of Nations, 8th Assembly, p. 116 (14th Plenary Meeting, 15 September 1927). The ballot for three seats, was as follows: Cuba 40, Finland 33, Canada 26, Greece was next out of seven other candidates, with 23 votes.

A draft reply to Amery was drawn up for the Executive Council on 17 June, with an explanatory note which read: 'every attempt to modify the present position in relation to the Privy Council in any sense likely to make its eventual abolition more difficult should be resisted.' Consequently the draft was of the opinion that:

> until the whole question of the Judicial Committee in its relation to the Irish Free State comes to be reconsidered, any modification in the present position of the kind suggested would not tend to facili-to the ultimate solution of the outstanding difficulties. With regard to the removal of the limitation on the number of Dominion Judges on the Committee, we feel that the attitude we have adopted on the general question does not leave us in a position to express approval or disapproval of the proposal.[12]

There was no question on this issue of the Free State trying to have the best of both worlds. There was simply a warning of an unequi-vocal and determined opposition to the Judicial Committee. It was a pointer to trouble ahead.

President Cosgrave opened the year 1928 with a visit to the United States and Canada. The visit had been initiated by an invitation from the American Government, and Cosgrave, accompanied by Desmond FitzGerald, made a very favourable impression on both sides of the American border. For a long time Irish societies* had been seeking a ministerial visit that might strengthen the image of the legitimate Irish government in America, and the arrival of the chief minister and one of his most senior deputies was a timely and effective answer to that plea.†

* For example, the Irish Fellowship Club of Chicago had made strong representations for such a visit, if possible for the St Patrick's Day celebrations in 1928, and had assured equally enthusiastic support in Washington and New York for any visiting Minister. See Memorandum, 7 December 1927, for Executive Council *re* 'Ministerial Visit to America' (FitzGerald Papers).

† A letter written on 14 May 1928, by an unidentified visitor to Chicago at the time of a visit there by the crew of the aeroplane *Bremen*, first to fly from Europe to America (Commandant FitzMaurice of the Free State being one of the three flyers), records: 'I had the opportunity of meeting many prominent citizens of Irish extraction, but who have not been mixed up with Irish political movements, and who expressed great pride at the fact that Ireland was gaining a prestige in this country of which they are proud. They attribute acceleration of this tendency to the recent visit of President Cosgrave and Mr Desmond FitzGerald who, by their appearance, behaviour, manners and addresses gave the average American an opinion of Irishmen which was not in conformity with the views that they had heretofore held, and impressed them with a sense of dignity and refinement which has made the better class of Irish in this country feel very proud' (FitzGerald Papers).

At home in Ireland a number of recurring problems demanded attention. Passports for Free State citizens were still the subject of negotiation with London. By March no agreement had been reached. The Irish were now determined to omit 'By the Grace of God' and 'Defender of the Faith' from the Royal Title, and discussions took place at the Dominions Office between Lord Lovat and the Minister for External Affairs. It was not found possible, however, to harmonise their different viewpoints.

In June it was proposed to increase Irish representation abroad. The Canadians had now expanded to cover Tokyo and Paris. The Irish decided to seek a legation in Paris, too, and also legations at Berlin and Ottawa. They decided as well to step up their Geneva office to the rank of legation and to establish a consulate in New York and to increase their staff in Washington. In the event, when the changes were made in 1929, the Vatican took the place of Ottawa.* 1928 closed with the illness of King George V, which necessitated the appointment of Counsellors of State. The Irish government rejected the British claim to appoint these Counsellors utilaterally, and were particularly indignant at the inclusion of such a political figure as the British Prime Minister.[13]

But the major international event of the year, in terms of Commonwealth significance, was the signing, in August, of the Paris Treaty for the Renunciation of War.[14] This treaty had grown out of the bilateral Franco-American discussions of June 1927. In April 1928 it was decided to add the other four great powers, and after Austen Chamberlain's letter of agreement in principle – an agreement in which the concurrence of the Dominions had been obtained – the Dominions were invited also to participate. The invitation to the Irish Free State was issued on 25 May 1928, and on 30 May Patrick McGilligan formally accepted. In July the Free State indicated its approval of the revised draft treaty and expressed the hope that all the powers of the world would accept also. The following month, on the 20 August 1928, President Cosgrave was issued with full powers with which to sign the Treaty on behalf of his country, and on the twenty-seventh, in Paris, he signed alongside the other signatories.

The importance of this treaty, in Commonwealth terms, is that it marks a new stage in their development. For the first time the

* South Africa, too, broke new ground in this year, by signing a trade Treaty with Germany on 1 September.

Dominions signed separately, their signature being confined to their own area of jurisdiction: and this applied equally to Great Britain.

When the debate on the ratification of the 'Kellogg Pact' took place in Dail Eireann, Mr McGilligan was at pains to emphasise the innovations which it contained. This was 'the first time that there has been an international agreement signed by any State member of the Commonwealth other than Great Britain as a separate instrument of ratification. It is the first time we negotiated and ratified an international agreement of this kind.'[15] He went on to stress that his government would ratify with an instrument signed by the King on the advice of the Executive Council, and that this would be presented to the American administration by the Irish representative in Washington. In the event, due to the King's illness, the ratification was signed by three Counsellors of State. But only the members of the royal family were acceptable to the Irish and this condition proved a workable compromise.[16] As a happy sequel to the Treaty, Mr Kellogg, the American Secretary of State who had given his name to this pact, visited Dublin after the signing, and thus accorded the Free State, towards the end of the year, a repetition of the favourable world publicity which had attended President Cosgrave's American visit at its beginning.

The following year, 1929, was, of course, the year of the Conference on the Operation of Dominion Legislation. But it was also a year of increased Domininion representation abroad. South African embassies were established at Washington, The Hague and Rome, with a permanent delegation in Geneva and a trade commissioner in Hamburg: Irish envoys were sent to Paris, Berlin and the Vatican.[17] In October of this year, too, Dominion status was announced to be the goal of British policy in India, and a London conference was promised to examine this as soon as the Report of the Simon Commission was completed. (The Report was published in the following June.) But apart from the 'O.D.L.' Conference, which met in October, the major Dominion development of the year occurred at Geneva. There, alone of the Dominions, the Irish Free State signed, without any reservation, Article 36 – the 'Optional Clause' – of the Permanent Court of International Justice.

The Optional Clause, by which member states agreed to submit their international disputes to the compulsory jurisdiction of the Permanent Court, had been a source of Commonwealth irritation since before the 1926 Imperial Conference. As early as 1925 there had been angry questions in Dail Eireann as to why the Saorstat had not yet adhered to the International Court.[18] The Irish delegation to Geneva the previous autumn had recommended immediate acceptance of the Clause, and Desmond FitzGerald then left no doubt that this advice was in accord with his government's wishes.[19] Why then was there delay? Kevin O'Higgins, who had written a 'considered statement'[20] on the advisability of Dominion membership of the Permanent Court, and who had, at Geneva in the autumn of 1925, denied Sir Cecil Hurst's claim to speak on this subject as though on behalf of the Empire[21] (as Hurst put it 'a very composite and peculiar political unit')[22] brings us closer to the cause of friction. To him it was a matter of the *inter se* controversy over again, no more, no less.

The problem had been tackled at the 1926 Conference. The Irish wished to proceed to sign the Clause: the British desired to safeguard the Commonwealth relationship by excluding intra-Commonwealth disputes. As Britain herself was the country most likely to be in dispute with the Free State, such a qualification would have made nonsense of the Irish case and so no agreement was reached. No bar was actually placed to Dominion signature but the Dominions did promise to take no action without further consulting one another.[23]

In May 1929, the Ramsay MacDonald government came to power in Britain pledged to adhere to the Optional Clause, and the promised 'further consultation' took place in August and September, during the tenth session of the League Assembly.[24] But it was soon clear that the British had not shifted their ground and that they were prepared to sign only with reservations – and these included the exclusion of intra-Commonwealth disputes.

According to the Australian, Sir William Harrison Moore,* it was at the insistence of Australia and New Zealand that the intra-Commonwealth reservation was made.[25] This may have been no more than habitual support for a traditional British view, though there is evidence of some wider Dominion disquiet concerning the rights of Indians.[26] What is certain is that the Dominions were far from unanimous over the issue. The Irish had argued that there should be no qualification of signature and they maintained their conviction by signing without reservation while the rest of the

---

* Professor Sir William Harrison Moore, of the University of Melbourne was Australian delegate to the League of Nations, 1927-8-9.

Dominions were still arguing.[27] Canada doubted whether the proposed reservations were consistent with the article under consideration and, according to the Irish, gave discreet support to the independent Irish line.[28] The Canadians had already shown themselves ready to 'pledge their faith to arbitration' and indicated their readiness to accept the jurisdiction of the Permanent Court.[29] The South African delegate, Eric Louw, wanted to give full support to the Irish and threatened to leave Geneva rather than oppose them, as his original instructions from home required.[30] He signed the Clause with the British reservations in the end, but he placed a very different emphasis upon the intra-Commonwealth exclusion. He recognised that 'such disputes are justiciable by the International Court of Justice' but he explained that his government preferred to settle them 'by another means'.[31]

The Irish, having delayed for nearly five years in deference to the Commonwealth connection, in the end made a dramatic, independent gesture. They made it because of their aversion to the Judicial Committee of the Privy Council, the only Commonwealth court, and because of their consistent desire to emphasise before the world the full international character of the Dominions. This indeed was the effect of their gesture, and this was more important than any benefit likely to accrue from the actual signature itself. It did draw straight away from a British minister an admission that the Dominions were 'international units individually in the fullest sense of the term',[32] an admission not hitherto given so public an expression. But there is one other reason for the Irish stand which has not received sufficient notice, and which has a validity not confined to Anglo-Irish manœuvrings. E. J. Phelan expressed it well in his lecture, *The British Empire and the World Community*. Including the British reservations in a general condemnation, the Chief of the Diplomatic Division of the International Labour Office pointed out:

> Those who regard the entry into operation of the Optional Clause as the most important step towards bringing the world under the rule of law are very much concerned at the amazing ingenuity displayed by States in accompanying adhesions to the Optional Clause with reservations so comprehensive that the legal value of those adhesions is so diluted as to render them almost meaningless.[33]

As a small power in a world of big blocs, the Irish had set an example of straightforward support for the only organs of international peace which were based on international democratic equality. B. C.

Waller, Secretary of League of Nations Society of Ireland, reporting to *Concord* from Geneva, added a further item of news: 'Our delegates have let it be known that the Irish Free State will stand for election for one of the non-permanent seats on the Council of the League.'[34] The Irish were ready to undertake the fullest international responsibilities.

A fitting postscript was added to the Optional Clause affair, on 26 February 1930, when the subject was debated in the Dail. Mr McGilligan related the history of the matter and explained that it was the Briand-Kellogg Pact which had finally persuaded the Irish to press for a signature of the Optional Clause, as a gesture of their good faith in renouncing war. McGilligan was fair to the British: he said that their signature with reservations was better than no signature at all. And he stressed that, notwithstanding its own unreserved adherence, the Irish Free State would always exhaust alternative peaceful solutions in any dispute with a member of the Commonwealth before going before the Permanent Court. It was Henry Grattan Esmonde, however, who made the most pointed observation. Congratulating his government and deploring the criticism levelled from across the water, he wondered how that criticism would stand in the future. 'If they had followed our good example', he said, 'they would have the protection and the prestige of the International Court to see that we, irrespective of any change of government, would not violate any of our undertakings to them.'[35]

(ii) The Committee on the Operation of Dominion Legislation

The 1926 Conference had not brought complete clarity or full recognition to Dominion pretensions even inside the Commonwealth itself. To the outside world it mattered little how much the British nations complimented one another: they still had the appearance of an imperial association dominated by Britain. The Irish Government was anxious to hasten the internal purification of Empire upon which it had embarked at the 1926 Conference. It had prepared its case and it knew what it wanted. Exactly two years after the Imperial Conference had ended, however, L. S. Amery was still writing to Dublin to say how much detailed preparation had yet to be done before the Expert Committee could assemble.[36] He explained that the next Imperial Conference would hardly meet before the autumn of 1930, suggested that the Expert Committee could most profitably meet towards the end of 1929, and asked for approval of this suggestion. A few days later Mr McGilligan, now Minister of External Affairs, explained to an impatient Dail that the detailed examination of matters contained in the Committee's terms of reference had taken considerable time, and pointed out that elections in some of the Dominions had caused delay. The Irish policy, he added, would be to consolidate the position of equality stated in 1926, and 'to seek to eliminate all the forms which in some Dominions more than others, and in most Dominions much more than here, are said not to be in accordance with the particular definition that was given'.[37] By the beginning of 1929 it was clear that the Conference would meet at the end of that year, and on 29 March Amery proposed 8 October as a suitable starting date.[38]

As that date approached McGilligan became more explicit. In a masterly speech to the Dail explaining his reorganisation of the Department of External Affairs and vigorously defending its record, he emphasised his Government's consistent policy, which would find further enunciation in the coming October. The Irish contribution to the doctrines formulated in 1926, he said, 'was positive, persistent and decisive'.[39] And he added of those same doctrines:

the vigilance and diligence which have been exercised in applying them to our routine relations with other states within and without the Commonwealth, in removing anomalous legal forms, in securing the discontinuance of practices that have no place in modern democratic life, and no justification in present constitutional theory, and generally in conforming every aspect of the Commonwealth scheme to the principles on which it rests, has been and must continue to be, the special work of the Department of External Affairs.

In the autumn of the present year a Committee of Experts from every State in the Commonwealth will meet to discuss the formal amendment or modification, or repeal of enactments still on the Statute Book of the United Kingdom which are inconsistent with the existing legislative powers of the member State Parliaments. Our purpose is that whatever remnants there may be of the old order of Imperial control will be removed and the last legal vestiges of the organisations now superseded swept away. The entire legal framework in which the old system of central rule was held together will be taken asunder and will never be put together again. A new legal structure will take its place, in which no bar or barrier to future constitutional development will be found. The free co-operation which is the basis of the Commonwealth idea, the instrument of its usefulness and the expression of the individual sovereignty of its members will be re-clothed in forms which reveal rather than conceal its reality.[40]

There was little doubt that McGilligan would be taking this Committee of Experts very seriously.

Patricia Hoey, also looking ahead to the Conference, in an article in *Review of Reviews*, stated that the two tasks of the Irish Delegation would be to safeguard both 'the future freedom of Ireland . . . and the future development of the Commonwealth'.[41] She saw the interests of England and Ireland at last in harmony, though she recognised that the Irish, under McGilligan, would have to bear the brunt of the attack on archaic institutions.

The Experts duly foregathered on 8 October 1929 at Westminster, in the Moses Room of the House of Lords. They met under the chairmanship of Lord Passfield, Secretary of State for Dominion Affairs in the new Labour Government; they sat – scarcely announced in the press and thereafter ignored – until 4 December. They held seventeen plenary meetings. They then reported back to their several governments, who in turn released their Report in the Dominion capitals concurrently, on 3 February 1930.

This Report was approved by the Imperial Conference of 1930 and was given legal expression by the Statute of Westminster in 1931. But it must be studied in the context of the Imperial Conference of 1926 which called it into being and established its terms of reference. The story from 1926 to 1931 is a continuous one and the Committee of 1929 is just a chapter. To estimate its importance, however, it is necessary to keep one eye on the Conference which went before and another on that which came after. The same arguments and counter-arguments ran through each and it is significant in terms of this continuous process that the government with the most consistent approach and the most determined attitude was also the government with the greatest continuity of office, the most experienced personnel, and the most developed delegation teamwork. It will help to explain their success if we study Mr McGilligan's team now before examining the Report.

McGilligan himself, friend and political heir of Kevin O'Higgins, was a tenacious lawyer with an acute grasp, remarkable memory and great breadth of knowledge. Still Minister for Industry and Commerce, he had used his experience of that Department to transform the tiny Department of External Affairs, both consolidating and expanding it. He had attended both the 1923 and the 1926 Imperial Conferences, the latter in a ministerial capacity. He was one of only two Dominion ministers on this committee, and he was the ablest, the most persistent and the best briefed man present.

Alongside him he had a unique team of friends, contemporaries and colleagues who had been with the department since the foundation of the State. Real teamwork was natural between Costello, O'Hegarty, Walshe and Hearne, Murphy and Boland. They were all young men, mostly with legal training. Civil servants or politicians they were of the same age and from the same class, and they were co-operating to build up a new State. Friends before, they were friends still. Together they understood the common aim just as they understood and anticipated one another. Costello, Attorney-General, skilled draftsman and protégé of Hugh Kennedy, was quick to spot and counter anything in the nature of a slur on the status of his country; he was as difficult as McGilligan to deflect from a principle. O'Hegarty, Secretary to the Cabinet, very astute and with a quickly expanding awareness of foreign affairs, brought a vast commonsense to offset the sometimes academic views of the lawyers. Joe Walshe, who had been a teacher and then retired through ill health, had become a solicitor. He had gone to Paris with S. T. O'Kelly in 1920 and was an extreme nationalist, but with great ability and political skill. He was the theoretician of the team, for he had the time and the leisure denied successively to Kevin O'Higgins, and to McGilligan and Costello.[42] J. J. Hearne, like Costello a skilled draftsman, had done an immense amount of legal preparation, drawing on a voluminous knowledge of British constitutional history: the former 'Boy Orator' of the Redmondite Party, he had a clarity of style that was invaluable to those delivering his briefs. Sean Murphy, a close friend of Walshe and Hearne, a trained solicitor who was later to become Secretary to the Department of External Affairs, was another strong nationalist, his father having been Redmond's election agent for twenty years. Freddie Boland, the only 'new boy' at this Committee, was later to achieve distinction in the United Nations. He completed a strong team, which was difficult to deter at the best of times. At this Committee it was to prove irresistible.

Apart from the United Kingdom delegation, which was very much on the defensive, the one which came nearest to the Irish was the delegation from Canada. Ernest Lapointe, Minister for Justice in the Liberal Government and French Canadian pioneer of

Dominion Treaty-negotiation, was an experienced Commonwealth statesman. It was O. D. Skelton, however, who made the running, here again working in close harmony with his Irish friends.* Skelton, as we have observed before, was not pro-British and he threw the weight of his country, the senior Dominion, behind the Irish proposals whenever possible.† Of the other Canadian delegates, Charles Burchell became chairman of the important sub-committee on merchant shipping. His excellent report proved acceptable *in toto* to the Irish, who had themselves concentrated on the Operation of Dominion Legislation.

For South Africa, Bodenstein and van den Heever, who were to spend so much time in 1930 keeping their leader, General Hertzog, abreast of the complexities then at stake, struck up a happy accord with the Irish team. Under F. W. Beyers, they followed up the pre-Committee liaison between their two governments. The Irish Free State had the policy and gave the Committee its momentum, for which Canada and South Africa were willing to provide valuable support in depth.

New Zealand was frankly uninterested in the Committee. Australia suffered the embarrassment of a change of government while the Committee was in session. But neither country had prepared a positive case: both attended solely to keep a watching brief on the extremists, to see that they did not go too far, a duty which the New Zealand delegation scarcely took seriously.

The scene, then, was set for a thorough implementation of that principle of equality enunciated in 1926. The British Conservative Government had not hurried to call the Committee into being; the Labour Government which found itself in power when the Committee met was equally reluctant to give the Dominions their heads. With their senior civil servant advisers they were suspicious of the logic of free association, and they were trained to cling where possible to the advantage of central control, or apparent control. But the Labour Government was a new government. It was unsure of itself and its leader was in America preparing for the coming London Naval Conference. It had other things on its mind when

* The Committee was always referred to as the 'O.D.L.' Committee. The Irish tried to give him a proprietorial interest in the Conference on account of his initials.

† F. H. Boland contends that neither was he anti-British. Rather he was pro-Commonwealth but with a clear idea of a Commonwealth consisting of fully autonomous Dominions, in accordance with the Irish view (Boland interview).

the O.D.L. Committee sat, and by the time the Committee Report was published the Naval Conference was fully absorbing its attention.*

(iii) THE O.D.L. REPORT

The O.D.L. Report is divided into eight parts, including an Introduction giving details of the Delegations, and a short, explanatory section. This section made it clear that the Committee desired to harmonise theory and practice in terms of the equality of status declared in 1926. It repeated its terms of reference. Its purpose was to 'enquire into, report upon, and make recommendations concerning –

(i) Existing statutory provisions requiring reservation of Dominion legislation for the assent of His Majesty or authorising the disallowance of such legislation.

(ii) a. The present position as to the competence of Dominion Parliaments to give their legislation extra-territorial operation.

b. The practicability and most convenient method of giving effect to the principle that each Dominion Parliament should have power to give extra-territorial operation to its legislation in all cases where such operation is ancillary to provision for the peace, order, and good government of the Dominion.

(iii) The principles embodied in or underlying the Colonial Laws Validity Act 1865, and the extent to which any provisions of that Act ought to be repealed, amended, or modified in the light of the existing relations between the various members of the British Commonwealth of Nations as described in this Report' (i.e. the Report of the Imperial Conference).[43]

The Merchant Shipping reference, added to these, required the Committee also to 'consider and report on the principles which should govern, in the general interest, the practice and legislation relating to Merchant Shipping in the various parts of the Empire, having regard to the change in constitutional status and general relations which had occurred since existing laws were enacted'.[44] As well as stating its terms of reference, this second part of the Report emphasised the Committee's origins in the 1926 Imperial Conference, summarised the advance made on that occasion, and

* The 'Committee of Experts' called into being by the 1926 Conference became the Committee on the Operation of Dominion Legislation and Merchant Shipping Legislation, 1929. It was referred to as the O.D.L. Committee for short and will frequently be so described below. It was also referred to as a Conference, because of its size.

made it clear that the intention of the Committee was to report its recommendations to 'His Majesty's Governments in the United Kingdom and in the Dominions' as 'a preliminary to further consideration'.[45]

Part Three of the Report dealt with the powers of Disallowance and Reservation, treating these two subjects separately. Disallowance, it explained, 'means the right of the Crown, which has hitherto been exercised (when the occasion for its exercise has arisen) on the advice of Ministers in the United Kingdom, to annul an Act by a Dominion or Colonial Legislature'.[46] Included in a statement of the present position was the observation that 'The Irish Free State Constitution contains no provision for disallowance'.[47] If not personally involved, however, the Irish Free State felt that the existence of this 'right', even in theory, was utterly incompatible with the Dominion status which it wished to see prevailing throughout the Commonwealth. Like other legal anomalies, Disallowance had meaning only in the context of a unified Empire under central control. Where it remained on the Statute Book it must be wiped off; it could only mislead the Courts and cloud the true position. Where it was exercised as of prerogative right, this right must be exposed as meaningless: for it was fundamental to the many arguments which the Irish had prepared for this Committee exalting the sovereign status of the Dominions, that the prerogative of the Crown – exercised in the United Kingdom by United Kingdom ministers – had passed to each Dominion on its assumption of self-government, to be exercised there only by the ministers of that Dominion.

In 1926 the Governor-General's office had been revised to conform with this very theory, and the fact that the representative of the Crown could act towards a Dominion only on the advice of the ministers of that Dominion made his initiation of Disallowance to the Irish 'an unsustainable and wholly illogical proceeding'.[48] This view was accepted and the Committee agreed 'that the present constitutional position is that the power of disallowance can no longer be exercised in relation to Dominion legislation'.[49] Immediately, however, it came up against another anomaly which the Irish held to be incompatible with full sovereignty. To recommend the implementation of its conclusion the O.D.L. Committee was forced to distinguish between those Dominions which possessed the power to amend their Constitution and those which did not possess that power. To the Irish Free State the possession of the power of constitutional amendment was essential to a status of sovereignty. It was prepared to offer a strong supporting case. The British Preliminary Memorandum, furnished to Dominions as a suggested basis for discussion at the Conference, had remained silent on the matter of Disallowance, but it did have some observations on this power.[50] Its views, however, were not in accord with those of the Irish Free State.

The British noted that there was no provision to enable Canada or Newfoundland to alter their Constitutions. In a further paragraph on 'Express Limitations in Dominion Constitutions as to the Subjects on which Legislation may be Enacted'[51] they ascribed positively colonial restrictions to New Zealand and argued that there was an *'express limitation'* on the Irish Free State that its legislation must conform to the terms of the 1921 Treaty. In defence of Canada and Newfoundland the Irish prepared an argument full of righteous indignation but allied to the facts of the contemporary situation, taking the opportunity to expose the basic nature of the whole Commonwealth association and of the king-function. Perhaps with their delicately balanced federal Constitution, the Canadians were embarrassed by this Irish frankness, but they could always take comfort that any restriction on their power to alter their own Constitution remained at their own request.[52] What Newfoundland thought scarcely mattered at this stage. In the Irish view, however, it was important to establish that the Dominions were now so completely independent that each one could validly amend its own Constitution by legistalation in its own Parliament as expediency required. The legislative sovereignty of a member-state of the Commonwealth must not be hampered by limitations which were appropriate to the imperial scheme of which the self-governing colony was a part. The Irish felt that it was colony-status which was at the root of the whole attempt to perpetuate the idea that the status of the member-states of the Commonwealth was a thing conceded by the British Parliament rather than 'a thing asserted, claimed and achieved by those States themselves'.[53]

Further, they claimed: 'A "State" which cannot alter its domestic institutions of government and administration is not sovereign: a "State" which cannot completely determine its external relationships is not sovereign. Any compulsory limitation at all upon its self-rule deprives it of the right to be recognised as a member of international society.'[54] The member-states of the Commonwealth had outgrown the scheme under which they had come into being, and their present association could only exist on the basis that it was a free association and readily recognisable as such to the outside world. The sovereignty of Canada, of South Africa, of the Irish Free State – of each of the Dominions – took precedence over the group known as the Commonwealth of Nations. Without the sovereignty of these separate states, the Commonwealth of Nations could no longer exist. Their sovereignty therefore must be guarded jealously. With incontrovertible logic the Irish repeated the theory of 'several' kingship, explaining their view of the king-function. Right from the start of this Committee they were determined to make their point and to invest every corner of the Commonwealth framework with that autonomy and equality declared in 1926. They recalled that it was the 'Crown in Parliament' which was the supreme legislative faculty in the old British Empire and they enunciated the only acceptable position: there must be no doubt that in Canada, for example, the supreme legislative authority was the King of Canada in the Parliament of Canada. And as in the United Kingdom itself the Executive and the Parliament and the Courts had become the realities and the King a constitutional form, so in the Commonwealth States the Governments and the Parliaments and the Courts were the realities also: there could be no authority whatever superior to the Government of Canada or the Legislature of Canada or the Courts of Canada so far as Canada was concerned. Because a Dominion Constitution contained no provision expressly enabling it to amend its Constitution, they concluded, this did not mean that it had not that power: rather it was true to say that where such enabling provisions did exist they were tautologous and should be removed. This was the logic of Dominion autonomy. In 1929 it was a logic not easy for the United Kingdom, or even some of the Dominions themselves, to grasp. As the appropriate Irish Free State memorandum put it:

> In view, however, of the fact that the Constitutions of all the Dominions other than the Irish Free State are contained in statutes of the British Parliament not accompanied by concurrent counterpart legislation on their own Statute Books the argument ... may be too formidable a morsel for the powers of deglutition of the representatives of those Dominions to dissolve.[55]

New Zealand provided a case in point. The limitation on its

Constitution referred to in the British Preliminary Memorandum was quite ludicrously comprehensive. The New Zealand Constitution Act, 1852, gave the General Assembly power to 'make laws for the peace, order and good government of New Zealand provided that no such laws be repugnant to the law of England';[56] and this, the Memorandum pointed out, was 'one of the sections of the Act of 1852 which the General Assembly of New Zealand has no power to alter'.[57] To the Irish it passed understanding that any member-state of the Commonwealth could allow such a proviso to remain in its Constitution. They bluntly stated in their brief that 'if that section cannot be amended by the deletion of the proviso, and if such an amendment cannot be made by the Parliament of New Zealand, New Zealand should not be a member-state of the Commonwealth of Nations at all'.[58] But then the Irish were always conscious of being at opposite poles to the New Zealanders. Imperial Conference Agreements had to be unanimous but had somehow to embrace their two opinions. Such company, the Irish felt, delayed Dominion progress and inhibited Conference action, and so they were resentfully scornful.

To the alleged limitation on its own legislative competence contained in the British Memorandum the Irish Free State paid even fuller attention. It did not deny that Article 50 of its Constitution contained a qualifying proviso. However, it interpreted this proviso not as an 'express limitation', but simply as an acknowledgement in the Constitution of what had been undertaken by the Treaty, which was then being given the force of law. The proviso did not enact that there was no power in the Oireachtas to legislate contrary to the Treaty. It simply declared that the Oireachtas would not so legislate, or would, in amending the Constitution have regard to the fact that there were outstanding mutual obligations between the Free State and the United Kingdom. There was no express limitation on the *power* of the Oireachtas to amend the Constitution.

Disallowance, simple of appearance, but, like every ancient constitutional practice, of iceberg proportion when probed, had gathered to itself many of the frustrations felt in some of the Dominion legislatures, and the Irish had used it to give a lesson in the facts of Commonwealth constitutional evolution. Disallowance had one further application, however, which received separate treatment (paragraphs 24 and 25) in the Report. This was the particular case of the Colonial Stock Act, 1900.

This Act allowed trustee status to be conferred on loans raised in London by the Dominions and Colonies, providing they complied with certain conditions. One of these conditions, as the Report related,

> is a requirement that the Dominion Government shall place on record a formal expression of its opinion that any Dominion legislation which appears to the Government of the United Kingdom to alter any of the provisions affecting the stock to the injury of the stockholder or to involve a departure from the original contract in regard to the stock would be properly disallowed.[59]

The Committee concluded that 'the right of disallowance in respect of such legislation must remain and can properly be exercised'.[60] It recognised the contractual nature of this condition and realised that no derogation of status was implied. It noted, however, that 'the condition regarding disallowance makes it difficult and in one case impossible for certain Dominions to take advantage of the provisions of the Colonial Stock Act, 1900'.[61] The one Dominion which found the condition unacceptable was the Irish Free State. It did recognise that the United Kingdom, when conferring a financial privilege, had a perfect right to insist on any conditions it cared to choose. But it tried to dissuade the United Kingdom from insisting on these particular conditions, which offended against dignity and were politically and constitutionally objectionable. Furthermore, trustee status in the United Kingdom was enjoyed by Land Bonds issued under the Irish Land Act, 1923. The principal and interest of these Bonds were guaranteed by the British Treasury under the Irish Free State Land Purchase (Loan Guarantee) Act, 1924, and the Bonds were therefore trustee securities by virtue of Section 1 (i) (*e*) of the Trustee Act, 1925. But the Treasury did not claim any right to disallow Irish Land legislation, so why insist here? Constitutional objections could be raised, too, against aspects of the Coinage Act, 1870, and the Irish Department of Finance desired a general clarification.

There were urgent practical reasons behind this desire, for the Irish Free State was anxious to raise another loan. It had not used the London market hitherto but conditions prevailing on the New York Stock Exchange were now unfavourable. Ernest Blythe, the Irish Free State Minister for Finance, would have preferred London this time but he simply could not afford the political capital at stake in any acceptance of the British conditions. He argued convincingly that Mr Cosgrave was unlikely to legislate to harm stockholders. The

British, however, could not accept that Mr Cosgrave was a permanent fixture. Already de Valera was breathing over his shoulder, and de Valera had time and time again vowed to withhold Land Annuities. The British stuck to their conditions and the Free State had to do without British money. Even so, the matter was raised in criticism in the Dail. The fact that some disallowance remained provided ammunition for the Irish Opposition. Mr McGilligan was able to point out its irrelevance to Ireland: there was no provision for Disallowance in the Constitution and they had never complied with the British conditions. Mr FitzGerald added that they never would comply. It would not have passed unnoticed, however, had they chosen to do so, and the incident illustrates the difficulties at home which faced even the aggressive Irish Government: difficulties which were too little appreciated in Britain.

Reservation was treated in the next part of the Report and it raised again the old bogies of Empire and of Westminster supremacy. The Committee defined Reservation as 'the withholding of assent by a Governor-General or Governor to a Bill duly passed by the competent Legislature in order that His Majesty's pleasure may be taken.'[62] It fell into two categories: Reservation at the discretion of the Governor-General, and Reservation which by statute the Governor-General was bound to impose. There were further provisions relating to Compulsory Reservation in both the Colonial Courts of the Admiralty Act, 1890, and in the Merchant Shipping Act, 1894, but these were due to receive separate treatment. In the case of the Irish Free State there was no provision for Compulsory Reservation, but, in Article 41 of the Constitution, Discretionary Reservation was included.

As with Disallowance, the 1926 Conference had agreed that Reservation was incompatible with the status of equality. The Dominions must be allowed to order their own affairs and the contradiction inherent in a discretion remaining to a Governor-General who was strictly bound to act according to the advice of his Dominion ministers was ridiculous. The Irish wanted to see such provisions removed entirely from the Statute Books. But for the complicating factor of Article 2 of the Treaty, which tied the Irish position to that existing in Canada, the Irish Constitution would doubtless have been purged already.

Accordingly, the Committee recognised that Discretionary Reservation was dead. In regard to Compulsory Reservation it repeated the 1926 pronouncement that it was the right of each Dominion to advise the Crown in all matters relating to its own affairs, and that it would be unconstitutional for the United Kingdom Government to tender contrary advice. In deference to the Irish it added: 'The same principle applies to cases where alterations of a Constitution are required to be reserved.'[63] In the actual matter of abolishing this offensive power, the Committee distinguished as before between the Dominions able to amend their own Constitutions and those requiring United Kingdom co-operation. Exactly as it had done in respect of Disallowance it recommended that where a Dominion needed assistance 'it would be in accordance with constitutional practice that if so requested by the Dominion concerned the Government of the United Kingdom should ask Parliament to pass the necessary legislation'.[64]

The view of the Irish Free State here had been admirably endorsed: no Reservation was to remain. It is fitting therefore that the last word on this section should be a summary of the Irish view from the pen of J. J. Hearne, legal adviser to the Department of External Affairs. To him, reservation in any form was:

> essentially inconsistent with the inalienable and inviolable constitutional right of the Parliament of the States of the Commonwealth to pass such laws as those Parliaments may determine for any purpose of peace, order and good government, that is to say for any purpose which expediency or policy may from time to time require. . . . Legal formulae having statutory authority which obscures the real relationships existing amongst the States of the Commonwealth should be formally removed, and where legislation by the British Parliament is for that purpose necessary or desirable such legislation should be passed without delay. The continuance of what are now anomalous and foundationless legal forms, while it may not endanger the principles upon which the future of the Commonwealth of Nations depends, must confuse those principles and postpone their final recognition in the world. They are commended by no practical values or advantages which may not readily be secured by a careful application of those methods of co-operation and reciprocal aid which are the chosen instruments of our polity.[65]

Part Four of the Report is entitled 'The Extra-Territorial Operation of Dominion Legislation', and it deals with parts (ii) (*a*) and (*b*) of its terms of reference. The Committee pointed out that, unlike Disallowance and Reservation, the territorial limitation of legislation was not specifically mentioned in any Dominion constitution.[66] The issue was confused and obscure. What was clear, however, was that in this respect there existed 'a radical difference between the position of Acts of the Parliament of the United Kingdom in the United Kingdom itself and Acts of a Dominion Parliament in the Dominion'.[67] General uncertainty, the Committee noted, was engendered in such matters as 'Fisheries, taxation, shipping, air navigation, marriage, criminal law, deportation, and the enforcement of laws against smuggling and unlawful immigration'.[68]

In nearly all these matters the Irish Free State had some dealings with Britain. The Irish, however, did not admit that there was any territorial limitation on their own legislative competence, and they recalled their vigorous argument of 1926. This argument had been directed primarily towards a clarification of the position throughout the Dominions, and the establishment of a uniform system of co-operation. The Irish required that Britain should be replaced as legislator by the several Dominions and it proposed that uniformity of practice should be maintained by reciprocal Dominion agreements.[69] They had come to this Committee determined to remove all anachronistic colonial concepts and this one offered peculiar scope for action, being based on thoroughly bad law.* Besides, the Dominions had already made a beginning. They all had power to regulate their armies and navies and to make provision for air defence. Canada had 'affirmed her undoubted power to regulate Canadian aircraft';[70] the Irish Free State had enacted and enforced fishery regulations effective beyond her territorial seas – and enforced them against British seamen.[71] South Africa, after the First World War, had legislated for her Mandated Territories (though New Zealand had thought fit to ask permission from Britain to do likewise). The point was that the Dominions were now sovereign states and therefore their legislation must be determined solely by the interests of their people. Even the British Foreign Secretary had been forced to admit that the Dominions were 'international units individually in the fullest sense';† and if they were 'international units' then they must have the power to regulate the details of international intercourse. But the Irish did not want the Dominions to appeal here to British Statute. Proud of the autochthonous redoubt from which they argued every issue, the Irish wanted the Dominions

* See above p. 112 (MacLeod's Case).
† See above Ch. 7, note 32. A. Henderson, Geneva, 14 September 1929. This is also quoted in Irish Memorandum; 'Additional Note on Ex-territoriality', for the O.D.L. Conference (McGilligan Papers).

to 'assert to themselves' the power to legislate exterritorially. They quoted Sir Wilfrid Laurier, when, in 1911, he had said: 'the United Kingdom has asserted to itself the power to disallow any legislation which it is in the power of the self-governing Dominions to pass.' He might, they argued, have gone further, had his purpose required it and added: 'The United Kingdom has asserted to itself the right to declare that any legislation passed in the Dominions and purporting to operate exterritorially is *ultra vires* the power of the Dominions Parliaments.'[72] That, the Irish proclaimed, is what the whole doctrine of the incompetence of the Dominion legislatures to enact exterritorial law came to. Britain in the colonial past had set an arbitrary limit to the powers of the Dominions. Let the Dominions now claim that, in the phrase of Mr McGilligan, 'whatever the Parliament of the United Kingdom can do, the Parliament of any other of the Associated States can do'.[73]

If the Committee did not adopt the Irish method, it fully executed the Irish aim. It drew no individual distinctions, recommending that a comprehensive 'declaratory enactment' be passed with the consent of all the Dominions by the Parliament of the United Kingdom. The clause, to which the Committee gave much thought, was to be untrammelled by any reference to 'provisions for the peace, order and good government' – to which the Irish had specifically objected – nor by reference to 'any particular class of persons (e.g. the citizens of the Dominion)'. It was to be short and simple:

> It is hereby declared and enacted that the Parliament of a Dominion has full power to make laws having extra-territorial operation.[74]

The Irish had this power already, but the Declaration, they argued, would at least end speculation and put all the Dominions on an equal footing with one another, Great Britain included. Even Britain found it easy to accept such a request. Had not Berriedale Keith just admitted that 'no real Imperial advantage attaches to this restriction on Dominion Legislation'?[75]

The next section of the Report, Part Five, though headed 'Colonial Laws Validity Act', covered many aspects of national and international sovereignty and was, as McGilligan told the Dail, 'the critical portion of the Report'.[76] As its title implies, however, its first task was to decide in what manner the generally agreed repeal of the Colonial Laws Validity Act, 1865, should be accomplished. By now it was clear that a Bill of some importance was going to be required of the United Kingdom Parliament in the manner of a self-denying ordinance. Only by such a measure could the statutes governing the Constitutions and later development of the Dominions legally be harmonised with the present position. The recommended removal of Disallowance and Reservation and the clarification of exterritorial powers would already form the nucleus of the projected Bill and the Committee was able now to concentrate on the most fundamental item of all. There was no argument about the need to repeal the Colonial Laws Validity Act, which was described, typically, by John Hearne as 'the sword of contingent invalidity hanging over Dominion legislation'.[77] The solution agreed as to the form of its repeal was finally set out as follows:

> (1) The Colonial Laws Validity Act, 1865 shall cease to apply to any law made by the Parliament of a Dominion.
> (2) No law and no provision of any law hereafter made by the Parliament of a Dominion shall be void or inoperative on the ground that it is repugnant to the law of England or to the provisions of any existing or future Act of Parliament or to any order, rule or regulation made thereunder, and the powers of the Parliament of a Dominion shall include the power to repeal or amend any such Act, order, rule or regulation in so far as the same is part of the law of the Dominion.[78]

To reconcile the existence of a legal power in the Parliament of the United Kingdom to legislate for the Dominions with the established constitutional position, the Committee of Experts further proposed that a statement of convention be placed on record in the proceedings of the next Imperial Conference, thus:

> It would be in accord with the established constitutional position of all members of the Commonwealth in relation to one another that no law hereafter made by the Parliament of the United Kingdom shall extend to any Dominion otherwise than at the request and with the consent of that Dominion.[79]

But the Committee also felt that statutory force should be given to this Convention and recommended that the proposed Bill should contain a declaration and enactment in the following terms:

> Be it therefore declared and enacted that no Act of Parliament hereafter made shall extend or be deemed to extend to a Dominion unless it is expressly declared therein that that Dominion has requested and consented to the enactment thereof.[80]

As the Committee observed, if the above recommendations were adopted, then 'the acquisition by the Parliaments of the Dominions of full legislative powers' would 'follow as a necessary consequence',[81] and,

> by the removal of all such restrictions upon the legislative powers of the Parliaments of the Dominions and the consequent effective recognition of the equality of these Parliaments with the Parliament of the United Kingdom, the law would be brought into harmony with the root principle of equality governing the free association of the members of the British Commonwealth of Nations.[82]

The *cri de cœur* of the Irish Memorandum of 1926 was close to being answered. Every sentence recommended by the Committee breathes the dignity of status and the freedom and equality which that document demanded, and which alone could inspire a true spirit of co-operation.

But there were many consequences of these recommendations other than the harmonising of legal theory with constitutional practice. Specific difficulties existed in connection with the acquisition of full legislative powers in particular Dominions. Also, if the Commonwealth association had value at all then its means of co-operative action would now have to be agreed. The Committee proceeded to tackle both the individual difficulties and the common needs; but first it devoted three paragraphs to that central bond of the Commonwealth which now stood out as its one visible link and symbol, the Crown.[83]

As the Dominions shared a common allegiance to the Crown it would have to be made clear that any laws relating to both the Succession to the Throne and the Royal Style and Titles were of equal concern to all. The representatives of all the Dominions here agreed that any such laws would require the assent 'as well of the Parliaments of all the Dominions as of the Parliament of the United Kingdom'.[84] This was a simple enough declaration of good manners and good intentions concerning the respected and widely loved symbol of Commonwealth unity. Though the declaration itself did not originate in the Irish Delegation, it was one to which they could fully adhere in the spirit of their 1926 Memorandum, and the description of the Crown as 'the symbol of free association of the British Commonwealth of Nations' – a new advance and hailed as such by Deputy Esmonde in the Dail[85] – was entirely their handiwork.[86]

As soon as this particular section of the Report was discussed in the South African Parliament, however, it was distorted and confused by General Smuts who tried to endow it with a quite insupportable element of compulsion. The Dominions, he maintained, had hereby declared that only by the agreement of all could any one member leave the Commonwealth. He had managed to confuse succession with secession.

In the Dail, McGilligan was asked outright whether the Free State could secede or not, and his reply was a sharp affirmative. In the Seanad he gave a more comprehensive outline of an Irish viewpoint which was as true at the Committee as it was when it was uttered, in July 1930. McGilligan explained:

> With all deference to the judgment of those who spoke in the South African Parliament, I still hold that the two questions of succession and secession are to be taken apart. One has no relation to the other. There is no relation between these two things. Certainly, so far as the 1929 Report is concerned, there is no relation. If any one of the present members of the British Commonwealth of Nations desires to secede, the only thing in my mind that is blocked by Article 60, is secession by way of alteration in the succession. If a Dominion does not want to bother about succession but simply wants to leave the Commonwealth, Article 60 presents no difficulty. Succession and secession are entirely different questions. If the Dominion wanted to become a Republic and to remain inside the Commonwealth, and wished to do so by changing the order of the succession to the Throne, then, undoubtedly, Article 60 would be a definite bar, but if some one member of the Commonwealth tried to get outside the Commonwealth, Article 60 would have no operative effect whatever in relation to that Dominion. A state which seeks to get outside an organisation which has certain rules and regulations, is careless as to what those rules and regulations are, in so far as they effect those who remain inside afterwards. What happens afterwards has no concern for such a State. Whatever happens concerns only those who remain within the partnership. I cannot understand that there should be any confusion of thought on these two questions of secession and succession.[87]

The Committee, to return once more to the Report, proceeded next with the difficulties of particular Dominions and designed Articles for the forthcoming Statute of Westminster, giving separate exemptions to Canada, Australia and New Zealand, to meet the peculiar requirements of each of these Dominions. Canada had a federal Constitution jealously balanced, and further consultation was desired between Ottawa and the Provinces: Australia and New Zealand could be brought to the waters of independence, but they could not be made to drink. The Committee did clarify some

Provincial and State powers in Canada and Australia before it passed to the more controversial outstanding problems of sovereignty and co-operation. The first of these problems was that of nationality.

The Committee recognised that there was ambiguity attached to the concept of nationality 'due in part to its use for the purpose of denoting also the concept of allegiance to the Sovereign'.[88] This was the problem which the Irish had encountered three years earlier when changing the Royal Title. Already, the Committee noted, two of the Dominions had passed Acts defining their nationals, both for national and for international purposes. At the same time common status also existed throughout the Commonwealth, based on the British Nationality and Status of Aliens Act, 1914. But there was no consistency, the Committee recorded, between this common status and the distinct nationality possessed by the individual Dominions.

In this matter the British Preliminary Memorandum had gone to considerable trouble to reveal the current position, not only of the 'Law of Nationality' (including nationality and citizenship), but also the 'Nationality of Married Women'; 'Disabilities to which a British woman becomes subject in the United Kingdom on Marriage with an Alien' and 'Pension and Franchise Rights in the Dominions of a British Woman Marrying an Alien'. The Committee, however, did not feel competent to lay down more than general principles on these subjects, and was content merely to add that 'steps should be taken as soon as possible by consultation among the various Governments to arrive at a settlement of the problems involved on the basis of these principles'.[89] The Irish Free State accordingly brought to the Imperial Conference of the following year, draft proposals for its own Nationality Bill. In the meantime it interpreted these paragraphs of the Report to embody one of the positive benefits of Commonwealth association. Ireland would legislate to make her nationality conform with her citizenship and would define the obligation of that nationality. But the wider advantages of membership would remain throughout the Dominions and in foreign lands the British consular services would continue to be of assistance.

Paragraph Eighty of the Report attempted to counter the consequences of the removal of the legal ties of Empire. Hitherto, uniformity of action had rested on the general application of United

Kingdom statute. Now unanimity, as the Irish had argued before, would rest on 'reciprocal action based upon agreement'.* This, it must be repeated, had been an integral part of their entire programme since 1926, and it refutes the suggestion that the Free State had no interest other than the destruction of imperial law. The principle of co-operation – 'the *fundamentum et radix* of the whole policy of the Commonwealth'[90] – should be

> translated into special agreements (less formal, perhaps than international conventions but not less effective for their purpose) to which the reciprocal enactments contemplated may give the force of law, or if that be unnecessary, upon which the reciprocal enactments contemplated may be based.

This was the new order which the Irish wished to establish. To make it effective was the primary reason for the removal of such statutes as the Committee had considered above, 'lest the new co-operation . . . at any time . . . be invalidated or impeded by Courts of Justice administering the unaltered but out of date law of the old'.[91]

This is the key to the creative aspect of the Irish vision, and it was not left simply to general theory. The Irish delegation had prepared a great quantity of memoranda on relevant imperial statutes. The British Preliminary Memorandum itself had detailed the existing position regarding 'The Fugitive Offenders Act, 1881', 'The Extradition Acts, 1870 to 1906', the 'Colonial Prisoners Removal Acts, 1869 and 1884' (all with a bearing on extra-territorial jurisdiction), 'Certain Acts Relating to Evidence', 'The Bankruptcy Acts, 1914 and 1926', 'The Companies Act', 'The Coinage Acts', and such general items as 'Industrial Property' and 'Air Navigation'.[92] The Irish covered not only these items but 'The Colonial Boundaries Act' and such matters as probates and maintenance orders. Their treatment of the Fugitive Offenders Act illustrates the underlying principle:

> The Fugitive Offenders Act, 1881 provided a simple and effective machinery for the return of fugitive offenders to the part of the Empire where they were 'wanted'. If the right and power of the Colonial legislatures to enact extra-territorial laws had been admitted there was no reason why the reciprocal statute should not have been the legal method of compassing the ends encompassed by the Fugitive Offenders Act, 1881.[93]

This Irish memorandum recognised that the 1929 Committee

* See above p. 157, note 69.

'may not in fact get down to the details of a general scheme of inter-state reciprocity. But it must definitely fix the lines along which the principle can be implemented'.[94] The Irish Free State, for one, came to the Committee prepared in the fullest detail. It observed that the several statutes of the Commonwealth Parliaments, which would follow the establishment of the reciprocity principle, would differ from those statutes of the British Parliament referred to above 'not so much in the resultant practices as in the source of their authority and the form in which they are framed'. It explained, with illustration, that 'the new Evidence Acts, Company Acts and Bankruptcy Acts of the various Parliaments of the Commonwealth will do little more than re-enact in those Parliaments provisions similar or corresponding to those of the existing statutes of the British Parliament'.[95] On the civil side, the Irish concluded, reciprocity in legal relationships was not a difficult ideal for the States of the Commonwealth to realise:

> All it means in the first instance is that the authority for the exercise of multifarious functions of a judicial or administrative nature should be founded in statutes of the States of the Commonwealth by the Executive Government of which the judges and administrative officers are appointed. All that it means in the second instance is that certain judicial and administrative acts done in one State should be recognised and given effect to in another or in more than one of the others as the case may be.[96]

If compulsion had been the hallmark of Empire, now co-operation would be the distinguishing feature of the Commonwealth of Nations.

This spirit of co-operation was to inspire the next part of the Committee's Report, concerned with Merchant Shipping Legislation and the Colonial Courts of the Admiralty Act, 1890. But before the Committee finally turned to this complex and important section, it took the opportunity presented to define the word 'Dominion' and to distinguish the Dominions from the remaining 'Colonial' territories. Then it closed Part Four of the Report with a statement of an assumption which had underlain the whole of the Committee's work so far:

> That the necessary legislation and the constitutional conventions to which we have referred will in due course receive the approval of the Parliaments of the Dominions concerned.[97]

Merchant Shipping, to the Irish, simply meant one requirement

As stated in the previous chapter they wished Irish ships to fly their own flag. The sub-committee, chaired by the Canadian, Charlie Burchell, realised this requirement in a report thoroughly acceptable to the Irish. It also provides us with one pleasant analogy illustrating the harmony of Irish and Canadian thought on some issues. John Hearne, in a memorandum on Nationality in the following year, referred to: 'Mr Lapointe, Canadian Minister for Justice in the late Mackenzie King Cabinet . . . [who had] in a singularly felicitous illustration given in the course of some remarks at the London Conference of 1929, likened the citizen of a State carrying his passport to a ship flying her national flag.'[98] Hearne went on to record that the Committee's Report on Merchant Shipping had suggested that once an agreement was reached within the Commonwealth as to the qualifications for owernship of a ship to govern admission to registration, a ship owned in any part of the Commonwealth within the terms of the agreement would, on being registered in that part, be entitled to all the benefits and privileges heretofore accorded to British ships generally; Irish nationality, he affirmed, would endeavour to copy this principle.

Briefly, the Merchant Shipping Section of the Report outlined the contemporary position, which, it agreed, was unsatisfactory. It then interpreted this position in the light of the recommendations made hitherto, and, as before, advised that concerted action be based on co-operation. Voluntary agreements were to be sought under a number of specific heads in the common interest.

Similar treatment was accorded to the 'Colonial Courts of the Admiralty Act, 1890'. Here the Irish position was different, being governed by the provisions of the Courts of the Admiralty (Ireland) Act, 1867, but both Acts required repeal and replacement according to modern requirements. The existence of International Conventions on mortgages, liens and limited liability, however, made it even more imperative in this instance that uniformity be retained, and United Kingdom law was suggested as a basis: a suggestion wholly in accord with the original Irish observations. Part Six closed with specific recommendations for the Statute of Westminster to clarify the situation, and with a short note on the position of India.

Only two parts now remained of the Report, both extremely short. Part Seven, entitled 'Suggested Tribunal for the Determination of Disputes', was a scant record of yet another abortive attempt to circumvent objections to the Judicial Committee of the Privy

Council by the creation of a more acceptable Court. The sub-committee which undertook this investigation was chaired by Sir Maurice Gwyer, and included H. W. Malkin, Legal Adviser to the Foreign Office, O. D. Skelton, Sir William Harrison Moore, Dr H. D. J. Bodenstein and J. A. Costello. Heightened importance was conferred on it by the recent division of opinion on the Optional Clause of the Permanent Court of International Justice. But the Committee could reach no conclusion. Technically speaking the Judicial Committee was outside the terms of reference of this Committee, and it was on such grounds that the Irish Delegation answered its critics in the Dail. But the British Preliminary Memorandum had included this controversial topic, and had denied to the Irish Free State, amongst others, the power to abolish the Appeal. The Irish, however, were content to hold their hand until the impending Imperial Conference, when, they felt sure, agreement to its abolition would amicably be attained.

The Report of the Committee on the Operation of Dominion Legislation and Merchant Shipping Legislation closed with a final part which reaffirmed the principles of the 1926 Conference and contained the signatures of the Heads of Delegations. On 4 December the Committee dissolved and its members reported back to their respective governments.

Before examining the reactions to this Report and endeavouring further to attribute responsibility for its recommendations, it is worth noting that one other matter besides the Judicial Committee was mentioned by the British Memorandum and was left over for solution until the 1930 Imperial Conference. This was the matter of the Prerogative of Mercy. The British noted that matters of the Prerogative were usually Reserved and that the Prerogative of Mercy itself, which was vested in the Governor-General, was exercisable according to the Letters Patent or Instructions constituting his Office. This section of the British Memorandum called forth a particularly scathing Irish reply.

The Irish Delegation had commissioned a voluminous memorandum, on the whole nature and history of the Royal Prerogative, from a Dublin barrister, A. A. Dickie. Some anomalies remained since the 1926 Conference and it was desirable to set the record straight. It was the forthright J. J. Hearne, however, who directed the Irish reply in the end. Hearne, as we have seen before, felt that the Colonial Governor should never have drifted down to the Dominion era, and he used this occasion to attack not simply the exercise of the Prerogative of Mercy, but the whole of the Royal Instructions upon which this exercise was based. First of all, he pointed out, these Instructions were not Royal, being drafted by a British Secretary of State. Furthermore they were authenticated by a Secretarial Seal – the Signet. (The introduction of the Seals as a matter of controversy is important here, for, as we shall see later, this issue itself grew to attain a Commonwealth-wide significance.)* Hearne summarised his argument with a characteristic burst of rhetoric:

> We have reached a stage in which the Royal Prerogative of mercy so far as the States of the Commonwealth of Nations are concerned is part of the 'discretionary authority of the executive'† in each of the States. It must be exercised accordingly; that is to say, its exercise must be controlled absolutely by the Executive Government of each of those States and the whole function must be stripped of the trappings and regalia of what is, so far as the Commonwealth of Nations is concerned, a defunct institution, namely, the Colonial Governor. Royal Instructions on the advice of a British Secretary of State must go the way of all anomalous constitutional literature, for us of no practical value, but for the constitutional historian, vastly interesting as illustrating one of those features of that intensely organised central rule upon which the old British Empire was constructed, and around which crystallised those fierce controversies which marked its climacteric and hastened its catastrophe.[99]
>
> † Dicey.

(iv) REACTIONS

The Report was published two months later, on 3 February 1930. The reaction of *The Times*, preoccupied as it was with the London Naval Conference, was aloof and scornful and revealed a complete unawareness of Dominion aspirations. General Smuts, remarked *The Times*, was right to warn against leaving the problems of Empire to 'the mercy of lawyers and legal formulas'. This report, *The Times* added, would 'not be read entirely without misgiving' for it had trampled on the sacred principles of Empire. There were anomalies in every living organisation which a statesman would be chary of touching 'fearing lest by too much tinkering with the tissues he may unwittingly injure the soul'. *The Times* apparently did not realise that it was the very soul of Empire that men such as McGilligan wished not merely to injure but to destroy. Querulously it admonished the Committee for having asked 'is this consistent with the formula for

* See below, Ch. 9.

equal status? And if not how must it be made to be so?' It proceeded
in similar vein:

> They have been comparatively little concerned to show any real practical necessity for the changes they recommend or that, on balance, these changes will be an improvement from the practical as well as the theoretical point of view. They seem even to have lost sight of the warning in the Balfour Report that the principles of equality of status does not necessarily apply to function.[100]

Seldom can a leading article have been so far from understanding the
issues involved. If no other justification existed for the stand which
the Irish Delegation had taken on the Committee, then this display
of myopic imperialism would have amply sufficed of itself.

The Times, having damned, passed on. The following days brought
no second thoughts, no further comment, no report of Dominion
reactions. Like historians afterwards *The Times* played down the
Committee's Report. There would be time to go into detail when
the whole matter came up again at the Imperial Conference in the
autumn.

In the South African and Canadian Parliaments, the Report was
received with favour. To Hertzog its acceptance appeared to be:

> the termination of the old conditions which prevailed in the past . . . by this not alone are new rights created, but a new position so far as the dominions are concerned, and they are put on a footing that they have never yet had in the past. . . . As soon as the British Government now does the needful we shall in actual practice be put on a completely equal footing with Great Britain.

He rejoiced that since 1926 'the wrangling has been got rid of, and
there is more co-operation than there has ever been'.[101] Smuts did
not react as *The Times* might have led us to anticipate, for he too
welcomed the Report in principle. But he seized upon his secession
error and in that touchy Assembly almost put the entire Report in
jeopardy. It was pointed out in the debate by Mr Coulter[102] that the
Irish Free State – which was said to stand on the left of South Africa
on this matter – had seen no limitation to its sovereignty in the
succession clause. In the end the matter was resolved harmoniously.

In Canada, Lapointe conducted the debate. He outlined the
work of the Committee and asserted that it had been done because
'the laws of empire must square with the facts of empire'.[103] There
was, however, some 'reactionary condemnation' of the Report, and
its description by the *London Post* as 'obscure, pedantic and

tedious' was quoted. But on the whole both understanding and approval were displayed. As Mr J. T. Thorsen pointed out:

> The future of our relationships with our equal sister British nations rests now upon the broad foundations of autonomy and self-government. That foundation is the strongest and safest foundation for the superstructure of the future that the genius of British [he might have said Irish] statesmanship has ever been able to devise.[104]

Canada and South Africa approved. For the sake of preserving the Empire, Australia and New Zealand reluctantly gave minimum acquiescence to this regrettable 'process of self-assertion',[105] this 'exaggerated self-consciousness' which made men chafe 'over trifling matters of theory'.[106] These phrases of Robert Menzies, in 1937, were as truly representative of Australasia in 1929. But then reality, to this continent, was still the Yellow Peril, and the safeguard was still the Royal Navy.

In America, W. Y. Elliott greeted the Report as a sharp and instantaneous rebuttal of the assertions which Berriedale Keith had included in his most recent work, *The Sovereignty of the British Dominions*.[107] It was in this book that Keith had derided the 'careless phraseology', 'exaggerated language' and 'rhetoric'[108] of the Balfour Declaration. Elliott pointed out enthusiastically, as *The Times* had done ruefully, that the Committee Report had taken the Balfour 'root principle' to heart.

Indeed one of the strongest arguments produced in favour of the Report was that it would end just the sort of aggravating speculation in which Keith indulged. In Dail Eireann, though the Irish had reason to be grateful to Keith for pointing out in succession every remaining hurdle to be cleared on the road to full sovereignty, Desmond FitzGerald could not resist rejoicing that the Report, resolving many things to the Irish point of view, had refuted the 'expert' lawyers and commentators who so often gave 'thoroughly misinformed' opinion 'against what we know to be a fact'.[109] On the same theme, in South Africa, Dr N. J. van der Merwe was more explicit. He resented 'men like Keith, Duncan Hall and Baker' who spread their interpretations of constitutional matters, wanting 'to inculate the group idea'.[110] J. W. Dafoe of the *Manitoba Free Press* was quoted in the Canadian House of Commons for his exposé of Keith as 'the chief' of a 'little group of hair-splitters' who since 1926, 'have been trying determinedly but ineffectively to deny the soundness of the constitutional doctrine embodied in that declaration'.[111]

Dominion annoyance was now mollified, for, as W. Y. Elliott concluded in the *American Political Science Review*, the discrepancy between law and practice would now end and there would be a clear field for co-operation on an equal basis.* If not in London, there was a great understanding of the Irish logic overseas.

To Mr Patrick McGilligan belongs the credit for bearing the burden of work in the Committee, and for so cogently and forcefully marshalling the admittedly excellent briefs of his colleagues. Both J. A. Costello and Sean Murphy have paid tribute to the achievement of their leader: 'It was McGilligan who bore the burden of the advance, proving himself a worthy successor to Kevin O'Higgins';[112] 'The Committee was the big Irish contribution and it was McGilligan's show.'[113] They have both agreed that McGilligan was well prepared, technically and politically, for his task, and they give credit to Dr Skelton for his assistance. But the physical stamina required, which, day after day on issue after issue, McGilligan displayed, was remarkable. He also proved immune both to persuasive temptations to compromise and to the pressures of the 'gentlemen's club'. McGilligan himself, a shy and retiring man with an encyclopedic memory, permits himself to retell the compliment paid at the end of the Committee by Sir (later Lord) Maurice Hankey. Sir Maurice, already veteran of so many Conferences and Cabinets, felt obliged to request a final meeting with McGilligan after the Committee had closed. Reluctantly, an exhausted McGilligan consented. To his astonishment the interview turned out to be no last minute British attempt to revoke or recant, but a sincere personal gesture of congratulation. Sir Maurice was warm and frank:

> I could not let you go without personally congratulating you and your delegation. I have been at every major Conference since Versailles and I have never met a delegation so consistently well briefed and which applied itself so rigorously to the job in hand. Small in number you were high in quality. Had the last government not fallen you would have received far more just treatment. I congratulate you all on your achievement.[114]

J. A. Costello has given other illustrations. Speaking of William

* W. Y. Elliott, in *American Political Science Review*, no. 24 (1930) pp. 971–88. Elliott, remarking that as international affairs became more important 'the Ministries of External Affairs may fall into competent hands' added 'as they have in the Irish Free State'. He also noted that if economic policies in the Dominions diverged 'An indivisible crown may prove more burdensome than the alternative of independent kingdoms united by an entente symbolised by the common King'.

Jowitt he recalled that gentleman's endeavour to advance the 'static theory' of the Treaty: that the Irish Free State received in 1921 only what Canada had attained at that time, and that any subsequent advance was irrelevant. 'Write that down please,' McGilligan asked him. Jowitt obliged. 'I will go home now. We have misinformed the Irish people in recommending the Treaty.' Jowitt took back the paper and tore it up.[115]

Nationality too, claimed Costello, was included in the Report on Irish initiative, while of succession, Costello affirmed that the Irish agreed willingly to the convention, as the view expressed was, they felt, implicit in their Treaty. But this was no bar to secession. After all if you are going to secede you do not do so by statute. Sir Keith Hancock could well observe later that the Royal Style and Titles section of the Report stressed the principle of unity, but it is clear that at no time had the Irish accepted that any element of compulsion had been incorporated into this unity.

The final statement remains with McGilligan himself. To Dail Eireann he asserted that this Report was the 'most comprehensive constitutional document that Dail Eireann has had to discuss since the Treaty was itself discussed'.[116] He recounted the problems of harmonising the individual views of the six Commonwealth States represented on the Committee and the difficulty of framing a report agreeable to all. Yet he and his colleagues had:

> brought forward definite things that we wanted ruling upon in accordance with the principles set out in 1926. We had limited terms of reference and within them we got the completest satisfaction that any delegation could get on these points.[117]

Personally he had always 'asserted the separateness of the nationhood of this country, the separateness of the people in a lot of their ideals and in the generality of their make-up'.[118] Now he brought them the fruits of his and their labour,

> we need not do anything about disallowance because that is gone. We need to do something about discretionary reservation because it is in our Constitution and out it comes. We need to do something about Merchant Shipping because we have legislation to pass and, when it is dealt with, our ships will fly the flag which we want and there is no contingent invalidity hanging over any statute we pass because of old time statutes. When we come to deal with our nationals it will be the same.[119]

Above all, he emphasised the break from the past which this Report would mean:

The frequency of the phrase 'the new position' is not accidental; it is deliberate. There is the ending of a chapter, an epoch – a history in which the legal and legislative predominance of the United Kingdom Parliament is plain to be seen. . . . The law, the legal position, is being made to square with the central and predominant political fact of absolute freedom and unequivocal co-equality.[120]

As Sir Keith Hancock summarised later, the Report 'would open the way for co-operation to secure in essential matters the coherence and uniformity which had been achieved hitherto by the legislative supremacy of the United Kingdom'.[121]

The Report was both an end and a beginning. It marked the destruction of the old Empire as well as the creation of the new Commonwealth.

8

The Imperial Conference 1930

(i) EXTERNAL AFFAIRS 1929–30

Between the O.D.L. Conference in 1929 and the Imperial Conference in 1930 a busy diplomatic year passed: a year which opened with the London Naval Conference in January. This Conference had been the subject of considerable Anglo-American preparation and it had been a constant distraction to the British Government during the O.D.L. negotiations. When it closed in April it was hailed by Ramsay MacDonald as an important foundation stone upon which to build international peace. Winston Churchill was less complimentary, four years later, when he dismissed it as an agreement which had 'crippled' Britain's power to equip herself and restricted America unnecessarily, while inhibiting the real menace, Germany, in no way at all.[1]

The Commonwealth significance of the Conference, however, is less open to controversy. The Dominions joined the negotiations and the Irish Free State, represented by Professor Smiddy, used the occasion to urge disarmament. But it was in the Irish ratification of the Treaty that a new departure was made. The Kellogg Pact had been ratified by the Dominions in six separate acts delivered simultaneously at Washington. On this occasion the whole Treaty was delayed from operation until 31 December 1930, by the Free State. The Dublin Government simply found it impossible to secure earlier legislative approval. But the effect was to highlight Dominion freedom and individuality; to emphasise the very Dominion qualities that the Free State was anxious to stress. The Dominions were full international entities. They could be taken for granted by no one.

There were other small incidents during the year. On 20 February a despatch from the Dominions Office informed the Free State of a *modus vivendi* between the United Kingdom and Russia Article

Four of this agreement made provision for the extension of its terms to any member of the Commonwealth by means of notes to the U.S.S.R., while Article Six provided a similar trade clause. The Irish objected to the principle of the British Government negotiating Treaties which affected the Dominions in any way, even if they might on occasion confer benefits. The South Africans, too, objected on this occasion, as they made clear at the 1930 Imperial Conference, but the other Dominions found the arrangement convenient. The Irish were in some difficulty with regard to Russia, for it was an essential requirement of the Ford Motor Company, whose factory at Cork was important to the Irish economy, that the Free State should have relations towards Russia similar to those which obtained between Great Britain and Russia. But the Irish favoured direct contact of their own. They would have preferred the establishment of a most-favoured-nation *modus vivendi*, pending the conclusion of a full Commercial Treaty between the Saorstat and the U.S.S.R., rather than mere attachment to a British agreement.* In the end the whole matter of treaty negotiation was given a thorough airing in October at the Imperial Conference.†

However, the principal Irish activity prior to the Imperial Conference was at Geneva, in September, when the Free State was elected to the Council of the League. Since their relatively snap decision in 1926 the Irish had nurtured ideas of Council membership, and when Canada was elected in 1927 they had begun to plan to succeed that country. The League of Nations Society of Ireland gave a hint of this hope in April 1928,[2] and in the League Assembly in the following year the Irish delegation let it be known generally that it was the Irish intention to stand in 1930.[3] In Dail Eireann, on 9 April 1930, replying to a remark by Deputy Esmonde, the Minister for External Affairs confirmed the Irish intention and assured the Deputy that there was no question of Australia standing as an alternative Commonwealth candidate. On the contrary, Australia would be supporting Ireland.[4]

* The matter had a sequel later in the year when the British arranged a Treaty with Roumania in August. This Treaty included a similar extension clause (Article 35) and on 1 October 1930, the Irish Government informed the Roumanian Government, through the British Legation, that it did not wish to take advantage of this clause. But it pointed out that most-favoured-nation treatment was in fact accorded by the Saorstat to Roumanian goods and it asked for a similar facility from the Roumanian Government. The Roumanian Government complied with this on 27 October. See A. B. Keith, *Speeches and Documents*, p. 455.

† See Imperial Conference discussion of this, pp. 216–19 below.

The Irish, of course, did not wish to stand as the representative of the Commonwealth or any other bloc, and firmly adhered to their support of the General Assembly and the absolute freedom of that body to choose its Council representatives. But they did recognise the facts of the situation, which would have made it impossible for two Commonwealth members to succeed. Technically Australia was the next senior Dominion to Canada, but in 1926 it had been adamantly against any Dominion candidature. It had now, however, come round more to the Irish Free State view, and it is interesting to read in a letter by Raoul Dandurand, the Canadian Council representative, some of the behind-the-scenes manœuvres on this matter. Writing in Canada, in 1931, Dandurand refers to a Geneva meeting early in 1930:

> We had a gathering of the 'Cubs' – as I used to call the Dominions – and Australia and the Irish Free State had expressed the desire of replacing Canada on the Council. Meeting later on Mr Henderson, I remarked that if we had two Dominions running they would both fail. He wondered if Australia could not claim precedence. I humorously reminded Mr Henderson that the old Kingdom of Ireland was somewhat older and its civilisation also, that Great Britain could hardly argue its own tyrannical domination towards that country for so many centuries. Some time later, I heard that Australia would not be a candidate and I had an interesting conversation with Mr Henderson. I asked him if the good Scot that he was could not make that gesture of good will towards Ireland by announcing his support for the Dublin Government. We were here in Geneva to maintain peace between nations. Was it not our primary duty to work for amity at home? Mr Henderson was looking out on the lake. He stopped a moment to reflect and turning towards me he said with a smile 'I think I can'.
>
> When the Irish Free State announced officially its candidature, Canada sent at once its adhesion. I was not at Geneva last September but I have the impression that Canada's lead was not ineffective.[5]

When, on 17 September 1930, the Free State was elected to a non-permanent Council seat, it was probably the Commonwealth vote which decided the issue. Nevertheless, it was as a small and independent State that the Irish stood. To Ernest Blythe, the chief Irish delegate, their success was no more than a recognition of their consistent honesty and loyalty to the League itself, and their fearless championing of justice irrespective of any group interests.[6] Indeed the Australian, Professor Harrison Moore, thought that the prevalent antagonism to group representation – there were already too many 'group seats' – and the fact that the Irish Dominion was appearing immediately after Canada, would have been sufficient to have ensured defeat for the Free State.[7] In the event, there were only four candidates and the Irish were elected comfortably. (China had applied to be eligible for re-election but did not secure the necessary proportion of votes to allow this.) The number of voting nations was 52, each nation having three votes. Guatemala received 41, Norway 38 and the Irish Free State 36. Portugal received 30 votes, in fourth place.[8] The Irish Free State had received the highest possible honour and it went forward to the Imperial Conference very conscious that its prior responsibility was now to the members of the League.

(ii) INTRODUCTION

The Irish Free State also came to the 1930 Imperial Conference with a particular purpose: to rubber-stamp its achievement of 1929, to record officially the advances of ten years, to close an era of struggle with a harmonious constitutional agreement. The Irish leaders had marshalled some arguments additional to those of the O.D.L. Report, and of course, the Appeal to the Judicial Committee had yet to be tidied away, but they were confident that the 1930 Conference would quickly dispose of all outstanding differences.

Confidence did not lead to a casual approach, however, and the Department of External Affairs prepared its usual thorough briefs. The British Government sent its customary 'Suggested Order of Procedure and Provisional Agenda',* and a close examination was made of this communication. A document was then drawn up of Irish reactions to the British suggestions and from this document and from the items they had already noted, the Irish sent their reply,† indicating to the Conference hosts what matters they specifically desired to settle.

The Irish document is in the nature of a Preliminary Note and it sets out clearly the Irish objectives.‡ Concentrating on the com-

* At the time of drawing up this paper the British anticipated 30 September as the opening day of the Conference. They proposed that the opening speeches – usually printed in full – should this year also be broadcast. The Irish regarded this proposed innovation as 'an attempt to put the Conference violently on the stage of British party politics'. Irish Free State Preliminary note on British suggestions (McGilligan Papers).

† See below, pp. 179–81.

‡ The Irish 'Preliminary Note' was a secret and confidential document prepared for the information of the Executive Council of the Irish Free State only.

prehensive 'Part One' of the Proposed Agenda – 'Questions affecting Inter-Commonwealth relations' – and noting a number of suggestions made by South Africa, the Irish Minister for External Affairs felt bound to propose at least one additional item, namely, 'The Relations between His Majesty the King and the Governments of the Member States of the Commonwealth other than His Majesty's Government in Great Britain'.[9] The Irish wanted to establish direct access to the King in order that the King might be in the Dominions a constitutional monarch in the fullest sense, as he was in the United Kingdom. The use of the British Government by the Dominions as a channel of approach to the King was a source of confusion. As the 1926 Irish Memorandum had pointed out, the King and the British Government were one, the King acting in relation to Britain only on the advice of the elected representatives of the people. Yet, in relation to the Dominions, the King appeared to act on the advice of advisers entirely outside the effective control of the Dominion electorates. Exequaturs, full powers and commissions for Consuls were issued under seals released by a formal executive act of a British Minister.* The entire machinery for the performance of these acts of State on behalf of the Dominions was within the absolute control of the British Government.

Thus, *vis-à-vis* the external world, the British Commonwealth remained an organic unit and it would continue so as long as the machinery of ultimate control in regard to external relations was centred on the British Government. The defective channel of access was at the root of all these difficulties and the Dominions must remedy the situation immediately. The Irish Preliminary Note outlined such a remedy. The most obvious solution would be to substitute the Governor-General for the King in the totality of his functions, but as that would remove all ambiguity as to the 'Personal Union' character of the bond between the nations of the Commonwealth, it would no doubt be unacceptable to the British at this stage. Therefore the Dominion High Commissioner should convey to the King the advice of the Government concerned. A special form signed and sealed by the Minister for External Affairs and stating the act which the King was being advised to perform, would have to be adopted for the purpose.

This Irish document 'while recognising that the form of our

---

* The Warrant authorising the use of the Great Seal, for example, had to be signed by a British Secretary of State.

relations with the King governs our external position more than any other factor',[10] went on to advise that the government was planning to give special attention to nationality, treaties and the intra-Commonwealth court. Under each of these headings followed a small but illuminating paragraph:

> 1. *Nationality* – Our object is twofold, to eliminate the description British Subject and to obtain for Irish, Canadian, Australia, etc., Nationals as such the recognition, rights and privileges at present attaching to British Subjects. The general principle was vaguely admitted at the 1929 Conference. A Nationality Bill is being prepared as the most practical basis for discussion.

[It may be noted that much ground here was covered earlier in the year when the Free State was preparing its brief for the First Conference for the Codification of International Law, the Preparatory Committee for which had been established by the Council of the League of Nations on 28 September 1927.]

> 2. *Treaties* – Apart from the forms connected with the issue of Full Powers and Ratification, there are other factors in the existing procedure which require altering. The *inter se* doctrine, the accession clauses inserted by the British into all their treaties as though they had some inherent right to act for the Dominions, and the granting of privileges to – or the acceptance of obligations for – all British subjects in treaties made by the British are elements in our international position which make it extremely difficult for us to claim that we possess real international status.
>
> 3. *The Intra-Commonwealth Court* – While, for strictly inter-Governmental disputes a Tribunal might be good in itself, for the moment we must regard it as a purely political expedient for getting rid of the Privy Council.

The Document then closed with a diatribe against the Privy Council itself, – a Court

> obnoxious because it is an Extra-State institution exercising judicial control over the internal affairs of the State without any form of democratic sanction.[10]

– and with the specific requirements which the Free State would make of any replacement Commonwealth Tribunal.

This document was modified for British consumption into a despatch (no. 233, 12 September 1930), sent to the Secretary of State for Dominion Affairs. The Despatch became one of the printed documents of the Imperial Conference and it is reproduced below. Perhaps not so fundamental a paper as the Memorandum of 1926, this Despatch nevertheless throws significant light on the Irish attitude in 1930, and its final clause goes a long way to counter later charges of complacency in economic matters which were levelled against the Free State by some British commentators.[11] Numbered E (30) 21 of the Imperial Conference, 1930, and headed 'Certain Questions Raised by The Irish Free State' it proceeds as follows:

Secret Despatch from the Minister for External Affairs of the Irish Free State to the Secretary of State for Dominion Affairs, dated September 12, 1930 No. 233.

Sir,
  I have the honour to refer to my confidential despatch of the 11th July, concerning the Agenda for the Imperial Conference, and to inform you that His Majesty's Government in the Irish Free State, while considering that the principal points which they wish to have specially considered at the Conference could be discussed within the general headings of the proposed Agenda, feel nevertheless that His Majesty's Government in Great Britain may desire to have some definite indication beforehand as to what these points are. They are set out in the following paragraph:—
    2. (1) Appeal to the Judicial Committee of the Privy Council.
       (2) The right of direct access to the King by all his Governments.
       (3) The position of the Members of the Commonwealth in relation to treaty-making, with special reference to the *inter se* application of treaties.
       (4) Communication between His Majesty's Governments other than the British Government and foreign Governments.
    3. The view of His Majesty's Government in the Irish Free State on the Judicial Committee of the Privy Council has been frequently stated. The existence of an extra-state institution claiming without any form of democratic sanction to exercise jurisdiction in the matter of the internal affairs of the Irish Free State remains a menace to our sovereignty. This exercise of jurisdiction constitutes one of the greatest obstacles to the acceptance of the Commonwealth position by a very large number of the citizens of the Irish Free State and it renders more difficult the growth of that close and friendly co-operation between Great Britain and the Irish Free State which is so strongly desired by all the Commonwealth peoples. It is accordingly the intention of His Majesty's Government in the Irish Free State to make known to the delegates of His Majesty's other Governments their desire that the wishes of the majority of their people in the matter of applications for leave to appeal to the Judicial Committee should be carried out.
    4. The right of the Government of each member of the Commonwealth to advise the King is at present exercised through the channel of the Dominions Office and the Foreign Office. This practice has in fact

created an impression that the effective advice in matters relating to the Member of the Commonwealth concerned is that of the British Government. The attendant procedure involves the executive act of a British Minister and the affixing of a seal controlled by a British Minister. The British Government thus act as a barrier between the King and his other Governments and prevent the normal functioning of the constitutional relations which should exist between them and him. The King, being cut off from the Governments of the Members of the Commonwealth and accessible only through the British Government, becomes so identified with the latter that it is impossible for the other Governments to distinguish where the functions of the British Government end and those of the King begin. In other words, whereas the Monarchy in relation to the United Kingdom is strictly constitutional, in relation to the other Members of the Commonwealth it has no existence distinct from that of the United Kingdom Government and is accordingly a very different institution. The resulting position is not merely a constitutional anomaly providing the text-writers with arguments against co-equality of status, but it is also calculated to lead in time to a lessening of the prestige of the Monarchy amongst the Members of the Commonwealth and a consequent weakening of the bond joining those Members together. His Majesty's Government in the Irish Free State therefore consider that the other Commonwealth Governments should be brought in practice into the same relationship with the King as the United Kingdom Government. As the procedure of advising must be entirely within the control of the Governments concerned, it is suggested that the High Commissioner should be used by the advising Minister as his substitute whenever it is impossible for that Minister to go to London for the purpose of tendering the advice. The adoption of this procedure – and it seems to be the most practicable – will entail the granting of a special position of dignity to the High Commissioners.

5. The *inter se* Statement contained in the Report of the 1926 Conference has given rise to a misconception of the international position of the Members of the Commonwealth of Nations. The reference to the statements made at the Arms Traffic Conference clearly implies that the nations of the Commonwealth constitute a single sovereign State. The application of treaties as between the Members of the Commonwealth is a question of convenience, and should depend on mutual co-operation. By agreement amongst themselves the Members of the Commonwealth can declare at the time of signing a treaty in which such a reservation can properly be made that it shall not apply *inter se*.

6. Communication between the Members of the Commonwealth and foreign countries takes place through the British Foreign Office except in the few cases where the Governments of other Members are represented by Ministers Plenipotentiary. The system is very slow, and it gives foreign Governments the impression that the British Government acting through the Foreign Office in London is the supreme authority in the international relations of the other Members of the

Commonwealth as if the Commonwealth were a Federal State. Invitations and communications of all kinds to the Governments of the other Members of the Commonwealth become mere addenda to a document addressed to His Majesty's Government in the United Kingdom. There is in the system an element of tutelage and want of trust unworthy of the position of co-equality of all the Members of the Commonwealth. It is therefore proposed that the Governments of those Members which have no representative in a particular foreign State should address their communications to the British representative for transmission to the Foreign Government. The reply, or any form of communication other than a reply, would be sent direct by the British representative to the Commonwealth Government concerned. As it is only proper that every Government should be fully informed of their representative's activities, it is suggested that a copy of the communication addressed to the Minister Plenipotentiary could be sent by the same post to the Foreign Office. The Minister Plenipotentiary would likewise forward a copy of communications received by him to his own Government.

7. His Majesty's Government in the Irish Free State believe that the elimination of the foregoing difficulties at the Conference will allow the delegates to examine with freer minds the important economic problems which are listed for their consideration.

> I have etc.,
> (Signed) P. McGilligan.
> Minister for External Affairs.[12]

One further document remains which throws an even clearer light on Free State intentions prior to this Conference. It must be remembered that the Canadian Liberal Government of Mackenzie King had fallen, being replaced by the Conservative Administration of R. B. Bennett. Ireland's strongest allies had been overthrown. At the end of August, therefore, a determined attempt was made to educate General Hertzog in the Irish views and to range this charming but often vague and unsuspecting South African Premier behind the Irish objectives. At the Hotel Metropole in Geneva, on Friday 29 August 1930, Patrick McGilligan, accompanied by the Secretary of his Department, Joe Walshe, argued Imperial Conference questions with the General during lunch and for two hours afterwards. The final document is the summary of their conversations, and it appears in full as Appendix D. Briefly, their discussion proceeded under seven main headings: '*inter se*'; 'The King and the Governments of the Dominions'; 'Communications with Foreign Countries'; 'Intra-Commonwealth Tribunal'; 'Nationality'; 'Secession'; 'Legislation by the British Parliament for the Dominions'.

On the *inter se* matter, Hertzog agreed with the Irish that the 1926 *inter se* statement must be altered.* It was not certain, however, that he fully realised its implication that the Commonwealth was a single sovereign state, the relations between its members not being international. This view had been repeated at the League† the previous year on behalf of Great Britain by Sir Cecil Hurst, who framed the original 1926 statement.

Regarding 'The King and the Government of the Dominions', McGilligan informed Hertzog that he would raise the whole question of direct access to the Sovereign. He explained the Irish plan and warned of possible British alternative proposals relating to the establishment of a central Buckingham Palace secretariat to control advice to the King. This alarmed Hertzog, reminding him of Smuts's 1921 proposal.‡ In the end the two leaders seemed to be in accord.

'Communications with Foreign Countries' covered the Irish dissatisfaction at the impression given abroad by Dominion usage of the Foreign Office and with delays occasioned by the procedure adopted hitherto. If Foreign Office officials were to be used, McGilligan maintained, the only proper method was direct correspondence between the Dominion and the plenipotentiary concerned, though copies could, he agreed, be sent to the British Government.

Brief discussion only was given to the proposed 'Intra-Commonwealth Tribunal'. Both agreed that it should be *ad hoc*, though clearly the Irish had thought out the Tribunal in much greater detail. 'Nationality' was also dismissed shortly, these subjects to be resumed at a later chat. Discussion of 'Secession' too was cut short through lack of time, though Hertzog seemed keen on a British declaration that the right of the Dominions to secede was not contested. The South African's passing reference to the Anglo-Irish Treaty is more interesting, indicating that he assumed that the principle of co-equality overrode the terms of that agreement. The continued British right to legislate for the Dominions brought a harmonious interpretation that this really did not apply to their two countries, and the interview concluded amicably with General Hertzog expressing his intention to visit Dublin for a further discussion in mid-September.

The South African did not manage to come to Dublin, in the event,

---

* See pp. 209–12, below, for full details of the Irish case.
† See Appendix D, p. 264.   ‡ See above, p. 7.

until 1 November, when the Imperial Conference was nearly over. He was not, himself, particularly worried by constitutional matters. Had not the O.D.L. Conference settled all these? What interested the General, and what interested the Canadians and the Australians and the New Zealanders, was economic progress. In the face of mounting economic recession the Dominion leaders looked to the Imperial Conference to provide urgently needed solutions. The Commonwealth must fight together in peace through trade, guaranteed markets, preferences and prices, as it had fought together in war through men and arms. In South Africa, General Hertzog had made it clear, as early as April 1930, that 'it will be the economic side which will be given the greatest importance',[13] and he expressed justifiable concern at the declared policy of the British Labour Government and its Chancellor, Snowden; a policy of doctrinaire Free Trade which not only seemed to preclude advances in Imperial Preference but also to threaten even such Preference as already existed.

In Canada, Premier Bennett was determined to advocate a policy of Empire (a word he used deliberately, regretting the loosening of imperial ties) Preference. He did not wish further constitutional advance and he recognised that the doctrines of Philip Snowden were the chief menace to his own economic vision. He came to Britain prepared for a showdown. Premier Scullin of Australia too, beset by enormous financial difficulties occasioned by years of Australian borrowing, had more important things on his mind than constitutional niceties. The new Prime Minister of New Zealand, Mr G. W. Forbes, was content to repeat, before leaving for the Conference, the old New Zealand formula:

> We have no complaints: no demands . . . the next important problem in inter-Empire constitutional relationships is no longer one of freedom and equality but of consultation and co-operation. . . . In Foreign Policy and Defence New Zealand must be largely guided by the experience and necessities of the United Kingdom.[14]

His Chief Justice, Sir Michael Myers, made a typical plea for the retention of the Privy Council as the final appellate tribunal of the Empire – 'the one remaining tangible link between Britain and the Dominions'.[15]

In Britain itself, though the Labour Government seemed committed to a Free Trade policy, no definite pronouncements were made. But, as General Smuts observed from his home Parliament, a feeling for Empire trade was growing there as the Imperial Conference approached. In London, the City became alarmed at the implications of Free Trade and in July urged a measure to promote inter-imperial trade. Bankers, supplemented by the Association of Chambers of Commerce, followed a month later, while in October the Federation of British Industries did likewise. The Economic Committee of the General Council of the T.U.C. in September urged that the 1930 Imperial Conference be used 'to press for as full a development as possible of the economic relations between the constituent parts of the British Commonwealth'.[16] These resolutions were vague enough, but they represented an uneasiness and an awareness that something must be done to weld together a strengthened Empire based on its undoubted resources and great market potential. *The Times* on 31 July explained that inter-imperial trade was the vital question. 'By comparison with the problem of how to re-establish our declining prosperity the discussion of academic legal and constitutional questions becomes a mere pedantic futility'.[17] As the Conference drew closer, so the urgency of concentration on economic matters became more obvious. On 1 October, the day the Conference opened, *The Times* was optimistic: the leaders of the Dominions were all endowed with a sense of purpose in the economic sphere. To the *Irish Times* too on that date, the problem was clear cut. The Conference, it pronounced in a leading article, 'will be remembered either as a turning point in the history of the British Empire or as a classic instance of the lost opportunity'.[18] Some constitutional matters remained, it conceded, but 'it will be a calamity if these and like issues are allowed to steal the Conference's time and to divert its attention from the paramount question of imperial trade'.[19]

The Commonwealth awaited economic developments to match the constitutional advances of the past decade. There was an expectation that the Cobdenite Snowden would be brushed aside. Even in France there was an alarmed regret that Britain appeared to be deflecting more and more from her European role. How then can the Irish have concentrated their preparation on mere constitutional issues?

The answer is simple. It is contained in the last paragraph of their reply to Britain. Let the Conference admit straight away the logic of the Irish constitutional demands and then let it get down to economic business. In his opening statement to the Conference Mr McGilligan did say clearly that for his country 'the recognition of our position as a free and sovereign State comes before all other considerations'. And, he went on to add:

> We desire to be able to devote ourselves entirely to the development of the prosperity of our people and to co-operation with the other Governments of the Commonwealth in raising the level of human happiness in other countries. While certain elements of the old system of Imperial control were maintained, even though it was only in form, the will to co-operate was correspondingly weakened. We most earnestly urge upon the present Conference the need of removing finally those last obstacles to harmonious and easy intercourse. So long as any form of control remained co-operation had to be tinged with some colouring of compulsion. That made it less wholehearted and less effective.
>
> I should not be frank with you if at this juncture I did not definitely place before you in what seems to my Government to be the proper perspective the considerations which should govern the proceedings of this Conference.[20]

He did emphasise his country's concern for constitutional matters. But he went on to affirm in his statement to the economic session on 8 October an equally fundamental belief:

> To the peoples of the States which are Members of the Commonwealth, the most effective test of the practical measure of co-operation to which we attain will be a test on the economic plane. It has been my duty during the past week to urge upon meetings of the heads of delegations an Irish Free State point of view in the political sphere sometimes more advanced than that adopted by some other delegations. The heads of some other delegations have asserted with emphasis that their relations within the Commonwealth involve the closest ties in outlook and aspiration. It will create, I imagine, some confusion in the mind of the ordinary citizen should he discover that the intimate character claimed for those ties is inadequately reflected in the economic sphere.[21]

The *Irish Times*, by no means a Government instrument, had already assumed on 1 October that constitutional issues would quickly be settled, and it had proceeded to make a sound additional comment:

> If Irish statesmanship helps the Conference to contrive a system that will give an enormous stimulus to Irish trade, the Free State Government will have won its greatest triumph and incidentally, will have confounded its domestic foes.[22]

It was in the Irish interest to see an economic settlement reached. But the Free State was in no position to make the running in the economic sphere. It could offer to Britain nothing more: already 80 per cent of Irish imports came from the Commonwealth, and 94 per

cent of its exports went to the Commonwealth, and in this context
the Commonwealth virtually meant Britain. Even if Britain was
now offered free entry into the Free State, this would not compen-
sate Britain for erecting tariff walls simply to benefit Ireland. The
Irish Free State could only wait for the major trading Dominions to
take the initiative and then try to tack Irish goods on to any preferential list which might emerge. This was the only possible Irish
economic policy now, as it had been all along.

But on the constitutional side it could and did take the lead.
When the Conference divided into constitutional and economic
committees, the Irish, under Patrick McGilligan, presented a clear
and forthright plan to the former. That the British chose to argue
with a medieval scholastic mentality was not the fault of the delegates from Dublin. That the British had nothing to offer on the
economic side was also no fault of the Irish. It was therefore quite
unfair, as some did afterwards, to accuse the Free State because the
Conference was a calamitous failure. Any achievements which were
recorded were on the constitutional side and for these, once again,
credit was due to the Irish. For the economic failure the British must
bear much responsibility.

But let us look at the Conference in detail: let us watch it develop
and let us analyse, from its Report, what was in fact achieved. It will
soon become clear why no economic progress was made, and if we
thereafter concentrate on constitutional matters it will be because,
once again, only in these matters were detailed solutions worked out
in advance, thereby making progress possible, and because, for want
of concrete alternatives, the Conference devoted so much time to
them.

(iii) THE CONFERENCE

The Conference opened on Wednesday 1 October 1930. That morning the death of Lord Birkenhead was announced in the press,
casting gloom over the proceedings but scarcely dimming the
exuberant newspaper expectations. Times were bad and the Conference afforded at least some hope of improvement. Further distress,
however, was occasioned by the loss of the Airship R101 on 5
October, at the cost of forty-eight lives. But it was not until a
considerable time after this tragedy that the newspapers and the
delegates themselves realised that the Conference too was going to
perish ignominiously.

It started off briskly enough. R. M. Smyllie, providing once again a detailed Conference diary in the *Irish Times*, described a scene of unprecedented urgency and determination to get down immediately to business. Yet the assembled delegates wore anxious faces as they set about their task. The front of the Prime Minister's house, wrote Smyllie, 'presented a lugubrious picture until Messrs. McGilligan and Hogan bounded up the steps with a merry jest'. He went on to describe the Irish leaders:

> Mr McGilligan possibly has not the constructive imagination of the late Mr Kevin O'Higgins, to whose memory many graceful tributes were paid to-day; but he has an incisive mind, a quick wit and a gift of analytical criticism which are likely to leave their mark upon the work of the Conference. . . . Mr Hogan in 24 hours has established himself as the most popular of all the delegates. His straightforward manner, impatience of nonsense and shrewdness of judgment coupled with a high order of imaginative intelligence have been recognised by all who have met him. Mr FitzGerald, I think, is the doyen of the Conference. He has been negotiating with British Governments for some nine years and his experience of the Conference table will be useful to the Free State delegation.[23]

Desmond FitzGerald, whose frequent letters home to his wife provide additional Conference information, explained the glum faces noted by Smyllie. 'The world slump', he wrote, 'has them all in a bad way. Each wonders if the other can do anything for them – conscious of a Press-doped public outside who expect what is obviously impossible.'[24] Mention of the press was to recur in Fitz-Gerald's letters, for he felt that the Tory papers were unfair in their coverage to the British Labour Government, and he suspected that they were in league with the Conservative Bennett in a plot to bring down the Labour Administration. He also mentions one other recurring feature in his first letters. Not only does he indicate the immense amount of Irish memoranda which he had to digest, but he also points out the poor equipment of the British leaders. On the second day of the Conference he could say:

> MacDonald and Thomas were badly briefed so the discussion wandered into byways, with self and P. McG. acting as general advisers to the whole lot. Fortunately it gave me a sense of confidence I have never had before, though I haven't read a document.[25]

And on the following day he was more explicit:

> it is irritating to be dealing with men who are badly briefed. They were discussing matters and had (or pretended to have) the wrong end of the

stick. I told them that I had dealt with the matter in '26 and what the
circumstances were. MacD. said I was wrong and proceeded to prove it
by reading from the report and landed on a sentence that just proved
what I said. That sort of thing happens constantly – and makes them
irritable.[26]

What happened at the beginning was to continue throughout the
Conference. FitzGerald's sympathies are constantly torn, feeling
that too much was being demanded of the British Government by a
hostile press, but also being convinced before long that bad faith and
double dealing as well as bad briefing characterised the British
delegation.

On Thursday 2 October a Committee under Lord Sankey was set
up to deal with 'Certain Aspects of Inter-Imperial Relations': the
'General Economic Committee' was also set to work, the Irish
representative on the latter being the Hon. Gordon Campbell.
Smyllie indicated that there seemed no likelihood of a change in the
British attitude to food taxes, while FitzGerald noted on Sunday the
fifth: 'I don't think anything will be done on the economic side here
that amounts to much. It is a peculiar position to have the newspapers
foretelling solutions that don't exist.'[27]

On the sixth the Heads of the Delegations, chaired by Scullin in
the absence of MacDonald, discussed the 'Judicial Committee' and
'Nationality' and then, following what was to become the general
pattern, passed these subjects on to the 'Sankey Committee'. By the
seventh an air of expectancy permeated every lobby: the second
plenary meeting was planned for the following day, when the
economic discussion would be opened by Mr Thomas.

On the eighth battle was firmly joined. The *Irish Times* had noted
how much the British leaders were hedging already on economic
matters and how they were trying to push these into the background.
But now the time had come. Mr Thomas made a good speech but it
was Bennett of Canada who bluntly and unequivocally brought
Empire Preference to the fore, condemned even Empire Free Trade
and demanded a straight British answer on economic policy. Policies
and personalities were now squarely in the ring and the most vital
Conference problems were at issue. Wide publicity was given to
Bennett's speech, and next day Baldwin endorsed its principle, on
behalf of the British Tory Party, by accepting the case for Preference.
On the ninth also, on behalf of the Labour Government, Snowden,
tight-lipped, doctrinaire Cobdenite and Chancellor of the Exchequer,

replied with brutal force. He banged the door firmly in Bennett's face. He told him that his Canadian proposals were as clear as mud, and that he could go and trade with the United States if dissatisfied with Great Britain.[28] Thomas added, in an unfortunately publicised phrase, that he regarded Bennett's speech as humbug.* FitzGerald paints the scene:

> Bennett came along with his big stick to the British Government. His speech was really outrageous. I imagine it was written in Beaverbrook's. I imagine also that Bennett will come a cropper. He talks too big and has probably been very bombastic in Canada and made general promises that certainly will not be fufilled.[29]

Snowden, unable to reply until the Economic Committee met on the ninth, had been observed by FitzGerald on the eighth.

> Snowden is not a cheerful looking man – but he got less and less cheerful. If he had to speak I imagine that he would have had to indicate what he thought of Bennett. I was quite indignant myself on behalf of the British Government. . . . I feel sorry for the Government here – Outside is the populace expecting great economic results – and I don't see that they can get anything. And inside are we, demanding constitutional changes – and some at least will have to be given – so that the Labourites may be denounced for busting the Empire as well as for economic failure.[30]

On Friday the tenth he was able to report with perhaps a misplaced satisfaction:

> Yesterday morning was the come back of Snowden on Bennett. It was masterly and courageous. Extremely so. When someone said – 'you were very frank' – he said 'I could be much franker'. He also stated he would like an opportunity to get the same publicity for his views as the others had for theirs. He faced up to facts in a way that is almost unknown to politicians. He certainly wiped the floor with Bennett.[31]

Three days later FitzGerald summarised his impression of this controversial exchange:

> I must say I think Snowden has been treated abominably. First of all he had to listen to a speech by Bennett (by many considered as made on behalf of the Conservative party *here* and to knock out the Labour

* Thereafter Thomas was known in Canada as 'Jimmy 'Umbug'. See for example Canadian Public Archives, 'Charles Murphy Papers: Correspondence', pp. 977–88. In a letter on 12 May 1932 to Prime Minister R. B. Bennett, the Canadian Senator refers to Bennett's invitation to de Valera in connection with the forthcoming Ottawa Conference . . . 'your method of dealing with the Irish Spaniard was a stroke of genius. But its political skill would not be apparent to stupid Anglo-Saxons like Jimmy 'Umbug who were trained in the methods of Bill Sykes. . . .'

Party). That speech reported in full. Then when S. replied to it – a reply that demolished Bennett – it was in a private session. But although it being a private session it was not reported, the Newspapers know enough about it to attack him for it, but the case he made is not public.[32]

FitzGerald's sympathy on the economic struggle was with the British. He saw that Bennett was not offering very much in return for the risks which were involved for Britain, 70 per cent of whose trade lay outside the Commonwealth. 'Bennett says', wrote Fitz-Gerald on the fourteenth:

that Britain banged the door by saying no tariffs – McG suggested that to say no other means of doing anything was banging the door . . . looks as though Bennett in close touch with Government's opposition. . . . Britain will make proposals for quotas etc. Not much in it probably – but there seems to be nothing in the other proposals so far.[33]

Thus the great opportunity, if it ever was one, was squandered. On the fifteenth FitzGerald recorded:

yesterday morning economic C'tee quite interesting. Bennett seems sulking and nursing grievances and Snowden watching him like a terrier. . . . The Labour alternatives to Bennett seem to be in the line of quotas, allocations of markets, bulk purchase and things like that, but it is doubtful if anything will be done on economic side. I hear that R. MacD., Jowitt and two others in the Cabinet lean towards tariffs – and the remainder are with Snowden. I would say that Snowden and those with him consider things on their merits while the former are intimidated by press and think of effect on fortunes of party.[34]

The next day he observed that:

Snowden determined to tell Bennett what he thought of his goings on here and prepared to fight his own colleagues who were trying to hinder him. Ramsay is doing the heavy milk of human kindness stunt – Snowden wants the codology cut out. I have sympathy with Snowden. He knows his own mind – and he knows a lot about economics while his colleagues – except Graham – are woolly. He knows just how little can be done – and doesn't see any use in pretending to be blind. . . . Snowden is all that a politician is supposed not to be. When he comes out in the open against Bennett it will be pretty straight if his colleagues don't tie his hands. When he talked about Bennett's speeches today B asked him would he like to write a speech for him. Snowden said 'certainly – if you promise to deliver it'.[35]

The blustering and the divisions went on. By the end of the Conference there was only bad feeling and resentment where so much optimism had been before. Bennett himself was indignant. On

11 December, as L. S. Amery reports him, he blamed J. H. Thomas, who had

> condemned beyond the possibility of further discussion and in language deeply resented by the Government of Canada, the proposal which I made in sincere desire to meet our individual and common needs . . . and he has condemned it without offering a single proposal . . . as an alternative.[36]

At the close of the Conference the exhausted FitzGerald was prepared to comment in support:

> Yesterday afternoon was economic affairs – Amusingly plain spoken. The British were told that they had been fooling the Dominions. Having told them to go off and examine various alternatives to tariffs they are told that the British will not legislate for any of them. Also having told the Dominions they will not put tariffs on food (the only thing of interest to the Doms) they turn around at the end and propose that all agree not to increase tariffs against England until three years hence – or after the Ottawa Conference whichever soonest. It is really all farcical – An awful display of ineptitudes. Trying to be clever they have only made things worse for themselves.[37]

But by now the Irish veteran had little sympathy left for his British opponents. 'Such a cowardly lot we have to deal with,' he wrote in despair. 'Won't ever say what their point of view is – only what the Die-hard opposition will say'.[38]

Clearly the British Government was divided against itself, and in the end the unyielding Snowden prevailed. Snowden was iron-willed and utterly uncompromising, and, as FitzGerald has indicated, he made no bones about his views. J. H. Thomas was his direct antithesis. An eloquent Trade Union Leader, to whom the letter *h* was unknown, he looked for results in any direction. To the Dominions he offered Defence and in return asked for Preference. To this Bennett in effect stated: We ask Preference for Preference and we want Defence for nothing (and, he had added later, We will put you out of office!). Bennett was supported by the Hon. Hugh Guthrie, an apoplectic-looking imperialist who wished to alter all mention in the O.D.L. Report of the 'British Commonwealth' to read 'British Empire'. The Canadians appeared at the Conference to threaten formidable opposition to Irish aspirations, particularly as they replaced the former Irish allies, King and Lapointe and Skelton. But even though FitzGerald wrote, half-way through the Conference:

The Government here is in terror of being landed in Parliament through anything we force them to – That and the defeat of MacKenzie King are our two handicaps,[39]

the Canadians turned out to be the most courteous and helpful friends. Once rebuffed on their economic schemes Bennett and Guthrie understood the Irish desire for complete constitutional autonomy and did everything they could to help.

The Australians too were a new proposition for the Irish. But when McGilligan saw the names Scullin, Parker Moloney and Brennan, he knew that the battle was half won. And so it turned out. Fellow Catholics, the Australians also proved loyal supporters. After a fortnight, FitzGerald was able to write:

> Scullin of Australia is very good. Though he wants things like Bennett, he is quite indignant at what he considers a plot against the Labour Government in the interest of snobbism. Also he recognises that on the constitutional side we are the authorities. He wants what we want – but has not thought it out in detail – and recognises that we have. When we meet people that have been in touch with the Australians we find that they have heard that we do the work. Scullin is amused at our direct brutal way – asks if we do politics that way in Ireland.[40]

Later in the week he added: 'Scullin is quite nice – simple – honest and a clear mind. Irish minds do shine by their clarity in the woolliness here', and he followed his line of thought to compliment the two British ministers who retained Irish respect, if not Irish support, all through the Conference: 'I don't know if Snowden has anything Irish about him – but if not he is an exception. I must admit that Graham (Bd of Trade) is very good also. . . .'[41]

There is no doubt, however, that FitzGerald's chief affection was reserved for Hertzog, and that it was the South Africans, in effect Bodenstein and van den Heever, who co-operated most closely on the constitutional issues which still caused concern to the Irish. Hertzog did not change:

> He is a fine loyal soul absolutely at one with us but sometimes he thinks that there will be no opposition and presumes that he hasn't to worry – and at others fails to see the ramifications of things. But his right point of view prevents him from going too far wrong.[42]

Earlier he had written:

> Hertzog is a dear – even though he sometimes goes entirely wrong through not understanding things. His staff want to get us after him more to keep him right. But he is a dear loyal man – even if a bit woolly. And when he has taken up a line and finds that it runs counter to us (and consequently to what he really stands for) he often tries to get back and

explain away what he said. Yesterday we had New Zealand supporting us – Hertzog had gone off the track. Te Water told me afterwards that he caught hold of the General and said – when Ireland and New Zealand are together for heavens sake back them.[43]

Here it is FitzGerald writing, but it might be either Murphy or McGilligan, both of whom confirm the efforts of van den Heever and Bodenstein to keep their leader up to the mark, and both of whom underline the frequent discussions which took place between the South African and Irish teams.

(iv) THE SANKEY COMMITTEE

No doubt much helpful detail was salvaged from the Economic Committee.* What there was is listed in the second half of the Conference Report. But the Commonwealth took little comfort from this. It had expected a major restorative operation and it was outraged at the prescription of a mere bottle of palliative pills.

The economic squabble, however, had direct repercussions on the constitutional negotiations. It lined up the Canadians behind the Irish, but it also put the British Government hard back against the wall and diminished the chances of compromise. Tempers were often frayed and intransigence and casuistry played an unprecedented part in these 'family' discussions. Personalities assumed an unusual degree of significance, not so much through their force as through their incompatibility. And all the time the innumerable social commitments forced an intense pressure on the time and stamina of the delegates. Day after day the discomfort of hotel life, the endless talks and interviews and the dinners and luncheons with their attendant wearisome speeches are bemoaned by Desmond FitzGerald. Sleep was at a premium: most members of a visiting delegation were on different committees, and at night, often in the early hours, all would meet, report and hammer out policy. The weeks wore on, the pace never slackened and still nothing was accomplished. The frustrations of time wasted through British indecision, personal vendettas, failure to understand owing to careless preparation, and downright recantation of agreed points added to the strain. New friendships, the occasional theatre, a little ice-skating, provided some compensation, but an Imperial Conference

---

* Smyllie refers to the General Economic Committee by its Conference name – 'the red herring Committee', *Irish Times*, 15 October 1930.

was never a soft assignment and this one was harder than most. FitzGerald is often off his food, has headaches, is exhausted: yet all the time he has room to pity and wonder at McGilligan, who had to withstand and to achieve so much more. For in spite of it all much was achieved.

The Sankey Committee provided the battleground upon which such achievements as there were, were won. This Committee was of major importance to the Conference. A communiqué* dated 6 October recounts its formation:

At Meetings of Prime Ministers, Heads of Delegations and other Delegates held at Number 10 Downing Street, S.W.1. on Thursday the 2nd October, and Friday the 3rd October, 1930, respectively it was agreed to set up a Committee under the Chairmanship of the Right Honourable Lord Sankey, to consider such aspects of Inter-Imperial Relations as might be referred to it by the Prime Ministers and Heads of Delegations.†

It was also agreed to refer the question of an Empire Tribunal to this Committee, which would consider the whole question in the light of the discussion which had taken place at the meeting of the Prime Ministers and Principal Delegates, and that the Committee should take into consideration, *inter alia*, the wording of the reservations made to the signature of the Optional Clause.†

It was also agreed to refer to the Committee the following questions included in the Provisional Agenda. (E. (30) 18 page 4):†
III (*a*) Advice to the King:
　　(*b*) Appointment of Governors-General:
　　(*c*) Issue of Full Powers:
　　(*d*) Issue of Exequaturs to Foreign Consuls:
VI‡　Form of Commercial Treaties.
VII‡　*Inter se* Applicability Agreements.
VIII‡　Phraseology in Official Documents.

The composition of the Committee is set out on the attached sheet.

Arrangements have been made for meetings of the Committee to be held in the Moses Room, House of Lords.

Lord Sankey hopes that it will be convenient to the Members of the Committee that the first meeting should be held on Tuesday, the 7th October, 1930 at 11.00 a.m. An Agenda paper for this meeting has been circulated.

Copies of this Notice have been sent to all Delegations.
(Signed) M. P. A. Hankey.
Secretary to the Conference.

Notes: † See P.M. (30) 2 Minutes 2, 3, 4.
　　‡ See P.M. (30) 3 Minutes 5. 6.
* All the quoted material below, pp. 194–7, is taken from the records of the 'Committee on certain aspects of inter-imperial relations', hereafter cited as the 'Sankey Committee' (McGilligan Papers).

On 6 October the subjects of 'Nationality', 'Nationality of Married Women' and the 'Judicial Committee of the Privy Council' were added to the Committee's Agenda. The Composition of the Committee was as follows:

CHAIRMAN:—The Right Honourable Lord Sankey, G.B.E., United Kingdom.

Representatives of United Kingdom		Sir William Jowitt, K.C., M.P.
„	„ Canada	Hon. M. Dupré, M.C., M.P.
		Mr J. E. Read, K.C.
„	„ Commonwealth of Australia	Hon. F. Brennan, M.P.
		Sir R. Garran, K.C.M.G.
„	„ New Zealand	Hon. G. W. Forbes, M.P.
		Hon. Sir T. Sidey, M.P.
„	„ Union of South Africa	Gen. Hon. J. B. M. Hertzog, M.P.
		Mr F. van den Heever
„	„ Irish Free State	Mr P. McGilligan, T.D.
		Mr D. FitzGerald, T.D.
		Mr P. Hogan, T.D.
		Mr J. A. Costello, K.C.
„	„ Newfoundland	The Rt Hon. Lord Morris, K.C., K.C.M.G.
„	„ India	The Rt Hon. Wedgwood Benn, M.P.
		Sir Muhammad Shafi, K.C.S.I., C.I.E.
Secretaries	United Kingdom	{ Sir H. Batterbee, K.C.V.O., C.M.G.
		Mr R. B. Howorth, C.B.

(Dominion Secretaries to be notified later)

It called upon the following advisers, among others:—

UNITED KINGDOM
Sir Claud Schuster
Sir E. J. Harding
Mr H. G. Bushe
Mr G. R. Warner

Sir Maurice Gwyer
Sir H. W. Malkin
Mr W. F. Dowson
Sir H. Fountain

CANADA
Mr C. P. Plaxton

COMMONWEALTH OF AUSTRALIA
Mr R. G. Casey

UNION OF SOUTH AFRICA
Mr H. T. Andrews

IRISH FREE STATE   Mr S. Murphy
Mr D. O'Hegarty   Mr J. J. Hearne
Mr J. P. Walshe

NEW ZEALAND
Mr C. A. Berendsen   [Publicity]
Mr Malcolm MacDonald
Mr C. Beckett Platt

And it split itself into a number of sub-committees, four of which are set out:—

Merchant Shipping	*Form of Commercial Treaties*
U.K.	Sir W. Malkin, K.C.M.G., C.B.
Sir Thomas Barnes, C.B.E.	
Mr G. H. Bushe	
Canada	
Mr C. P. Plaxton	Mr J. Read
Australia	
Sir R. Garran	
S.A.	
Mr F. P. van den Heever	Dr H. D. J. Bodenstein
I.F.S.	
Mr J. J. Hearne	Mr S. Murphy
Newfoundland	
Lord Morris, K.C., K.C.M.G.	Lord Morris
India	
Sir G. Corbett, K.B.E., C.I.E., I.C.S.	Sir G. Corbett
New Zealand	
Mr C. A. Berendsen	Mr C. A. Berendsen
CHAIRMAN	
Sir C. Hipwood, K.B.E., C.B. (U.K.)	Sir R. Garran (Australia)

The Great Seal	*Nationality*
U.K.	Sir C. Schuster
CHAIR: Sir C. Schuster	Sir M. Gwyer
Sir H. F. Batterbee	Sir W. Malkin
(G. R. Warner)	Mr W. F. Dowson
Canada	
Mr J. E. Read	Mr J. E. Read
Australia	
Mr R. G. Casey	Sir R. Garran
South Africa	Mr F. P. van den Heever
Dr H. D. J. Bodenstein	

The Great Seal—cont.

Irish Free State
Mr J. A. Costello

New Zealand
Mr F. D. Thomson

Nationality—cont.
Mr J. J. Hearne
Mr S. Murphy

Mr C. A. Berendsen

The Sankey Committee was an imposing body, and, as the Conference Report indicates, its primary task was to review the O.D.L. Report. But it did not make rapid progress; nor was it noted for its harmonious discussions. By 13 October FitzGerald wrote that he would not go to the Lord Chancellor's breakfast:

> Last night when talking about him I said that he couldn't stand the sight of me. Most of them had not noticed but Dermot* saw that that was so. Had noticed that he was offensive when I explained circumstances of appointment of last Canadian G.G. That he habitually interrupted me. Of course he does that with everyone – when they are demolishing what he wants. He had done it worse with Tody† than with me. But in general however I can see that he can't stand me.[11]

On the fifteenth he added:

> Sankey Committee this afternoon. S. up to his usual dodges. Poor S. African (van den Heever) who has very sound ideas – but almost stammers when speaking so seems very shy and nervous, interrupted with a view to bewildering him. But anything he left vague was made very clear by Tody and me. Old S. much more civil to me, but probably doesn't feel it – He read out a form of words for agreement, and I suggested an amendment by deleting 3 words. Thanked me and said he quite understood my point and then added that he was rather afraid of me and would like to consider the suggestion between now and next meeting. Dermot said that he was very annoyed at having worded the thing in the way he did that was so simple to amend to give what I wanted.[45]

On Friday the seventeenth, Lord Sankey himself outlined their work to date. 'He understood that the position was as follows:

> Nationality: had been referred to a sub-committee.
> Empire Tribunal: had been discussed.
> Defence questions: had been referred to a sub-committee (he had taken note of Mr McGilligan's objection to the use of the word 'defence' but he thought that that word was convenient as a short description of the only two subjects involved, namely Prize and Discipline of the Armed Forces).

* Diarmuid O'Hegarty.
† P. McGilligan: a childhood nickname (corruption of Paddy) which stuck.

Advice to the King: had been discussed.
Appointment of Governors-General: had been discussed.
Exequaturs to Foreign Consuls: had been discussed.
Channels of Communication with For. Govts: was on Agenda for
to-day.
Communication and Consultation: was also on Agenda.
Technical phraseology: had been discussed.
There remained the O.D.L. Report and Merchant Shipping.'[46]

The Lord Chancellor thought that the technical subject of Merchant
Shipping ought to be referred to a sub-committee on which each
Dominion had a representative, but did they want the sub-committee
to elect a chairman or an official of the Board of Trade with technical
knowledge to be supplied? Sir Thomas Sidey said the latter, and Sir
Charles Hipwood was appointed. Finally:

> The Lord Chancellor observed that this left the consideration of the
> O.D.L. Report and Mr McGilligan's point regarding appeals to the
> Privy Council as the only outstanding items on the Agenda, and they
> would be taken as soon as the discussion of the existing agenda was
> completed.[47]

It is interesting to note that on the same day that Lord Sankey was
giving his summary Desmond FitzGerald records the dissatisfaction
felt by the British Premier:

> MacDonald said how worried he was as Parlt. is to meet week after next
> and he has to speak – and it will not be enough to tell them that we are
> still discussing matters. He went on to say how disappointed he was at
> the slowness of the Sankey Committee – I made it perfectly clear that
> greatest hindrance to progress was Sankey. . . . We have done practi-
> cally nothing here so far though we haven't had much spare time. But
> we are reaching the stage when it is felt that we must get a move on. It
> is always the same in these things.[48]

A week later – on the twenty-fourth – the situation had not improved:

> Things are rather crucial at the moment – and it looks as though we may
> be minority reporting on most subjects – and things are now being
> rushed that will tend still more in that direction as it takes time to
> agree.[49]

On the twenty-eighth he could not say how things would go:

> Spoke to Hertzog about the need to postpone his departure. But he is
> blandly oblivious and thinks all is well – and that it is straight running.
> Of course we may bust quickly not agreeing.[50]

There was of course particular pressure on the Irish:

> Things are very trying here . . . it is awful trying to get agreement here
> to things without yielding anything that will be harmful at home. . . .
> At the same time there is a rush to get reports agreed – and an im-
> patience at objections that make difficulties and delay. And even the
> delegations that really have our point of view have gone into things so
> carelessly that they are prepared to accept things without realising what
> they mean.[51]

According to Smyllie, in the *Irish Times*, the Sankey Committee
ended its labours at noon on 4 November. It made 'a number of
minor recommendations' and made an exhaustive survey of the
O.D.L. Report, but it 'shirked the Judicial Committee of the Privy
Council'.[52] But this issue was taken up, with others, by the Heads of
Delegations in an atmosphere of increasing acrimony. On 6 November FitzGerald wrote home in exhaustion to his wife:

> Yesterday was appalling. Massed British guns directed on us – I never
> had such a day. . . . Faced with dishonesty, treachery and cowardice.
> Only satisfaction is that no one could have any doubt as to who won the
> arguments – or who had right on their side. Scullin and Hertzog
> splendid. (I am referring to the Privy Council matter) British have
> consulted the Tories and are told they will be . . .* if they meet us on
> that point. Don't know what the outcome will be. They may make some
> proposition – but I don't know what. They got some plain speaking
> from us. On another matter (*inter se*) we just broke. . . . Plainer speaking
> than yesterday. Tody told off old Sankey so much in the morning – that
> he did not appear in the afternoon. Probably told that his presence
> might annoy us. Discussion might be said to be satisfactory from one
> point of view – that the other Dominions should at least be impressed
> by our case. But wearing and depressing for us.[53]

On the eleventh, when the Conference was almost over, he could
still summon up indignation:

> We get no peace at all for even when we have fought our end out in
> Conference we have to watch the report of the meetings – and if we have
> got away with anything in one – Thomas will bring it up again at the
> next and try to confuse it . . . I am in an irascible mood. I find it very
> hard to be civil to people like Thomas – or MacDonald.[54]

On the constitutional side, then, as on the economic, this Imperial
Conference displayed an unusual degree of temper and engendered
unprecedented bitterness. As the *Irish Times* observed indignantly,
this was 'the first Imperial Conference under a Labour Government
in Great Britain. We hope it will be the last'.[55] *The Times* condemned

* Word indecipherable, but general sense is plain.

the utter indecision, lack of preparation and procrastination of the British Government.[56] But it is time to leave the atmosphere and the back-biting and to turn to the Report. Like the Report of 1923, it failed to mention some of the more significant items discussed, but it did include some valuable work, particularly its endorsement of the O.D.L. Report, with which it began.

(v) THE CONFERENCE REPORT

To the Irish, the O.D.L. Report had seemed an excellent document. But now, in 1930, they found that the British were less happy about it. However, it was not until the Conference was nearly three weeks old that proper discussion of it was joined, 20 and 21 October witnessing arguments on the Colonial Laws Validity Act and a number of other items covered by the O.D.L. Committee. The British had little room to manœuvre as substantial agreement had been reached in the previous year, and in the end the Imperial Conference made no major alterations. The recommendations for a Statute of Westminster were officially approved and the Articles of that Bill were scheduled to the Conference Report, with a number of resolutions designed to expedite its enactment.' 1 December 1931, was proposed as the date from which the Statute would become operative* and a request was made for Supporting Resolutions, passed by both Houses of the Dominion Parliaments, to be forwarded to the United Kingdom Parliament before 1 August. Thus the main part of the O.D.L. Report moved forward towards fulfilment. The Conference, if it did nothing more, had at least justified its existence. But there was in fact a little more.

Nationality problems, for one thing, demanded attention. In the Conference Report these are treated immediately after the Statute of Westminster recommendation, and the general principles of nationality, laid down the year before,[57] were confirmed in the face of strong British opposition. Here in fact lay another Irish victory, but then nationality had always been one of the Free State Government's long suits. From the moment of its establishment the Free State had used every available opportunity to emphasise the difference between Irish and British citizenship, and it had now brought to this Imperial Conference the draft of its own proposed Nationality Bill. This Bill

* This was partly to suit the Irish Free State in view of the General Election due there in 1932.

would be based on the British 'Nationality and Status of Aliens Act, 1914', but it would be redrawn to fit Irish requirements. When preparing for the Conference for the Codification of International Law, the Free State had expressed the keenest interest in such questions as the acquisition and loss of nationality, statelessness, dual nationality, the effect of marriage and the dissolution of marriage upon nationality, and the diplomatic protection of nationals,[58] and J. A. Costello had come straight from that Codification Conference at Geneva to the Imperial Conference with these topics fresh in his mind. Meanwhile, John Hearne had prepared an interpretive memorandum for his Irish colleagues on the major sections of his proposed Irish Nationality Bill, to help them at the conference table. This Nationality Bill was in accordance with the O.D.L. conclusions which were summarised thus:

> Heretofore the law of nationality radiated throughout the Commonwealth from the British Statute Book, which was its ultimate authority. In future the citizens of each State will look to the law of that State itself for the ultimate legal basis of their status. And that status will, notwithstanding the change in its legal foundation be the same as heretofore by reason of the nature of the Commonwealth Association and the agreement reached. . . . (First) an agreed basis of citizenship will have to be worked out. Once the agreed basis is fixed the question of status is solved.

Hearne underlined the basis of the Irish Bill in relation to the common status sought after for all Commonwealth citizens:

> A fundamental term of the agreement would, it is thought, relate to the group or class to be enfranchised as natural born citizens and for that purpose section 1 of the Nationality and Status of Aliens Act, 1914 may be suggested to us as a basis of discussion. . . .

With reference to naturalised citizens he drew the important distinction that

> the form of oath (if any) to be taken by applicants for naturalisation in Saorstat Eireann could not be in the form contained in the second schedule to the N. and S. of A. Act, 1914 [but he assumed that] . . . the granting of certificates of naturalisation . . . will be in accordance with procedure and subject to conditions similar to these laid down in Part 11 of the Nationality and Status of Aliens Act, 1914.

The policy of the Irish Free State begins to emerge:

> Our law should provide that British subjects and Canadian subjects etc., living in Saorstat Eireann shall have the same status as citizens of Saorstat Eireann. The status of such persons will not depend upon any resort to the naturalisation procedure but rather will be automatic by

virtue of a section in our Nationality Act itself declaring the status of these persons to be the same as, or of a like character to, the status of our own nationals. . . . The Department of External Affairs hopes . . . that by virtue of their citizenship of Saorstat Eireann our nationals will be entitled to the status of British subjects while in London, of Canadian subjects while in Ottawa, and of South African citizens while in Pretoria.[59]

This basis was infinitely preferable, the self-conscious Dominion felt, to the old, all-embracing category of 'British Subject'. It represented a more acceptable position than that posed by the British 'umbrella' theory, or the latest manifestation of that theory, the 'orange skin' theory (that the Dominions could have their own citizenship nestling inside an outer skin of British subjecthood). The Irish Free State representatives explained to the Sankey Committee that they wanted their own citizenship first and would be happy to add the superstructure of a Commonwealth agreement on top of this. Once more the struggle turned on British theories of allegiance to the Crown and imperial unity, and there were bitter exchanges. As the debate did not go smoothly, Hearne, on 31 October, summarised the position regarding the actual status to which the Irish proposed to give statutory effect in their Act. Draft section One of the Irish Bill proposed 'to confine the group to be called Irish Nationals (who would have "common Status") to the same group who would have become British subjects if the Act of 1914 remained in force', but draft section three would be in the following or similar terms:

> Every person who is by or under the law relating to nationality for the time being in force in any of the States mentioned in the Schedule to this Act a national of that State shall, by reason of the fact that that State is a Member of the British Commonwealth of Nations, have, while ordinarily resident or being in the Irish Free State, the same status as a national of the Irish Free State and, subject to compliance with the conditions imposed by law in relation to such persons may exercise all and every of the rights and privileges conferred by law on nationals of the Irish Free State and shall be subject to the same obligations as such nationals.[60]

(The Schedule would set out the States of the Commonwealth other than the Irish Free State.)

The British, however, sought a different emphasis. On behalf of the Home Office, Mr W. F. Dowson 'insisted' that no agreement would be possible unless Irish law contained some such section as the following:

Every person who is a subject of His Majesty by nature of the laws in force throughout the British Commonwealth of Nations, by reason of the fact that he possesses a status in common with the nationals of the Irish Free State as defined in this Act, be entitled in the Irish Free State to the rights and privileges and be subject to the obligations to which an Irish Free State national is entitled or subject.[61]

Sir Claude Schuster also drafted a version of the Irish section Three and this in turn was modified by Mr McGilligan. In the meantime the battle raged over what was to be included in the Conference Report. Mr Hearne resumes the story:

> You have a copy of the draft Report on Nationality produced by the Sub-Committee. I dissented from the Report. The Minister feels that he should in the last resort (i.e. failing agreement on a Report) put in a minority Report as follows:
> 'The Conference having carefully considered the paragraphs relating to the subject of Nationality contained in the Report of 1929 recommends that the several Governments of the Commonwealth should have regard to the recommendations contained in the said paragraphs when preparing any legislation on nationality which they may consider necessary.'
> But we have *not* reached the minority stage in this subject yet. You will recollect however that at this afternoon's meeting a suggestion was made that disagreement on nationality might hold up the passing of the Statute of Westminster. You will recall the context and know what importance to attach to that suggestion.[62]

Mr Hearne throws further interesting light on the negotiations with the closing paragraph of his letter:

> Sir H. Batterbee suggested to me some days ago that Mr McGilligan and Mr MacDonald would have to have a private conversation together (no one else present) and would probably be discussing nationality *and* the Privy Council at the same moment. It suggested some sort of bargain. It is impossible to say precisely how far any particular suggestion of that kind made by officials will be adhered to or abandoned or how far it represents actual instructions. You are aware of the stampede by the officials.[63]

Though these excerpts from the negotiations on nationality are patently incomplete they do shed light on the way business was conducted. In the end, the Conference did approve the 1929 paragraphs and added three further points of general co-operative intent, including the statement that 'the possession of the common status in virtue of the law for the time being in force in any part of the Commonwealth should carry with it the recognition of that status by the law of every other part of the Commonwealth'.[64] On the subject of Nationality of Married Women, the Conference could reach no further agreement than had been achieved at the Nationality Convention signed at the Hague earlier in the year by all Commonwealth members. Thus confusion remained. Even in 1937 a French girl marrying an Irish official became British, and not Irish, on assuming the nationality of her husband.[*]

The next item on the Conference Report is the Commonwealth Tribunal, a matter inextricably entwined with the Irish rejection of the Judicial Committee of the Privy Council. It is unnecessary to repeat here the Irish views on the established Court of Appeal. They had made these views well known in 1926 and they had been persuaded then to postpone their demands only by the eloquence of Lord Birkenhead and the promise of his future support. Now he was dead. But the Irish were still confident that the Appeal to the Privy Council would be removed. They looked for an amicable solution, but they took the trouble to outline the continuing failure of this court to honour the agreed principles of 1926. In April 1930 they had noted the case of the Performing Right Society versus the Bray Urban Council, which was heard in London against the wishes of the Free State Government. They had determined then that:

> His Majesty's Government in the Irish Free State will, at the next Imperial Conference, elaborate for the information of His Majesty's other Governments the considerations which render the removal of this provision from the Irish Free State imperative:[65]

and as the introductory brief demonstrated at the beginning of this chapter, they regarded the Commonwealth Tribunal as a mere political gambit which might make the removal of the Privy Council easier for the British to face.

Smyllie, in the *Irish Times* – an organ which represented the old Unionist minority who tended to be in favour of the retention of the Privy Council – buttressed the arguments for a Commonwealth Tribunal by quoting a Conference delegate to the effect that it was useless to talk of brotherhood if the members of the Commonwealth were going to submit their domestic disputes to foreigners.[66] Some, he added, as the struggle warmed, could not be satisfied with the Privy Council but preferred to run to Holland with Imperial tittle-tattle.[67]

---

[*] Wife of Dr Michael Rynne, who supplied this example in interview.

To the Free State leaders, however, this was a matter of the highest principle. They were no longer prepared to suffer this very real derogation of their national sovereignty. They sought agreement but they would take unilateral action if thwarted. Their whole approach to the projected Tribunal was dictated by their determination to remove the Privy Council:

> the only operative Imperial institution which can be said to make of the Commonwealth a legal and constitutional unit, as distinct from the Diplomatic Unit created by the unified control of the King's external acts.[68]

Before the Conference the Irish set out their attitude to the Commonwealth Tribunal and explained their confidence of victory:

> It is . . . of the first importance to ensure that the jurisdiction of the new Court be strictly limited to the settlement of inter-Governmental disputes which the Governments concerned shall have failed to settle by diplomatic means. There must be no single persisting Court. Its mere persistence might encourage an enlargement of its functions and an encroachment on matters internal to the Individual States of the Commonwealth. But there is no reason – if tactics dictate such a course at the Conference – why we should not suggest a whole series of panels for Courts to come into existence only in the contingency mentioned. Thus the Saorstat and Great Britain could agree to appoint five members on a panel constituted as follows: Great Britain and the Saorstat would each choose one member from its own country, one member from another State of the Commonwealth and both together would select the fifth member likewise from another State of the Commonwealth. Canada and Great Britain, the Saorstat and Canada, etc., would all select their panels in similar manner. This method is that followed in the American conciliation treaties. It has the advantage of giving a definitely equal share in the constitution of the Court to the potential disputants, and of allowing the Court to operate within a reasonable space of time.
>
> Anything in the shape of a permanent Court would be dangerous to us. The British could hardly fail to use it for the purpose of maintaining control or enforcing their views on constitutional matters, and even though mutual consent in each case were a condition precedent to acceptance of the Courts jurisdiction, we might find ourselves forced into a position of isolation by a series of constitutional decisions accepted by the other Members of the Commonwealth.
>
> The Privy Council must disappear and is already decaying because of its inherent incompatibility with the constitutional evolution of the Commonwealth and it need not cause us serious anxiety. But any single permanent Court, or any single permanent panel appointed for setting up an *ad hoc* tribunal is a danger for us because five-sixths of its membership and considerably more than five-sixths of its operations would

be completely independent of our will. No matter what form its original constitution might take, we could not prevent its being moulded to the will of the most powerful member of the Commonwealth.[69]

The Irish wished to take no chances, and it is interesting to see that the paragraphs which the Conference eventually agreed exactly mirror this plan for the Tribunal. A voluntary *ad hoc* body to settle inter-governmental differences was approved, and the machinery for selecting its five members was that outlined above. But on the matter of the Privy Council there was no similar success.

From the very beginning the British dug their heels in. Desmond FitzGerald was not dissatisfied at the start of the second week. He wrote on Monday the sixth: . . .

> Conference this a'noon.
> It was tough but generally satisfactory. I did most of the talking – and at the end every Dominion came to congratulate me and Tody.* As a matter of fact, though the matter (P. Council) looked bad for us in the beginning we got support in varying degrees from all Dominions.[70]

Two days later he noted that 'the P.C. discussion was very forceful'.[71] Patrick McGilligan also contributes to the story. He has related how, soon after this, he was having his say against Thomas, Havenga already having indicated South African support, when he was interrupted by an irate Guthrie. Fearing that the Canadian might throw his weight against him, McGilligan endeavoured to hold the floor, but at last he was forced to yield. Guthrie addressed the Dominions Secretary in forceful terms:

> Mr Thomas, you say that the Irish Free State can do in this matter what Canada can do. You say that Canada can get rid of it if it wants. And your amazing conclusion is that the Irish Free State CAN'T! Tell me Mr Thomas, why?

When questioned later why he had thrown in his support, after the hostility he had shown at the opening of the Conference, the Canadian Minister of Justice explained with all the disillusionment of his leader's economic rebuff: 'Ah, that was ten days ago.'† The Free State had now new allies.

Yet they could not make the British move. The British were perhaps convinced that to yield here was to destroy the Labour Party. So they tried every trick and every expedient to mollify the

* P. McGilligan.

† P. McGilligan, recounted in interview. Of course the Anglo-Irish Treaty did contain the requirement that the Appeal should remain (Article 66).

Irish delegation. An exhausted, angry and disgusted FitzGerald hints of deep intrigue as the bitter argument neared its end. After an all-out battle the day before, he noted on the morning of 6 November:

> Haven't seen Tody this morning yet – but I imagine he will be suffering from reaction. There was consternation among the British when he said it might be necessary to publish correspondence about case where British Government undertook to square the Judicial C'tee of the P.C. – but we with foresight had told them that if things went wrong they would have to do the paying. And when British Government thought they had the P.C. squared the P.C. doublecrossed them, and they, the British Government, had to pay. But I am too fed up to go over the whole argt again.[72]

The British refused to yield, although the retention of the Privy Council Appeal was by now but a hollow safeguard in the Free State itself. The Irish, as a result, became angry and resentful. They felt that they had been treated scandalously and they determined to press on unilaterally with the abolition of the Appeal. Their Bill to achieve this was taken over and enacted in 1933 by the de Valera Administration.[73]

The Report continues on its desultory way. Not enough time was devoted to Defence for anything but the loosest generalities to be agreed. Conclusions were reached on the Appointment of Governors-General, in response to South African pressure. Simple and logical rules were laid down so that Dr Bodenstein's plea, at the third meeting of the Sankey Committee, that 'constitutional forms should reflect the constitutional position'[74] was satisfied. The Sankey Committee had agreed that 'Sir Claude Schuster, Doctor Bodenstein and Mr Costello should be asked to confer as to a practical solution of the question',[75] but if these men further explored the associated and more controversial matter of the use of Seals, no record of their conclusions is contained in this part of the Report. They left no doubt, however, that in future no ambiguity could exist as to who was responsible for appointing a Governor-General.*

'Communication and Consultation' and 'The Channel of Communication between Dominion Governments and Foreign Governments' received the attention of the delegates and contributed to the written material of a Report obviously conscious of its meagre

---

* The Irish were already satisfied that no ambiguity could exist, but the example of the Australian Government's difficulties no doubt prompted the South Africans to seek clarity. See below p. 304 (note 5 to Appendix G), for references to this affair.

content. This, the major section of the Report, closed with an essay on the status of High Commissioners. This was another issue raised by the South Africans, who were anxious that the High Commissioner should be accorded a status at least equal to that of a representative of foreign governments; the same status, privileges and immunities. It was agreed that a Dominion High Commissioner should rank next to a British Secretary of State, and it was hoped that the Dominions would accord a similar position to any British High Commissioner appointed to them.

Annexed to this section of the Report was a 'Draft Agreement as to British Commonwealth Merchant Shipping' and the remaining non-economic sections included 'Arbitration and Disarmament', 'The Antarctic', 'Defence' and 'Imperial War Graves'.

The 'Arbitration and Disarmamemt' Committee listed the following as its agenda for business: the General Act for the Pacific Settlement of International Disputes; the Draft Disarmament Convention; and the proposed revision of the Covenant of the League of Nations. Mr McGilligan made it clear that

> in the opinion of the Irish Free State a discussion of the pacific settlement of disputes could not be dissociated from the discussion of disarmament. They felt that the Covenant of the League should be the main if not the only instrument for the preservation of peace and should not depend for its efficiency on external agreements. . . . The Irish Free State was in favour of the principle of the General Act, but they were in general opposed to attaching reservations to League documents. They would like to accede to the General Act without reservation. Finally the Irish Free State must reserve the question of their own accession. Once the principle of acceptance was admitted they felt it unwise to attach undue importance to common action, and that failure to reach agreement on the form of accession should not be a bar to action on the part of any member of the Commonwealth.[76]

To the last the Irish minister would resist any suspicion of group action.

The report of this meeting also mentions that

> some discussion then took place on the reservations proposed by His Majesty's Government in the United Kingdom: it was pointed out that the first four reservations were identical with those attached to the acceptance of the Optional Clause by all H.M. Govts. except the Irish Free State.[77]

The third of these reservations referred to disputes between mem-

bers of the Commonwealth and revived the whole *inter se* controversy. It was denounced as unacceptable to his country by Mr
McGilligan in the resumed discussion at the second meeting
of the Committee.[78]

None of the other conclusions of the Report merit attention. It is
a thin report once the O.D.L. recommendations are passed, and the
simple reason for this is the number of topics which were excluded
as no agreement was ever reached. The FitzGerald letters have
already shown that an angry breakdown occurred on the *inter se*
controversy referred to above, but there was disagreement also on
the whole range of matters connected with the issue of 'Advice to
The King' (Seals), 'The Issue of Full Powers', 'Commercial
Treaties', 'Phraseology in Official Documents' (the use of 'Britannic
Majesty'), and 'The Issue of Exequaturs'. These matters were all
specifically on the agenda of the Conference,[79] and the fact that no
mention of them could be made in the Report is a further indication
of the temper of the Conference and the assertive individuality of
some of the Dominions. They also provide, however, a clear picture
of Irish Free State views and require careful examination.

(vi) MATTERS UNDECIDED

As it is fundamental to the outlook of the Irish Free State, and as it
coloured Irish foreign policy from the moment of the formation of
the State in 1921 onwards, it is logical to examine the *inter se* controversy first.

The *inter se* doctrine, discussed so fully with Hertzog,* was concerned with the applicability or non-applicability of international
treaties and agreements to the members of the British Commonwealth *inter se*. It also involved the international status of the
Dominions, their relationship to the League of Nations, and the
concept of the British Commonwealth as a single unified State. It was
an issue upon which the Irish and British Governments held dia-
metrically opposed views, which had first come out in the open in
1924 with the registration of the Anglo-Irish Treaty at Geneva.

Since the Barcelona Convention of 1921 it had been British practice to insert an *inter se* clause in all League Conventions, making it
clear that such conventions were not binding between the members
of the Commonwealth, but by implication admitting that without

* See Appendix D.

such a clause the Conventions would be binding. When in 1924 the Irish Government sent the Treaty to be registered – a move to secure the international recognition of their State* – the British immediately declared:

> Since the Covenant of the League came into force, His Majesty's Government have consistently taken the view that neither it nor any convention concluded under its auspices are intended to govern the relations *inter se* of the various parts of the British Commonwealth.†

This declaration was of course, in the Irish view, simply a matter of opinion, of no more force than their own contrary opinion. The Treaty was registered as an international treaty; and the British continued up to 1926 to insert the *inter se* clause in League Conventions.

At the 1926 Conference however, the British sought to impose an unambiguous settlement:

> a form of treaty such as to prevent there being any risk of an international body maintaining that the treaty does operate between the various parts of the Empire.[80]

The solution reached, it will be recalled, was that all League Treaties should be made in the name of the King 'as the symbol of the special relationship between the different parts of the Empire', and this, the report continued,

> will render superfluous the inclusion of any provision that its terms must not be regarded as regulating *inter se* the rights and obligations of the various territories on behalf of which it has been signed in the name of the King. In this connection it must be borne in mind that the question was discussed at the Arms Traffic Conference in 1925, and that the Legal Committee of that Conference laid it down that the principle to which the foregoing sentence gives expression underlies all international conventions.[81]

Though in some ways this section represented an improvement over the existing system it was in fact self-contradictory and contained implications quite unacceptable to the Irish. As they pointed out in 1930, the Legal Committee of the Arms Traffic Conference, 1925, had dealt simply with a query by the Dutch delegate who wished to make clear the point that 'trade between two territories (Holland and the Dutch East Indies) belonging to the same State would naturally

---

* See above, Ch. 5, Section i.   † See above, p. 59.

remain outside the provisions of the Convention'. As he had then explained:

> the Convention dealt only with the regulation of international trade, and trade between two parts of *one and the same State* did not fall within this category. By the term 'international trade' must be understood the transfer of arms and ammunitions from the possession of *one political unit to that of another*.[82]

What the Legal Committee of that Conference had in fact decided underlay 'all international Conventions' was the principle expressed thus in their verdict:

> the provisions of the present Convention *shall not be interpreted as applying* to the despatch of arms, munitions and implements of war from the territories forming part of, or placed under, the protection of one and the same *sovereign state*.[83]

The 1926 section, then, was in fact implying that the members of the Commonwealth were merely parts of one sovereign state. But this was quite incompatible with the accompanying Balfour Declaration. It was therefore quite useless, the 1930 Irish brief argued,

> for Great Britain or any other member of the Commonwealth to declare that all the members of the British Commonwealth are international units in the fullest sense of the word, if at the same time we declare that the relations between these so called international units are not international relations.[84]

It may be asked how the Irish came to accept such a remarkable clause in the 1926 Report in the first place. Light is thrown on this from correspondence between Desmond FitzGerald and E. J. Phelan. On 18 February 1927 Phelan wrote to FitzGerald to congratulate him, by and large, on the Imperial Conference Report. But he was understandably alarmed at the *inter se* development:

> I must say the para relating to the *inter se* clause in League Treaties to me is unintelligible. The Imperial Conference cannot amend the Covenant. The Covenant does not provide for two classes of Members of the League. And League treaties are binding on all members who ratify them unless there is an *inter se* clause.* How the Imperial Conference could decide that they weren't and that the *inter se* is superfluous beats me.[85]

---

* The point being that any treaty signed with an *inter se* clause was obviously acceptable to the contracting parties. For the British Commonwealth of Nations simply to agree amongst themselves that there was no *inter se* applicability was quite another matter.

In his reply Desmond FitzGerald explained:

> I may as well admit that it is one of the worst features of the report, but it was a matter of give and take and we gave the minimum and took the most. In that matter we were gravely handicapped by General Hertzog. He came over with a theory which he thought could be the basis of a great triumph. Inherent in his theory was the idea that the League of Nations knew that a special relationship existed among the members of the British Commonwealth as they entered the League under conditions unlike other members. I argued this matter with him before the Conference began but his mind was so utterly wedded to his pet theory which led nowhere that nothing could be done; and I should say that at the end of the Conference, he regarded as a triumph that one point which I regard as a defeat and that we must try to remedy sometime.[86]

By 1930 the time for remedy had arrived. And the Irish were ready to stress the implications of the British doctrine at which Phelan had hinted in his letter: the effect which it was creating in the League. There was no doubt that the members of the British Commonwealth were full and complete members of the League of Nations, having equal rights and obligations along with all other members. And there was no suggestion anywhere in the Covenant that the whole of its provisions were not to apply generally to the mutual relations of all members of the League. Yet this 1926 constitutional convention appeared to be an agreement – this was what the British interpretation meant – between members of the British Commonwealth of Nations to exclude the application of the Covenant to their *inter se* relations. And such an agreement was directly in conflict with Article 20 of the Covenant.*

This was the Irish argument in 1930 and it was the argument used nine months later in Geneva by Mr Phelan in an address he gave to the Geneva Institute of International Relations, entitled *The British Empire and the World Community*.[87] Phelan was in London during the 1930 Imperial Conference – Desmond FitzGerald pays tribute there to his 'remarkable brain'[88] – and it is tempting to think that he was behind the Irish case. The argument went further. It held that

---

* 'The members of the League severally agree that this Covenant is accepted as abrogating all obligations or understandings *inter se* which are inconsistent with the terms thereof and solemnly undertake that they will not hereafter enter into any engagements inconsistent with the terms thereof. In case any Member of the League shall, before becoming a Member of the League, have undertaken any obligations inconsistent with the terms of the Covenant, it shall be the duty of each Member to take immediate steps to procure its release from its obligations' (Article 20 of the League of Nations Covenant).

this Convention left two courses open to the Dominions. They must either choose their duty to the general peace of the world and denounce the Convention, seeking to conclude some new arrangement in conformity with the obligations of the Covenant, which would protect the particular interests of the Commonwealth when such interests seemed likely to be adversely affected by international Conventions concluded under the auspices of the League, or they must withdraw from the League on the grounds that essential intra-Commonwealth arrangements were in conflict with the articles of the Covenant. The Irish would denounce the 1926 Convention. The future of the League demanded it; the dignity of their own international position required it.

They recognised that the British case was founded on a natural anxiety to preserve the organic unity of the Commonwealth. This was what led the British to deny that intra-Commonwealth relations were international; this was what inspired them to cloud their signature of the Optional Clause in 1929 with reservations; and this was why they would endorse the General Act with similar reservations. The British had everything to gain by preserving the image of unity. But the Dominions, struggling to assert their international integrity, had everything to lose. As the Irish brief concluded:

> The relationships between members of the Commonwealth are already sufficiently difficult for the foreigner to understand, without increasing the difficulty by declaring that while the members of the British Commonwealth of Nations are full international units, nevertheless, the relations between those units are not international relations.[89]

It was Mr McGilligan who had to present this argument to the Sankey Committee. He did so with eloquence. He pointed out that Professor Noel Baker[90] had accepted the British viewpoint and he quoted M. van Eysinga, who thought that the 'interrelationship between the various Members of the British Commonwealth, that is to say whether or not it was a single sovereign State, was of considerable importance to foreign States'.[91] It was a matter not simply confined to treaties: judgeships on the Permanent Court, for instance were affected. McGilligan's plea was that '*inter se* applicability should be regulated by a special provision and not be deduction from a general constitutional doctrine'.[92]

He was supported at length by Dr Bodenstein, fresh from detailed research into the minutes of the 1926 sub-committee which had agreed the contentious Convention. 'It was never intended to lay down the legal principles which were in the background of that form', Bodenstein maintained.[93] He took pains to deny that the Dominions could have accepted any organic implications, asserted that General Hertzog had continually denied that very conception, and insisted that though Sir Cecil Hurst had argued the idea of the King as the one contracting party (unitary crown), the Dominions in 1926 had not accepted this idea nor the conception that there could be one ratification only. General Hertzog had said specifically that the King was to be considered 'as having performed so many different acts as there were Dominions participating in the Treaty'.[94]

Sir William Jowitt tried to pour oil on the troubled waters by assuring the Dominions that the United Kingdom had no wish to prejudice any member's point of view: it was merely a matter of agreeing a solution, of using such forms as would maintain the special relationships existing between the Dominions.

Dupré of Canada added his condemnation of the 1926 formula. It was most unfortunate that reference had been made to the 1925 Arms Traffic Conference 'which was based on patently fallacious reasoning'.[95] Sir H. W. Malkin assured the Conference that there was no intention in the reference to the Arms Traffic Conference to imply all that Mr McGilligan had said, and he begged that things be left as they were in the interests of clarity.

McGilligan and Costello then both sought, in addition, a clear statement that the King was several and could contract with himself, just as he sued himself daily in the Courts. The British had denied this view in 1926 and it looked as though that denial still held sway in some quarters.

Thus the debate went on. The British proposed a draft agreement, the first three paragraphs of which were quite acceptable to the Irish. The fourth paragraph, however, indicated that the British Government had not moved an inch, and it inspired a nine-page memorandum from the Irish attacking every phrase contained in it. The British draft reads as follows:

> The Report of the Inter-Imperial Relations Committee of the Imperial Conference of 1926 contained a sentence referring to the Arms Traffic Conference 1925 on the subject of the applicability of treaties as between the members of the British Commonwealth, which has given rise to some discussion regarding the international position of the several members of the Commonwealth.
>
> In our opinion neither the sentence in question nor the practice based on it were intended to detract from the position of the several members

of the British Commonwealth as international units individually in the fullest sense of the term.*

It follows that there was no intention of developing by that sentence any theory as to the status of the British Commonwealth inconsistent with that status as described in the second section of the Report of 1926.

In view, however, of the special relationship between the members of the Commonwealth, we think that it should be placed on record that no international convention (whether made between Heads of States or between Governments) shall apply as between members of the Commonwealth participating in it, except in so far as such members may be willing to apply between themselves the convention or any of its provisions.

We recommend that the present Conference should agree to place this on Record.[96]

The British had not budged. As a matter of principle treaties would not apply *inter se*. The Commonwealth nations were to be preserved as a distinct and privileged group within the League – or as integral parts of the British Empire.

There could be no agreement on such terms: they denied the Dominions the power to conduct treaties between themselves and automatically invalidated the Irish claim that the 1921 Treaty was an international document. The Irish proposed three alternative drafts to replace the fourth British paragraph, each one an expansion of the one before. The final one follows below, containing the first draft (the first sentence) and the second draft (the first three sentences):

We think that it follows from the previous paragraphs that the non-applicability amongst the members of the Commonwealth of any international treaty cannot depend upon the fact that the treaty is concluded in a particular form and that the non-applicability of any such treaty amongst those members must depend upon an agreement to that effect made between any two or more of the members of the Commonwealth at the time which the treaty is concluded and embodied in the terms thereof. We recognise, however, that there are special common interests existing between the members of the Commonwealth which may render it desirable that international treaties should not in every case apply between them *inter se*. We are satisfied that the procedure of full consultation which has been accepted at previous Conferences will allow for the consideration of cases of this kind. Where members of the

* This paragraph expressed the opinion of the South African delegation which submitted the following draft: 'We wish to place on record that there was no intention in 1926 of developing in that paragraph any theory as to the relation of the members of the Commonwealth *inter se* inconsistent with their position and mutual relationship as decided in the second section of the Report of 1926, or of derogating in any way from the position of the members of the British Commonwealth of Nations as international units in the fullest sense of the term' (FitzGerald papers).

Commonwealth are of opinion that a treaty to which they are parties should not apply *inter se*, it is considered that, as suggested in the 1926 Report, the Heads of States form of treaty should be employed.[97]

The Irish delegation finally settled for the second draft – (to 'this kind.') but in the end no agreement at all was reached. The Irish angrily rejected the British form and the British interpretation of the special relationship which undoubtedly existed. For there were in fact two interpretations of this special relationship, according to Irish reasoning:

> The British maintain that it is a relationship which has as a consequence to make the Dominions an international enclave. Within that enclave international conventions cease to have any effect. How they arrive at that theory I do not profess to be able to follow. But it is an easy and convenient theory which preserves a spectacular unity which is politically advantageous. There is to be a block of seven great and growing nations participating in international life, but the commitments within the bloc are to be of no international concern and are not even to be known (since they cannot be registered like other commitments).
>
> The other view is that there is a special relationship which consists in having one King and certain common procedures as regards the expression of the national authority. A series of Free Nations which, because of common interests and certain historical factors, have found a way of working together in friendly union with an obligation of consultation which does not diminish their absolute freedom.
>
> Surely that absolute freedom implies their right to enter into international contracts and to contract among themselves?[98]

Ireland was at the time sitting on the Council of the League. It could not countenance the buttressing of this distinct group inside the League. The memorandum concluded with the following warning:

> It is all very well to assume that the Commonwealth and its members will always be peaceful and pro-League and that everything will always work smoothly. But supposing a 'Hitler' Government of Die-Hards were to take military action against the Saorstat in an economic quarrel, should we leave it open to them to plead before world public opinion that it was a 'domestic matter' that the Covenant did not apply and that we had agreed that this was so?[99]

Allied to the failure to reach agreement on *inter se* applicability was the failure to agree on the form of Commercial Treaties. One of the most objectional consequences of the British *inter se* theory, expressed in the 1926 convention, was that foreign powers, regarding the British Commonwealth as a unit, dealt only with Britain as representing that unit.* There were factors inherent in most of the British methods of conducting treaties which tended to reinforce this situation and though some of these methods may have saved the Dominions time, may have facilitated a uniform Commonwealth policy and may even have conferred benefits upon the Dominions, the Irish regarded them as unconstitutional, illogical and misleading in a way detrimental to the international Dominion image. It was, for instance, a common British practice when making a commercial treaty to include an accession clause enabling the various Dominions to participate if they so desired. The Irish submitted a memorandum to the Conference on this point as follows:

Property of His Britannic Majesty's Government.

SECRET   COPY NO. 163
E.(30).25   *IMPERIAL CONFERENCE 1930*
                     Form of Commercial Treaties

Memorandum by the Irish Free State Delegation

1. In the Memorandum on the Form of Commercial Treaties (Paper No. E.(30) 8) circulated by the United Kingdom delegation, the several Governments of the Commonwealth are asked to consider whether they could prefer:
   (*a*) that the existing practice as regards the accession clause and the 'nevertheless' clause should be maintained, or
   (*b*) that the Dominion should be omitted from both clauses.

2. His Majesty's Government in the Irish Free State prefer that the existing practice as regards the accession clause and the 'nevertheless' clause should not be maintained.

3. Treaties must be confined in their entire application to the area and citizens under the jurisdiction of the Government on the advice of which a full power is issued and the treaties are concluded. The present practice implies that His Majesty when advised by the Government of the United Kingdom alone has authority to contract for the nationals of the other countries of the Commonwealth. The fact that such a contract does not involve active obligations on the part of any of His Majesty's Governments other than that of the United Kingdom does not affect the implication. Since the geographical limitation of full powers recommended in the Report of 1926 was intended to prevent any misconception arising as to the scope of a treaty concluded on the advice of any one of His Majesty's Governments no part of the treaty, whether the preamble or the articles thereof, should purport to extend its scope beyond the limits of full power.

The practice whereby His Majesty's Government in the United

* The most recent instance of this had been the U.S. Government in connection with the London Naval Treaty, 1930. Also see McGilligan/Hertzog conversation. Appendix D, p. 266.

Kingdom purport to act for the nationals of all the members of the
Commonwealth is opposed to the principle which should govern the
internal and external relations of the members of the Commonwealth,
namely, that the British Commonwealth of Nations is not a single
sovereign state.

4. The principles above stated appear to His Majesty's Government in
the Irish Free State to be fundamental to the conception of the British
Commonwealth and to the individual sovereign state-hood of the
several members.

5. His Majesty's Government in the Irish Free State do not believe
that considerations based on mere expediency should be allowed to
obscure the indefeasible and exclusive right of each of the Commonwealth Governments to order the internal and external relations of the
people whom it represents. In the absence of a Commonwealth federal
system in which a central government would possess real representative
powers, no one of His Majesty's Governments can act for the nationals
under the jurisdiction of another of His Majesty's Governments without
violating the root principle of democratic rule. The nations of the
Commonwealth, having definitely and finally rejected federation, His
Majesty's Government in the Irish Free State would view with grave
concern any endorsement of a practice which is in opposition to the
principles which inspired that decision.

GROSVENOR HOUSE, PARK LANE, LONDON W.1.

October 8th 1930.[100]

This memorandum came under withering British fire in the
Sankey Committee. Jowitt, however, explained that the British did
not wish to preserve the accession clause unless the Dominions wanted
it, which he thought they did. Dupré of Canada and Sidey of New
Zealand agreed with Jowitt's assumption. Australia, too, deemed
the clause very useful. Dr Bodenstein, however, supported McGilligan. The clause might cause political difficulties in South Africa, he
said, and before making it the United Kingdom should consult the
Dominions in every case so that those desiring could then be
mentioned by name. He instanced the Soviet Treaty. South Africa
had not wanted to be associated with this treaty, and much against
its will it had had to make a provocative dissociative declaration,
whereas it would have preferred to have had to say nothing at all.
Here was a fundamental practical example of objection to the
existing system. McGilligan summarised the Irish view, regarding it
as just as unconstitutional for the United Kingdom to stipulate
benefits as it was for it to impose obligations on other parts of the
Commonwealth. Lord Sankey urged the Irish Minister repeatedly

not to 'jeopardise the advantages which other Dominions enjoyed'[101] but no agreed solution could be reached.

The Irish had reviewed the whole field of treaty making and the effect which the disputed 1926 convention had upon it. The accession clause was an objectionable feature of all British-conducted Bilateral Treaties and with the 'nevertheless' clause,* formed an integral part of the whole British *inter se* doctrine, which was perpetuating the Commonwealth-unit image. Most of the remaining subjects upon which agreement could not be reached were also allied to that image and formed part of the campaign which the Irish were conducting to bring clarity to the status of the Dominions and logic to the international role of the Commonwealth *entente*.

Of these subjects a relatively minor one was 'Phraseology of Official Documents'. Like the 'Several Monarchy' and '*inter se*' this was a special concern of Joe Walshe, the Secretary of the Department of External Affairs and the 'thinker' of the Irish Delegation. Basically, the objection under this pretentious title was to the use of the word 'Britannic' to describe His Majesty the King. The objection fell on stony ground and received little Dominion support. However, Lord Sankey did at least circulate his Committee with a 'revised formula relating to the use of this word'[102] in the King's title. Perhaps that was as much as could have been expected.

The question of 'Official Seals', however, was not such a minor affair, and, though no satisfaction was gained at the Conference, it became a major issue the following year,† being part of the mounting desire for direct Dominion access to the King. Entwined with this question were the questions of the 'Issue of Full Powers' and the 'Issue of Exequaturs'.

These last two matters were raised by the South Africans who wanted the Governor-General to have the power to sign Exequaturs in cases where foreign Governments made their request directly to their Government, and who objected to the implications of the use of the Great Seal of the Realm in the issue of full powers to Dominion plenipotentiaries. With regard to the former, Lord Sankey persuaded Dr Bodenstein that no major inconvenience existed and that it would be better to leave things as they were. The South African objection to the Great Seal applied also in the matter of

---

* Though Britain held that Treaties did not apply between Dominions it allowed that 'nevertheless' they could be applied as an administrative measure.
† See Ch. 9 below.

Ratification of Treaties and it was simply an echo of the Irish case on Seals in general. In the words of Dr Bodenstein, in the Third Meeting of the Sankey Committee:

> His Majesty's Government in the Union consider a procedure by which the intervention and co-operation of one of His Majesty's Ministers in the United Kingdom* is rendered essential in regard to acts performed by the King in respect of one of His Majesty's other Governments, now inappropriate and merely conducive to confusion.[103]

The Irish brief was more explicit in its rejection of this procedure. It pointed out that the intervention of a British minister, no matter how formal this might be declared to be by the British Government,

> was regarded by Keith, Corbett and Smith, and other writers on Dominion Status, as a restriction on the Dominions for the purpose of maintaining unity. It is a part of the machinery to ensure unity in foreign relations.[104]

Keith had even gone so far as to suggest that if a treaty concluded by the King, for one Dominion, is broken, the other party to the treaty might require the British Government to put pressure on the Dominion to carry out its obligation, on the ground that the ratification of the treaty involved the personal action of the King, who could only act on the authority of the British Government.[105] But whatever the theorising might be, the Irish had 'ascertained that the Department of State in Washington regard the British Government as having responsibility for treaties between the U.S.A. and the Dominions'[106] for the above reasons. The Irish brief ended with the following definite conclusion:

> It is submitted that the only way in which the position of the Dominion in relation to these documents can be cleared up is by their being submitted to the King through some channel other than a Secretary of State, and are [sic] sealed with the Seal of the part of the Commonwealth concerned.[107]

The subject had been brought up at the second meeting of the Sankey Committee and it inspired a comment from FitzGerald. After lunch with George Bernard Shaw, he wrote in a letter to his wife, he had rushed back to the Sankey Committee:

> Not much done there but seems to be moving in pretty good direction. It was amusing that we had to explain to Lord Chancellor and Attorney

---

* E.g. the Great Seal of the Realm could be used only on the authority of a warrant signed by a Secretary of State in the British Government.

General of England all about Seals. They had an expert there (Lord Shuster) [*sic*] but he was asleep when called on and couldn't grasp what was being discussed so he came round to us. Jowitt asked about the privy seal but we told him it was abolished in 1851.[108]

The matter was not to reach a successful conclusion and in the end three separate reports were drawn up. 'The representatives of the United Kingdom, Canada, the Commonwealth of Australia, New Zealand and Newfoundland' presented a report setting out the historic role of the Great Seal – reserved for documents 'which it is desired to invest with the highest degree of importance such as Letters Patent, Full Powers, and Instruments of Ratification'[109] – and the Signet in its Greater and Lesser forms. To assist foreign understanding while leaving a British Secretary of State in control of the Great Seal, these Dominions agreed to have a counter-signature of a Dominion minister on the Warrant of Authority, if convenient.

South Africa, on the other hand, wished to concentrate attention on the King's signature, and in a separate report explained that it had not made up its mind whether any seal was necessary in addition. If it decided in favour of a seal then it would use one appropriate only to South Africa, but stressed that as the King was the Commonwealth link, 'the Chief Executive Officer of the Dominions and the *persona agens* in a particular instrument',[110] it was the royal sign manual which was important.

As usual it was the Irish Free State which had alone prepared its brief from the beginning and formulated a definite policy. It submitted a short separate report stating:

> the manner in which the King's signature is confirmed is for the Government concerned to decide.
> If the Government concerned decides to use signets and a Great Seal the form of signets and of the seal is for that Government to decide. In the Irish Free State the seals have been established by law, and if the Irish Government decides to use seals the seals would be those so established.[111]

It is a cautious and non-committal report but the expansion of it was not slow in appearing.*

* See Ch. 9 below (access to the King).

(vii) REACTIONS

Thus with much disagreement the 1930 Imperial Conference ended. The Committee disbanded after listing their compromise conclusions, and these conclusions became the Conference Report. Then the delegates dispersed. There was a momentary show of conviviality as the farewells were made, but dissatisfaction and failure hung over the proceedings and characterised the Press reactions in Britain and the Dominions overseas.

The leading Empire statesmen were shocked and depressed. General Smuts, in Opposition, expressed a widespread despair at the missed opportunity:

> If the final settlement of Dominion Status could have gone hand in hand with a great gesture of fellowship and comradeship, with the holding out and grasping of a helping hand all round in the common hour of trial, what a landmark the Conference would have been in the history of the Empire.[112]

There was disillusion instead. General Hertzog also expressed his disappointment, before leaving for home, though he did have this satisfaction to bring to his people:

> With the formal renunciation by the British Parliament of all its claims or legal rights the independent position of South Africa, equal in extent and purport with that of Great Britain or any other free State, not only in theory but equally in its practical application, stands at the free disposal of the people of South Africa to use or misuse at their own free will. No state knows greater freedom.[113]

Canadian disillusionment was sharper and more personal, but at least the agreement to meet again at Ottawa had been salvaged. The Economic Conference was not ended but merely adjourned. Mackenzie King attacked Bennett for his interference in British affairs and his brusqueness of method. Bennett defended himself and looked to Ottawa to achieve progress: it was inconceivable that the Empire could waste this second opportunity.

In New Zealand call after call was made in Parliament for Empire Preference and the development of Empire markets and resources. New Zealand, the farthest of the Dominions, was nearest to Great Britain in heart and spirit, it was lamented, while the Irish Free State, the nearest physically, was spiritually the most remote.[114] Premier Forbes explained that on the constitutional side 'the New Zealand representatives were more concerned to consolidate the unity of the British Commonwealth than to lay down any principles of status or of freedom for this Dominion'.[115] On the economic side the failure was all too evident, and the New Zealand leader poured tremendous scorn on the British Government for its lack of preparation and its lack of thought and effort. Views in Britain were changing, however, and without saying as much, he obviously looked forward to a Conservative victory which would bring new hope to the Empire.

Scullin, in Australia, stressed the value of personal contacts and the sense of fellowship which was genuinely induced by the Conference meetings. But he could not hide his disappointment on the economic side. He too looked hopefully towards Ottawa. The groundwork had now been done and the foundations were laid for closer economic co-operation.

In Britain there was recrimination, accusation and counter-accusation. Sir Edward Grigg wrote in December what was a more than individual reaction. 'I detest this government so much', he complained, 'and feel that they are doing so much harm to the Empire everywhere that I must get at them if I can.'[116] Leo Amery was filled with indignation at the rudeness and cowardice of the Labour Government, and with despair at the listless leadership of Baldwin on the Conservative side. Labour angrily retorted that they were committed to Free Trade and it was no use shouting now: the Protectionists had been in power in 1926, and if they were so keen, why hadn't they done something then? J. H. Thomas threw the economic blame squarely on the shoulders of his colleague, Snowden.[117]

In *United Empire*, Sir J. Sandeman Allen, M.P., was appalled at the unnecessary and criminally negligent failure. The Congress of the Federation of Chambers of Commerce, the Association of British Chambers of Commerce, the Federation of British Industries and the Chamber of Shipping, as well as the separate Dominions had submitted reports to the Conference on economic matters. But all the British Government could decide was to rule out discussion on tariffs – a matter which 80–90 per cent of British businessmen had agreed was the most vital question.[118] One is tempted to recall Smyllie's *Irish Times* contention that it was no part of the British Government's job to resist anything which might weaken the Empire: only Bennett's proposal which might bring it strength.[119]

Amongst the Free State delegation, although there was disappointment that no economic breakthrough had been made and there

was anger that some of the constitutional issues had not been finally
settled, nevertheless there was considerable satisfaction at what had
been achieved. The Irish delegates, perhaps more than most, had
made real friends at the Conference and had understood the value
of personal contacts which ranged the world over and brought
fellowship and sympathy to problems both common and individual.
Though President Cosgrave's illness had meant that General Hertzog was the only attending Prime Minister left from the 1926
Conference, the Irish delegation remained one of the most experienced. On constitutional matters they were the acknowledged
masters. Even Smyllie, more reluctant to bestow praise than in 1926,
and seeming to depend more on British delegates for his information, had to admit this point. On constitutional affairs, he acknowledged, 'the fine Italian hand of Mr P. J. McGilligan will be
traced on every line. He is the "big noise" in the Constitutional
band.'[120]

He added on 29 October:

> A member of another delegation told me today, 'that he was much
> impressed by the way in which the Free State delegation had prepared
> its case on the constitutional side and by the manner in which it had
> been presented by Mr McGilligan. From the logical point of view no
> fault can be found with this case. Indeed, it is a triumph of constitu-
> tional logic; but some of the members of the Conference have not been
> able to appreciate the skill of Mr McGilligan's arguments, and even are
> inclined to take the view that he has been wasting their time.'[121]

Desmond FitzGerald took less time to sum up the situation. Inside
the first ten days he had determined to his own satisfaction that: 'It
is obvious that as a delegation we are head and shoulders above the
others. We do at least know our subject.'[122]

Knowing their subject added to their confidence and stressed
their authority. FitzGerald's letters contain many references to the
fruitful co-operation which took place between the Irish delegation
and their Dominion colleagues. On 9 October he wrote: 'Bodenstein
of S.A. was here to have a talk. Talk very satisfactory. He came
because he realised poor Hertzog was off the track on a number of
points. On most things he found that he agreed with us thoroughly.'[123]
On the twenty-third it was the Australians: 'In the morning
Tody and I were due round to see the Australians. Very satisfactory
talk there (10.30–12.30). . . . Had talk and tea with Hertzog . . . very
satisfactory.'[124] On the twenty-fifth FitzGerald records that the

veteran Canadian Nationalist, J. S. Ewart, author of *Independence Papers*, and confidant of Mackenzie King, had arrived.* Ewart, FitzGerald found, 'Has become very old – hand shakes when he holds a paper. He had tea and talked a long time.'[125] Ewart was back again before the close of the Conference wanting 'to help us with Bennett cf. Privy Council matter – probably will be useless or harmful – but he means well – and one must appreciate that'.[126]

There is yet one other field in which a new co-operation marked this Conference. It is in a special category of its own and it deserves to be recorded. It is the remarkable degree of understanding which the Irish delegates reached with the Royal family.

Much of the credit for this redounds to the Prince of Wales. At his formal dinner for the Commonwealth delegations he took the trouble to sit the 'two recalcitrant members of the Commonwealth'[127] on either side of him: General Hertzog on his right, Patrick McGilligan on his left. Dividing his attention equally between the two, the Prince fired many probing questions. McGilligan was, of course, Minister for Industry and Commerce as well as External Affairs, and he found the Prince extremely well informed on labour and trade problems in Britain. He was, McGilligan concluded, an able and sympathetic man and would one day make an acceptable king. But it was on the constitutional side that the new accord was struck. McGilligan was forced to explain the Irish attitude towards the Commonwealth, which he did by stressing the Royal link. 'We don't object to the Monarch or the Monarchy,' he emphasised, 'but we do object to the British Parliament using the Monarchy. The King advised solely by our Ministers is what we want, and we will then be strongly monarchic.'[128] The Prince was pleased to learn this. He reported his conversation later to the King and the King sent for McGilligan to talk the whole matter over fully. But before the dinner was over the Prince of Wales had explained to McGilligan that he felt that he now knew him well: he said that he also felt he knew Mr FitzGerald opposite, so would he please send Mr Hogan so that he could get to know him.[129]

This story, told by Mr McGilligan himself, over thirty years later, is remarkably well born out by FitzGerald's account at the time. The

* While on this side of the Atlantic, Ewart spoke to the College Historical Society (Trinity College, Dublin) 5 November 1930, explaining the 'Several nature of Monarchy' and hailing the 'Irish Kingdom'.

dinner was on Thursday, 16 October. On Tuesday the twenty-first, FitzGerald reported to his wife:

> The other night P. of W. commented to Tody on youthful appearance of Hogan and me – Tody said that in spite of that we were His Majesty's oldest ministers – P. said glad to hear him say that. T. said: 'That we are oldest Govt?' No, said P. but to hear you refer to my father – I thought you – or at least your people wanted to cut him out. T. suggested that though some might have thought about various forms of govt. and decided against monarchy – that the real thing had always been against English control and that what we were occupied with was getting rid of every form of real or apparent power of British Govt. P. said – hadn't last vestige gone? Tody said a few other things occupied us still. P. said – you have referred to an individual – I may be that individual sometime – so I am interested to have all those things cleared up – again later he said – 'as I said, I may sometime occupy the position now held by my father – you and your colleagues there will be my advisers – I am glad to know that I shall be getting good advice'. He also made it clear that if anything, he thought that we were on the right line in our constitutional demands.[130]

FitzGerald's account had been sparked off by an accusation by Thomas that the Irish were upsetting things. The Labour Government 'are worried – or say they are –' recounted the Irish delegate, 'that we are going so strong that we are attacking the whole existence of monarchy. We are not doing that at all. But we are attacking everything else.'[131] FitzGerald then proceeded on a valuable summary of the work of the Irish Government, not alone at this Conference, but since its coming to power:

> I think we shall get a certain amount and what we don't get will be postponed a short while. Knowing the history of these last years as I do I am amazed at the way we have changed the situation . . . the Free State is (or will be in a couple of years – without even a vestige of any form even to mar it) just a constitutional monarchy – with only that to make the difference between it and an Irish Republic. In the matter of Independence and sovereignty there is no whittle of difference. Of course what the future may do I cannot say. But accepting the Treaty we certainly are getting all that the most perfervid supporters were claiming for it – and more. And we have educated the British and the Dominions in a very short time. Points of view that previously were attributed to our revolutionarism are now just presumed as natural by the others. The trouble is they don't always realise the implications of things. Of course another trouble is that the Govt. here is conscious that it is in momentary jeopardy – and are in terror of anything that could be presented in an unpopular light, and used against them. And I suppose that knowing that there will be disappointment on the economic side –

They want to prevent its being said that having got nothing on that side they gave away everything (or anything) on the other.[132]

Two days later FitzGerald again alluded to the Prince of Wales's dinner: 'It is quite apparent', he wrote, 'that the P. felt easier with us owing to youthfulness and that he was able to get freer talk than usual with Dominion ministers – it was political among friends rather than formal or official.'[133] The Imperial Conference was always more than just an inter-governmental struggle over economic and constitutional forms.

In Dublin reaction to the Conference was not very marked. In the following July the Report was debated in both Houses of the Oireachtas. In the Seanad, Johnson, former Labour leader in the Dail, made an observation that rings as true now as it did in 1931. Believing that the Free State was as free from British influence as the most radical republic would be, he added: 'the Governor of the Bank of England, the Board of the Prudential Assurance Company, or the financiers who are able to manipulate the share and stock markets and the prices of wheat, petrol and other things [had more influence on Ireland] . . . than the Government or the monarchy of Great Britain.'[134]

Senator O'Farrell, giving support to the Cosgrave Government, brought the issue squarely to the level of domestic politics. The Cosgrave Government, he admitted,

> have assisted other members of the Commonwealth and led them in asserting their independence as co-equal members of that Common-wealth.

But, he added, turning on the Opposition:

> The minority in some peoples' minds must be always right, but they have got to submit until the majority comes round to their point of view. Infinitely more objectionable than a King, whom the people never see and who never interferes with our affairs, would be a truculent minority who would impose its views on the majority, irrespective of their interest.[135]

Mr McGilligan spoke fairly and frankly in this debate but it was in the Dail, naturally, that he made his greatest effort. McGilligan it was who had fought longest on the Conference battle-fields, often standing alone against intimidating odds. On 16 and 17 July 1931, in two typical speeches, he summarised not only the Conference achievement but also the whole continuous and successful policy of the Cosgrave Government in the sphere of constitutional relations. This policy would be crowned by that 'Act of Renunciation by the British Parliament' – that 'most complete Act of Renunciation that any Parliament has passed in regard to any country or countries'[136] – to which he had referred the previous year, following the O.D.L. Report. Anticipating that Statute and its effects, McGilligan's words belong more properly to the following chapter. They form a fitting conclusion to a commentary on the closing event of Commonwealth significance in this decade.*

The Irish Government recommended the 1930 Conference Report because it removed many recognised Commonwealth anachronisms. If it did not yet complete the necessary removal of all anomalies,[137] there was a clear year for such action before the Statute would become law. 1931 might yet see the complete conversion of the old Empire into the new Commonwealth of Nations.

* See Ch. 9 below, pp. 245–8.

9

1931

(i) Access to the King: Change of Seals

The year 1931 ended with the enactment of the Statute of West-minster, a Bill providing the constitutional seal to an era of Commonwealth development: an era of which the final decade, as we have seen, had been distinguished by considerable Irish effort. The Statute of Westminster was in real terms a milestone and it provides a fitting termination to our examination. But it was not the only achievement of 1931. The Statute tackled many of the constitutional tangles which confused the reality of the Commonwealth relationship, but it did not solve all the practical problems. Though much attention had been devoted to outstanding constitutional anomalies, some of the apparent facts of subservience remained, so that at the beginning of 1931 the Dominions were still not seen to be free: and the area of their lingering subordination was that which included their relationship to the Monarch and their dependence upon the royal and national Seals of England. The Irish Free State had been unsparing in its efforts to root out the British Government from all the State affairs of the Dominions, and it had borne the major responsibility of drawing up the Statute of Westminster from 1926 onwards. The Free State Government now determined that before the Bill came into effect at the end of 1931, it would remove these last examples of official British involvement once and for all.

The Irish objections to the use of British Seals, strongly expressed in the 1930 Conference and echoed there by the South Africans, had been formally drawn up in preparation for the 1929 Committee. No matter how much the British argued to the contrary, the affixture of a Secretarial Seal made the responsibility for the document issued a British Government responsibility. Clearly, the Irish argued, the 'history of the Seals was a record of the progressive restraint imposed on the expression of the Royal Will by the interposition of responsible Ministers':[1] it was essential that these ministers must not be British ministers when the affairs concerned were the sole responsibility of the Dominions. Hancock admits that the Great Seal, by virtue of its control by the British Government, was regarded as a safeguard by the legal experts who made the constitutional concessions of 1929.[2] Keith, too, argued the importance of the Seals in the preservation of British control, and his arguments were echoed by Corbett and Smith.[3] Even the sympathetic W. Y. Elliott was convinced that on no occasion could Dominion ministers advise the King, and he held that 'British Ministers are not merely channels of communication. They are ultimately responsible for every royal act, such as the release of the Great Seal, for the full powers issued to plenipotentiaries, and for the ratification of Treaties.'[4] It was not mere petty imagination which motivated the Irish External Affairs Department. The Irish knew that these arguments existed, and that they were the prevailing sentiments in no less a place than the State Department in Washington,* and they were determined to remove any doubts on the matter.[5]

The Imperial Conference of 1930 was the turning-point. The Dominions failed to reach agreement and the Irish submitted a minority resolution. They made it clear that it was upon this resolution that they would act in future and they defended the right of each Dominion to determine its own practical arrangements. On 3 January 1931 the Executive Council of the Free State decided to make the occasion of their new procedure an unimportant Treaty of Commerce and Navigation with the Portuguese Republic.† The King would be advised directly by his Irish ministers, and the Treaty would be authenticated by a newly-struck 'Great Seal of the Irish Free State'.‡

This intention was notified to Downing Street and immediately a tough British rearguard action was commenced. The British clung desperately to the single Great Seal, so important a feature of the unity of the Commonwealth and of its image abroad. The documents available concerning the struggle which was then joined are incomplete, but they do paint much of the picture with a vividness difficult to recapture at second hand; and they reveal in full measure

---

* See Ch. 8 (particularly note 106) above.
† The Draft Instrument of this Treaty is contained in Appendix E.
‡ See Memo to Executive Council, Irish Free State, 3 January 1931, set out in Appendix F.

the strength of British resistance to Irish pressure even yet, and the sort of tactics employed by both parties in their determination to prevail.

The first revealing Irish salvo – Despatch no. 17, of 24 January 1931 – is a counter-attack to a British telegram of 21 January. The Irish Despatch, signed by Sean Murphy, for the Minister of External Affairs, sets the scene:

Sir,

I have the honour to refer to your confidential telegram of 21 January in reply to my despatch of the 17 January on the subject of the ratification of the Treaty of Commerce and Navigation between the Irish Free State and Portugal.

2. It will be remembered that the Irish Free State representative on the Sub-Committee on Seals at the Imperial Conference 1930, expressed the views of this Government in the following terms:—

'The manner in which the King's signature is confirmed is for the Government concerned to decide.

If the Government concerned decides to use signets and a Great Seal the form of the signets and of the seal is for that Government to decide. In the Irish Free State the seals have been established by law, and if the Irish Government decides to use seals the seals would be those so established.'

3. At the meeting of heads of delegations on the 10 November, I made it quite clear that the position of the Irish Free State was that stated by its representatives on the sub-Committee. At a subsequent meeting I stated that the manner in which the King's signature was confirmed was for the Government to decide.

4. It will be remembered that conclusion (C) originally read:

'The subject should be postponed on the understanding that the whole question should be reviewed at the next Imperial Conference.'

and that it was subsequently amended on the suggestion of General Hertzog to read as follows:

'The subject should be postponed on the understanding that the whole question should be left for further discussion between Governments should occasion arise.'

5. It was not my understanding of that conclusion that no change in the procedure could be effected until a full discussion had taken place between His Majesty's various Governments. Had I thought so, I should not have concurred in the conclusion on behalf of the Irish Free State.

6. The object of General Hertzog's amendment was clearly to permit of a change being made without awaiting the next Imperial Conference.

If a question in regard to which it was not possible to find a solution around the Conference Table, was to be discussed between the various Governments by correspondence, the likelihood of a solution being found would be remote indeed. In view of the statements made by the Irish Free State it is clear that the interpretation of Conclusion (C) expressed in your telegram under reply was not, and could not have been contemplated by us.

7. Our understanding of conclusion (C) was that any Government desiring a change in the existing procedure would naturally raise the question with His Majesty's Government in the United Kingdom, in view of the fact that it was through the instrumentality of that Government that part of the procedure was carried out.

8. In my despatch No. 301 of the 22 December transmitting the instrument of ratification of the London Naval Treaty I intimated that henceforth His Majesty's Government in the Irish Free State intended to adhere to the principle set out in the statement made at the Imperial Conference.

9. His Majesty's Government in the Irish Free State consider that their attitude on this question is completely in accord with the constitutional position of the Irish Free State as a member of the British Commonwealth of Nations and with the conclusions reached at the Heads of Delegations meeting.

I have the honour to be,
Sir,
Your most obedient servant

Signed S. Murphy, for Minister for External
Affairs.[6]

Concurrently with this notification the Irish Government pressed ahead with the rest of its plan. It instructed its High Commissioner in London to negotiate direct access to the Monarch.

The Irish were concerned with principle and were determined that their advice to the King would not have to pass through any British Government channels. The actual form of their direct access was less important. The High Commissioner was ordered to open discussions.

The form of instruction sent to Dulanty, the High Commissioner, is not available, but a copy of the alarmed reply received by him from the King's Secretary indicates that the British were no more ready to concede this right than that of the official seals. Written on 26 January 1931, at Buckingham Palace, the reply reads as follows:

BUCKINGHAM PALACE
26th January, 1931

Dear High Commissioner,
   Since the receipt of your letter of the (19th)
inst, the matter to which it refers has been most
carefully considered.
   Am I not right in assuming that the proposal it
contains regarding the presentation to His Majesty the King
of the Instrument of Ratification of the Treaty of Commerce
and Navigation between the Irish Free State and Portugal
is a new procedure? And one which, I venture to think the
King should not have been asked to follow in any particular
case until His Majesty's approval had first been obtained.
No antecedent step of this nature has been taken, nor any
opportunity sought for ascertaining the King's wishes in
a matter in which His Majesty has a close personal interest.
   Would you be good enough to represent this
aspect of the question to your Government: and, in the
meantime, it would, perhaps, be premature for you to see me.

Yours very truly,

(Sgd) STAMFORDHAM.

John Whelan Dulanty Esq., C.B., C.B.E.,
   High Commissioner for the Irish Free State,
   33–37 Regent St. London S.W.1.[7]

The next stage of the engagement is best told in the words of J. P.
Walshe, the tactician of the Irish Department of External Affairs,
who went over to London to conduct an unofficial exploration with
his British counterparts. His account, unfortunately undated, is
taken from a copy of the official Departmental memorandum. His
delightful frankness illuminates many aspects of Anglo-Irish relations at that time, both the spirit as well as the letter. He proceeds:

My dear Minister,
   I was with the British yesterday from 11 o'clock until 7.45 in the
evening (having lunch with four of them). Batterbee was the principal
on the British side. They let me open the discussion. I did so on the
following lines, which I hope you will approve, notwithstanding the
inaccuracies and exaggerations.
   My Minister thought that their method of arguing about the meaning

of the text in the Imperial Conference minutes relating to seals was not serious. They misconceived the whole situation. The issue between us did not concern the interpretation of a particular text, nor indeed the general conclusions of the Imperial Conference. The vital issue at stake was the whole relationship between our two countries in the future. It was a fundamental error on the part of the British to suppose that there was even a remote similarity between our position and that of the other Dominions:—which were still evolving out of the colonial stage. No apparent acquiescence on our part in the past in such an artificial assimilation should have deceived them as to the real needs of our essentially distinctive and separate nationality. Let us therefore get away from trivial texts of Reports in which apparent common agreement and uniformity covered the most radical divergence of views. It would be for ever impossible for Ireland and New Zealand to take the same view in national matters, and the last Conference was a failure because the British Ministers did not realise that simple truth.

My Minister and his colleagues, long before the Imperial Conference, had been watching with pained surprise a new and dangerous phase in the policy of the British Government in relation to inter-Commonwealth matters. The Conservative Government, following the desire of the Dominions, and not least of the Irish Free State, had formulated the principle of co-equality, and had accepted the conclusions urged on them by ourselves and Canada that co-equality could only become an operative principle through the complete equating of the relations between each Dominion Government and the King with the relations between the United Kingdom Government and the King.

In his speech at the Oxford Raleigh Club, and in his speech on the Dominions estimate in the House of Commons, Mr MacDonald had practically declared the policy of his Government to be the direct opposite of that of the Conservatives. The Dominions, he said, must stop their progress on the co-equality road. There must be an organic unity. The Imperial Conference of '26 had gone too far. My Minister and his colleagues could only draw one conclusion from that attitude. The Labour Government had decided to restore the position of the British Government as a supreme controlling power over the Dominion Governments and to eliminate the King from the *inter se* relations of the Commonwealth. They had apparently decided that the monarchy was bound to disappear within a relatively short time and it was not their desire to add to the power and prestige of the King by allowing the Dominions to have direct relations with him. Such a policy was, no doubt, due to the influence of the Republican doctrinaires who appear from time to time in the Labour Party. (This insinuation seemed to have a powerfully worrying effect on Batterbee and Co., and he disappeared soon after to have half an hour's talk with Mr Thomas.)

My Minister and his colleagues believed that the King and the King alone could keep the Commonwealth together and they were determined to establish their own relations with the King on a proper basis, unless they were forced away from him by the British Government. If the British Government adopted that line they would have themselves to blame if the Government adopted non-monarchical methods in their future intra-Commonwealth and external relations. They had the means of doing so, and they were not going to be held up, especially in their policy of developing friendly relations with foreign countries. What did my Minister want? Complete untrammelled control of our external relations and everything remotely appertaining thereto. There must be no British control, not even in the form of control over documents relating to our external affairs, and there must be the completest freedom of access to the King. No British Minister should, in future, be used as the channel between our Government and the King.

My Minister must be able to say without any shadow of reservation that the advice tendered to the King was the advice of his Government, that that advice was tendered either by him in person or through a properly accredited agent, that the seals and documents used were in the complete and absolute control of the Irish Government. That was the only possible condition in which a complete and friendly understanding could begin to exist between the two countries. Continued interference meant continued friction, and the people who were responsible for the interference must take the consequences.

After this discourse which was very frequently interrupted and broken by long arguments the British came down to fundamentals, dropped all talk about interpretation of texts of Imperial Conference Reports, about the need of uniformity and all the usual dope with which they have been annoying and boring us for such a long time. I repeated again and again that you would never again have anything to do with British seals of any kind and that you would brook no further interference in the relations of our Government with the King. In fact I did my best to produce the impression that you and all your colleagues were in exceedingly bad temper owing to the attitude of intransigence and intolerance adopted by the British Government for the last twelve months.

How far have we got? I presumed your good will to let me discuss the last details, while making it quite clear that I was speaking unofficially and without powers. In the circumstance it was the only way to discover their entire mentality – if that is ever possible. The enclosed draft secret report of our conversation on the seals to be given by B. to his Government represents after much chopping and changing on both sides the bare bones of the conclusion. I gathered on Batterbee's return that Thomas was ready to go almost the whole way with us. B. Himself and Schuster appeared to be the chief opponents to surrender on the question of the single physical Great Seal and I think without being quite sure that the *mot d'ordre* came from Thomas after consultation with MacDonald to both of whom all my remarks has been detailed by Batterbee.

I am personally convinced that the King himself would not consent nor would the British Government to let us have a seal for the purpose of confirming the King's signature which did not contain some representation of the King; some sort of indication that he was an operative

factor in the act to which his signature was appended. I urged as strongly
as I could that the signature was quite enough, that the form of the seal
was indifferent. They wanted to insist that the only possible indication
were the royal arms as at present appearing in the signet. I replied that
such a symbol represented the British Crown in a sense in which we
could not accept it, and the only possible compromise which my
Minister might consider accepting was a Seal having on one side a
representation of the person of the Monarch for the time being, with
his title round the margin, and on the other the Irish Harp and inscrip-
tion as at present appearing on our seals. That compromise would show
the relationship between the Monarch and the Irish Free State to the
exclusion of the British Government. The representation of the King
could be exactly the same as on the present British Great Seal i.e. the
side on which George V appears sitting on his throne. The signet for
use on foreign documents would be a miniature of the new seal and like
it would be affixed in double embossed wax to a ribbon attached to the
document. The seals would take the place of the British seals on all our
external instruments signed by the King. The British said that the
King could not and never does waive all his personal feelings in dealing
with his Ministers, that he was of a highly argumentative and somewhat
victorian disposition. He might, they said, want to hand you these seals
himself. In fact if you agreed to his doing so it would help both him
and the British Government to fall in with our demands. I expressed
the view that if the King desired to hand the seals to you I could not
conceive you accepting the proposal unless it was done in a completely
informal way. You might, I suggested, be ready to hand the seals to
Stamfordham on your way in to the King and the latter could then
hand them back to you or you might agree to send them to the King
beforehand through Dulanty but under no circumstances could you
agree to any publicity either for your visit or for the handing over of the
seals. They acquiesced in that condition.

In insisted that the seals must be created entirely by ourselves. There
need be no name for the seals. We have a Great Seal and Ministerial
seals. The new seals would be created by legislation, if you thought it
necessary for the purpose of sealing documents signed by the King. The
British thought that the King might ask you – as he sometimes asks
British Ministers – whether you were sure of the legal side of your
proposals. In that case, I said that you would send our Attorney General
to explain to the King the legal basis of the new seals. In this country
the Attorney General is sometimes sent to the King at his request to
explain points of law, and the British admitted that there is no reason
why we should not do likewise.

Let me recapitulate shortly the entire procedure to be adopted if you
think well of the proposals.

Having agreed with the British Government as to the design (as
explained) you would prepare a document called a 'Submission' setting
out quite simply and shortly that your Government regard the present
system of seals and advice as out of harmony with the constitutional

relations between the Government of the Irish Free State and the King, that you propose to create new seals (telling him the design), and in future to communicate with him directly or through your High Commissioner in London. You would tell him, to make things easy for him, that the difficulties with the British Government have been eliminated. You would send the document to the King and a few days later you would go to the Palace, explain the situation verbally and advise. Measures would be taken to prevent publicity. The Seals would be struck at once, and you could get your documents signed by the King through Dulanty and Stamfordham. The Ministers here do not in the ordinary course present documents for signing. They go through the Private Secretary.

The British have thrown up the sponge. Our real *coup de maître* in this whole matter was getting Dulanty to approach the Palace. That convinced the British that we were ready to go any length. I think they have made up their minds not to class us any more with the other Dominions.

Can you accept the compromise? To put the image of the existing monarch on an Irish Free State seal used only for confirming the King's signature is to my mind a safe and logical constitutional procedure. If legislation and a full explanation is necessary you will have an opportunity of making a first-class political and international statement. You will be able to say that you have eliminated the last shadow of control of the British Government over the Irish Free State – that there is now no flaw internally or externally in the independence of the Saorstat. It would be of great advantage to be able to intimate to foreign countries that the seals on our external documents are now purely Irish seals. You remember that the State Department regards the seal as the measure of our independence. We shall have advanced further than any Dominion, placed ourselves in a different and better category. I most earnestly hope that you will find it possible to get the proposal accepted. I believe it solves our difficulty and if we reject the idea of the King's photograph on the back of the seal we cannot any longer use the King as a means of further independence. We have broken the unity which they attached to the physical oneness of the seal, and I think that achievement is worth while.[8]

Walshe rounded off his report with some unrelated matters which were also at issue between the two Governments. The logic of equality had led onward, and the Irish Free State was now removing the last obscuring barrier. The Dominions would surely soon be seen to be free.

On 19 March 1931 Mr Patrick McGilligan himself arrived at Buckingham Palace and carried through his Government's purpose. His task was fourfold: to establish direct access to the King; to advise him to sign the particular treaty; to take this document away;

and to put upon it the authenticating Great Seal of the Irish Free State. His appointment had been arranged by Dulanty and he went to the Palace unsure of the type of reception that awaited him. He was shown into King George alone.

After enquiring about the Irish minister's sea journey from Ireland, the King glanced briefly at the document before him and then asked McGilligan where he would like him to sign. McGilligan was taken aback, so the King explained the British convention. 'If I am signing to denote that I have read and approved,' he said, 'I sign at the bottom. But if I am signing to denote that I am under orders to sign, I sign along the side. I expect you would like me to sign along the side?' McGilligan indicated that this was so.

The King then smiled, signed and remarked that while it may have been a bit rough for McGilligan's night journey over, this night would no doubt be a good one.

McGilligan agreed that the weather had improved, but the King explained that he had been referring to the Irishman's great constitutional victory and to the celebration that would no doubt be following it.

Charmed, McGilligan informed King George that his Government preferred to regard these matters as constitutional developments, nowadays, rather than victories, and the interview ended. At the personal level the matter had been amicably and successfully concluded.[9]

On 27 March, the Irish Government revealed the importance of the visit which McGilligan had made to London and outlined the new procedure which had been established.[10] To Professor Berriedale Keith this action was of 'fundamental importance' for it had removed 'a power which the British government formerly possessed in law of securing consideration of any proposed action which might injure the rights of other Dominions or of the United Kingdom'.[11] To the Canadian historian, R. M. Dawson, this step 'decisively settled a controversial point of many years standing'[12] and placed responsibility for Dominion action squarely on the shoulders of the Dominion Governments – at least those which followed the Irish example. To the *Round Table* Irish correspondent the Irish action established the Kingdom of Ireland and was 'another stage in the success of the policy of the Free State in bringing constitutional forms into conformity with constitutional realities'.[13] But to the Irish Government itself it was simply a clinically logical excision of

British governmental power from the affairs of the Irish Free State. The last major step would be the removal of the Privy Council.

(ii) Other Events

The Cosgrave Administration did not in fact achieve the abolition of the Appeal to the Judicial Committee of the Privy Council before its own mandate expired, early in 1932. Ernest Blythe, in 1929,[14] had pointed out that the Appeal was effectively dead and had called upon the British Government to give it a decent burial. McGilligan had promised to end the Appeal, in December 1930, and again in March 1931.[15] In Canada, Ernest Lapointe deflected criticism of the Appeal in his country by saying that it was 'of our own free will', and by pointing out that the British Government had made it clear that 'when one of the sister nations of the Empire wants to do away with that appeal, it is for her to decide'.[16] On 17 July 1931, McGilligan told the Dail that a Bill was in the course of preparation.[17] Meanwhile, as we have seen, J. P. Walshe had argued the issue in uncompromising terms in London. He told the British Government that the Irish had been treated scandalously on this issue at the 1930 Conference and that they were very angry and had now no alternative but to eliminate the Appeal by unilateral legislation. Political and constitutional reasons compelled swift action and the Irish Government would not hesitate to take such action.[18] The British Government refused to co-operate.[19] In the event, however, action was not taken. The legal technicalities may have delayed the Bill or there may have been a change of mind on political priorities: whatever the reason, the Appeal remained until de Valera removed it, in November 1933.[20]

Another controversial issue which the Cosgrave Government attempted to tackle in this pre-election year was the Oath of Allegiance, which members of the Dail were required to take. This was an integral part of the Treaty Settlement and as such the Irish tried to settle it by negotiation. Sean Murphy* was sent over by the Department of External Affairs to explain the situation to the British in London. He pointed out that removal of the Oath had become a major political issue in Ireland and one of the chief planks of the Opposition Fianna Fail platform. If the British would agree now to remove this oath, de Valera would not come to power. If they did not

* Assistant Secretary, External Affairs Department. He recalled this in interview.

agree, then he would be elected and he would proceed to remove it unilaterally. It was a clear-cut decision but the British either did not believe Murphy's case or they underestimated de Valera's intransigence. The Oath was not removed and Murphy's forecast became fact.

On 23 June, to turn to European affairs and the rest of the year's events, the Irish Free State replaced the many existing Anglo-French Conventions, to which it was attached, by a Treaty of Commerce and Navigation between France and the Irish Free State. Three days later Dail Eireann debated the 1928 General Act for the Pacific Settlement of International Disputes. This Act, as McGilligan explained, was a further development in line with the League Covenant. It had been adopted by the General Assembly of the League on 26 September 1928, and the Irish Government now proposed to accede to it. The British, along with Australia and New Zealand had already acceded in May, and Canada had followed in June, but all these with the by now customary reservations.[21] The Irish Free State did not believe that these reservations were in keeping with the League Convenant and it followed its own previous example by acceding unconditionally. Once more it held an independent view and stood by it.

1931 was of course a year of almost universal economic recession, and this was one of the main preoccupations of the League of Nations. Great Britain was forced to go off the Gold Standard, and throughout the Commonwealth the effects of the world economic disorder became more acute. But the outstanding Commonwealth event of 1931 remained in the constitutional sphere: the enactment in the Imperial Parliament, on 11 December, of the Statute of Westminster. In a sense it was no longer news when it was enacted, so much of it having been prepared and argued out in previous years. But it did embody tremendous endeavour and it remains of signal significance to the Commonwealth today. Although most of its content has already been discussed, the final passions which it aroused are important, and the Statute itself brings to a suitable conclusion a decade of constitutional development.

(iii) THE STATUTE OF WESTMINSTER

The Statute of Westminster, that 'one great legal landmark in the history of the Commonwealth',[22] 'the most important of the rules of strict law which define Dominion Status',[23] was enacted 'to make clear the powers of the Dominions' and 'to promote the spirit of free co-operation amongst the members of the British Commonwealth of Nations'.[24] It was a controversial Statute and discussions of it distracted Dominion Parliaments throughout the Commonwealth during the summer months of 1931. These discussions mirrored the several Dominion reactions to 1926 and 1929, and nowhere were divisions of opinion more marked than in the Imperial Parliament itself. In Britain, in and out of Parliament, the Statute was analysed, condemned or accepted, politicians, historians, commentators and constitutional lawyers all airing their views. In the Dominions, also, opinion was divided and particular reservations were imposed to safeguard minority or provincial rights or to meet peculiar conditions or requirements. Federal Australia and Canada perforce trod more warily than unitary South Africa and the Irish Free State; New Zealand remained regretfully aloof.

New Zealand in fact, to take the least enthusiastic first, approved the Statute on 21 July. But Mr Forbes, premier since the previous year, 'was far from enthusiastic'.[24] The Imperial Conference of 1930, he claimed, was 'more concerned to consolidate the unity of the British Commonwealth than to lay down any principles of status or freedom for the Dominions'.[25] Neighbouring Australia was not much keener, but the Scullin Government felt that it was less dangerous to approve the Statute than to do nothing. Attorney-General Brennan proposed this approval on 3 July, and J. G. Latham, Deputy Leader of the Opposition, subjected it to an anxious and detailed analysis. He did not want it to cause trouble in the Australian Commonwealth and he proposed a provision to safeguard the rights of the States.[26] He also recommended a clause similar to that made by the New Zealand delegation at the 1930 Conference, namely that the Statute should not apply to Australia until the Parliament of Australia deemed it necessary. Latham regretted that family relationships which had brought so much benefit should now be written down in legal terms, and this view was very forcibly endorsed by ex-Premier Hughes in characteristic language. Hughes considered the whole affair an act of supreme folly and he proposed his own alternative to the Statute.[27] He obviously resented the success of Irish and South African agitation, deploring 'the fact that the British Government listened to these tempters – these men who, in some instances were newcomers to the table of the Empire'.[28]

There were others less fearful of the proposed Statute, and its approval – with Latham's provisions – was secured. Out of Parliament, ex-Premier Bruce confessed that he too was worried but thought it best that the poison of discontent should be removed.[29]

In Canada, provincial representatives met in April and recommended modifications to safeguard their powers. These were accepted by the Bennett Government. In the Canadian House of Commons Bennett himself moved the resolution of approval with 'utmost pleasure',[30] as it was the culmination of the long progress from Colony to self-governing Dominion. Ernest Lapointe, now in Opposition, but formerly so deeply concerned in that progress, supported the Statute and denied that any practical restrictions which might remain on the sovereignty of the Canadian Parliament or Courts entailed inequality of status, so long as these restrictions remained at the request of Canada herself to suit her complex federal position. Others were not so sure and while the ultra loyalists regretted the formalisation of the family bond, nationalists like Bourassa jeered at this half measure and prayed 'for the day when Canada will once more be in the vanguard instead of the rearguard of enfranchisement and autonomy'.[31] R. M. Dawson, was among the unenthusiastic. The goal of self-government had been reached within the Empire and legal theory had now caught up with events: but the measure was passed 'chiefly to satisfy those sensitive Dominions and fussy persons who were not content with constitutional practice as enunciated in 1926 but who demanded legal as well as practical equality'.[32]

In South Africa the constitution was uncomplicated by a federation of states and controversy turned on the important entrenched clauses which the South Africa Act contained. Guarantees were sought by the Opposition, led by Smuts, that these clauses would not be revoked, once the Government received unfettered powers under the Statute. General Hertzog gave the required assurance, Smuts's amendment was accepted, and approval was given for the Statute to be enacted. To Hertzog this was the great step which crowned all his labours, which removed 'ninety-five per cent of the accumulated grievances and misunderstandings of the last hundred years'[33] and which provided the country at last with a basis for unity.

At Westminster, the Statute was discussed with heat. Introduced to the Commons on 12 November, it was debated at length on both the twentieth and twenty-fourth. The Lords debate was on the twenty-sixth. Both British and Irish attitudes revolved around the relationship existing between their two countries, which was complicated by the still surviving and contrary interpretations of the Anglo-Irish Treaty, and the subsequent legislation establishing the Free State.[34] Few in Britain considered Irish nationhood autochthonous, assuming that it derived from British statute; but would this Statute affect the Treaty, or was this safely entrenched in the Irish Constitution? Could the Irish Government be trusted? If not, could special legislation limiting the Statute in respect of Ireland really secure British interests? Why not leave well alone, instead of committing to paper the beautiful mysteries of the imperial relationship? These questions were asked in debate: harsh words were spoken in answer. Each suggestion of mistrust, each demand for safeguards alienated sympathy in Dublin and finally brought forth a dignified and unanswerable protest from President Cosgrave.

J. H. Thomas, Secretary of State for Dominion Affairs, opened the debate in the Commons on 'the most important and far reaching [Bill] that has been presented to this House for several generations'.[35] He traced the story of Colonial and then Dominion advance up to its culmination in this Statute, but emphasised that, far from being merely the end of the road, this was 'the beginning of a new system'.[36] Sir Stafford Cripps rose next to support the Bill. He pointed to the necessity of full trust in and freedom for the Dominions. 'Face the facts' was his plea: it was wiser to 'make the legislative provisions fit in with those facts, than to have the law in a state which does not accord with either the desires of the people of the Empire or the stage of evolution which the Empire has reached.'[37]

Cripps did his best to steer the debate away from areas of Anglo-Irish controversy. He was wasting his time. He was succeeded by Winston Churchill who opened up a magnificent salvo of condemnation in three directions: the Empire, India and above all Ireland. Churchill anticipated the amendment to be proposed by Colonel Gretton, designed to protect both the terms of the Anglo-Irish Treaty and the constitutional position of Northern Ireland.* In a 'most impressive, thoroughly mischievous and wrong-headed, but

* Col. Gretton's amendment involved the insertion of a new clause: 'Nothing in this Act shall be deemed to authorise the legislature of the Irish Free State to repeal, amend or alter the Irish Free State Agreement Act, 1922, or the Irish Free State Constitution Act, 1922, or so much of the Government of Ireland Act, 1920, as continues to be in force in Northern Ireland.' 260 H.C. deb. 5s. col. 303.

most effective'[38] speech he argued that the Irish Free State Constitution Act, 1922, should, like the British North America Acts, 1867 to 1930, be excluded specifically from the operation of the Statute, apparently considering that such a measure would have the effect of preventing the Irish Government from legally repudiating the Treaty.[39] Ireland was now squarely in the ring and it remained there until the close of the debate.

It fell to Sir Thomas Inskip, the Solicitor-General, to reply on behalf of the Government at the end of the first day. Outlining the facts of the Commonwealth relationship, he pointed out that the imperial parliament could not go against express Dominion wishes. He recognised that 'undoubtedly the crux of this discussion this afternoon has been the position of Ireland'[40] and he hinted at the confusion of interpretation concerning the Treaty and the Constitution which were, nevertheless, 'irrevocably woven together'.[41] His views may not have been in accord with Irish legal opinion, but he did emphasise the necessity of showing confidence in the present Irish leaders, paying tribute to the integrity of the Cosgrave Government.

Allegations, however, had been made, and the Secretary for the Dominions had been ambiguous in his final statement.* The Irish Government could not sit idly by. President Cosgrave deemed it necessary to pen a word of warning to his opposite number in Britain. A passage of his letter was read out to good effect when the debate resumed on the twenty-fourth. Written on the twenty-first it was unequivocal:

> I have read the report of last Friday's debate in the House of Commons on the Statute of Westminster Bill, and am greatly concerned at Mr Thomas's concluding statement that the Government will be asked to consider the whole situation in the light of the debate. I sincerely hope that this does not indicate any possibility that your government would take the course of accepting an Amendment relating to the Irish Free State.
>
> I need scarcely impress upon you that the maintenance of the happy relations which now exist between our two countries is absolutely dependent upon the continued acceptance by each of us of the good faith of the other. This situation has been constantly present in our minds, and we have re-iterated time and again that the Treaty is an agreement which can only be altered by consent.

* 'Every consideration', Thomas had promised, 'will be given between now and Tuesday to all that has been said here today and . . . the Government will be asked to consider the whole situation in the light of the Debate that has taken place.' Ibid. col. 1253.

I mention this particularly because there seems to be a mistaken view in some quarters that the solemnity of this instrument in our eyes could derive any additional strength from a Parliamentary law. So far from this being the case, any attempt to erect a statute of the British Parliament into a safeguard of the Treaty would have quite the opposite effect here, and would rather tend to give rise in the minds of our people to a doubt as to the sanctity of this instrument.[42]

To Colonel Gretton's amendment, this letter provided the *coup de grâce*.* In spite of persistent support the proposed clause was overwhelmingly defeated by 360 votes to 50.[43]

Official Irish reaction to the debate at Westminster is well characterised by President Cosgrave's letter. As to the Irish Government's response to the Statute itself, no better indication exists than the statement of political faith which was delivered by Patrick McGilligan urging approval of the Statute in July. Bearing in mind what had yet to be done, McGilligan took pride in his country's work: work of an imperial significance, the strong domestic motivation of which he clearly revealed. By combining below his two speeches to the Dail, opening and closing the debate, a full record of the Irish achievement is portrayed:

> You cannot approach the consideration of this subject – the subject of the relationship between Great Britain and the other members of the Commonwealth of Nations – as if it had no history, no genesis, no development, no chequered background of alternate controversy, constraint, concession and ultimate progress. When the Irish Free State came into existence in 1921 we happened to strike in at a definite stage in the evolution of the other members of the Commonwealth. But their evolution, though politically rapid, had been slow from the point of view of legal expression of the political facts. There was a whole hinterland of highly anomalous law to be cleared out of the way, and an elaborate system of administrative practice to be transformed or discontinued.
>
> Deputies will agree with me when I say that there can be no two views on the question that when this country accepted the status of Canada in certain respects in 1921 the status of Canada then accepted was not a stereotyped legal formula. Therein lies the kernel of the whole Treaty position and the key to the progress that has gone on – I will not say at our whole behest, or even always at our instance – since 1926. How well the founders of this State builded, the developments which have since taken place go to show. The task begun in 1926 – the first Commonwealth Conference since the Treaty in which we took an active

---

* Reactions in the House were recorded in *The Economist*: the letter 'did not move' Churchill; it 'shook' Lord Hugh Cecil, and 'mollified' Austen Chamberlain. *The Economist*, 28 November 1931, p. 1000.

part – is completed in the paragraphs written down in Part VI of this Report.* [44]

Mr McGilligan proceeded in detail to display the merits of the Report. He referred to the declaration that British Statute would no longer apply in the Dominions, except by their request:

> That declaration will not remain merely as a record in the report of a conference of delegates from the various parts of the Commonwealth. It will become at the end of this year an enactment in a British statute. And its effect then will be to destroy as a matter of law what has already been destroyed as a matter of practice, the legislative sovereignty of the British Parliament in the Commonwealth in the sense in which it existed and functioned since the foundations of the Colonial Empire were laid. The importance of that achievement is beyond question. I do not want to overstress it but I do not want to have the effect of it minimised. [45]

He then outlined the reason behind this forthcoming British Statute:

> . . . this declaration must be understood in two senses, or rather it must be viewed from two angles. It must be viewed from the point of view of the history which it ends as well as from that of the history which it begins. The last words in the long story of British legislative supremacy occur nowhere more fittingly than in a statute passed as its own deliberate act by the assembly most closely associated with that phenomenon. Lastly there were the courts – you had to put an end to speculative judicial thought. . . . [46]

But the Irish minister was careful to emphasise a most important aspect of the impending statute. Relating his general remark to the specific clause in the Statute upon extra-territorial legislation, he was emphatic:

> I do not mean that the object or effect of this statute is, or will be, to write a new legal Constitution for the Commonwealth of Nations. Let there be no mistake about that. This clause illustrates very clearly the declaratory character of the whole statute. The House will observe that the clause is cast in a form which assumes the existence of the extra-territorial power at the present time. This statute will confer no new legal powers as far as the Irish Free State is concerned. It merely declares their present existence in the States of the Commonwealth. It is a direction: a definition, and a demonstration and proof in the most solemn form possible by the British Parliament that an entirely new situation has come into existence and that the former legal unitary State has gone the way of the former political unitary State and of the former diplomatic unitary State so far as States like Canada and ourselves are concerned. [47]

* I.e. the proposed Statute of Westminster.

In concluding his second speech, the Irish Minister for External Affairs again pointed the historians' context:

When we came into existence as a separate State in 1921, the new system of State relationships under the aegis of the League was hardly two years old. We came into it during its formative period. The Nations of the Commonwealth who sat at the Peace Table in 1919 were beginning their international life. The founders of the Irish Free State were quick to see the course of world events and the inevitableness of the developments which were to make Canada and South Africa and the others co-sharers in the international destiny of the post-war States of the world. The very method chosen for the creation of this State was the international method of a bilateral treaty. If we came into existence untrammelled and unimpeded by so many of those legal forms and anachronistic practices which remained to Canada and South Africa and so on, nevertheless, these things had by reason of their different origins and history survived to those States with whom we had entered into relationships and we accordingly played our part in removing them. The principles laid down in 1926 – or rather formulated in that year – were applied with ruthless logic to the whole field of inter-State relationships within the Commonwealth. And this part VI of this Report shows where the cables strained and where, by force of the political facts and the pull of international events, they smashed right through.

I want to add a personal word as to the pride I have in being associated with the later stages of this Report, because I regard this Report as being the end now achieved to the work which the then Vice-President of this State (the late Mr Kevin O'Higgins) started in 1926. And I want to confess to a great happiness at having been allowed to be associated with the end of the work which he started so well in that period.

There was one big task before the delegates who went to the Conference of 1926. They laid down certain lines. The principles were accepted. They were even accepted as having for some time previously ruled the existence of the States of the Commonwealth but it was declared that certain laws were still not in harmony with the particular facts, and certain laws were passed over to what was described as a committee of experts in 1929 to decide upon, and their report showed that the law should be brought into harmony with the facts. We who were not experts, but who, as representatives of the Governments of the different parts of the Commonwealth, met together and agreed that the principles of 1926 should be applied right down even to the very small pieces of legislation that were caught up by the conference of 1929, and this Report, when it is carried further by statute for these countries that want it carried further will have at last, as I said in the beginning, brought to an end the whole chapter of the single legislative sovereignty and the central Government of the old Empire.

We had one purpose in 1926, and that was that there must be uprooted from the whole system of this State the British Government; and in substitution for that there was accepted the British Monarch. He is a King who functions entirely, so far as Irish affairs are concerned, at the will of the Irish Government and that was the summing up on the whole aim and the whole result of the conferences of 1926, 1929 and 1930.[48]

10

Conclusion

The Statute of Westminster, to some contemporaries the key-stone of a new Commonwealth of freely co-operating, equal States, to others an ominous expression of divisive forces, portent of disunity and imperial demise, was duly passed and made law on 11 December 1931.[1] Two months later – on 16 February 1932 – the Cosgrave Administration was voted out of office* and Mr de Valera became President of the Executive Council of the Irish Free State: the State he had opposed so vehemently and which he had been so reluctant to acknowledge. He was soon to admit the remarkable strides forward which this State had taken since the dark December days when the Treaty was signed.[2] But the honeymoon period with Britain was now at an end. The Commonwealth as a positive Association conferring benefits and safeguards was no longer to be appreciated in Ireland.

For ten years the successors to Griffith and Collins had worked to establish the State on a broad base and had nursed it through successive trials. They had vindicated the rule of law at home and had established the integrity of public service, resisting the temptations of office in the interests of ultimate national unity and union. Abroad they had attained international recognition, relentlessly constructing a national stature out of all proportion to the territorial area within their borders. They had indeed 'redeemed' the 'pledges'[3] of their dead leaders, basing their achievement on the twin rocks of League and Commonwealth. At first apprehensive of their membership of the latter, they had nevertheless recognised its potential and had set out to ensure the rapid and acceptable evolution of that anomalous British Empire towards a clearly visible association of

* For an analysis of this election see W. W. Moss, *Political parties in the Irish Free State*. Professor Hancock summarised the result as follows: 'Scientific, objective, neutral, the Cosgrave State was found wanting in drama and colour. Economic nationalism was sought by many interests and de Valera promised just this.' W. K. Hancock, *Survey of Commonwealth Affairs*, p. 323.

free and equal partner-states.[4] In the ten years allowed to them they had done their work well.[5]

Contemporary apologists and commentators accorded them many tributes. The legal and political stability of the State was remarkable in an era of European unrest and following upon such emotional conflicts in Ireland itself.[6] But stability did not just occur. It was Cosgrave who provided the steadying continuity of experience in public affairs which made it possible. It is said that he was the only politician in a Government of talented individuals. He modestly argues that he simply gave his ministers their heads and they did the rest, but there is no doubt that to his wisdom and moderation much of the early success is due. Internal security on the other hand was the first achievement of Kevin O'Higgins, before he turned to wider horizons.* To Ernest Blythe belongs the credit for orthodox financial stability,[7] while Patrick Hogan radically reorganised the agricultural economy, in some measure realising the Plunkett maxim: 'better farming, better business, better living'.[8] Finally the persistent and penetrating McGilligan, after launching the Shannon hydro-electric scheme, turned to external affairs to round off the work of FitzGerald and of his departed friend O'Higgins. McGilligan, Costello, Walshe, Murphy, Hearne and their subordinates constituted the most formidable team in a highly qualified Government.†

Subsequently, historians have added further comment. Professor Mansergh pays tribute to the 'legislative output and administrative reorganisation'[9] of Cosgrave's Cumann na nGael Party. K. C. Wheare prefers to emphasise, with respect to the Irish Dominion, that 'the principles which its founders asserted, though rejected by other Members of the Commonwealth at the time, came to have a

---

* The Lord Bishop of Killaloe, unveiling a portrait of Kevin O'Higgins at Leinster House, 21 Jan. 1944, made direct reference to his contribution in the imperial field, designating him a 'young Irishman of supreme talent . . . intellectually, perhaps the ablest of them all. He took up the Treaty, unfolded its implications, and, mainly to the exercise of his brilliant and powerful mind at the Imperial Conference, we owe what is now known as the Statute of Westminster. That memorable Statute may be said to have put the goblet of freedom into Ireland's hands to be drained at her discretion.' *Forum*, December 1946 (Treaty Commemoration Number).

† W. B. Yeats also recorded his feelings about these men:
> Had Cosgrave eaten Parnell's heart, the land's
> Imagination had been satisfied,
> Or lacking that, government in such hands,
> O'Higgins its sole statesman had not died.

W. B. Yeats, *Poems* (Variorum Edition, ed. Allt and Alspach, Macmillan, N.Y. 1957) p. 543, 'Parnell's Funeral'.

strong influence on the course of the development of the constitutional structure of the Commonwealth, particularly after 1945. It is clear also that this influence is by no means exhausted.'[10] He puts their achievement in a modern context. It was no mean achievement. Cosgrave's team deserves well of both Country and Commonwealth.

In the sixteen years following Cosgrave's defeat, years during which de Valera remained firmly in power, Ireland made further contribution to the Commonwealth Association, in the process demonstrating particularly the flexibility of its membership. Ireland now stood upon its dignity, self-righteous upon a platform of fundamental national right. Free Ireland was too novel. Irish nationalism in such pure terms was yet too adolescent to exemplify that spirit of Mazzini commended by Professor Coupland at the beginning of our period* and now increasingly relevant to our shrinking mid-century planet.

We may observe that Hancock also invoked Mazzini,[11] showing how in accord with the great European liberal of the last century was General Smuts: Smuts of the League of Nations, of the Commonwealth of Nations, of Humanity, and interdependence of peoples. Mansergh, too, emphasises that it was Mazzini above all who pointed beyond nationality[12] (even though his views on geographical boundaries could be useful to the Irish in a different context). But whilst it may be certain that the 'first duties' of man 'are to Humanity',[13] it is also true that 'Nations are the individuals of Humanity',[14] and that 'Before associating ourselves with the Nations which compose Humanity we must exist as a Nation'.[15] The trouble for Ireland was its continuing struggle to exist as a nation. Under Cosgrave it had perhaps begun to feel something in which the *Round Table* passionately believed: that inside the Commonwealth there lay the opportunity for a co-operation and a true fulfilment which narrow nationalism denied. Perhaps here there was, in embryo, a healthy, practical experience of an extra-national association. But Ireland was dismembered. Ireland did not yet exist as a whole instrument to play in that great orchestra of Humanity. The Ireland of de Valera blamed Britain, and drew apart from the British Commonwealth.

Nevertheless, in so withdrawing, Ireland created precedents which remained, whether the deliberate or accidental results of its policies, as Commonwealth realities. The removal of the Oath of Allegiance and the abolition of the Appeal to the Judicial Committee

* See pp. 12–13 above.

of the Privy Council – both unilateral actions – sprang from interpretations of Anglo-Irish agreements contrary to those obtaining in London. The parallel economic dispute, waged over similarly contradictory interpretations concerning Land Annuities, prevented from the start Irish co-operation at the Ottawa Conference of 1932, and led in the end to a serious diminution of Anglo-Irish trade.* Negotiation was abandoned and bitterness and hostility replaced co-operation. Even more significant, the Irish Nationality Bill, 1935, the Executive Authority (External Relations) Bill, of December 1936, and the new Constitution of 1937 (ratified by the Irish people and thus free of any doubt as to its autochthonous derivation) underlined the separate nature of the Free State, or Ireland, as it now styled itself. Neutrality in the Second World War, unavoidable in a state of such divided loyalties, further emphasised this separateness. And Ireland no longer played an active part in the direction of Commonwealth affairs.

Ireland did not attend the Imperial Conference of 1937. De Valera's External Association had become a reality and Ireland's Commonwealth position had become in every sense exceptional. This has led Mr Gordon Walker to conclude that the Irish role in reshaping the Commonwealth was a limited one, 'was not as great as is often supposed'.[16] By 1937 Ireland's main work had been done, but even its latter demonstrations of independent action had their importance, studied as they were in India, where they created the basis for the acceptance by India and Pakistan of continued Commonwealth membership after independence. 'A bitterness and an intransigence'[17] may have marked de Valera's relations with Britain, but however much they may be regretted they cannot simply be ignored. That so many new African States have since felt able to remain Commonwealth partners must, in some considerable measure, be due to the conscious work of transformation undertaken in the Cosgrave period and to the admittedly more negative decisions of de Valera.

* McGilligan, veteran of Commonwealth Conferences where his constitutional expertise was all-important, had looked forward to this Ottawa gathering which would have allowed his other main interest great scope. He was bitterly disappointed in the Fianna Fail performance and he echoed in interview the view expressed by his leader Mr Cosgrave at the time: 'It is difficult', Mr Cosgrave had observed, 'to realise that such a chance was deliberately thrown away, and that the material advancement of the country was callously subordinated to the pursuit of political futilities.' Dail Eireann debates, XLIV, col 1609.

Cosgrave had worked unremittingly to remove from Irish affairs any form of interference by the British Government. This work was seen to be effective. De Valera carried it on to a conclusion. To the civil servants of the Department of External Affairs there was no dramatic break in 1932.* Work proceeded in a straight line until December 1936, when External Association became a reality. Yet de Valera's touchy and uncompromising nationalism was hardly compatible with Commonwealth co-operation. From 1937 until 1948 the position of the undeclared Republic was illogical.

Both Cosgrave and de Valera had laboured in the hope of ultimate national unity: the reincorporation of the lost six counties. Those counties contained the only Commonwealth vote, but this vote was of little electoral use to the Dublin politicians, and no gesture ever came from the North to help the pro-Treaty Party. It became clear that Dominion status and External Association alike were irrelevant to national re-union. The Northern Irish would accept Leinster House only by rejecting Westminster, and this decision would be dictated, if ever, by factors more fundamental than Commonwealth attachment. Though it had done much to shape the Commonwealth, the Irish Government had never succeeded in inspiring enthusiasm for it amongst its own people. Ireland did not wish to remain connected, and on 18 April 1949, Costello, successor to Cosgrave and former Attorney-General, formally severed the link.

The Ireland of the sixties, the Ireland of peace-keeping in the Congo and Cyprus, is less preoccupied with its British neighbour than was the case in the twenties. Paradoxically, however, co-operation is closer, and the special relationship which exists between such close peoples is recognised not only in Britain but throughout the Commonwealth, by a reciprocal 'non-foreign' status.

The Commonwealth of the sixties, be it observed, has taken decisions surprising in the light of its earlier development. A secretariat has been formed. Canadian Arnold Smith is first Commonwealth Secretary-General, intent on improving consultation and releasing the Premiers from trivia to concentrate on major issues.†

---

* Several senior civil servants have testified that this is so, e.g. F. H. Boland, Sean Murphy, Dr Rynne, Miss Sheila Murphy.

† 'My first step', he has said, 'will be to encourage consultation at all levels inside the Commonwealth. I would like to see the scope of intra-Commonwealth dialogue broadened. This will serve to take the pressure off the Prime Ministers, who will meet less often to talk longer on fewer subjects. We'll look after the details while they deal with the major problems.' *Maclean's Magazine*, 21 August 1965, p. 40.

Laudable evidence though this may be that the Commonwealth dynamic survives, it was not a foreseeable development in the era of Laurier or Mackenzie King. On the other hand, familiar habits have not vanished. The *cri de cœur* of Premier Williams of Trinidad and Tobago after the 1965 Conference has a ring of the twenties about it:

> There is a curious attitude and I was not the only visiting Prime Minister to remark on this – which regarded our Conference either as a sub-committee of the British Parliament or of the British Cabinet.
>
> There is no real value to these meetings if statements are to be made reducing the gathering of Commonwealth leaders to the status of a football of British party politics. From conversations, I know that many Prime Ministers took this view and I happen to be one of them.
>
> Certain topics were ruled out by the chair. The most important was migration, which both Jamaica and Trinidad wanted to raise as a matter of urgency. This is a paramount issue which could break up the Commonwealth.
>
> It was made clear that certain ideas contributed by various Prime Ministers at this Conference could not be incorporated into the communiqué because they would be unacceptable to certain segments of opinion in Britain.
>
> Several of us object strongly to a system of putting up something and saying it represents the consensus of views of those present, unless someone positively objects and asks to have it taken out.[18]

Arnold Smith may perhaps effect the desired changes.

The British Government and the other governments of the State-members of the Commonwealth of Nations do enjoy now a proper conception of the relationship which exists between them: a relationship rooted in free co-operation. The recognition of this conception owes much to the work of the Irish Free State: more than to the single-track South Africa or to the conciliatory and often complacent Canada. In 1921 the British Empire lay shrouded in constitutional mists. By 1931 almost every area of doubt and conflict had been replaced by clarity and accord.* Where mystery or division remained, the Irish Free State had made known its views and prepared the ground for eventual solution. The main achievement of the twenties was that the Commonwealth association was seen to be based on a mutual interest, and the organs which served this interest were modified to accord therewith.

* For a summary of the position of the Commonwealth in 1931, similar to that undertaken for the Commonwealth in 1921, on pp. 8–11, see Appendix G, pp. 271–2.

In ten years an Empire had become a Commonwealth, but should any single Dominion claim to have been responsible for developments which in the end were accepted by all? At the half-way stage in that decade, Desmond FitzGerald made some pertinent observations:

The War, the Treaty of Versailles, and the League of Nations marked the definite entry of the Dominions into the International fellowship. But there were still remaining certain anomalies. Great Britain breaks very reluctantly with forms no matter how devoid of objective meaning. Internally the Governor-General could hold up bills for the pleasure of the Monarch acting on the advice of his British Ministers alone. Externally treaties made by Great Britain were deemed *ipso facto* to include the Dominions unless they were formally excluded therefrom by the act of the British signatory. The British signatory held unlimited powers from the King and accordingly acted for the entire extent of the King's territories. The full power unlimited as to territory issued on the sole advice of the King's British Ministers was of course, objectively, a flagrant violation of the principles of representative government, as was every act of the King in relation to the affairs of a Dominion when he acted independently of the advice of his Dominion executive.

The Saorstat, being an ancient kingdom with a great past, could not acquiesce in a state of things which could be tolerated, temporarily at least, by direct offspring of Great Britain. From the beginning we have striven to emphasise the principle of equality and to persuade Great Britain that the Commonwealth of Nations to which we both belong can only find secure and lasting foundations on the will of the peoples composing it.

The States of the Commonwealth must cling together for their mutual interest, they must co-operate for the furtherance of the interest of the whole group, but that co-operation can never be entirely sincere and whole-hearted until the last vestige and form of control over the Dominions ceases to be vested in the British Parliament. We believe that the continued existence of this association of states is for the good of the individual members composing it, and for the good of the whole family of nations. We believe that its continuance depends entirely on the completion, down to the last formula, of the powers of government in each state of the Commonwealth, and any agency which may be at work, whether in Great Britain or in the other states of the Commonwealth, to put obstacles in the way of that development is an enemy of the Commonwealth and of all the nations that are striving for peace.

We have never claimed any special credit for the achievements of the Imperial Conference. I don't think it is right that any individual or any group of individuals should do so. They were the achievements of the Commonwealth group as a whole and it would be just as harmful for one state of the Commonwealth to take special credit for them as it would be harmful and dangerous for one state of the Commonwealth to endeavour to go back by whatever methods on the principles of *freedom* and *democracy* formulated at the Conference.[19]

FitzGerald's words, based on a thorough knowledge of his government's achievements and intentions, show a proper regard for the developing Commonwealth society. Adopted resolutions were the achievement of all. But since the twenties many claims have been made. Biographers – and there have been none from Ireland – have set out to relate the part played by their subject hero. In isolation each part appears in an exaggerated light. Hertzog, Smuts, Amery, Mackenzie King in turn illumine the Commonwealth scene, while South Africa, Britain and Canada in turn seem to play a predominant role.

Commonwealth commentators have added their authority to this or that interpretation. Because Ireland did not follow the accepted 'rule' of Dominion evolution, Mr Gordon Walker for one dismisses it as an exception, even contending that Ireland serves to prove his rule.[20] He is happy to ignore completely the Irish contribution of the twenties, claiming instead for Canada, the decisive modern role 'down to the Second World War'.[21] He would prefer, though, to assert that 'the history of the Commonwealth discloses, not a series of rearguard actions and retreats, but an orderly and steady advance towards the fulfilment of the inherent nature of the Commonwealth, latent in it from its earliest beginnings.'[22] To such an assertion it is hoped that the story above provides its own answer. Such, at least, was not the case in the period from 1921–31. Here rather was a decade of persistent Irish negotiation directed skilfully towards a desired end: the transformation of an Empire dominated by the Westminster Parliament into a Commonwealth of free and equal partner nations.

Application for Membership of League[1]

To:

The Honourable Sir Eric Drummond 17 April 1923
      Secretary-General
   To the League of Nations
      Geneva.

Sir,

In accordance with the terms of Article 1 of the Covenant of the League of Nations, I have the honour to request that the Free State of Ireland may be admitted as a Member of the League of Nations, and that this request may be placed on the agenda of the next Meeting of the Assembly of the League.

The Government of the Irish Free State is prepared to accept the conditions laid down in Article 1 of the Covenant, and to carry out all the obligations involved in Membership of the League.

The Government will send representatives, empowered to give all necessary explanations, to the Assembly, and it will be glad in the meantime to give any information relevant to this application which may be required.

It is requested that this application may be brought without delay to the knowledge of all the Members of the League.

      I have the honour to be,
        Sir,
           Your obedient Servant,

           (Signed) DESMOND FITZGERALD.
               Minister for External Affairs.

First Draft of Suggested Reply to Despatch No: 628 of 4th November, 1924[1]

REGISTRATION OF THE TREATY

I have the honour to refer to your Despatch No: 628 of the 4 November with reference to the registration of the Treaty.

2. My Ministers find it impossible to accept a view which interprets in a distorted and restricted sense the rights and obligations of the Members of the League of Nations. They can see no clause in the Covenant which in any way purports to differentiate as between the various States Members of the League. There is nothing, in their view, to justify any one Member in withholding or attempting to withhold from any other Member or group of Members any of the rights conferred by the Covenant on all Members of the League without exception.

3. My Ministers having carefully examined all the implications of the action which you propose taking regarding the registration of the Treaty are driven to the conclusion that it must eventually be fatal to the existence of the League itself as it constitutes a definite denial of the equality on which alone the existence of the League is based.

4. It is also their profound conviction, as you are no doubt aware, that the strictest adherence to the principle of perfect equality amongst its members in all circumstances whatsoever is an essential condition for the continued existence of the British Commonwealth of Nations. My Ministers fully recognise the need for the maintenance of the right to make special intra-Commonwealth arrangements, but they do not admit that this end can be legitimately attained at the instance of one member of the Commonwealth alone by general or particular declarations which can only serve to lessen the status and dignity of the other Members in the eyes of the World.

I have the honour to be, etc.

Draft of Suggested Reply to Colonial Office Despatch No: 628 of the 4 November, 1924[2]

Sir,

I have the honour to acknowledge receipt of your Despatch No: 628 of the 4 November concerning the Registration of the Treaty at the Secretariat of the League of Nations. My Ministers desire me to reply as follows:

2. It is quite clear from Article 18 of the Covenant that it is binding upon States Members of the League of Nations to deposit for Registration all Treaties and international agreements. Inasmuch as Great Britain and the Irish Free State are Members of the League and as the Treaty is the basis of the relations between these two States, it was eminently the duty of the Irish Free State Government to register the Treaty. They accordingly entered the Treaty for registration and it was duly registered on 11 July of this year.

3. An attempt now to obtain the withdrawal of this registration must necessarily be regarded as a disavowal of the Covenant or as a declaration that the Dominions are subject States to Great Britain, and in the latter case it must necessarily question the right of the Dominions to membership of the League.

4. Therefore My Ministers cannot in any way agree to the action proposed in your Despatch.

I have the honour to be, etc.

No. 3

Irish Free State Government to League of Nations, 18 December 1924[3]

Saorstat Eireann
18 December 1924

... The Government of the Irish Free State cannot see that any useful purpose would be served by the initiation of a controversy as to the intention of any individual signatory to the Covenant. The obligations contained in Article 18 are, in their opinion, imposed in the most specific terms on every Member of the League, and they are unable to accept the contention that the clear and unequivocal language of that Article is susceptible of any interpretation compatible with the limitations which the British Government now seek to read into it. They accordingly dissent from the view expressed by the British Government that the terms of Article 18 are not applicable to the Treaty of 6 December 1921.

I have the hour to be,

Sir,

Your obedient servant,

J. P. WALSHE,
Secretary.

The Honourable,
Sir Eric Drummond, K.C.M.G.,
    Secretary-General,
        League of Nations, Geneva.

Letter from FitzGerald to Skelton

9 June 1926

My dear Skelton,

I wonder if you could let me know what your arrangements are for this year? I presume that Mr Mackenzie King will be coming over for the Imperial Conference, which is due to begin on 5 October, and I presume that you also will be at the Imperial Conference.

Can you tell me if you will attend the League of Nations, and give me a rough idea as to when Mr Mackenzie King and you will be arriving in Europe?

I feel that the Imperial Conference this year should deal with many constitutional anomalies, and go a long way towards removing at least the majority of the many remnants of a previous state of affairs which are not consistent with the declared equality of the status of the States forming the British Commonwealth of Nations.

I am enclosing a memorandum on some of these points. No doubt you have others in mind. I should be very glad if you could let me know how many of the points in my memorandum are likely to interest your Delegation, and I should also be glad to hear of any points that you are interested in and are not included in the enclosed memorandum.

It seems to me that these inconsistencies can be classed roughly under three headings, viz: Governor General, Extra Territorial Powers and the unqualified right of the Governments of Dominions to be sole and direct Advisers to the Crown on all the affairs of that Dominion, one might say both internal and external. To give an instance under each heading:

The Governor General should clearly now be the Representative of the King – that and nothing but that. If he were that and that only and co-equality were unqualified, and the Dominion Government were sole advisers to the Crown on all matters relating to the Dominion, then it seems that the Governor General should be appointed on the advice of the Dominion Government: also his resignation should be tendered to the Dominion Government or direct to the Crown, or to the Crown through the Dominion Government.

Obviously, too, despatches passing between Dominion Governments and British Ministers should not go through the channel of the Governor General.

Extra Territorial Powers : The most obvious instance here is the fact that Dominion ships sail under the Red Ensign. The fact of the Red Ensign being defaced by the Dominion Arms makes no difference whatever.

It appears that the moment a Dominion ship leaves Dominion territorial waters the ship and all aboard are governed by the laws made by the British Parliament. The same thing applies, of course, to Dominion citizens going abroad, the theory clearly being that once they are outside Dominion territory they are British Subjects – that, and nothing more, and their home Government is the British Government.

The sole and direct right to Advise the King : The most clear instance under this case is the system whereby Dominions (other than the Irish Free State) send certified copies of their Acts when bound, to the British Government, and receive a reply informing them that His Majesty will not be advised to dis-allow the Acts.

I give these merely as instances under the three heads.

You will see in the memorandum other matters referred to, such as the fact that when Great Britain makes a Treaty we are presumably included unless it is specifically stated that we are excluded. Obviously we should be excluded unless we are specifically stated to be included.

I am not wanting to rush things unduly, but I feel that the most of these points can be settled amicably, while their non-settlement can easily lead to friction and misunderstanding.

I think that your Government and ours will have, to a very large extent, a common point of view, and I feel that it would be very useful if we could talk these matters over together as soon as possible. For that reason if I knew when Mr Mackenzie King was due to arrive in London I should do my utmost to be there with a view to arranging as far as possible a common programme between us. And if it is your intention to be present at Geneva this year I think you and I might have some useful talks over these matters.

By the way, you will notice that the recent pronouncement of Lord Cave in the King versus Nadan brings out the danger of relying too entirely on advancement through constitutional usage.

I should be very glad if you can let me know as soon as you know yourself what your plans are, and any ideas you may have about the Imperial Conference.

Best wishes to you and Mrs Skelton.

Yours very sincerely,

MINISTER FOR EXTERNAL AFFAIRS[1]

O. D. Skelton, Esq.,
Office of the Under-Secretary of State for
        External Affairs,
Ottawa, CANADA.

The Minister's Interview
with General Hertzog

The Minister for External Affairs, accompanied by the Secretary of the Department, lunched with General Hertzog at the Metropole on Friday 29 August. During lunch and for two hours after lunch the conversation was entirely on Imperial Conference Questions. The following is a summary of the conversation:

1. *Inter Se.*[1] General Hertzog agreed with the Minister's view that the *inter se* Statement in the 1926 Report, if it expressed something inherent in the constitution of the Commonwealth and inalienably associated with it by virtue of the common Kingship, must be altered because it presupposed a unitary crown and a single international unit. Neither the General nor the Minister thought that there would be anything derogatory to the status of the Members of the Commonwealth if they agreed that they should make a formal declaration *toties quoties* of non-applicability *inter se* in treaties the terms of which would not serve the best interests of the Commonwealth if applied as between the Members. General Hertzog was inclined to regard the Statement as a kind of Agreement only requiring slight modifications, and there was therefore in his view no obstacle in the way of revision. The Minister pressed his point that the 1926 Report merely stated that if the treaty were made in the name of the King the *inter se* non-applicability should be presumed. It was therefore a statement of doctrine and in no sense an agreement. The view that it was a statement of principle and that this principle had the worst possible implications was strengthened by the reference to the discussion at the Arms Traffic Conference of 1925 in the next sentence of the same paragraph of the Report.

The question at issue at the Arms Traffic Conference was the definition of '*International* Trade', and the Dutch delegate proposed that the despatch of arms, munitions, etc. from and to territories *forming part of or placed under the protection of the same Sovereign State* should not be regarded as International Trade, and should not accordingly come within the terms of the Convention. The delegate added that 'International Trade' in arms should be understood as the transfer of arms from the possession of *one political unit to that of another*. That reference clearly indicated that the making of multilateral treaties in the name of the King was intended by the British to convey to the world that the members of the Commonwealth of Nations constituted a single sovereign state. In other words, the Report of 1926 said: According to a principle laid down by the Arms Traffic Convention, relations between two parts of the same sovereign state are not international and cannot be regulated by international conventions. Now the relations between the Members of the British Commonwealth of Nations come under the principle formulated by the Arms Traffic Convention. Therefore these relations are not international, and the members of the Commonwealth form a single sovereign state. The making of Treaties in the name of the King is to be the method of indicating to foreign Governments that internationally the Dominions and Great Britain act as a single state.

During the discussion the Minister for External Affairs also referred to the statement made by Sir Cecil Hurst at the meeting of the Committee of Jurists in 1929. At that meeting 'Mr Raestad asked whether the constitution of the British Empire prevented a dispute between Great Britain and a Dominion or between two Dominions from being brought before the Court. Sir Cecil Hurst replied that the matter had been discussed in London, where the view was that no question arising between Great Britain and a Dominion could be brought before the Permanent Court owing to the provisions of Article XIV of the Covenant, which laid down that the Court possessed jurisdiction only in regard to international disputes. This provision excluded the submission to the Court of disputes between two of the units composing the British Empire, because the relations between them were different from the relations between two foreign states, and for this reason the relations between them were not international. Although the Dominions were autonomous, a dispute between two of them or between a Dominion and Great Britain was not an international matter and could not be brought before the Court.' (The whole passage between quotation marks is taken from the official League of Nations Report C 166, M.66. 1929 V.) The Minister pointed out that this reply of Sir Cecil Hurst, who was the framer of the 1926 *inter se* Statement, showed clearly that that Statement was intended to be a doctrinaire assertion of a supposedly inherent principle which left no freedom for agreement, and was therefore contrary to the other principle of freedom of co-operation upon which the Commonwealth is so frequently declared, in the same Report, to have its real basis. Mr Henderson's declaration about the international position of the Dominions as individual states did not, the Minister thought, effect any change in the position created by the *Inter Se* Statement. It is not certain to what extent General Hertzog is convinced of the seriousness of the *Inter Se* Statement. Further discussions will be necessary.

THE KING AND THE GOVERNMENTS OF THE DOMINIONS

The Minister told General Hertzog that it was his intention to raise formally the question of the right of direct access to the King. Before the

Minister could explain what his procedure was to be, General Hertzog exclaimed: 'That is the key to the whole situation. Direct access will make the personal union a reality.' The Minister went on to outline his suggested procedure. Either the Governor-General should become the substitute for the King in the totality of his functions, and that would be the simplest, though, no doubt, to the English, the least acceptable solution, or the High Commissioner in London should advise the King as the Minister's substitute, it being always understood that the Minister himself could approach the King any time he wished to do so. The High Commissioner would present the document to be signed to the King, who might affix a purely personal seal, but the only State seal to be used would be that of the member of the Commonwealth concerned.

It could still be argued that the King acted on the effective advice of his British ministers in all the major acts (Full powers, Exequaturs, Commissions, Ratifications) through which a Dominion had relations with foreign States. This system raised the strongest presumption in favour of a Unitary State, and taken together with the *inter se* doctrine, it provided all the text writers with a cogent argument against the external sovereignty of the Dominions. The Minister further indicated that a species of Buckingham Palace Secretariat might be suggested by the British as the next best method of exercising control over the advice tendered to the King. Each member of the Commonwealth would be represented thereon, and the document to be signed would be presented by the representative of the member State concerned. Such a secretariat would have many obvious disadvantages, chief amongst which would be its tendency to become an imperial political clearing-house, no matter how minor the officials might be. On the other hand, from the purely constitutional point of view, it would be infinitely better than the present system. General Hertzog said that he would not mind telling the Prime Minister of Great Britain in each case before advice was tendered by him. In this connection, he recalled with disapproval a secret memorandum presented by General Smuts to the 1921 Conference advising the setting up of an Imperial Committee presided over by the British Prime Minister through which all imperial matters (apparently whether having relation to the King or otherwise) should pass. The Minister, referring to General Hertzog's remark that the Prime Minister of Great Britain might be given notice on each occasion when advice was being tendered to the King, urged that the result of following that course would be to leave the real control in the hands of the British Cabinet. Moreover, the principle of co-equality would require that all the Prime Ministers should receive notice. In any case, as the Commonwealth was founded on mutual trust and co-operation, the British would have to take it for granted that no member of the Commonwealth would advise the King contrary to the general interest. The General finally appeared to agree with the Minister's point of view, and added that if the British refused to implement the principle of co-equality in these matters he would have to tell them that co-operation would not be forthcoming. General Hertzog appeared to desire to raise formally the whole question of the personal union as the only possible solution of existing difficulties. The Minister preferred, by eliminating the incidents of the unitary Crown and creating countervailing facts, to reach the same goal without making it a formal issue.

COMMUNICATIONS WITH FOREIGN COUNTRIES

The Minister further informed General Hertzog of his desire to change the present system of communicating with foreign countries in cases where there was no direct diplomatic channel. It was our experience that communications transmitted through the Foreign Office were held up for weeks, sometimes for months. That was true of communications both ways. Apart from the delay there was the more important factor of the impression created abroad as to the position and status of the Dominions. The Foreign Office is regarded by most foreign States as the central Foreign Office of the whole Commonwealth. Very frequently communications intended for the Dominions took the form of a request at the end of a letter or *note verbale* to the British Government that the Dominions were also to be informed, invited, etc. Sometimes the Dominion Governments were referred to as local authorities, at all times the implication of subordination of some sort to the Foreign Office was present. The only proper method, in the Minister's view, was to send the communication direct to the British Minister on the spot. He in turn should send the reply to the Government of the Commonwealth concerned. General Hertzog suggested that there should be no objection to sending a copy of the communication to the British Prime Minister on each occasion. The Minister agreed that, the Minister Plenipotentiary concerned being an agent of the British Government, there could be no serious objection to sending the communication to the British Government but not to the Prime Minister. The Minister emphasised the point that the new system of communication would be in accord with the usual international practice. General Hertzog appeared to realise the difficulties, but the degree to which he would accept the proposed changes was not quite clear. He had himself on some occasions used the channel suggested, but he was asked not to continue doing so.

INTRA-COMMONWEALTH TRIBUNAL

The proposed Tribunal was discussed shortly. General Hertzog held the same view as the Minister as to the *ad hoc* character of the Court, but he seemed to envisage disputes other than inter-government disputes coming before it, for instance, disputes between citizens of two different members of the Commonwealth. The Minister urged the necessity of eliminating every form of non-inter-State dispute. Otherwise the Court might become part of the mechanism of the organic unity which we were trying so hard to avoid. For him the disappearance of the Privy Council in relation to the Saorstat was a condition precedent to the acceptance of any tribunal. The panel for each particular dispute might be selected there and then, or the members of the Tribunal might be taken from some previously agreed general panel. The selection of the Court panel would have to be a matter solely for the disputant States. The body of law and conventions forming the basis for the judgements of the International Court would serve likewise for the Tribunal. General Hertzog did not seem to have given much thought to the Tribunal, but he agreed generally with the Minister's proposals. The Minister reserved further reference to the Court for another chat.

NATIONALITY

The Minister explained to General Hertzog his general line of approach to the solution of the nationality difficulty, his main purpose being to secure that all the incidents of the nationality of each member of the Commonwealth should derive from the legislation of that member following a general agreement as to the elements of common status acceptable to all. In other words a South African was in future to be a South African only, but that description should henceforth connote all the incidents previously proper to a British subject as such, as well as those belonging to the description South African. The Saorstat would have a draft Nationality Bill ready at the time of the Conference. The Minister will also have further discussion with General Hertzog on this matter.

SECESSION

General Hertzog seems to be taking a declaration of the right to secede as a matter of course offering no difficulty whatever. The Minister did not wish to ask General Hertzog what impressions he received from Mr MacDonald in this connection, but the General's easy optimism warranted the conclusion that all was well. He was obviously delighted that General Smuts had given him the opportunity of winning such an easy party victory. He declared that General Smuts's lieutenants were disgusted with their leader for his bad tactics. The Minister had little opportunity of developing his ideas on the Secession question, or of getting more definite information from General Hertzog, as the time for leaving had almost come. In any case, he felt it would be unwise to divert the General from his idea so long as there was no risk of losing the fruits of the 1929 Conference by insistence on getting a further declaration from the British. The leading article in *The Times* of 23 August on the right to secede is an indication that the demand for a declaration would not cause any revulsion of feeling in Great Britain. The Minister further felt that a declaration of the right to secede would be a further strengthening of the Government's constantly reiterated view that the Treaty contained in it all the principles of the most complete freedom. The right to secede once admitted, anti-State politicians would have very little to talk about except humdrum economics. Here, as in South Africa, any party which supported the exercises of the right to secede would find itself up against the instinct of economic self-preservation of the majority of the people. In connection with the Treaty position, General Hertzog remarked to Professor Smiddy a few days ago that, in his view, any restrictions imposed by the Treaty were overridden by the principle of co-equality. General Hertzog, like Mr Beyers, refuses to consider the legal past of the Dominions. For him the basis of Dominion evolution is entirely political and must be divorced from existing law. He brushes aside any reference to the Acts by which the Dominions were established, and concentrates on the principle of co-equality alone.

LEGISLATION BY THE BRITISH PARLIAMENT FOR THE DOMINIONS

The Minister asked General Hertzog what he thought of the right of the British Parliament to legislate for the Dominions which was expressed in paragraphs 54 and 55 of 1929 Report, that right being independent of constitutional exigencies. The General thought the request and consent qualification saved the Dominions' face and left their sovereignty intact. When the Minister suggested that the Dominions should feel their sovereignty infringed by asking France or Holland to legislate for them, the General replied that he understood that the right was restricted to the constitutional requirements of certain Dominions. After further argument he agreed that, if paragraphs 54 and 55 had reference to anything other than the constitutional requirements of Australia, Canada and New Zealand, the wording of these paragraphs should be changed so as to restrict the right to those particular cases.

CONCLUSION

General Hertzog promised the Minister that he would come to Dublin on his return from Geneva about 17 September. The Minister will then discuss all the points over again with him, and he will endeavour to secure General Hertzog's co-operation in detail. It is already secured in principle.

1 September 1930.[2]

APPENDIX E

Draft Instrument of Treaty with Portugal[1]

GEORGE, by the Grace of God, of Great Britain, Ireland and the British Dominions beyond the Seas King, Defender of the Faith, Emperor of India, etc.

To all and singular to whom these Presents shall come Greeting!

WHEREAS a Treaty between Us in respect of Our Irish Free State, and Our Good Friend the President of the Portuguese Republic, relative to Commerce and Navigation, was concluded and signed at Dublin on the Twenty-Ninth day of October in the Year of Our Lord One Thousand Nine Hundred and Twenty-Nine by the Plenipotentiaries of Us and of Our said Good Friend duly and respectively authorised for that purpose.

AND WHEREAS the Dail and Seanad of Our Irish Free State have approved of the said Treaty which is word for word as follows:—

AND WHEREAS the Executive Council of Our Irish Free State have advised Us to ratify the Treaty aforesaid,

WE having seen and considered the Treaty aforesaid, have approved, accepted, and confirmed the same in all and every one of its Articles and Clauses, as we do by these Presents approve, accept, confirm, and ratify it, in respect of Our Irish Free State, for Ourselves, Our Heirs and Successors; Engaging and Promising upon Our Royal Word that We will sincerely and faithfully perform and observe all and singular the things which are contained and expressed in the Treaty aforesaid, and We will never suffer the same to be violated by anyone, or transgressed in any manner,

as far as it lies in Our Power. For the greater testimony and validity of all which,

We have caused the Great Seal of Our Irish Free State to be affixed to these Presents, which

We have signed with Our Royal Hand.

Given at Our Court of Saint James
the   day of   in
the Year of Our Lord One Thousand Nine Hundred and Thirty and in
the Twenty First Year of Our Reign.

Change of Seal Procedure[1]

In a memorandum to the Executive Council, 3 January 1931, the intention was made clear that the procedure for ratification of the Treaty with Portugal would be used to inaugurate the new procedure respecting the Seal.

The memorandum contained the background to, and the form of the Treaty to be used. It proceeds.

'The Letters Patent creating the office of Governor-General of the Irish Free State provide for a Great Seal of the Irish F.S. in the following terms:

'There shall be a Great Seal of and for the said State which We do hereby authorise and empower Our said Governor-General to keep and use for sealing all things whatsoever that shall pass the said Great Seal. Provided that, until a Great Seal shall be provided, the private seal of the Governor-General may be used as the Great Seal of the said State.

'This article does not specify what things are to pass the Great Seal, nor does it restrict in any way the use of the Great Seal. It is quite clear that the seal is the Seal of the State, and in no sense that of the Governor-General. Its use depends entirely on the discretion of the Executive Council. In practice it is affixed to certain documents which are signed by the Governor-General on the advice of the Executive Council. It would appear appropriate that the King's signature to a document confirming an agreement between Him as head of the Irish Free State and the Head of another State should be confirmed by the Seal of the Irish Free State. The affixing of the Great Seal will be at the same time confirmation of the constitutional steps taken to effect ratification and evidence of the acceptance by the State of the obligation undertaken in its name.

'The Minister of External Affairs accordingly proposes that the instrument of ratification of the Commercial Treaty between the Irish Free State and Portugal should be sealed with the Great Seal of the Irish Free State, and should then be transmitted to His Majesty for signature.

'Copies of the draft instrument are enclosed herewith.'

Signed Sean Murphy.

The Commonwealth 1931

1. DOMINION STATUS

The successive developments of the twenties had totally altered Dominion status, and this was recognised both inside the Commonwealth and in the world at large.

So far as *inter se* dealings were concerned, the Dominions Office had replaced the Colonial Office in 1925.

International activity had grown apace. Ambassadors, following the Irish example of 1924, had multiplied. Canada had appointed her representative to Washington, at last, in 1927, and had followed this in 1928 with an envoy to Paris and in 1929 to Tokyo. In 1929, also, Irish legations had opened in the Vatican, Paris and Berlin, while the South Africans had begun their diplomatic representation at the Hague, Rome and Washington. Diplomatic unity was ended. The treaty-making power too was now unfettered, following Canada's example of 1923. The right of individual Dominion negotiation, signature and ratification had been agreed in that year at the Imperial Conference. The clear establishment of the right of independent advice to the Monarch and the final affixture of separate Dominion Seals, achieved in 1931 by the Irish Free State, removed any doubts remaining. Britain was no longer able to include the Dominions in her own treaties: the British *inter se* interpretation had been repudiated.

The Statute of Westminster had completed the definition of autonomy: 'the fundamental principle', as Harold Nicolson observed, 'was thus established that a Dominion Parliament could legislate without reference to the laws of the United Kingdom, and that the British Parliament could not legislate for a Dominion without the consent, previously given, of the Dominion concerned.'[1]

The Appeal to the Judicial Committee of the Privy Council, apparently circumscribed in 1926 but unaccountably still frustrating certain Dominion sentiment, remained in being, but due to the Statute of Westminster would only continue to do so at the will of the Dominions.

The anomalies and anachronisms had been ruthlessly cleared away. Dominion status, for all the world to see, rested upon only three principles: the maintenance of allegiance to the Crown;[2] the absence of any element of subordination of one Dominion to another; an acceptance of free association with the other members.[3]

2. THE GOVERNOR-GENERAL

The position of this official had been harmonised with full independent status. He now represented the Monarch. It was now finally established that he was appointed by the Monarch on the advice of the ministers of the Dominion concerned. Here again the Irish had led the way, though commentators show a considerable reluctance to quote Irish precedents.[4] The issue however had been settled beyond question by the Australian appointment of 1930.[5]

3. CONSTITUTIONAL AMENDMENT

Here again, though the Statute of Westminster was not uniformly adopted, no ambiguity remained. Certainly no derogation of status existed where an individual Dominion by its own choice might prefer to retain a procedure for altering its Constitution which still involved the British Parliament. Thus Canada and Australia protected the complex balance of their federal constitutions and New Zealand, by its own choice, ignored the powers available to it.

4. CONSULTATION

The new clarity of Dominion Status was reflected in the more logical way in which the Dominions did their common business. In his handbook on *Consultation and Co-operation in the British Commonwealth*, G. E. H. Palmer has outlined the organs through which the Dominions kept in touch and executed their combined decisions as they stood in 1932. The machinery for consultation had never been adequate but this no doubt suited the purpose of the Dominion governments. Professor Mansergh has observed that all efforts to improve consultation and co-operation fell through because of the lack of underlying interest. The Dominions were never keen on imperial policies.[6]

Palmer nevertheless sets out in order the channels of co-operation: the Governor-General; the Imperial Conference: correspondence and personal contact between governments; inter-imperial bodies, including those for defence and disputes. Great Britain continued, by virtue of its resources and experience, to play a preponderant part in the field of diplomatic services, providing a number disproportionate to those, if any, which it received in return.

Bibliography

The place and date of publication of published works is given, except in the case of those published in London, when the date only is given.

Note on Archival Material
The text of this book was largely completed before the British Fifty-Year secrecy rule concerning official documents was reduced to thirty years, on 1 January 1968. While the proofs were being corrected, however, I was able to check through much of the relevant new material. I found nothing to alter my views, which were in any case based on much of this same material obtained privately. I have, however, been able to attribute some source-references to the Public Record Office, and where small errors of detail emerged I have incorporated the required changes into the text.

In Ireland I was unable to use any official archives, but I did use papers of an archival nature, as mentioned in the Acknowledgements above, and as indicated in the Notes.

1. Manuscripts

Balfour, A. J.	Papers	British Museum, Additional Manuscripts
Costello, J. A.	Papers	Dublin
FitzGerald, D.	Papers	Dublin
Grigg, Sir E. W. M.	Papers	London
McGilligan, P.	Papers	Dublin
Murphy, Charles	Papers	Public Archives of Canada, Ottawa.

2. Personal Interviews

Adams, W. G. S.
Batterbee, Sir H. F.
Blythe, Ernest
Boland, F. H.
Butler, Sir J. R. M.
Cosgrave, W. T.
Costello, J. A.
de Valera, President E.
Dixon, Sir Charles W.

Hancock, Sir W. K.
Hayes, Senator Michael
McCracken, J. L.
McGilligan, P.
Morrah, D.
Murphy, Sean
Murphy, Sheila
Rynne, M.
Wheare, Sir K. C.

3. Parliamentary Debates

Commonwealth of Australia, Parliamentary debates, Senate and House of Representatives, 1921–37.

Dail Eireann debates and Seanad Eireann debates, 1921–31.

Dominion of Canada, Official report of debates, House of Commons, 1921–31.

New Zealand Parliamentary debates, Legislative Council and House of Representatives, 1921–31.

Union of South Africa, debates of the House of Assembly, 1921–31.

United Kingdom Parliamentary debates, House of Commons and House of Lords, 1920–31.

4. Parliamentary and League of Nations Papers

British Parliamentary papers

Address to His Majesty on Irish Affairs from the House of Commons of Canada, and the reply thereto (Cd. 1697) H.C. 1903, XLIV 121.

Correspondence relating to the future organisation of the Colonial Conferences (Cd. 2785) H.C. 1906, LXXVII 53.

Address from the House of Representatives (Australia) and Resolution of the Senate on the subject of Home Rule for Ireland, and the replies thereto (Cd. 2821) H.C. 1906, LXXVII 217.

Published proceedings and précis of the Colonial Conference, 15 to 26 April 1907 (Cd. 3404) H.C. 1907, LV i.

Minutes of the proceedings of the Imperial Conference, 1911 (Cd. 5745) H.C. 1911, LIV 103.

Extracts from proceedings and papers laid before the Imperial War Conference, 1917–18 (Cd. 8566) H.C. 1917–18, XXIII 319.

Conference of the Prime Ministers and representatives of the United Kingdom, the Dominions and India, held in June, July and August, 1921. *Summary of proceedings and documents* (Cmd. 1474) H.C. 1921, XIV 3.

Imperial Conference, 1923. *Summary of proceedings* (Cmd. 1987) H.C. 1923, XII, part i, i.

Imperial Economic Conference of representatives of Great Britain, the Dominions, India and the Colonies and Protectorates, held in October and November 1923. *Record of proceedings and documents* (Cmd. 2009) H.C. 1924, X 313.

Treaty between Canada and the United States of America for securing the Preservation of the Halibut Fishery of the North Pacific Ocean, signed at Washington, 22 March 1923 (Cmd. 2377) H.C. 1924–5, XXX 898.

Imperial Conference, 1926. *Summary of proceedings* (Cmd. 2768) H.C. 1926, XI 545.

Imperial Conference, 1926. *Appendices to the summary of proceedings* (Cmd. 2769) H.C. 1926, XI 607.

Report of the Conference on the Operation of Dominion Legislation and Merchant Shipping Legislation, 1929 (Cmd. 3479) H.C. 1920–30, XVI 171.

Imperial Conference, 1930. *Summary of proceedings* (Cmd. 3717) H.C. 1930–1, XIV 569.

Imperial Conference, 1930. *Appendices to the summary of proceedings* (Cmd. 3718) H.C. 1930–1, XIV 701.

The Statute of Westminster, 22 Geo. V, c. 4.

Canadian Parliamentary papers:
Canadian Sessional Papers, 118, 16 March 1926.

League of Nations papers:
League of Nations General Assembly and Committee Reports and Minutes, 1923–30.
League of Nations Journal.

5. NEWSPAPERS, PERIODICALS

Fine Gael newspapers:
The Freeman
Forum
The Star

Gazette (Montreal)
Irish Times
Manchester Guardian
The Times
Annual Register
British Dominions Yearbook
Concord
The Economist
Journal of the Parliaments of the Empire
Round Table
United Empire

6. MEMOIRS, SPEECHES AND ADDRESSES

Amery, L. S. 'Some Aspects of the Imperial Conference' (an address to the Royal Institute of International Affairs, 30 November 1926) in *Journal of R.I.I.A.*, VI (1927).
— *My Political Life*, II (1953) and III (1955).
Balfour, A. J. *The Imperial Conferences with Special Reference to Commerce and Trade*, Cust Foundation lecture (Nottingham, 1924).
Borden, R. 'Address to R.I.I.A., 14 June 1927', in *Journal of R.I.I.A.*, VI (1927).
Hughes, W. M. *The Splendid Adventure: A review of Empire relations within and without the Commonwealth of Britannic Nations* (1929).
Lloyd George, D. *War Memoirs* (1938 ed.).
Massey, V. *What's Past is Prologue* (1963).
O'Connor, F. *An Only Child* (1961).
Smuts, J. C. *Wartime Speeches: a Compilation of Public Utterances in Great Britain* (1917).

7. ARTICLES

Allen, J. S. 'The Imperial Conference and the Future', in *United Empire*, XXII (1930).
Balfour, A. J. 'The Report of the Imperial Conference, 1926', in *The Commonwealth Story* (Nottingham, 1932).

Brady, A. 'The New Dominion', in *Canadian Historical Review*, IV (Toronto, September 1923).

Bromage, A. W. 'Constitutional Development in the Irish Free State and the Constitution of Eire', in *American Political Science Review*, XXXI (Washington, 1937).

Conway, J. 'The Round Table – A Study in Liberal Imperialism' (unpublished thesis, Harvard, 1951).

Cook, R. 'A Canadian Account of the 1926 Imperial Conference', in *Journal of Commonwealth Political Studies*, III, no. 1 (Leicester, 1965).

Costello, J. A. 'The Long Game', in *The Star* (Dublin, 24 December 1932).

Crisp, L. F. 'The Appointment of Sir Isaac Isaac as Governor-General of Australia, 1930: J. H. Scullin's Account of the Buckingham Palace Interviews', in *Historical Studies, Australia and New Zealand*, XI, no. 42 (Melbourne, April 1964).

Cumpston, M. (Some early Indian Nationalists and their Allies in the British Parliaments, 1851–1906', in *English Historical Review*, LXXVI (1961).

Dafoe, J. W. 'Did the Conference Fail?', in *Maclean's Magazine* (Toronto, 15 January 1924).

Elliott, W. Y. 'The Sovereignty of the British Dominions: Law Overtakes Practice', in *American Political Science Review*, XXIV (Washington, 1930).

Fletcher, A. S. 'South Africa and the British Empire', in *Harris Foundation Lectures* (Chicago, 1927).

Glazebrook, G. P. de T. 'Permanent Factors in Canadian External Relations', in R. Flenley (ed.) *Essays in Canadian History, presented to G. M. Wrong* (Toronto, 1939).

Hall, H. D. 'The Genesis of the Balfour Declaration' in *Journal of Commonwealth Political Studies*, I, no. 3 (Leicester, 1963).

Hoey, P. 'The Irish Free State and the British Commonwealth', in *Review of Reviews*, LXXIX (1929).

Hogan, J. 'Ireland and the Commonwealth' in *Ireland Today* (Dublin, September/October 1937).

Hone, J. M. 'Ireland since 1922', in *Criterion Miscellany*, no. 39, 1932.

Kennedy, H. 'The Association of Canada with the Constitution of the Irish Free State' in *Canadian Bar Review*, VI (Toronto, 1928).

Law, H. A. 'The Irish Free State in 1929', in *Review of Reviews*, LXXIX (1929).

McDougall, D. V. 'Canada and Ireland', in R. Flenley (ed.) *Essays in Canadian History presented to G. M. Wrong* (Toronto, 1939).

Mackintosh, W. A. 'O. D. Skelton', in R. L. McDougall (ed.) *Canada's past and present: a dialogue* (Toronto, 1965).

Malone, A. E. 'Party Government in the Irish Free State', in *Political Science Quarterly*, XLIV (New York, Setpember 1929).

Mansergh, P. N. S. 'Commonwealth Membership', in *Commonwealth perspectives* (Durham, N.C., 1956).

Mills, J. S. 'The Imperial Conference', in *United Empire*, XVII (1926).

Moore, W. H. 'The Dominions in the League of Nations', in *International Affairs*, X (1931).

Morgan, J. H. 'The Statute of Westminster', in *United Empire*, XXIII (1931).

Mulcahy, R. 'The Treaty', in *Forum* (Dublin, December 1946).

O'Sullivan, D. J. 'Ireland and Appeals to the Judicial Committee of the Privy Council', in *Neuphilologische Monatsschrift*, I (Leipzig, 1930).

O'Sullivan, M. D. 'Eight Years of Irish Home Rule', in *Quarterly Review*, CCLIV (no. 504).

Smiddy, T. A. 'The Position of the Irish Free State in the British Commonwealth of Nations', in *Harris Foundation Lectures* (Chicago, 1927).

Waller, B. C. 'Impressions of the Tenth Assembly', in *Concord* (Dublin, 1929).

Zimmern, A. E. 'The British Commonwealth and the League of Nations', in *Problems of peace*, II (1928).

8. Books

Aitken, W. M. (Baron Beaverbrook). *The Decline and Fall of Lloyd George* (1963).

Amery, L. S. *Thoughts on the Constitution* (1947).

Baker, P. J. N. *The Present Juridical Status of the British Dominions in International Law* (1929).

Batterbee, H. F. *The Idea of Commonwealth* (1960).

Blake, R. N. W. *The Unknown Prime Minister* (1955).

Borden, R. *Canada in the Commonwealth: from Conflict to Co-operation* (Oxford, 1929).

Cambridge History of the British Empire, I–VIII (1929–63).

Chadwick, St J. *Newfoundland: Island into Province* (Cambridge, 1967).

Childers, E. *The Framework of Home Rule* (1911).

Churchill, W. S. *The World Crisis: the Aftermath* (1929).

— *The Second World War*, vol. i, *The Gathering Storm* (1948).

Cook, R. *The Politics of John W. Dafoe and the Free Press* (Toronto, 1963).

Corbett, P. E. and Smith, H. A. *Canada and World Politics: the Constitutional and International Relations of the British Empire* (1928).

Coupland, R. *Story of the British Commonwealth: an Inaugural Lecture* (Oxford, 1921).

Curtis, L. *The Problem of the Commonwealth* (1915).

— *The Commonwealth of Nations: an inquiry into the nature of citizenship in the British Empire and into the mutual relations of the several communities thereof* (1916).

Curzon, G. E. (Marchioness Curzon of Kedleston) *Reminiscences* (1955).

Dawson, R. M. *William Lyon Mackenzie King*, I (1958).

— *The Development of Dominion Status, 1900–36* (1937).

— *The Government of Canada* (Toronto, 1948).

Dewey, A. G. *The Dominions and Diplomacy: the Canadian Contribution* (1929).

Digby, M. *Horace Plunkett* (1949).

Elliott, W. Y. *The New British Empire* (1932).

Encyclopaedia Britannica, 1963 ed., VI (1963).

Fawcett, J. E. S. *The British Commonwealth in International Law* (1963).

— *The 'inter se' Doctrine of Commonwealth relations* (1958).

Fiddes, G. V. *The Dominions and Colonial Offices* (1926).

Figgis, D. *Irish Constitution explained* (Dublin, 1922).

Gallagher, F. *The Indivisible Island* (1957).

Gathorne-Hardy, G. M. *A Short History of International Affairs, 1920–39* (4th ed., 1950).
Gordon Walker, P. *The Commonwealth* (1965 ed., paperback).
Griffith, A. *The Resurrection of Hungary* (Dublin, 3rd ed., 1918).
Gwynn, D. *The Irish Free State* (1928).
Hall, H. D. *The British Commonwealth of Nations: a Study of its Past and Future Development* (1920).
Hall, W. P. *From Empire to Commonwealth* (1929).
— *Thirty years of British Imperial History* (New York, 1928).
Hancock, W. K. *Survey of British Commonwealth Affairs*, vol. i, *Problems of Nationality* (1937).
— *Smuts*, I (1962), II (1968).
Hanna, H. *The Statute Law of the Irish Free State* (Dublin, 1929).
Harrison, H. *Ireland and the British Empire, 1937: Conflict or Collaboration?* (1937).
Heever, C. M. van den. *General J. B. M. Hertzog* (Johannesburg, 1946).
Hodson, H. V. (ed.) *The British Empire. A Report on its Structure and Problems by a Study Group of the R.I.I.A.* (Oxford, 1938).
Holt, E. *Protest in Arms* (1960).
Hughes, H. *National Sovereignty and Judicial Autonomy in the British Commonwealth of Nations* (1931).
Inglis, B. *Story of Ireland* (2nd ed., 1965).
— *West Briton* (1962).
Jebb, R. *Studies in Colonial Nationalism* (1905).
Keith, A. B. *Responsible Government in the Dominions* (1909).
— *The Constitution, Administration and Laws of the Empire* (1924).
— *The Sovereignty of the British Dominions* (1929).
— *Speeches and Documents on the British Dominions 1918–31* (1932).
— *The Governments of the British Empire* (1936).
Knowles, L. C. A. *The Economic Development of the British Overseas Empire*, I (1924) and II (1930).
Kohn, L. *The Constitution of the Irish Free State* (1932).
Macardle, D. *The Irish Republic: a Documented Chronicle of the Anglo-Irish Conflict and the Partitioning of Ireland with a Detailed Account of the Period, 1916–23* (1937).
Mackay, R. A. *Changes in the Legal Structure of the British Commonwealth of Nations* (Worcester, Mass., 1931).
McCracken, J. L. *Representative Government in Ireland: a Study of Dail Eireann, 1919–48* (1958).
McNeill, R. *Ulster's Stand for Union* (1922).
Macready, N. *Annals of an Active Life*, II (1924).
Madden, F. *Imperial Constitutional Documents 1765–1965, a Supplement* (Oxford, 1966).
Manning, C. A. W. *Policies of the British Dominions in the League of Nations* (1932).
Mansergh, P. N. S. *The Irish Free State; its Government and Politics* (1934).
— *Survey of British Commonwealth Affairs. Problems of external policy, 1931–9*, I (Oxford, 1952).

Mansergh, P. N. S. *The Name and Nature of the British Commonwealth: an Inaugural Lecture* (Cambridge, 1954).
— *The Irish Question, 1840–1923* (1965).
Mazzini, G. *The duties of Man, and other Essays* (Everyman ed., 1907).
Miller, J. D. B. *The Commonwealth in the World* (3rd ed., 1965).
Moss, W. W. *Political Parties in the Irish Free State* (New York, 1933).
Mullett, C. F. *The British Empire* (1938).
— *The British Empire – Commonwealth: – its Themes and Character – a Plural Society in Evolution* (Washington, 1961).
Neame, L. E. *General Hertzog: Prime Minister of the Union of South Africa since 1924* (1930).
Neatby, H. B. *William Lyon Mackenzie King*, II (1963).
Nicolson, H. *King George V: His Life and Reign* (1952).
O'Brien, C. C. (ed.) *The Shaping of Modern Ireland* (1960).
O'Hegarty, P. S. *The Victory of Sinn Fein* (1924).
O'Sullivan, D. *The Irish Free State and its Senate* (1940).
Pakenham, F. (Lord Longford). *Peace by Ordeal: the negotiation and signature of the Anglo-Irish Treaty, 1921* (1935).
Palmer, G. E. H. *Consultation and Co-operation in the British Commonwealth: the methods and practice of communication and consultation between the members of the British Commonwealth of Nations* (Oxford, 1934).
Phelan, E. J. *The British Empire and the World Community* (1931).
Phelan, J. *The Ardent Exile. The Life and Times of Thomas D'Arcy McGee* (Toronto, 1951).
Phillpott, H. R. S. *The Right Honourable J. H. Thomas: Impressions of a Remarkable Character* (1932).
Pirow, O. *J. B. M. Hertzog* (1958).
Shaw, A. G. L. *The Story of Australia* (1955).
Sinclair, K. *A History of New Zealand* (1959).
Smith, F. W. F. (Lord Birkenhead) *Frederick Edwin, Earl of Birkenhead*, I (1933) and II (1935).
Stewart, B. *Treaty Relations of the British Commonwealth of Nations* (New York, 1939).
Strauss, E. *Irish Nationalism and British Democracy* (1951).
Thornton, A. P. *The Imperial Idea and its Enemies* (1959).
Toynbee, A. J. *Conduct of British Empire Foreign Relations since the Peace Settlement* (1928).
— (ed.) *British Commonwealth Relations: Proceedings of the first unofficial Conference at Toronto, September 1933* (Oxford, 1934).
Ward, N. *The Canadian House of Commons* (Toronto, 1951).
Wells, W. B. and Marlowe, N. *The Irish Convention and Sinn Fein: in Continuation of 'A History of the Irish Rebellion of 1916'* (1918).
Wheare, K. C. *The Statute of Westminster and Dominion Status* (Oxford, 1938).
— *The Constitutional Structure of the Commonwealth* (Oxford, 1960).
White, T. de V. *Kevin O'Higgins* (1948).
Williams, A. F. B. *Botha, Smuts and South Africa* (1946).
Williams, D. (ed.) *The Irish Struggle: 1916–26* (1966).
Williamson, J. A. *A short History of British Expansion* (1958).

Winks, R. (ed.) *The Historiography of the British Empire-Commonwealth* (Durham N.C., 1966).

Wiseman, H. V. *Britain and the Commonwealth* (1965).

Woodruff, P. *The Men Who Ruled India* (1953).

Yeats, W. B. *Poems* (variorum ed., New York, 1957).

Zimmern, A. E. *The Third British Empire* (1926).

— *The League of Nations and the Rule of Law, 1918–35* (1936).

Notes

PREFACE

1 149 H.C. Deb. 5s, col. 48.
2 A. Brady, 'The new Dominion', in *Canadian Historical Review* (September 1923), IV 204.
3 Canada, H. of C., 1926–7, II 1884.
4 See, for example, T. A. Smiddy, 'The position of the Irish Free State in the British Commonwealth of Nations', in *Harris Foundation Lectures* (1927) p. 109.
5 P. N. S. Mansergh, *Survey of British Commonwealth Affairs; Problems of external policy, 1931–9.* Hereafter cited as Mansergh, *Survey of Commonwealth Affairs, 1931–9.*
6 Ibid. p. 14.
7 Ibid. p. 10. The Latham quotation is from his essay 'The law and the Commonwealth', in W. K. Hancock, *Survey of British Commonwealth Affairs,* I 513.
8 Ibid. p. 26.
9 In R. Winks (ed.), *The Historiography of the British Empire-Commonwealth.*
10 Ibid. p. 326.
11 A. B. Keith, *Speeches and Documents on the British Dominions, 1918–31,* p. xlvii.
12 Dail Eireann debates, XXX, col. 793.
13 'To write a history of those Conferences would be a lengthy task but one of absorbing interest.' J. A. Costello, 'The long game', in *The Star,* 24 December 1932.
14 Dr M. Rynne in interview.

INTRODUCTION

1 *Cambridge History of the British Empire,* II 677 (hereafter cited as *C.H.B.E.*).
2 *C.H.B.E.* III 4.
3 Keith Sinclair, *A History of New Zealand,* p. 216.
4 *Correspondence relating to the future Organisation of the Colonial Conferences,* p. 14 [Cd. 2785] H.C. 1906, LXXVII 66.
5 Cd. 3404, 1907, p. 16.
6 *C.H.B.E.* III 456.
7 58 H. C. Deb. 5s, col. 378.

8 Australia, H. of R., 1937, CLIV 84 (R. Menzies).
9 W. K. Hancock, *Smuts*, I 149.
10 Cd. 8566, 1917–18, pp. 40–1. (See also D. Lloyd George, *War Memoirs*, p. 1045.)
11 Cd. 8566, 1917–18, p. 47.
12 Ibid. p. 41.
13 Ibid. p. 59.
14 J. C. Smuts, *Wartime Speeches*, pp. 32–3.
15 Ibid. p. 34.
16 Cmd. 1474, 1921, p. 9.
17 This he did on 30 September 1921, but while still in London he picturesquely informed his colleagues at home that he had 'soldered up the constitutional tinkers in their own can'. See H. Duncan Hall, 'The genesis of the Balfour Declaration', in *Journal of Commonwealth Political Studies*, I (no. 3) p. 182 (1963).
18 Cmd. 1474, 1921, pp. 22–3.
19 H. Duncan Hall, *The British Commonwealth of Nations*.
20 Cited in H. Duncan Hall, 'The genesis of the Balfour Declaration', in *J.C.P.S.* (no. 3) I 180.
21 J. C. Smuts, 'The Constitution of the British Commonwealth' (1921), quoted by H. Duncan Hall, in *J.C.P.S.* (no. 3) I 174.
22 Ibid. pp. 175–6. (See also W. K. Hancock, *Smuts*, II 44–8.)
23 Ibid. p. 176.
24 L. S. Amery, letter to J. C. Smuts, 20 June 1921 (copy in Hughes Papers, seen and quoted by Hall, *J.C.P.S.* (no. 3) I 178).
25 A. B. Keith, *The Constitution, Administration and Laws of the Empire*, p. 29.
26 Ibid. p. 30.
27 Ibid. pp. 30–1.
28 R. T. E. Latham, in W. K. Hancock, *Survey of British Commonwealth Affairs*, I 552.
29 A. B. Keith, *The Constitution, Administration and Laws of the Empire*, pp. 22–3.
30 Ibid.
31 Ibid.
32 Ibid.
33 Keith Sinclair, *A History of New Zealand*, p. 239.
34 Canada, H. of C., 1924, III 2936.
35 N. Mansergh, *The Name and Nature of the British Commonwealth* (Inaugural Lecture at Cambridge, 1954) p. 9.
36 R. Coupland, *Inaugural Lecture* (Oxford, 1921) pp. 12–13.
37 J. C. Smuts, *Wartime Speeches*, p. 31 (speech at banquet given in his honour by members of both Houses of Parliament 15 May 1917).
38 Dail Eireann, Treaty debates, p. 32.
39 Mary Cumpston, 'Some early Indian Nationalists and their allies in the British Parliaments, 1851–1906', in *English Historical Review* (1961), LXXVI 282.
40 *Address to His Majesty on Irish Affairs from the House of Commons of Canada, and the reply thereto*, p. 3 [Cd. 1697] H.C. 1903, XLIV 123.

41 *Address from the House of Representatives (Australia) and Resolution of the Senate on the subject of Home Rule for Ireland, and the replies thereto*, p. 4 [Cd. 2821] H.C. 1906, LXXVIII 220.

42 Erskine Childers, *The Framework of Home Rule*, p. 340.

43 'The Sinn Feiners will regard a Constitution as a mere ticket-of-leave, unless it leaves the Irish Parliament as free as any of the Dominion Parliaments. I am now speaking of a Constitution in the sense of a Home Rule Act, not of an unwritten, or rather partly written free and elastic arrangement....' G. B. Shaw to Sir H. Plunkett, 30 July 1917, quoted in M. Digby, *Horace Plunkett*, p. 222.

44 Ibid. p. 227.

45 F. W. F. Smith, *Frederick Edwin, Earl of Birkenhead*, p. 383.

46 R. Mulcahy quoting Collins, quoting de Valera, in *Forum* (Treaty Commemoration Issue, December 1946), p. 2.

47 Dail Eireann, Treaty debates, p. 41.

48 Ibid. p. 33.

49 Ibid. p. 46.

50 Ibid. p. 63.

51 Ibid. p. 103.

52 Ibid. p. 104.

53 Ibid. p. 86.

54 Ibid. p. 149.

55 Ibid.

CHAPTER I

1 L. Kohn, *The Constitution of the Irish Free State*, p. 16.

2 *Encyclopaedia Britannica* (1963 ed.) VI 172.

3 Canada, H. of C., 1926–7, II 1679.

4 Articles of Agreement for a Treaty between Great Britain and Ireland, Article 3.

5 Ernest Blythe, Minister of Finance 1923–32 and Vice-President of the Executive Council 1927–32, made this point clear in interview.

6 Comment by Ernest Blythe (see also note, pp. 24–5 above).

7 W. K. Hancock, *Survey of British Commonwealth Affairs*, I 146.

8 Canada, H. of C., 1926–7, II 1679.

9 Constitution of the Irish Free State, Article 2.

10 L. Kohn, *The Constitution of the Irish Free State*, p. 1.

11 Ibid. p. 80.

12 Ibid. p. 97.

13 Ibid. p. 80. Note also: When asked by an American in 1932 if he believed in a Republic, W. T. Cosgrave replied: 'You in America have a Republic. If your Parliament passes an Act and sends it up to your President, he can refuse to pass it. If we in Ireland pass an Act and send it to our Governor-General, he cannot refuse it. We have in fact a republican Monarchy: you have a monarchical Republic.'

14 The Constitution of the Irish Free State (Saorstat Eireann) Act, 1922.

15 Ibid. Preamble.

16 *Hull* v. *McKenna*, [1926] I.R. at p. 409.
17 Constitution of the Irish Free State, Article 49.
18 This view was expressed by J. A. Costello in interview.
19 W. K. Hancock, *Survey of British Commonwealth Affairs*, I 322.
20 Dail Eireann debates, XVII, cols 712–13.
21 Ibid. cols 1645–6. For an entirely contemporary exhortation of this nature, see three articles by J. C. Sheridan in the *Irish Times*, 8, 16, 23 September 1922.
22 Dr Michael Rynne in interview.
23 Terence de Vere White, *Kevin O'Higgins*, p. 83.
24 Dail Eireann debates, I, col. 544. See also Gavan Duffy's article of explanation in a letter to the Editor, *Irish Times*, 23 September 1922.
25 Dail Eireann debates, I, col. 1459.
26 Ibid. col. 1066.
27 Ibid. col. 574.
28 Dail Eireann debates, II, cols 13–14.
29 L. Kohn, *The Constitution of the Irish Free State*, p. 16.
30 Seanad Eireann debates, XV, col. 938.
31 Dail Eireann debates, XXX, col. 792.

CHAPTER 2

1 G. Gavan Duffy, Irish Free State Department of External Affairs Memorandum, 20 June 1922, in the Desmond FitzGerald Papers, hereafter cited as FitzGerald Papers.
2 C. A. W. Manning, *The policies of the British Dominions in the League of Nations*, p. 11.
3 See Sir William Harrison Moore, 'The Dominions in the League of Nations' in *International Affairs*, X (1931) 379.
4 L. S. Amery, *Thoughts on the Constitution*, pp. 126–7. Also commented upon by P. N. S. Mansergh, *Survey of Commonwealth Affairs, 1931–9*, p. 72.
5 W. M. Hughes, *Splendid Adventure*, p. 164.
6 C. A. W. Manning, *The policies of the British Dominions*, p. 8.
7 John MacNeill, 'Report of Irish Free State Delegate to the League of Nations Assembly', dated 4 October 1923 (FitzGerald Papers).
8 See Appendix A.
9 Dail Eireann debates, XVII, col. 732 (Deputy Johnson quoting Preamble to the Act authorising the Executive Council to make application to the League).
10 W. T. Cosgrave, League 4th Assembly Plenary Session, p. 25. Cited in C. A. W. Manning, *The policies of the British Dominions in the League of Nations*, p. 153.
11 John MacNeill, 'Report of Irish Free State Delegate to the League of Nations Assembly', dated 4 October 1923 (FitzGerald Papers).
12 Ibid.
13 See *Treaty between Canada and the United States of America for securing the Preservation of the Halibut Fishery of the North Pacific Ocean, signed at*

Washington, 22 March 1923 [Cmd. 2377], 1924–5, xxx 898. Also cited in A. B. Keith, *Speeches and Documents on the British Dominions, 1918–31*, pp. 311–14.

14 R. M. Dawson, *W. L. M. King*, I 432–4 (background) and p. 435.
15 Ratifications were exchanged after some Senate hesitation at Washington, 21 October 1924.
16 W. K. Hancock, *Survey of British Commonwealth Affairs*, I 253.
17 W. T. Cosgrave interview.

CHAPTER 3

1 Dail Eireann debates, XVI, col. 257–8.
2 Ibid. col. 264.
3 Ibid. XVII, col. 711.
4 R. M. Dawson, *W. L. M. King*, I 465. This was actually part of King's speech on Foreign Affairs at the 1923 Conference.
5 Canada, H. of C., 1926–7, II 1701–2.
6 Ibid. p. 1677.
7 See Dafoe, 'Did the Conference Fail?', *Maclean's Magazine*, 15 January 1924 (cf. R. M. Dawson, *The Development of Dominion Status 1900–36*, pp. 277–83).
8 See P. N. S. Mansergh, *The name and nature of the Commonwealth*, p. 25, and *Survey of British Commonwealth Affairs, 1939–52*, I 415.
9 Australia, H. of R., 1928, CXVIII 4674 (Duncan-Hughes).
10 New Zealand, H. of R., 1927, CCXVI 808 (Mason).
11 McGilligan interview. See bibliography.
12 R. M. Dawson, *W. L. Mackenzie King*, I, ch. 15. See, for example, pp. 474–7, King's observations in his Diary from 5 November to 7 November 1923.
13 Telegram 23 June 1924, Ramsay MacDonald to the Dominions. See A. J. Toynbee, *The Conduct of British Empire Foreign Relations since the Peace Settlement*, p. 76.
14 New Zealand, H. of R., 1927, CCXVI 794.
15 Ibid. pp. 805–6.
16 Canadian reply, 8 August 1924, to Ramsay MacDonald's telegram. See A. J. Toynbee, *The Conduct of British Empire*, p. 79.
17 *Saturday Review*, 29 November 1930, quoted by Mr G. C. C. Black, New Zealand, H. of R., 1931, CCXXVIII 627.
18 P. Gordon Walker, in *The Commonwealth*, having classified the Irish Free State as an exceptional case, tends to forget its existence thereafter and to ignore the very real impact of its presence.

CHAPTER 4

1 *Irish Times*, 1 October 1923 (report of Cosgrave speech before leaving for London).
2 *The Times*, 2 October 1923.
3 Cmd. 1987, 1923, pp. 18–19.

4 *Round Table*, XIII 484–5. See also J. Conway, 'The Round Table—A Study in Liberal Imperialism', Harvard unpublished thesis, 1951.
5 Canada, H. of C., 1923, v 4661.
6 *The Times*, 12 November 1923.
7 Ibid. 10 November 1923.
8 Secretary of State for the Colonies.
9 Mackenzie King described this speech as 'the finest intellectual treat I have ever witnessed'. R. M. Dawson, *W. L. M. King*, I 464.
10 See R. M. Dawson, *W. L. M. King*, I 475.
11 *The Times*, 12 November 1923.
12 See J. W. Dafoe, 'Did the Conference Fail?' in *Maclean's Magazine*, 25 January 1924. Cited in R. M. Dawson, *The Development of Dominion Status, 1900–36*, pp. 277–83.
13 Cmd. 1987, 1923, p. 13.
14 Cmd. 2009, 1924, p. 228.
15 W. K. Hancock, *Survey of British Commonwealth Affairs*, I 253–4.
16 H. B. Neatby, *W. L. M. King*, II 7.
17 Mackenzie King Diary, 16 December 1923, cited in H. B. Neatby, *W. L. M. King*, II, p. 7.
18 R. M. Dawson, *W. L. M. King*, I 480.
19 Before the Conference Dafoe had written to Sir Clifford Sifton that he had 'little confidence in King. I am afraid his conceit in his ability to take care of himself is equalled only by his ignorance, and I should not be surprised if he should find himself trapped'. Dafoe papers, Dafoe to Sir Clifford Sifton, 12 November 1923, cited in R. M. Dawson, *W. L. M. King*, I 453. See also H. B. Neatby, *W. L. M. King*, II 7.
20 R. M. Dawson, *The Development of Dominion Status, 1900–36*, p. 85.
21 R. M. Dawson, *W. L. M. King*, I 454.
22 Isabel Skelton, *Life of Thomas D'Arcy McGee* ('the definitive biography', as Josephine Phelan points out in *The Ardent Exile*).
23 The FitzGerald Papers contain some of these letters.
24 Vincent Massey, *What's Past is Prologue*, p. 135. But see also note, p. 148 below.
25 G. E. Curzon, *Reminiscences*, p. 183.
26 A. J. Balfour, *The Imperial Conferences, with special reference to Commerce and Trade*, pp. 6–7 (Cust Foundation Lecture, 1924).
27 See D. Gwynn, *The Irish Free State 1922–7*.
28 Cmd. 1987, 1923, p. 62.
29 Cmd. 2009, 1924, p. 49.
30 *Irish Times*, 3 October 1923.
31 *The Times*, 3 October 1923.

CHAPTER 5

1 M. McWhite, to Department of External Affairs, Dublin, 17 September 1923 (no. NS 103/23) FitzGerald Papers.
2 J. P. Walshe, Department of External Affairs, Dublin to M. McWhite, 22 September 1923 (no. 234/23) FitzGerald Papers.

3 M. McWhite, Geneva (NS 107/23) to Ministry of External Affairs, Dublin, 25 September 1923 (FitzGerald Papers).
4 League Council Memorandum, 'Registration of Treaties' 1920 (FitzGerald Papers).
5 Dail Eireann debates, VI, col. 3038.
6 Both included in Irish Free State Memorandum (SPB/RCM) of Department of External Affairs, written by J. P. Walshe, 1 December 1924 (FitzGerald Papers).
7 J. H. Thomas, 4 November, Despatch to Dublin. Quoted by J. P. Walshe in Irish Free State Memorandum (SPB/RCM) 1 December 1924 (Fitz-Gerald Papers). See also A. B. Keith, *Speeches and Documents*, p. 347, and J. E. S. Fawcett, *The 'inter se' Doctrine*, p. 16.
8 Irish Free State Memorandum (SPB/RCM) 1 December 1924 (FitzGerald Papers).
9 League of Nations Treaty Series (1924) XXVII 450.
10 A. B. Keith, *Speeches and Documents*, p. 347.
11 E. J. Phelan, from Irish Free State office in Geneva, 15 December 1924, to D. FitzGerald (FitzGerald Papers).
12 Ibid. 29 December 1924, to D. FitzGerald (FitzGerald Papers).
13 L. S. Amery, despatch no. 81, 9 March 1925, to Dublin (FitzGerald Papers).
14 Letter from Desmond FitzGerald to Professor Kennedy, 9 April 1925 (FitzGerald Papers).
15 *The Gazette* (Montreal) 27 February 1923. On the occasion of a visit by Smiddy to Ottawa, where he consulted the Canadian Cabinet.
16 Authority: Minister of Finance, no. E72/1, 20 March 1923.
17 Dail Eireann debates, VI, cols 3029 and 3026.
18 Cited in A. B. Keith, *Speeches and Documents*, pp. 349–50.
19 Ibid. pp. 350–1.
20 Senator Belcourt to D. FitzGerald, 25 July 1924 (FitzGerald Papers).
21 *London Gazette*, 10 October 1924.
22 D. FitzGerald to Senator Belcourt, 13 August 1924 (FitzGerald Papers).
23 D. FitzGerald to Senator Belcourt, 13 August 1924 (FitzGerald Papers).
24 J. P. Walshe: Irish Free State Memorandum (SPB/RCM) 1 December 1924 (FitzGerald Papers).
25 Canada, H. of C., 9 June 1924. Cited in A. B. Keith, *Speeches and Documents*, pp. 332–41.
26 H. B. Neatby, *W. L. M. King*, II 34.
27 Ibid. p. 36 (King's diary, 2 April 1924).
28 Ibid. p. 37.
29 W. K. Hancock, *Survey of British Commonwealth Affairs*, I 256–7.
30 R. M. Dawson, *The Development of Dominion Status, 1900–36*, p. 301.
31 A. Zimmern, 'The British Commonwealth and the League of Nations', in *Problems of Peace*, II 1027.
32 Dail Eireann debates, XI, cols 1453–4: see also cols 1417–20.
33 Hugh A. Law, T.D., 'The Irish Free State in 1929', in *Review of Reviews* (no. 474) LXXIX 194 (15 July 1929).
34 H. B. Neatby, *W. L. M. King*, II 39.

35 Dail Eireann debates, VI, cols 3027–8.
36 A. J. Toynbee, *The conduct of British Empire foreign relations since the Peace Settlement,* section V, pp. 75–80, in particular.
37 Article 9, Locarno Pact. See A. B. Keith, *Speeches and Documents*, p. 356.
38 188 H.C. Deb. 5s, col. 454.
39 Ibid. col. 456 (D. Lloyd George quoting Smuts's speech as reported in *The Times*).
40 *Round Table*, XVI 16–19.
41 N. Mansergh, *Survey of Commonwealth Affairs, 1931–9*, p. 60.
42 Desmond FitzGerald to Dr O. D. Skelton, 16 June 1925 (FitzGerald Papers).
43 C. A. W. Manning, *The Policies of the British Dominions in the League of Nations* (lecture III (a) Optional Clause). See also League Assembly, 6th Session, First Committee, p. 24.
44 T. de V. White, *Kevin O'Higgins*, p. 191.
45 Ibid. p. 192.
46 191 H.C. Deb. 5s, col. 1242 (11 February 1926).
47 Dominions Office Despatch, 25 February 1926 (FitzGerald Papers).
48 Dominions Office Despatch, 5 March 1926 (FitzGerald Papers).
49 League of Nations, 7th Assembly, Special Supplement no. 44, pp. 73–4 (10th Plenary Session).
50 T. de V. White, *Kevin O'Higgins*, pp. 189–90.
51 Secretary of Irish Free State Delegation to all Dominion Delegations, 14 September 1926, Geneva (FitzGerald Papers).
52 Austen Chamberlain to Irish Free State Delegation, 15 September 1926, Geneva (FitzGerald Papers).
53 D. FitzGerald to his wife, 17 September 1926 (FitzGerald Papers).
54 Ibid. 19 September 1926.
55 Telegram, Irish Free State Delegation to Department External Affairs Dublin, 17 September 1926 'received' (FitzGerald Papers).
56 Irish Free State Delegation Report on 7th Session League Assembly (FitzGerald Papers).
57 *Round Table* (1926–7), XVII (no. 65) 139.
58 Ibid. p. 39.
59 Ibid. p. 44.

CHAPTER 6

1 *The Times*, 10 November 1926 (Stanley Baldwin at the Guildhall).
2 H. B. Neatby, *W. L. M. King*, II 179.
3 See note, p. 113 below.
4 P. N. S. Mansergh, 'Commonwealth Membership', in *Commonwealth Perspectives*, p. 5 (Duke University Commonwealth Studies Center, 1956).
5 L. S. Amery, *My Political Life*, II 380.
6 H. B. Neatby, *W. L. M. King*, II 178.
7 Sir M. Hankey to Sir E. Grigg, 25 May 1926 (Grigg Papers).
8 *Round Table*, XVI (no. 64) 675. The latter phrase belongs to Sir Wilfred Laurier.
9 *Round Table*, XVI (no. 62) 231.

10 L. E. Neame, *General Hertzog*, p. 251.

11 O. Pirow, *J. B. M. Hertzog*, p. 111.

12 H. B. Neatby, *W. L. M. King*, II 176: 'Mackenzie King had been an ardent advocate of Dominion autonomy and he left for the Conference expecting to continue his efforts.'

13 Telegram, Governor-General of Canada to Secretary of State for Dominion Affairs, Ottawa, 8 January 1926 (Canadian Sessional Paper 118, 16 March 1926).

14 Ibid. 19 February 1926.

15 H. B. Neatby, *W. L. M. King*, II 178 (M. King observation is dated 10 October 1926).

16 Ibid. p. 178.

17 Ibid.

18 J. Saxon Mills, 'The Imperial Conference', in *United Empire*, XVII (new series), no. 12, 652 (1926).

19 O. Pirow, *J. B. M. Hertzog*, p. 109.

20 Dail Eireann debates, XVI, col. 259.

21 Ibid. col. 264.

22 *Round Table*, XVII (no. 65) 135.

23 V. Massey, *What's Past is Prologue*, p. 112.

24 Ibid.

25 *The Times*, 19 October 1926.

26 *Irish Times*, 19 October 1926.

27 Ibid. 23 October 1926.

28 Ibid. 8 November 1926.

29 Ibid.

30 Ibid.

31 D. Gwynn, *The Irish Free State*, *1922–7*, p. 112.

32 Cmd. 3718, 1930–1, p. 19.

33 T. de V. White, *Kevin O'Higgins*, pp. 220–1.

34 Ibid. pp. 221–2.

35 L. S. Amery, *My Political Life*. See particularly vol. II, ch. 12, 'The New Commonwealth Conception'.

36 *Irish Times*, 11 November 1926.

37 Ibid. 13 November 1926.

38 Ibid. 20 November 1926.

39 Ibid.

40 Ibid.

41 Ibid.

42 Ibid. 24 November 1926.

43 Cmd. 2769, 1926, p. 411.

44 *Irish Times*, 24 November 1926.

45 Ibid.

46 Cmd. 2768, 1926, p. 13.

47 Ibid.

48 Ibid.

49 Ibid.

50 C. M. van den Heever, *General J. B. M. Hertzog*, p. 210.

51 C. M. van den Heever, *General J. B. M. Hertzog*.
52 O. Pirow, *J. B. M. Hertzog*. See also CAB 32/56 (P.R.O.).
53 H. B. Neatby, *W. L. M. King*, II 182.
54 K. C. Wheare, *The Statute of Westminster and Dominion Status*, p. 28 (1938 ed.).
55 Duncan Hall, 'The Genesis of the Balfour Declaration' in *J.C.P.S.*, I (no. 3).
56 H. B. Neatby, *W. L. M. King*, II 187.
57 Duncan Hall, *J.C.P.S.*, I (no. 3).
58 P. N. S. Mansergh, *Survey of Commonwealth Affairs, 1931–9*, pp. 10–11.
59 J. A. Costello, 'The Long Game' in *The Star*, 24 December 1932. The title of the article is derived from a comment by Kevin O'Higgins at the end of this Conference: 'It's a long game and I'd like to see the end of it.' Perhaps he had already a premonition that he would not.
60 C. M. van den Heever, *J. B. M. Hertzog*, p. 216.
61 A. E. Malone, 'Party Government in the Irish Free State', in *Political Science Quarterly*, XLIV 375.
62 E(IR/26)3, in 'Reports, Proceedings and Memoranda', E(IR/26) series, in CAB 32/56 (P.R.O.).
63 L. S. Amery, *My Political Life*, II 385–6.
64 Cmd. 2768, 1926, p. 14.
65 Dail Eireann debates, VI, cols 2919–20 and 2922–6 (Complaint by Deputy Osmond Grattan Esmonde).
66 L. S. Amery, *My Political Life*, II 395. See also his considered views of this topic recorded in 1946 in *Thoughts on the Constitution*, pp. 151–3.
67 *Irish Times*, 22 November 1926.
68 Terence de Vere White, *Kevin O'Higgins*, p. 222.
69 Ibid. p. 225 (Carson is recorded as saying: 'Mr O'Higgins, each of us loves Ireland. We can shake hands on that').
70 *Irish Times*, 2 November 1926.
71 Ibid. 12 November 1926.
72 Ibid. 26 November 1926.
73 Ibid.
74 Ibid. 30 November 1926.
75 Cmd. 2768, 1926, p. 15.
76 J. C. Sheridan (then lately Commissioner for Finance, Union of South Africa), *Irish Times*, 23 September 1922.
77 Canada, H. of C., 1924, III 2931 (J. S. Woodsworth).
78 H. B. Neatby, *W. L. M. King*, II 160.
79 Ibid. p. 180.
80 Ibid. pp. 180–1.
81 L. S. Amery, *My Political Life*, II 387.
82 H. B. Neatby, *W. L. M. King*, II 188.
83 A. A. Dickie, Memorandum for Irish Free State Government on 'The Doctrine of the Prerogative' in the papers of Patrick McGilligan, hereafter cited as McGilligan Papers.
84 The appointment was announced in Dublin and London on 15 December 1927. Mr Blythe's statement is in *Irish Times*, 16 December 1927.

85 Cmd. 2768, 1926, p. 16.
86 Ibid. p. 17.
87 Ibid. p. 16.
88 Ibid. p. 17.
89 Ibid.
90 Ibid.
91 Irish Free State memorandum 'Exterritorial jurisdiction', 1929 (McGilligan Papers).
92 Cited in above Irish Free State memorandum.
93 Cd. 5745, 1911, p. 394.
94 Cited in above Irish Free State memorandum.
95 Cited in an appendix by Charles Green, B.A., Dept. of Fisheries, Irish Free State, to 'Report of Inter-Departmental Committee on the limits of territorial waters' (1925), from Colonial Office Despatch no. 495 of 17 August 1923, to Governor-General, Irish Free State (McGilligan Papers).
96 MacLeod's Case (1891) A.C. 455.
97 2 I.R. 1925, p. 193 (this the basis of Irish Memorandum Clause).
98 Cmd. 2768, 1926, p. 18.
99 Imperial Conference 1926, Irish Free State memorandum 'Appeals to the Privy Council', Conference Paper E.115 (FitzGerald Papers).
100 H. B. Neatby, *W. L. M. King*, II 189.
101 Cmd. 2768, 1926, p. 19.
102 Ibid.
103 Ibid. p. 20.
104 Irish Free State Memorandum E(I.R./26)3. See above p. 103.
105 H. B. Neatby, *W. L. M. King*, II 179.
106 Ibid. p. 188 (King's Diary 18 October 1926).
107 Ibid. p. 189.
108 Cmd. 2768, 1926, p. 21. See also Dail Eireann debates, XVII, col. 719.
109 Dail Eireann debates, XVII, col. 721.
110 Ibid.
111 Ibid. col. 720. This was the Irish view. It was capable of the opposite inter-pretation, as the Irish fully realised.
112 Cmd. 2768, 1926, p. 22 (para. 4).
113 Ibid. p. 27.
114 Ibid.
115 Ibid.
116 H. B. Neatby, *W. L. M. King*, II 180.
117 Stenographic notes of Meetings, E (1926) series 12 Meeting, in CAB 32/46 (P.R.O.).
118 J. A. Costello in interview.
119 *The Times*, 22 November 1926.
120 Cmd. 2768, 1926, p. 19.
121 *The Times*, 22 November 1926.
122 Ibid.
123 Ibid. 24 November 1926.
124 A. J. Balfour to Sir George Foster, 4 May 1927. B.M. Add. MSS. Balfour Papers, XV 49697.

125 A. J. Balfour, 'The Report of the Imperial Conference 1926', in *The Commonwealth Story*, p. 265 (International University Society Reading Course).
126 L. S. Amery, 'Some aspects of the Imperial Conference' in *Journal of R.I.I.A.*, VI (30 November 1926) 10.
127 S. M. Bruce to A. J. Balfour, 21 December 1926. B.M. Add. MSS. Balfour Papers, XV 49697.
128 Australia, H. of R., 1927, CXV 62.
129 Ibid.
130 *The Times*, 24 November 1926.
131 W. M. Hughes, *Splendid Adventure*, p. 164.
132 Australia, H. of R., 1931, CXXXI 4074.
133 Ibid. p. 4062.
134 W. K. Hancock, *Survey of British Commonwealth Affairs*, I 263.
135 *The Times*, 24 November 1926.
136 New Zealand, H. of R., 1927, CCXVI 790.
137 Ibid. p. 789.
138 South Africa, H. of A., 1927, VIII, col. 1482.
139 *The Times*, 23 November 1926.
140 *Annual Register*, 1926, p. 313.
141 Canada, H. of C., 1926–7, II 1648.
142 H. B. Neatby, *W. L. M. King*, II 190–1.
143 See particularly the debate on the Governor-General's Address 1928.
144 Canada, H. of C., 1926–7, II 1657.
145 Ibid.
146 Ibid. p. 1667.
147 Ibid. p. 1679.
148 Ibid. p. 1680.
149 Ibid. p. 1755.
150 Ibid. pp. 1891–5.
151 R. M. Dawson, *The Development of Dominion Status, 1900–36*, p. 112.
152 Sir George Foster to A. J. Balfour, 8 April 1927, B.M. Add. MSS. Balfour Papers, XV 49697.
153 Sir Robert Borden, G.C.M.G., K.C., M.P., 'Address to R.I.I.A.' (14 June 1927), in *Journal of R.I.I.A.*, VI 206.
154 T. de V. White, *Kevin O'Higgins*, p. 237.
155 *Round Table* (no. 66), XVII 340–7.
156 Dail Eireann debates, XVII, col. 891 (Baxter).
157 In the Dail, such deputies as Johnson and Magennis for example. Dr Michael Rynne was an opponent outside politics.
158 Dail Eireann debates, XVII, col. 733 (Johnson).
159 Ibid. col. 711.
160 Ibid. col. 714.
161 Ibid. col. 728.
162 Ibid. col. 897.
163 T. de V. White, *Kevin O'Higgins*, p. 223.
164 J. A. Costello, 'The long game', in *The Star*, 24 December 1932.
165 Ibid.
166 W. K. Hancock, *Smuts*, I 549–50.

167 See W. Y. Elliott, 'The Sovereignty of the British Dominions: law overtakes practice', a review in *American Political Science Review* no. 24 (1930) of A. B. Keith's *The Sovereignty of the British Dominions.*

168 W. T. Cosgrave interview.

169 H. B. Neatby, *W. L. M. King*, II 186.

170 N. Mansergh, *Survey of Commonwealth Affairs, 1931–9*, p. 16.

171 H. B. Neatby, *W. L. M. King*, II 177.

172 W. K. Hancock, *Survey of British Commonwealth Affairs*, I 284.

173 Irish Free State memorandum, 'Report on 1926 Imperial Conference', by J. P. Walshe (FitzGerald Papers).

174 W. K. Hancock, *Survey of British Commonwealth Affairs*, I 268.

CHAPTER 7

1 Irish Free State memorandum, 'Ratification of Arbitration Treaty with Siam and Treaty of Friendship with the Hedjaz', by J. P. Walshe, 1 January 1927 (FitzGerald Papers).

2 E. J. Phelan to D. FitzGerald, 21 March 1927 (FitzGerald Papers).

3 Ibid. 18 February 1927.

4 Ibid. 3 April 1927.

5 Downing St. despatch (FitzGerald Papers).

6 Notes on Department of External Affairs, 1 June 1927 (FitzGerald Papers).

7 T. de V. White, *Kevin O'Higgins*, p. 237.

8 Notes on the Department of External Affairs, 1 June 1927 (FitzGerald Papers).

9 V. Massey, *What's Past is Prologue*, p. 127.

10 *Concord*, September 1927.

11 Ibid. October 1927.

12 Draft Memo for Executive Council, 17 June 1927 (FitzGerald Papers).

13 See Dail Eireann debates, XXX, cols 874–5. P. McGilligan outlines the Irish Free State reactions.

14 See A. B. Keith, *Speeches and Documents*, pp. 398–409 and pp. 442–3.

15 Dail Eireann debates, XXVIII, col. 278.

16 See A. B. Keith, *Speeches and Documents*, pp. 443–4 for the Instrument of Ratification.

17 The Minister for External Affairs had gone to the Holy See in April to initiate *pourparlers* for an exchange of diplomatic relations, a move which was greeted with particular enthusiasm by the Irish people.

18 Dail Eireann debates, X, col. 1354.

19 Ibid. XI, cols 1474–6.

20 T. de V. White, *Kevin O'Higgins*, p. 190.

21 League of Nations, 6th Assembly, 1925, 1st Committee, pp. 24–5.

22 Ibid. p. 22.

23 See Desmond FitzGerald after the Conference: Dail Eireann debates, XVII, col. 724 (15 December 1926). There had been a question from Johnson before the Conference (Dail Eireann debates, XVI, col. 259) to which FitzGerald had replied (Dail Eireann debates, XVI, col. 348). In 1928 Patrick McGilligan, now Minister for External Affairs, reiterated the Irish

view in Dail Eireann (Dail Eireann debates, XXVII, col. 493, 21 November 1928). It had not changed during this time.

24 W. Harrison Moore, 'The Dominions in the League of Nations' in *International Affairs*, X 377 (1931).

25 Ibid. p. 379.

26 See A. B. Keith, *Speeches and Documents*, p. 416 (footnote). The Dominions were worried about immigration and residence laws with respect to Indians.

27 See C. A. W. Manning, *The policies of the British Dominions in the League of Nations*, p. 39. The I.F.S. signed 16th: G.B. on 19 September.

28 P. McGilligan in interview.

29 See Dail Eireann debates, XXXIII, col. 885. McGilligan refers to this.

30 P. McGilligan in interview.

31 10th Assembly, *League of Nations Journal*, p. 293.

32 Ibid. This was triumphantly noted in *The Star*, 28 September 1929. Also see Keith, *Speeches and Documents*, p. 416, 'Memorandum on the signature by His Majesty's Government in the U.K. of the Optional Clause of the Statute of the Permanent Court of International Justice 1929'.

33 E. J. Phelan, *The British Empire and the World Community*, pp. 25–6. (Lecture to Geneva Institute of International Relations, 8 August 1931. Published in Great Britain by G. Allen & Unwin, reprinted from *Problems of Peace*, 6th series.)

34 *Concord*, October 1929.

35 Dail Eireann debates, XXXIII, col. 905.

36 L. S. Amery, telegram from Dominions Office, 16 November 1928 (FitzGerald Papers).

37 Dail Eireann debates, XXVII, col. 432.

38 L. S. Amery, telegram to all Dominions from Dominions Office, 23 March 1929 (FitzGerald Papers).

39 Dail Eireann debates, XXX, col. 792.

40 Ibid. cols 792–3.

41 Patricia Hoey, 'The Irish Free State and the British Commonwealth', in *Review of Reviews*, LXXIX (1929) 188.

42 F. H. Boland in interview spoke very warmly of the contribution of Joe Walshe.

43 Cmd. 3479, 1929–30, p. 9.

44 Ibid.

45 Ibid. p. 10.

46 Ibid. p. 11.

47 Ibid.

48 Irish Preparatory Memorandum on 'Reservation Disallowance and the Suspensory Clause', 1929 (McGilligan Papers).

49 Cmd. 3479, 1929–30, p. 12.

50 O.D.L. Conference, 1929, 'British Preliminary Memorandum', furnished to Dominions as a suggested basis for discussion at the Conference (McGilligan Papers).

51 Ibid.

52 See Cmd. 3479, 1929–30, pp. 21–2, para. 63.

53 Irish Preparatory Memorandum, 'Provisions enabling Dominions to alter their Constitutions' based on section of that title in British Preliminary Memorandum (McGilligan Papers).
54 Ibid.
55 Irish Free State Preliminary Memorandum, 'Exterritorial Jurisdiction' (McGilligan Papers).
56 New Zealand Constitution Act, 1852, Article liii, 15 & 16. Victoriae, cap 72.
57 O.D.L. Conference, 1929, British Preliminary Memorandum (McGilligan Papers).
58 Irish Free State Memorandum 'Express limitations in Dominion Constitutions as to the subjects on which legislation may be enacted', p. 3 (McGilligan Papers).
59 Cmd. 3479, 1929–30, p. 12.
60 Ibid.
61 Ibid. p. 12.
62 Ibid. pp. 12–13.
63 Ibid. p. 15 (para. 34).
64 Ibid. p. 15.
65 Irish Preparatory Memorandum, 'Reservation, Disallowance and the Suspensory Clause' (McGilligan Papers).
66 See Irish Free State Memorandum 1926 (E/IR/26)3, Clause 5, pp. 102–3 above.
67 Cmd. 3479, 1929–30, p. 16.
68 Ibid.
69 See Irish Free State Memorandum, 1926, E.(IR/26)3, Clause 6 (see above p. 103) and also Cmd. 3479, 1929–30, Articles 80 and 94.
70 Irish Free State Preliminary Memorandum, 'Exterritorial Jurisdiction' (McGilligan Papers).
71 Ibid.
72 Irish Free State Preliminary Memorandum, 'Exterritorial Jurisdiction' (McGilligan Papers).
73 P. McGilligan, cited in above Memorandum.
74 Cmd. 3479, 1929–30, p. 17.
75 A. B. Keith, *Responsible Government in the Dominions*, I 336.
76 Dail Eireann debates, XXXIII, col. 2064.
77 P. McGilligan recollection (the phrase also occurs in an unsigned Preliminary Memorandum for this Conference).
78 Cmd. 3479, 1929–30, pp. 19–21.
79 Ibid. p. 20.
80 Ibid.
81 Ibid.
82 Ibid. pp. 20–1.
83 Ibid. paras. 59–61.
84 Ibid. p. 21.
85 Dail Eireann debates, XXXIII, col. 2294.
86 J. A. Costello, interview.
87 Seanad Eireann debates, XIII, col. 2030.

88 Cmd. 3479, 1929–30, p. 24.
89 Ibid. p. 25.
90 Irish Free State Memorandum, 'Commonwealth Co-operation: mutual assistance in enforcement of laws', p. 22 (McGilligan Papers).
91 Ibid.
92 British Preliminary Memorandum (McGilligan Papers).
93 Irish Free State Memorandum, 'Commonwealth Co-operation: mutual assistance in enforcement of laws', section A, The Fugitive Offenders Act, 1881 (McGilligan Papers).
94 Ibid. section B, The Bankruptcy Act, 1914 (McGilligan Papers).
95 Ibid. General section, p. 19 (McGilligan Papers).
96 Ibid. p. 22.
97 Cmd. 3479, 1929–30, p. 26 (para. 82).
98 J. J. Hearne, Memorandum for guidance of Irish Free State Imperial Conference Delegation, *re* 'Irish Nationality Bill', dated 21 August 1930 (McGilligan Papers).
99 J. J. Hearne, Preparatory memorandum 'The Prerogative of Mercy', Section C (the Prerogative of Mercy in the Colonies and Dominions), p. 18 (McGilligan Papers).
100 *The Times*, 4 February 1930 (leading article).
101 South Africa, H. of A., 1930, XV, cols 4425–6.
102 Ibid. col. 4452.
103 Canada, H. of C., 1930, III 2570.
104 Ibid. p. 2600.
105 Australia, H. of R., 1937, CLIV 92.
106 Ibid. p. 92.
107 W. Y. Elliott, 'The Sovereignty of the British Dominions: law overtakes practice' – a review of A. B. Keith, *The Sovereignty of the British Dominions* – in *American Political Science Review*, no. 24 (1930) pp. 971–88.
108 Ibid.
109 Dail Eireann debates, XXXIII, col. 2200.
110 South Africa, H. of A., 1930, XV, col. 4437.
111 Canada, H. of C., 1930, III 2623. Here Mr Lapointe is quoting *Manitoba Free Press*, 28 February 1930.
112 J. A. Costello's description, in interview.
113 S. Murphy's description, in interview.
114 P. McGilligan, in interview.
115 J. A. Costello, in interview.
116 Dail Eireann debates, XXXIII, col. 2050.
117 Ibid. col. 2326.
118 Ibid. XXXIV, col. 2354.
119 Ibid. XXXIII, col. 2324.
120 Ibid. XXXIX, col. 2302, P. McGilligan, in debate on 1930 Conference Report refers to the achievement of 1929 (16 July 1931).
121 W. K. Hancock, *Survey of British Commonwealth Affairs*, I 274.

CHAPTER 8

1 W. S. Churchill, *The Gathering Storm*, p. 74.
2 *Concord*, April 1928.
3 See B. C. Waller, 'Impressions of the 10th Assembly', in *Concord*, October 1929.
4 Dail Eireann debates, XXXIV, col. 689.
5 R. Dandurand to Senator Charles Murphy (Ottawa, 27 May 1931), Canadian Public Archives, 'Murphy Papers. Correspondence', p. 2663.
6 *Concord*, no. 23 (December 1930).
7 Sir William Harrison Moore, 'The Dominions in the League of Nations', in *International Affairs* (1931) X 380–1.
8 League of Nations, 11th Assembly Records (14th Plen. Meeting, 17 September 1930) p. 127.
9 Irish Free State Preliminary Note for 1930 Imperial Conference (McGilligan Papers).
10 Ibid. pp. 4–5.
11 E.g. *The Times*, 15 November 1930.
12 Imperial Conference, 1930: E(30)21, in CAB 32/81 (P.R.O.).
13 South Africa, H. of A., 1930, xv, col. 3020.
14 Cited in *Annual Register*, 1930, pp. 143–4.
15 Ibid. p. 144.
16 L. S. Amery, *My Political Life*, III 32. See also Sir J. Sandeman Allen, M.P., 'The Imperial Conference and the Future', in *United Empire*, XXII (new series) no. 1, p. 23.
17 *The Times*, 31 July 1930.
18 *Irish Times*, 1 October 1930.
19 Ibid.
20 Cmd. 3718, 1930–1, p. 21.
21 Ibid. p. 72.
22 *Irish Times*, 1 October 1930.
23 Ibid. 2 October 1930.
24 D. FitzGerald to his wife, 20 October 1930 (FitzGerald Papers).
25 Ibid.
26 Ibid. 3 October 1930.
27 Ibid. 5 October 1930.
28 P. McGilligan interview (also recalled by Mr S. Murphy).
29 D. FitzGerald to his wife, 9 October 1930 (FitzGerald Papers).
30 Ibid.
31 Ibid. 10 October 1930.
32 Ibid. 13 October 1930.
33 Ibid. 14 October 1930.
34 Ibid. 15 October 1930.
35 Ibid. 16 October 1930.
36 L. S. Amery, *My Political Life*, III 34.
37 D. FitzGerald to his wife, 12 November 1930 (FitzGerald Papers).
38 Ibid. 10 November 1930.
39 Ibid. 23 October 1930.

40 D. FitzGerald to his wife, 13 October 1930 (FitzGerald Papers).
41 Ibid. 17 October 1930.
42 Ibid. 23 October 1930.
43 Ibid. 8 October 1930.
44 Ibid. 13 October 1930.
45 Ibid. 15 October 1930.
46 Imperial Conference 1930, Sankey Committee, minutes of 6th meeting, 17 October 1930 (FitzGerald Papers).
47 Ibid.
48 D. FitzGerald to his wife, 17 October 1930 (FitzGerald Papers).
49 Ibid. 24 October 1930.
50 Ibid. 28 October 1930.
51 Ibid.
52 *Irish Times*, 5 November 1930.
53 D. FitzGerald to his wife, 6 November 1930 (FitzGerald Papers).
54 Ibid. 11 November 1930.
55 *Irish Times*, 15 November 1930.
56 *The Times*, 15 November 1930.
57 Cmd. 3479, 1929–30, sections 73–8.
58 Irish Free State Memorandum for Executive Council, 18 February 1930, 'The First Conference for the Codification of International Law' (Fitz-Gerald Papers).
59 J. J. Hearne, Memorandum for Imperial Conference Delegation, 21 August 1930 (FitzGerald Papers).
60 J. J. Hearne, 'Various drafts of proposed sections relating to the status of nationals', dated 31 October 1930 (FitzGerald Papers).
61 Ibid. (quoted by Hearne).
62 Ibid.
63 Ibid.
64 Cmd. 3718, 1930–1, p. 22.
65 Irish Free State Memorandum, 'Appeals to the Judicial Committee of the Privy Council', 17 April 1930 (FitzGerald Papers).
66 *Irish Times*, 3 October 1930.
67 Ibid. 18 October 1930 (the Irish Free State did prefer the Permanent Court of International Justice at The Hague).
68 Irish Free State 'Preliminary Note on British suggestions', pp. 4–5 (Fitz-Gerald Papers).
69 Ibid. pp. 5–6.
70 D. FitzGerald to his wife, 6 October 1930 (FitzGerald Papers).
71 Ibid. 8 October 1930.
72 Ibid. 6 October 1930.
73 Became law, 16 November 1933: Constitution (Amndt no. 22 Bill).
74 Sankey Committee, draft conclusions, third meeting, 10 October 1930 (FitzGerald Papers).
75 Ibid.
76 Imperial Conference 1930, sub-committee on Arbitration and Disarmament, first meeting, draft conclusions (FitzGerald Papers).
77 Ibid.

78 Ibid. second meeting.
79 Suggested order of Procedure and Provisional Agenda for Imperial Conference, Section A, September 1930 (FitzGerald Papers).
80 Sir Cecil Hurst in Minutes of Inter-Imperial Relations Committee, 1926 Imperial Conference, cited in Irish Free State 'Draft Memorandum on Treaties', Section 1 (League Treaties) p. 3 (FitzGerald Papers).
81 Cmd. 2768, 1926, p. 22.
82 Dutch delegate to the sub-committee of the Legal Committee, Arms Traffic Conference 1925, in 'Report of the Legal Committee', cited in Irish Free State 'Draft Memorandum on Treaties', Section 1 (League Treaties) p. 2 (FitzGerald Papers). The italics are Irish.
83 Cited in above Irish Free State Memorandum, p. 2 (para. 2).
84 Ibid. p. 3 (para. 5).
85 E. J. Phelan to D. FitzGerald, 18 February 1927 (FitzGerald Papers).
86 D. FitzGerald to E. J. Phelan, 24 March 1927 (FitzGerald Papers).
87 E. J. Phelan, *The British Empire and the World Community.*
88 D. FitzGerald to his wife, 27 October 1930: 'Phelan is here and he loves arguments on these points. In these arguments one realises that he has a remarkable brain – though on other occasions he may seem dull' (FitzGerald Papers).
89 Irish Free State 'Draft Memorandum on Treaties', section one (League Treaties) p. 7 (FitzGerald Papers). Considerations of Empire Trade Preference did complicate the British position.
90 P. J. Noel Baker, *The Present Juridical Status of the British Dominions in International Law*, p. 298.
91 Sankey Committee, draft conclusions, fifth meeting, 16 October 1930 (*Inter se* Applicability of Treaties) FitzGerald Papers.
92 Ibid. (See also above, p. 211, footnote.)
93 Ibid.
94 Ibid.
95 Ibid.
96 Imperial Conference 1930, Sankey Committee documents (FitzGerald Papers). See also CAB 32/88 P.R.O. (Committee on Inter-Imperial Relations, Report and Proceedings, pp. 25–6).
97 Ibid. (Irish Free State reply to British draft *inter se* clause).
98 Irish Free State Memorandum on draft *inter se* clause (FitzGerald Papers).
99 Ibid.
100 Imperial Conference 1930: E(30)25 in CAB 32/81 (P.R.O.).
101 Imperial Conference 1930, Sankey Committee, draft conclusions, fifth meeting, 16 October 1930 (FitzGerald Papers).
102 Imperial Conference 1930, Sankey Committee, draft conclusions, fifth meeting, 16 October 1930 (FitzGerald Papers).
103 Ibid., third meeting, 10 October 1930. (The phrase occurs in the South African Preliminary Suggestions sent to the Dominions from Pretoria, July 1930. FitzGerald Papers.)
104 Irish Free State 'Draft Memorandum on Treaties', section on 'Full Powers', p. 18, para. 25 (FitzGerald Papers).

105 Ibid. (para. 26).

106 Ibid. (para. 27). See also pp. 8–9 (para. 11).

107 Ibid. (para. 28).

108 D. FitzGerald to his wife, 10 October 1930 (FitzGerald Papers).

109 Sankey Committee; documents arising from the discussion on Seals (FitzGerald Papers).

110 Ibid.

111 Ibid.

112 See L. S. Amery, *My Political Life*, III 34 (citing Smuts at Bloemfontein).

113 See *Annual Register* (1930) p. 131.

114 See, for example, M. Waite, New Zealand, H. of R., 1931, CCXXVIII 563. There are very frequent references to the Irish Free State in this debate. Most deplore her individual attitude but Mr Holland is glad to see a Dominion standing on its own feet.

115 New Zealand, H. of R., 1931, CCXXVIII 548.

116 Sir E. Grigg to H. M. N. Moore, 9 December 1930 (Grigg Papers).

117 'Had Snowden gone to the House of Lords a couple of years before he did the Conference might have ended differently. . . .' H. R. S. Phillpott, *J. H. Thomas*, p. 203.

118 See Sir J. Sandeman Allen, 'The Imperial Conference and the Future' in *United Empire*, no. 1, XXII (new series) 24–5.

119 *Irish Times*, 22 October 1930.

120 Ibid. 23 October 1930.

121 Ibid. 19 October 1930.

122 D. FitzGerald to his wife, 9 October 1930 (FitzGerald Papers).

123 Ibid.

124 Ibid. 23 October 1930.

125 Ibid. 25 October 1930.

126 Ibid.

127 P. McGilligan recollection.

128 Ibid.

129 Ibid. Hogan must have been very relieved. According to Desmond Fitz-Gerald he was placed near Rudyard Kipling and only answered him when he spoke. D. FitzGerald to his wife, 16 October 1930 (FitzGerald Papers).

130 D. FitzGerald to his wife, 21 October 1930 (FitzGerald Papers).

131 Ibid.

132 Ibid.

133 Ibid. 23 October 1930.

134 Seanad Eireann debates, XIV, col. 1615.

135 Ibid. cols 1640–2.

136 Dail Eireann debates, XXXIII, col. 2298.

137 See K. C. Wheare, *The Statute of Westminster and Dominion Status*, pp. 133–4: 'The Statute was a part of the process of re-adjustment and redefinition; the terms did not cover the whole of the subject.'

CHAPTER 9

1 Irish Free State memorandum, 10 January 1929 (by J. J. Hearne): 'Warrant granting leave of absence to Governor General', p. 2 (McGilligan Papers).
2 W. K. Hancock, *Survey of British Commonwealth Affairs*, I 287.
3 See A. B. Keith, *Speeches and Documents*, pp. xxxvii–viii, and also P. E. Corbett and H. A. Smith, *Canada and world politics*.
4 W. Y. Elliott, 'The Sovereignty of the British Dominions: law overtakes practice' in *American Political Science Review*, no. 24 (1930) pp. 971–88.
5 Speaking in Seanad Eireann, 23 July 1931, McGilligan outlined the situation and put it in proper perspective: see A. B. Keith, *Speeches and Documents*, pp. 251–5.
6 Irish Free State Despatch no. 17, 24 January 1931, Department of External Affairs, Dublin (FitzGerald Papers).
7 Lord Stamfordham to J. W. Dulanty, 26 January 1931. (Royal Archives, Windsor Castle: reproduced by the gracious permission of Her Majesty the Queen.)
8 J. P. Walshe, Memorandum to Minister for External Affairs, Irish Free State, 'Change of Seals' (FitzGerald Papers).
9 P. McGilligan interview.
10 See *Irish Times*, 28 March 1931.
11 A. B. Keith, *Speeches and Documents*, p. xxxviii.
12 R. M. Dawson, *The Development of Dominion Status, 1900–36*, p. 121.
13 *Round Table* (no. 83) XXI 628.
14 Seanad Eireann debates, XIII, col. 44.
15 Dail Eireann debates, XXXVI, cols 1229–30; XXXVII, cols 1620–1.
16 Canada, H. of C., 1931, III 3204. (See A. B. Keith *Speeches and Documents*, p. 263.)
17 Dail Eireann debates, XXXIX, col. 2360.
18 J. P. Walshe, Memorandum to Minister for External Affairs, 'Change of Seals' (FitzGerald Papers).
19 For British view see debate in House of Commons, 20 November 1931, in Keith, *Speeches and Documents*, p. 296. Keith discusses this view as 'technically open to criticism'.
20 Constitution (Amendment no. 22) Act, 16 November 1933.
21 See A. B. Keith, *Speeches and Documents*, pp. 440–1.
22 P. N. S. Mansergh, *Survey of Commonwealth Affairs, 1931–9*, p. 16.
23 K. C. Wheare, *The Statute of Westminster and Dominion Status*, p. 3 (1938 ed.).
24 King's Speech 1931. (See K. C. Wheare, *The Statute of Westminster*, p. 303.)
25 *Annual Register* (1931) p. 148.
26 Statute of Westminster, Article 9, pt. 2. See Statute reprinted in A. B. Keith, *Speeches and Documents*, and also pp. 263–74, for the whole of Latham's speech (or Australia, H. of R., 1931, CXXXI 4061–70).
27 Australia, H. of R., 1931, CXXXI 4074 (see above, Ch. 6, pp. 124–5).
28 Ibid. p. 4075.
29 See J. H. Morgan, 'The Statute of Westminster' in *United Empire*, XXIII (1931), pp. 653–9.

30 Canada, H. of C., 1931, III 3193.
31 Ibid. p. 3221.
32 R. M. Dawson, *The Development of Dominion Status, 1900–36*, p. 122.
33 South Africa, H. of A., 1931, XVII, col. 2759.
34 See K. C. Wheare, *The Statute of Westminster and Dominion Status*. Ch. 4
   sets out the rival points of view and their supporting legal decisions.
35 259 H.C. Deb. 5s, col. 1173.
36 Ibid. col. 1183.
37 Ibid. col. 1186.
38 L. S. Amery, *My Political Life*, III 75. In his own speech he was less severe,
   'one of the most powerful and impressive speeches', being his comment.
   259 H.C. deb. 5s, col. 1199.
39 See 259 H.C. deb. 5s, cols 1191–7, in particular.
40 Ibid. col. 1249.
41 Ibid. col. 1250.
42 260 H.C. deb. 5s, col. 311.
43 Ibid. cols 353–4.
44 Dail Eireann debates, XXXIX, cols 2291–2 (16 August 1931).
45 Ibid. col. 2293.
46 Ibid. col. 2294.
47 Ibid. cols 2296–7.
48 Ibid. cols 2306–8.

CHAPTER 10

1 Reprinted in A. B. Keith, *Speeches and Documents*, pp. 303–7.
2 Seanad Eireann debates, xv, col. 938. (Also see p. 29 above.)
3 W. K. Hancock, *Survey of Commonwealth Affairs*, p. 327.
4 P. N. S. Mansergh reports their conviction that they had 'greatly contributed to the reshaping of the Commonwealth' and recognises that they had
   'worked for the transformation of Empire into Commonwealth', P. N. S.
   Mansergh, *Survey of Commonwealth Affairs, 1931–9*, pp. 255–6.
5 'In discouraging circumstances the twenty-six counties Dominion . . . has
   done extraordinarily well.' J. M. Hone, 'Ireland since 1922' in *Criterion
   Miscellany*, no. 39 (1932) p. 32.
6 See W. K. Hancock, *Survey of Commonwealth Affairs*, p. 62.
7 See, for example, A. E. Malone, 'Party Government in the Irish Free
   State', in *Political Science Quarterly*, XLIV 375.
8 See M. D. O'Sullivan, 'Eight years of Irish Home Rule', in *Quarterly
   Review*, CCLIV (no. 504) 237–8.
9 P. N. S. Mansergh, *The Irish Free State ; its government and politics*, p. 284.
10 K. C. Wheare, *The constitutional structure of the Commonwealth*, p. 90.
11 W. K. Hancock, *Smuts*, I 310.
12 P. N. S. Mansergh, *Survey of Commonwealth Affairs, 1931–9*, p. 298.
13 Mazzini, *The duties of man* (Everyman Library ed. of Mazzini, *Essays*), pp.
   41–9.
14 Ibid. *To the Italians*, p. 241.
15 Ibid. *The duties of man*, p. 55.

16 P. Gordon Walker, *The Commonwealth*, p. 112.
17 R. M. Dawson, *The Development of Dominion Status, 1900–36* (2nd ed., 1965) p. 123.
18 The *Guardian*, 17 July 1965.
19 D. FitzGerald, 'Notes for a Speech', subsequent to 1926 Conference (FitzGerald Papers).
20 P. Gordon Walker, *The Commonwealth*, p. 76.
21 Ibid. p. 95.
22 Ibid. p. 82. Mansergh (*Survey of Commonwealth Affairs*, p. 15) is also too generous to Britain. It was not always true that 'Great Britain, far from fighting to the last ditch for the old Imperial order, was forward in her desire to give substance to the new'.

APPENDIX A

1 FitzGerald Papers.

APPENDIX B

1 FitzGerald Papers.
2 Ibid.
3 See A. B. Keith, *Speeches and Documents*, p. 348. And also in R. M. Dawson, *The Development of Dominion Status, 1900–36*, p. 316.

APPENDIX C

1 FitzGerald Papers.

APPENDIX D

1 See Ch. 8, pp. 209–11, above, for the full Irish case. The statement of the 1926 Report discussed here, is reproduced on p. 210. It may be helpful to an understanding of this topic, discussed here with General Hertzog to read it in conjunction with the arguments on pp. 209 ff.
2 FitzGerald Papers.

APPENDIX E

1 FitzGerald Papers.

APPENDIX F

1 FitzGerald Papers.

APPENDIX G

1 H. Nicolson, *King George V : his life and reign*, p. 472.
2 This did leave subtleties such as 'active' and 'passive' belligerency – indeed the whole question of neutrality – somewhat in doubt.

3 See Professor Coupland's letter to *The Times*, 20 February 1935.

4 T. M. Healy was doubtless appointed under the old procedure of joint consultation but there seems little doubt that Irish wishes prevailed. That he was a commoner and an Irishman was significant. Mr Gordon Walker in his book *The Commonwealth* seems inclined to ignore even the second Irish Governor-General, MacNeill, another Irish commoner, this time appointed solely on the advice of the Irish Government (*The Commonwealth*, p. 106).

5 Harold Nicolson tells the 1930 Australian story in outline in his biography of King George V (pp. 477–82) but fascinating new material has been made available by L. F. Crisp, in *Historical Studies* (*Australia and New Zealand*) no. 42, XI 253–7. Here Scullin's views are set out and the British rearguard action is put in its context. It may be noted that Harold Nicolson, in *George V*, shows that a surprising unawareness that 1926 had changed the situation existed in the British camp. Further, the Law Officers of the Crown advised that 'since the Commonwealth of Australia did not permit Australian Ministers to advise the King, and since the 1926 resolutions did not permit British Ministers to tender advice on Dominion matters, there was nobody who could constitutionally tender advice' (p. 479). This is quite contrary to the Irish contention that such aspects of the Royal prerogative which had in time passed to British Ministers automatically devolved upon the appropriate Dominion Ministers. See Ch. 7 p. 167, above.

6 P. N. S. Mansergh, *Survey of Commonwealth Affairs, 1931–9*, p. 63.

Index

Adderley, C., 1

Alexander *v.* County Court Judge of Cork, 112

Allen, J. S., 223

Amery, L. S.: Imperial Conference (1921), 6, 8; League of Nations, 34; the Imperial Conference, 41–2; Dominions Secretary, 43; Imperial Conference (1923), 49, 53; registration of 'the Treaty', 62; Imperial Conference (1926), 73, 82–4, 92–3, 104–5, 107, 123–4; Balfour Declaration, 97–8; Governor-General, 108 n.; U.S.A. ambassador to I.F.S., 137; Judicial Committee of Privy Council, 138–9; O.D.L. Committee, 144–5; Imperial Conference (1930), 191, 223; Commonwealth figure, 256

Arms Traffic Conference (1925), 210–211, 214

Arnold, Lord, 64

Article 10, League of Nations Covenant, 34

Articles of Agreement for a Treaty between Great Britain and Ireland, xi, 12, 13, 15–17, 22, 56–63, 69, 72, 81, 131, 182, 206 n., 209–10, 243, 245, 249

Asquith, H. H., 2

Baldwin, S.: Imperial Conference (1923), 46–7, 52; Imperial Conference (1926), 80, 88, 94 n., 106; King's title, 106; Imperial Conference (1930), 188; Conservative leadership, 223

Balfour, Lord: Imperial Conference (1923), 52–3; Imperial Conference (1926), 91–2, 94, 96–7, 119, 123–4; correspondence, Sir G. Foster, 123, 129; Declaration questioned, 133

Balfour Declaration, 96

Baker, P. J. N., 169, 213

Bankruptcy Acts (1914, 1926), 163

Barcelona Arms Traffic Conference (1921), 59–60, 209–10

Batterbee, H. F., 195, 203, 233, 235

Baxter, 106 n.

Belcourt, N. A., 64–6

Bennett, R. B.: P.M. Canada, 181; Empire policy, 183; Imperial Conference (1930), 187–90, 192, 222; Ottawa Conference, 222; Statute of Westminster, 242

Beyers, F. W., 148

Binchy, D., 74

Blythe, E.: on the Commonwealth, 26; League Council, 74–5 (1926), 175 (1930); Governor-General position, 109; loan projected (1929), 154; appeal to Privy Council, 239; financial stability, 250